MOSCOW 1956

MOSCOW 1956
THE SILENCED SPRING

KATHLEEN E. SMITH

HARVARD UNIVERSITY PRESS

Cambridge, Massachusetts

London, England

2017

First printing

Library of Congress Cataloging-in-Publication Data

Names: Smith, Kathleen E., author.
Title: Moscow 1956 : the silenced spring / Kathleen E. Smith.
Description: Cambridge, Massachusetts : Harvard University Press, 2017. |
    Includes bibliographical references and index.
Identifiers: LCCN 2016046251 | ISBN 9780674972001 (hardcover : alk. paper)
Subjects: LCSH: Political rehabilitation—Soviet Union. | Soviet
    Union—Politics and government—1953–1985. | Soviet Union—
    History—1953–1985. | Khrushchev, Nikita Sergeevich, 1894–1971.
Classification: LCC DK277 .S64 2017 | DDC 947.085/2—dc23
LC record available at https://lccn.loc.gov/2016046251

*In memory of my father, Michael Price Smith (1941–2016),
who instilled in me a love of travel and who never said "Don't go"
when I planned another trip to Russia.*

CONTENTS

The Soviet Union in 1956.

PROLOGUE

As the year 1956 dawned in Moscow, Joseph Stalin had been dead for nearly three years. His preserved corpse lay alongside Vladimir Lenin's in the mausoleum on Red Square. Just over the wall in the Kremlin, however, pressure had been building for months among members of the Communist Party's ruling presidium about how to handle the late dictator's mixed legacies. Stalin had aggressively promoted industrialization and led the Soviet Union to victory in World War II, but he had also purged his rivals, sanctioned mass arrests of innocent people, and built a monopoly on power centered on a "cult of personality." After Stalin's death, his heirs had quickly backed away from a looming show trial and reined in the secret police. However, they had acted with little commentary. Nikita Khrushchev was about to change that.

On February 29, 1956, writer Lidiia Chukovskaia, whose husband had been executed during the purges, wrote in her diary: "Rumors, rumors, you can't make out anything. Can it be that we've lived to hear the Word?"[1] It would be another month before she heard Khrushchev's "Secret Speech" read out loud at the Writers' Union. But she had indeed survived to learn that judgment on Stalin had been pronounced from on high. Four days earlier, the party's own first secretary had stunned a closed gathering of the political elite by recounting appalling facts about the terror that had been unleashed in the name of the revolution. Over the course of a few hours, Khrushchev shattered the myth of Stalin's infallibility and promised that a restored collective leadership would bolster socialist legality and undo the harmful practices of the Stalin cult.

Starting in March 1956, Khrushchev's confidential report to the Twentieth Party Congress would be read out to a broader audience of party and youth league members and civically active persons across the Soviet Union. For the cult of Stalin to be dissolved, its millions of adherents had to learn how the late leader had violated Marxist-Leninist norms. Before they encountered survivors of the gulag, Soviet citizens needed to know that the party had already recognized and corrected its errors.

Khrushchev acted out of conviction that the party would be strengthened by acknowledging and addressing problems caused both by the erosion of collegiality within its ranks and the elevation of Stalin to godlike status. In his report to the special session of the Congress, the first secretary did not delve into the larger record of coercion and violence that marked the span of Soviet rule; he recognized only a few of the worst abuses of the Stalin era. However, Khrushchev believed that a dose of truth telling could emancipate the post-Stalin leaders emotionally and practically from their adherence to past practices and policies. Well aware of the people's dire need for housing and their desire for a higher standard of living, Khrushchev gambled that promoting peace abroad and reinvigorating management at home would boost the economy and with it popular support. He expected the restoration of "the great moral and political strength of our Party" promised in the Secret Speech to produce a cascade of positive outcomes.[2]

However, while Khrushchev's bold act spawned genuine admiration and enthusiasm in some quarters, it also gave birth to myriad unintended and sometimes profoundly unwelcome consequences. The "wide practice of criticism and self-criticism" that Khrushchev claimed ought to characterize party life proved hard to handle in practice, especially as the "Report on the Cult of Personality and Its Consequences" raised questions about the accountability of the current party leaders. Moreover, the denunciation of the practice of whitewashing flaws in the Soviet economy encouraged writers, journalists, and engaged citizens to tackle current issues more bluntly. Chukovskaia and other members of the intelligentsia in particular would struggle in 1956 to understand what it meant to lift the constraints of the cult of Stalin within the framework of a monopolistic ruling party. How far did the limits of criticism stretch? Who would be the regime's new heroes and villains? How could "liberation" be combined with "renewal"—and under whose terms?

While the Soviet government coped with pressure from its intelligentsia for more freedom of speech and more access to the outside world, genuine popular unrest broke out in two of its central European satellites in 1956. The year would end with Khrushchev scrambling to defuse discord in Poland and suppress an armed uprising in Hungary. These events would strengthen the position of those who feared that the Secret Speech had damaged the regime's standing. In December, with Khrushchev's acquiescence, they would turn the party apparatus against reformers who had taken up the tasks laid out by Khrushchev and against young "freethinkers" who had begun to call for more popular control over politics. The spring would be silenced at least temporarily.

For the Soviet Union, 1956 became a year of optimism and disillusionment, of painful revelations and gratifying debates, of hopes raised and disappointed. During this intense period of social, cultural, and political turmoil, people from all walks of life attempted to sort out what it meant that the patriotic narrative of progress toward a communist utopia had been tarnished—but presumably not upended—by Stalin's megalomania, paranoia, and mass persecution of innocent people. Meanwhile, Khrushchev and other party leaders wrestled with challenges to their notion that political changes could and should be orchestrated and directed from above. Khrushchev assumed the masses would respond enthusiastically to a fresh commitment to a more approachable and responsive government. He did not expect that young people especially would demand more freedom and more trust than he was ready to yield.

Half a century later, veteran human rights activist Ludmilla Alexeyeva would recall of her generation, "Of course, our development began before the Twentieth [Party] Congress, [but] it constituted a shock for us, because we all knew but had never heard [about Stalin's repressions] from the lips of the leader of the country. We instantly sided with Khrushchev—psychologically we were already children of the Twentieth Congress." Other intellectuals participating with Alexeyeva in a 2006 seminar on the "Sixties Generation" concurred that although some reforms predated

Khrushchev's speech and while cultural liberalism had thrived most vigorously in the 1960s, one could fairly say that: "The sixties generation was born on the day of the Twentieth Congress."[3] The self-censorship ingrained under Stalin had taken a major blow, and as a result a new culture of discussion and debate emerged among artists, writers, scientists, university students, and the like. Pent-up questions and fresh opinions would spill over into the public sphere in 1956 as people were emboldened by Khrushchev's disparagement of Stalin's practice of labeling critics as "enemies."

Both the buoyant Khrushchev and more critical intellectuals understood the deed of tearing away the fabric of lies covering the terror propagated under Stalin as an act of liberation and a signal of transformation. This book explores many aspects of the social, political, and cultural changes initiated by Khrushchev in the course of a single year. In 1956 Khrushchev would release political prisoners and recruit youthful volunteers to replace them in tackling grand economic projects on the outskirts of Soviet civilization. He would crack open the Iron Curtain dividing the Soviet Union from the West, allowing travel in both directions, as well as numerous cultural exchanges. While many intellectuals and young people would embrace the spirit of openness, others mistrusted the sudden "slandering" of Stalin and viscerally rejected Khrushchev's own domineering style and blustering confidence. In short, top-down reform would turn out to be neither straightforward nor unidirectional.

This book is built on the premise that 1956 marked neither a simple turning point nor a sharply drawn line between one era and the next. Instead, I expose a complicated and fraught revelatory period in which the possibilities and challenges of reform from above unfurled as different voices tried to answer the questions of what could and should come next for the Soviet Union. Over the space of roughly twelve months, I argue, actors inside and outside the party elite faced up to the burden of the past and some cautiously tested out the principles of the Secret Speech. The cumulative interaction of enthusiasm for and resistance to de-Stalinization in universities, publishing houses, and government offices and among gulag survivors and bureaucrats, students and teachers, and idealists and cynics pushed reform out of the bounds envisioned by Khrushchev and created a disequilibrium that threatened his control of the party apparatus. For those who are interested in how dictatorships stumble into reform and cope with ambiguity of their own making, 1956 provides a case study of the obstacles to controlled liberalization.[4]

The central argument of this book is that the arc of the year 1956 in Russia encompassed multifaceted reform from above, scattered, sometimes intemperate reactions from below, and ultimately a reassertion of top-down control that did not (and could not) restore the status quo ante. I contend that 1956 constituted just one year of a post-Stalin "thaw," but one that marked a mental threshold that forever after hobbled the Soviet Communist Party. Khrushchev's endorsement of a return to Leninist principles of democracy and self-criticism combined with his denunciation of the unquestioning obedience demanded by Stalin invoked ethical norms that could neither be lived up to by the party-state nor lightly set aside. Revelations about the scale of injustices carried out under Stalin, even though they addressed only part of the dislocation and cruelty wrought by the modernizing Soviet state, permanently altered people's understandings of the party's self-congratulatory autobiography. Hence, on the one hand, 1956 marked just the beginning of a long and unresolved tug-of-war over the boundaries of acceptable criticism within the Soviet system. On the other hand, the sequence of change from above sparking intellectuals especially to push the bounds of "permitted dissent," only to instigate a new freeze, encapsulated a political pattern that recurred until it triggered the final demise of the USSR.[5]

The next great reformer from within the Soviet Communist Party, Mikhail Gorbachev, would number himself among the "children of the Twentieth Party Congress." Thirty years later, he proved to share some of Khrushchev's optimism about the capacity of reformers to initiate and guide change from within, as well as the assumption that the Soviet people would readily mobilize behind a democratic socialist vision prescribed from above. Gorbachev, however, would encounter a more jaded, consumerist, and worldly public in 1986 when he launched perestroika. Moreover, his efforts clashed with others of the post-Stalin generation who took a different lesson from the Secret Speech. For Ludmilla Alexeyeva, the moral of the Twentieth Party Congress was: "I don't want to lie or to say in public that in which I don't believe. And I don't want people whom I don't respect to dictate to me how to live. I will decide for myself how to live, whom to befriend, what to say, and what books to read."[6] She did not need a tutelary regime to think for her. She and other dissidents would step outside the system in the 1970s to openly question whether socialism could be reformed. Their numbers were few, but the sense that the party should not dictate taste and other matters spread from 1956 onward.[7]

By tracking the first steps toward dismantling one of the most notorious dictatorships in modern history, *Moscow 1956* exposes the immediate political and psychological legacies of Stalinism for rulers and subjects alike. However, the lurching progress in 1956 away from a regime of terror and ideological orthodoxy arguably not only shaped the generation that would make perestroika in the late 1980s but also continues to influence Russia today. In the new millennium, Russia's leaders have re-created the challenges of managing a single-party system, constraining an unwieldy and insular bureaucracy, and coping with dissenting views. Moreover, the long shadow cast by a strong state historically intolerant of criticism continues to depress civic activism.

While the post-2000 Russian government lacks the sort of ideology that inspired and united the Communist Party elite, it views its own survival as paramount. Therefore, its members continue not only to perceive change as perilous but to relate to outsiders with insecurity and to question the motives of even well-intentioned domestic critics. In recent years contact with foreigners has again begun to attract suspicion and surveillance. Once more, those who point out gaps between the avowed principles of the regime and its real practices place themselves at risk for harassment and selective prosecution. In short, Vladimir Putin has demonstrated that one can draw cautionary lessons from moments of liberation and liberalization. Unpacking the multifaceted repercussions of the Secret Speech then may prove quite useful in trying to understand how talk of democratization and a common European home in Gorbachev's Russia shifted to rhetoric about "foreign agents" and demands for vigilance over the public sphere.

Understanding the extent and shape of the changes that took place in Russia in 1956 is not easy. Events were hard for contemporary outside observers to make out from the other side of the Iron Curtain. They were also often hidden from those present in the moment in a country where censorship choked information flows and common sense dictated against discussing touchy subjects. Westerners got a one-sided peek at inner-party struggles when during his forced retirement Khrushchev recorded his own version of his eventful time in power. More recently, the opening of many official archives of the former USSR has allowed for a more nuanced view of elite politics, though mostly through a narrow lens of carefully composed memos and reports rather than direct or extemporaneous speech. Fortunately, the last two decades have also brought to light diaries, correspondence, and memoirs that give voice to multiple and different perspectives on cultural and political developments of the time.

With access to once-classified materials from party archives, a spate of Russian-language memoirs about the 1950s, new secondary works by Russian and Western historians, plus my own interviews with some who came of age at the time, I have striven to provide a fresh and complex look at the post-Stalin liberalization. I have triangulated between publications from 1956, archival traces, and retrospective accounts to paint a detailed picture not of the entire "thaw" but of its most intense moment of flux and uncertainty. Balancing a narrative of high politics with the stories of principled students, former prisoners, persecuted scientists, and audacious writers, I have attempted to reveal the drama that marked the lives of ordinary and extraordinary Russians as they navigated the rocky first year of pronounced de-Stalinization and to demonstrate how disparate responses to reform added up to a crisis.[8]

My research benefited greatly from the labor-intensive work and thoughtful analyses of numerous post-Soviet historians who have been exploring the 1950s and 1960s through wide-ranging and scrupulous investigations of a variety of topics ranging from the nature of the university system to the development of cybernetics. I also profited from new investigations of Khrushchev's life by Western scholars and members of his own family.[9] Rather than pursue a single theme or focus on elite politics, however, I have chosen to examine and to present the year 1956 in the form of a montage, a mixture of panoramic shots and close-ups. To this end, I tell the story of reform and retreat through a series of biographies intermixed with national events. Some of my subjects shaped liberalization with their words and deeds; others were buffeted by forces beyond their control. To organize their lives against the backdrop of tempestuous politics and to capture the momentum of events, I have shaped the narrative into twelve roughly chronological chapters, each presenting one aspect of the year's events and showing the cumulative effects of reform and resistance.

Even with the deliberately narrow framework of a calendar year, however, *Moscow 1956* is not a comprehensive account of Soviet society or politics. Rural life, nationalities issues, relations with China, welfare policy, music, and many other topics might have been included. As a political scientist who has long studied memory politics, I was drawn to concentrate on the impact of the Secret Speech in the political sphere and especially the emergence of independent, sometimes anti-Stalinist discourse among educated persons. My desire to examine the lives of the politically engaged tilted the year's account toward the intelligentsia. And even within the segments of society I focus on—party elites, historians, urban youth, writers, and scientists—I had to pick and choose to keep the cast of characters manageable. When possible, I selected protagonists for whom diverse source bases existed or whose lives intersected with those of other featured persons. Finally, I occasionally stretched the time frame to provide necessary context or complete individual stories. Nonetheless, this is in essence the story of a memorable year and a reflection on the long-term impact of stunted reforms.

Chapters 1 to 3 probe the Stalinist system Khrushchev inherited, his decision to make the Secret Speech, and the fallout for propagandists as they tried to answer the myriad questions Khrushchev ducked. Chapters 4 and 5 present the sharpest consequences of the rejection of Stalinism—the dismantling of the gulag and rehabilitation of Stalin's victims. Here I illustrate the complexity of reform from within by revealing the hidden role of old Bolsheviks, especially two former inmates turned policy makers, as they faced constant hurdles in streamlining the review of prisoners' sentences. Then, by delving into the lives of four writers of different ages and genres—all of whom served long terms in labor camps—I map the difficulties of survivors in reentering a barely reformed society. The selective nature of accountability and the secretive aspects of rehabilitation deprived survivors of the clout that might have allowed them fully to recover their lives and tell their stories.

I then turn in Chapters 6 to 8 to the experience of young people—students, aspiring writers, would-be geneticists, and adventurers—as they explored the opportunities the system had given them to study, travel, and work. From the universities out into the countryside, they threw themselves into Khrushchev's grand schemes for developing the socialist economy, including the planting of fallow lands in Siberia and Kazakhstan. A generation raised on high ideals grappled with the reality of the planned economy, including corruption, administrative fiat, and waste, coping at the same time with demands for unquestioning loyalty and restraint. I maintain that they took seriously the promises of more free speech in 1956 and kept alive dreams of a just society.

A partial opening up to the West, to Eastern Europe, and to pluralism created difficulties for managing reform. In Chapter 9, I shadow Khrushchev and a boatload of pioneering Soviet tourists as they encounter capitalist lands and confront their own ignorance and insecurities. Chapter 10 explains why a novel about a stymied inventor produced intolerable attacks on the Soviet bureaucracy, and Chapter 11 analyzes young students' obsession with developments in other socialist states, a curiosity that led them into danger as 1956 ended with Soviet intervention to quash the Hungarian uprising. Together, these stories demonstrate how small doses of freedom inspired a quest for greater liberties that strained the regime's tolerance for independent activity and critical thinking and forced it to once again bare its own flaws.

In Chapter 12, I trace how Moscow's spring withered as more orthodox actors blamed the Secret Speech for disorder in the bloc and disarray at home and Khrushchev retreated from his bold talk against Stalin. The unsteady course of reform in 1956 reinforced skeptics' fears that the system could not heal itself. Yet I argue the regime's step back from reform was not a reversal of the thaw. Many aspects of liberalization could not be undone, and others remained in favor with authorities and citizens. Instead, the official if semisecret repudiation of Stalin launched a cycle of authorities seeking, and often rejecting, new policies centered on maintaining control with less recourse to repression. In 1956 the Secret Speech simultaneously undermined Soviet rule and stimulated a search for ways to strengthen it.

1 JANUARY

AFTER THE ICE

January is a harsh month in Russia. Subzero temperatures dominate across the north and central regions, and short hours of daylight make the days seem even colder. Celebrating the New Year in this frigid climate seems like an act of faith. Amid snow, wind, and darkness, it is hard to believe that spring will ever come, that the black-and-white landscape will take on shades of green, that there will be a time of new life and reawakening.

In January 1956, however, New Year's dreams of spring may have been more vivid than usual. Two years earlier, the prominent writer Ilya Ehrenburg had published a novella about artistic independence with the suggestive title *The Thaw*. From that moment on, Russian intellectuals had taken up this metaphor as a way to describe the changes they had begun to see in the USSR. They were on the lookout for traces of melting of the harsh dictatorship that had grown up over twenty-five years under Joseph Stalin's leadership of the Communist Party of the Soviet Union (CPSU).

Stalin's sudden death in March 1953 had been followed by some important changes: the quick end of an anti-Semitic campaign that threatened to mark the start of a new round of terror, the replacement of a one-man dictatorship with the apparent rule of a collective, and a sweeping criminal amnesty that partially emptied Siberian prison camps.[1] But could Stalin's demise herald even bigger change? While some writers, artists, and even scientists had begun to test the limits on expression imposed by strict dogmas and harsh censorship, others kept their heads down. For many Russians, the deep freeze of Stalinism remained the dominant reality. In January 1956 the intentions of the new Soviet leadership were unclear. Although official paeans to Stalin had grown ever more subdued, no harsh words had been uttered publicly against the old dictator. Yet this was the last month in which Stalinism reigned unchallenged. Behind the scenes, those who would denounce him were preparing.

A Holiday Mood

Looking at the surface of Soviet society and at what lay below, one can see elements of stability and hints of change as Soviet leaders and citizens ushered in 1956. In Moscow for New Year's Eve, the members of the presidium, the highest body of the CPSU, hosted a diplomatic reception. Out of the eyes of the press, the party's elite representatives mingled amiably with foreign ambassadors and their wives. That same day, privileged children had come to the Kremlin for a party complete with a towering "New Year's tree" and gifts for all. And late into the night in the great hall of the Kremlin, a few select students from the capital's most prestigious university danced with a different set of distinguished guests—young settlers of the "Virgin Lands," Khrushchev's term for previously untilled steppe lands of Kazakhstan. Such balls had begun only in 1954 after the leadership reversed Stalin's closure of the Kremlin grounds to all tourists and unofficial visitors.[2]

Ordinary students partied more modestly. Girl students from Moscow State University's language and literature department (*Filologicheskii fakul'tet* or *filfak*) created a holiday mood in their dorm room by sticking a pine branch decorated with tufts of cotton in an old bottle. They pooled their money to buy wine and snacks and spent the evening singing popular favorites as well as unrecorded student songs. A group of geology students abandoned their dormitory, where behavior was monitored, to greet the New Year in the only private space they could find, the one-room apartment a classmate shared with her grandmother. There they

drank and danced to the one modern record in their possession. Decades later the two songs they listened to that night remained engraved on their memories.[3]

In its first edition of 1956, the main newspaper of the land, *Pravda,* published workers' pledges to increase production in honor of the upcoming twentieth congress of the CPSU. The newspaper's editorialists hailed the start of the first year of a new five-year plan for the economy. A photograph presented readers with happy economic news of a lesser but enviable sort: a Moscow factory worker's family decorated a tree for the holidays in their new apartment. A lamp with a fringed silk shade could be seen hanging over a dining table covered with a fancy tablecloth and laden with crockery. Indeed, the new residents appeared quite settled in—the walls were papered and pictures hung. The image demonstrated an ideal level of material comfort—albeit one consisting of standard goods without style or distinction.[4] This lucky family had achieved the new dream of domesticity and privacy in a country where several generations frequently crowded into cramped quarters, often in barracks or "communal apartments" where multiple families shared a single kitchen and bathroom.

The central newspaper further spread holiday cheer with a photo featuring children and Grandfather Frost, the secular Soviet substitute for Saint Nicholas. A poem told of first graders celebrating the New Year with a new classmate, a girl from India: the children include her in their circle as they dance, and the tree "shines and sparkles, and speaks of friendship and of peace."[5] In words and images, *Pravda* promised that the New Year would be one of progress, peace, and prosperity for the Soviet Union.

Outside the enchanted circle of the Kremlin and the idealized world of posed news photos, however, frost and dark prevailed in some realms of Russia and its empire. In the oddly named settlement of Turkmen—not a Central Asian outpost, but a peat-processing factory town one-hundred-plus kilometers from Moscow—a supply agent, former prisoner, and erstwhile writer spent the first days of the New Year alone with a book, or, more precisely, a future book. On January 8, 1956, Varlam Shalamov

Fig. 01-01 New Year's Party for children in the Great Kremlin Palace. Photograph by Semyon Fridlyand. Courtesy Dalbey Photographic Collection at the University of Denver.

penned a letter to his idol, Boris Pasternak, to thank him for the privilege of reading the manuscript of *Doctor Zhivago*.

Four years earlier Shalamov had written to Pasternak from Kolyma, one of the most far-flung outposts of the Soviet penal system. In his letter, sent via friends, Shalamov had confided that Pasternak's poems helped sustain him through three terms of hard labor; he had enclosed a handmade notebook of his own poetry. After years in which he had not held a pen or seen a printed page, a lighter regime, followed by release in 1951, had allowed Shalamov to resume his creative life. Now with some distance from the gulag, Shalamov felt driven to convey some of what he had witnessed, first in poetry and later in painfully stark, masterfully laconic short stories. He wrote without ceasing, and Pasternak was one of his few trusted readers.

On January 1, 1956, Shalamov had been in Moscow visiting friends and relatives. His ex-prisoner's passport barred him from staying overnight in the major cities of the Soviet Union. Nevertheless, since his first daring visit to the city in 1953, he had frequently broken the rules. How else could he find his way back to civilization and to his family? Shalamov's wife had been exiled to Central Asia as a consequence of his second arrest, but she had since managed to return legally to Moscow with their daughter, a young woman who did not remember her father. He had been arrested when she was eighteen months old. Now these women were a key link to the world he longed to rejoin. His wife helped arrange his meetings with Pasternak and passed parcels of precious manuscript back and forth between the dull village of Turkmen and the exclusive dacha community of Peredelkino, where the great writer lived.

A week after receiving the draft of *Doctor Zhivago*, Shalamov wrote to its author: "Thank you for the marvelous New Year's present. For me, nothing in this world could have been finer, dearer, and more necessary. I feel as though I can live on, as long as you are alive, as long as you exist—forgive me for such sentimentality."[6] Then he got down to the work of the letter, a detailed review of the novel with special attention to the parts that touched on the camps. Shalamov's letter radiated both deep respect for Pasternak and sincere gratitude. Shalamov knew that he himself was never going to be a literary star in the Soviet Union. His biography, his topic, his uncompromising moral stances all dictated against success in the official system. But Pasternak, he was sure, valued him for his literary talent. After all, Pasternak had invited him to critique his novel. Still, for Shalamov, Moscow, the writer's dacha in Peredelkino, and the world of ideas and literature remained frustratingly far away.

The day after Shalamov sent his review to Pasternak, another Russian poet also dreamed of Moscow, of old friends, and of an unobtainable refuge. On January 9, 1956, Anna Barkova was released from a labor camp near the far northern coal-mining city of Inta. She had undoubtedly spent New Year's preoccupied with her future. Perhaps twisting a strand of her once-copper curls, she had sat in a drafty barrack and worried that life on the outside might possibly be worse. In 1939 Barkova had completed a five-year sentence for political crimes and found herself condemned to a life of provincial poverty. Barred from Moscow, Barkova had spent the 1940s in small provincial towns working as a street sweeper and a cleaning woman in a school. She had scarcely earned enough money to feed herself and rent a corner of a room. She had dressed in rags and only twice scraped together enough money to travel to Moscow. Now, once again, she would have a passport that kept her out of the Soviet Union's major cities.

Did Barkova guess that poverty in some provincial hellhole would make the labor camp of 1956 look good? Since the July 1953 arrest of Lavrenty Beria, who had served as minister of internal affairs at the height of the purges and again after Stalin's death, Barkova had served her term in relatively tolerable conditions. She received meager but predictable meals and had a small but appreciative audience for her poetry. In camp her poor health had exempted her from heavy work. Now, at age fifty-five, she feared she would be too weak to eke out a living in the "big zone" and that no one there would dare listen to, let alone publish, her poems.[7]

Nearby in Inta, but already on the other side of the barbed wire, two young would-be writers greeted 1956 with more optimism. Iulii Dunskii and Valerii Frid were camp veterans, too, but of a different generation. The two friends, both thirty-four years old, had grown up in Moscow in similar middle-class Jewish families. They had become friends in primary school and together had entered the Soviet Union's only film school. They also had been arrested together in 1944 before they could graduate and start their screenwriting careers. Dunskii and Frid had been part of a group of young friends, including daughters of repressed parents, who had hung out together in the evenings in an apartment on the capital's central Arbat Street. Accused of plotting to shoot Stalin as he was driven to his dacha, Dunskii and Frid each got ten years, even though it came out during the investigation that the windows of the apartment in question faced the building's inner courtyard and not the street.

Dunskii and Frid celebrated New Year's Eve 1956 with twenty-five guests crammed into the small wooden house they had bought upon being released in 1954. "Liberation" had come with a sentence of "eternal exile," so they were trying to make a home in Inta. The friends worked for the big coal-mining trust during the day and tried to write at night, hoping that their scripts would pave their way back to Moscow. They still possessed youth and ambition. Moreover, in the labor camp they had made an important friend, the well-known film director Aleksei Kapler. Arrested for too close a friendship with Stalin's daughter, Svetlana, by 1956 Kapler had already won rehabilitation and begun to rebuild his career. He promised to help them land a contract and insisted they continue petitioning for rehabilitation.

Meanwhile, in the rough little house in the godforsaken north, Dunskii and Frid spent a lively New Year's. As if trying to revive their lost youth, they celebrated like the students they had been before their arrest. They wrote and illustrated a satirical broadsheet with jokes at the expense of their friends, composed limericks to entertain the guests, laid on food and drink, and even set up a "radio station" for fun. A microphone was rigged next door, and every thirty minutes the hosts ducked out to "broadcast the latest news, radio reports, concerts, and so forth." They were marooned far from home but not without comforts and good company. "If you believe that greeting the New Year's well means that you'll live that whole year well," Iulii wrote to a friend afterward, "then this year ought to be outstanding all-around for us."[8]

Writers were not the only ones trying hard to predict the future. On January 5 a once-prominent geneticist newly released from exile wrote to a friend in Moscow, welcoming the news that science was "stirring" and that the "'recovery' of biology" from limitations imposed under Stalin was gaining speed.[9] For many intellectuals, the search for terms to capture the small signs of change led to Ehrenburg's meteorological metaphor of a "thaw." The term *thaw* gives us several ways to think about what might have been happening in Russia in 1956. One might think of Stalinism as a sort of terrible ice age. The end of the deep freeze could

Fig. 01-02 Dunskii and Frid's house on Coal Street in Inta. Courtesy Zoya B. Osipova.

mean a return to life and warmth. Like a "recovery," it might hark back to a previous good condition; or like the retreat of glaciers, it might leave a distorted, scarred landscape, but it at least carried the promise of long-lasting change. Thaws, however, can also be seasonal, part of a bigger cycle. The breaking of ice in the Neva River, for instance, has always been seen in Leningrad/St. Petersburg as a happy harbinger of spring. The melting of winter snow and ice signals change, but change of a temporary sort, part of a familiar cycle rather than a promise of eternal spring.[10] Change, in other words, can be transformational and long lasting, cyclical and predictable, or precarious and perhaps untenable.

While scholars debate exactly when the "thaw" began and ended, 1956 marks its clear takeoff. "Rapid ideological change" was, as historian Stephen Bittner puts it, "the common denominator of Khrushchev's contradictory, uneven, and sometimes ill-planned reforms."[11] Khrushchev's so-called Secret Speech in February would disrupt the official narrative of Soviet history and send propagandists and policy makers scrambling to answer tough questions about blame for the cult of Stalin and to deal with prisoners whose guilt had been cast into question. The rehabilitation of victims of the purges and renunciation of slavish adherence to Stalin's every word marked the start of a renaissance of intellectual searching. The year would be full of criticism, exuberance, and debate until political and ideological crises in Poland and Hungary sparked Soviet intervention to preserve the socialist bloc and kindled a backlash at home.

To understand the impact of Khrushchev's choice to more openly break with Stalin and his repressive policies, we must first examine where the Soviet Union stood in 1956. The pivotal nature of this tumultuous year in Russian history rests on the fundament of Stalinism, a complex and shifting phenomenon in its own right. Nearly forty years had passed since the Bolshevik seizure of power in October 1917. During those decades the Soviet Union had experienced revolutionary upheaval, class conflict, civil war, collectivization, industrialization, purges, world war, victory, famine, and recovery. Despite all the changes wrought by the revolution in economics, politics, and culture, one constant stood out: the dominance of the Communist Party and, between 1928 and 1953, the personal leadership of Stalin. No brief summary can fully capture the complexities of Stalin, his reign, or the ideology and practices he promoted. I offer some generalizations and then let the biographies of some who lived through Stalinism, most notably Stalin's successor Nikita Khrushchev, speak for themselves.

"Life Is Getting Happier"

When Stalin began to accumulate power in the years after Lenin's death, the Communist Party was a diverse organization of revolutionaries and strivers, a motley crew of ideologues, organizers, bureaucrats, connivers, and idealists. Big questions stood before them: How should the economy be organized? Could world revolution be fomented quickly? How could industrial development be accelerated? What means could most effectively turn illiterate peasants and first-generation workers into new communist men and women? By the end of the 1930s, the answers to many of these questions had been formulated, and the party stood powerful, monolithic, uncompromising, and humorless. Revolutionary schemes had given way to technical plans for loyalists and prison sentences for dissenters.

In the countryside peasant plots had been forcibly replaced with collective farms; in the cities new industrial enterprises churned out heavy machinery. In the universities sons of peasants studied alongside the daughters of intellectuals, and, regardless of their chosen discipline, all university and trade school students crammed the doctrines of Marxism-Leninism-Stalinism. Soviet schoolchildren learned they were the luckiest in the world, growing up in the most progressive nation on earth under the care of the kindly Stalin. Even those who lived badly could take pleasure at the nation's gains.

Future physicist Yuri Orlov spent his boyhood dwelling in a damp "apartment" made of converted monastery cells and using a filthy communal toilet, but he remembers thinking his home "marvelous," much better than the barracks one saw in many places. Similarly, his neighbor in Moscow took pride in the accomplishments of collective farms as reported in the newspapers. When a skeptic reminded him of how he bemoaned the state of the village in which his relatives lived, the neighbor replied: "That's only one place. But you've got to look at other places."[12] Personal disappointments had to be held up against the big picture, and here the flood of positive information in the press and on the radio gave scoffers little ammunition. "Life is getting happier" was the slogan drummed into Soviet citizens in the 1930s. Indeed, the Soviet regime excelled in some areas: teaching basic literacy, providing opportunities to study, promoting public health, ensuring employment, and mandating basic wage equality.

The life of the future first secretary reflected many of the positive developments of these years. Born in 1894 into a peasant family in the Kursk region in southwest Russia, Khrushchev received meager schooling as a youngster and tended livestock before moving to the Ukrainian factory town of Yuzovka, now known as Donetsk. In his native village, few people could read and write. They lived in small huts and eked out a living. As Khrushchev later recollected, "Every villager dreamed of owning a pair of boots. We children were lucky if we had a decent pair of shoes. We wiped our noses on our sleeves and kept our trousers up with string."[13] Khrushchev got his taste of urban life at age fourteen. He started out cleaning boilers and advanced to working as a fitter, assembling machinery. Yuzovka was a tough, dirty town full of impoverished workers, disease, and crime, but Khrushchev never pined for the village. He had his heart set on improving his social situation through skilled work and study.

Before the revolution, Khrushchev was busy mastering new jobs, wooing a worker's daughter to be his wife, and learning a bit about politics in his quest to win better working conditions for himself and his co-workers. The revolution, however, upended Khrushchev's personal plans. Although he continued to aspire to become an engineer or factory director, he was sidetracked by the business of building Soviet power. Khrushchev had a reputation in Yuzovka for being involved in left-wing politics. He did not join the Bolshevik Party until 1918, but he supported the revolution and immediately became an activist in his district. Before long Khrushchev found himself fighting on the side of the Red Army against the monarchist Whites.

When the civil war ended, Khrushchev returned to Yuzovka to help restart the mines. His upward mobility might have stalled there—back in his home area, back at familiar work—but the new government promoted workers' training, and Khrushchev seized on the chance to improve his credentials. At a new school for adult workers, Khrushchev combined his studies with leadership of the local party cell and soon with membership in the city party committee. Already a widower, he once again married up—this time to an educated party worker. Throughout the 1920s Khrushchev took up ever-higher positions in the Ukrainian party organization.

The magnitude of changes in Khrushchev's life and in those of some of his countrymen can be appreciated only with attention to some details. In 1925, at the age of thirty-one, Khrushchev held the post of party secretary for a rural region. In describing one good commune in his district, he noted, "They had no tractors. I myself had only ever heard about tractors at the time; I had heard that they existed but had never, as they say, set eyes on one."[14] It was Khrushchev's job to exhort the peasants to sow more grain, all the while making promises about a utopian future replete with these mythical tractors. That same year Khrushchev traveled to Moscow for the first time to attend the Fourteenth CPSU Congress. His strongest memory of the occasion was an embarrassing one: how he got lost trying to take a streetcar to the Kremlin. After that mishap

Khrushchev chose to rise early and walk to the Kremlin. He preferred to solve his problem with extra physical effort, rather than risk letting his ignorance show again.

The grandeur of the Kremlin conference hall and the apparent humility that Stalin and other leaders showed toward the provincial delegates made a huge impression on Khrushchev. Such events fed his ambition but also sparked self-doubt. Could a poorly educated provincial fellow such as he ever become an influential person, ever gain Stalin's confidence? It seemed that under socialism the answer might be yes. Just three years later, Khrushchev was sent to head up the party organization in Kiev, the capital of the Ukrainian Soviet Socialist Republic. Khrushchev related, "This was the first time in my life I had been in Kiev, a very large city. Before that, strictly speaking, and not counting Moscow, I had seen only Kharkov, Yekaterinoslav [Dnepropetrovsk], and Mariupol."[15] He rightly feared that Kievans would regard him as a country bumpkin. But Khrushchev soldiered on, compensating for his lack of education and cultural savvy with energy, determination, and party loyalty.

Khrushchev's advancement did not stop in Kiev. He still harbored a strong desire to become an engineer, a respected and useful profession. In 1930, at age thirty-four, he wangled permission to leave his party post to study at the Industrial Academy in Moscow. An indifferent student, Khrushchev shone as a party activist at his institute. Before long he was tapped to return to full-time party work as a secretary for a region of Moscow. Khrushchev never became an engineer, but he learned how to run a city. Khrushchev's biographer William Taubman describes the task of party secretaries in the 1930s thus: "They weren't just administrators but Soviet-style politician/managers."[16] They had to become knowledgeable about industry, construction, food supply, housing, transport—in short, everything. Khrushchev proved himself in part by overseeing the construction of the Moscow Metro. He recruited labor, exhorted workers, helped organize supplies, and weighed in on technical issues as he shepherded to completion the first stage of the capital's subway system. The party framed metro construction as one of the heroic tasks of the day, and Khrushchev's role in it won him an Order of Lenin and the post of party secretary for all of Moscow.

But the revolution had its dark side. Under Lenin, during revolution and civil war, the Bolsheviks had fought to "exterminate class enemies."

Their measures ranged from executing the tsar and his family to driving petty traders out of the cities. By the 1930s it seemed as if the exploiting classes had been vanquished, yet the violence continued. Collectivization targeted "rich" peasants, the so-called *kulaks*, who had their land and household property confiscated. Many were sent into exile or imprisoned. It also contributed to an unacknowledged famine that took millions of lives. Meanwhile, political opponents of Stalin, real and imaginary, also suffered increasingly sharp persecution. The Soviet public was treated to the spectacle of show trials of foreign experts and high-ranking communists accused of sabotage and treason. The party fought internal enemies on the right and left, winnowing its own ranks, suppressing diversity, and stifling debate. Rewards awaited party officials who played Stalin's game by conducting witch hunts against oppositionists. Indeed, Khrushchev first came to the leader's attention when he helped identify and expel alleged deviationists from the Industrial Academy, where Stalin's young wife was a fellow student.

In 1934 the assassination of Leningrad party boss Sergei Kirov by a lone gunman, a crime soon linked to show trials of Stalin's rivals, served as a pretext for strengthening the power of the secret police and ramping up vigilance and arrests.[17] Stalin decided that those accused of terrorism now could be executed without full trials. The Soviet secret police, the NKVD, was secretly authorized to use torture to extract confessions. Leningrad and Moscow were quickly emptied of suspicious types. Former aristocrats and petty traders, anyone who had belonged to another political party, and those who had fallen afoul of authorities in the past faced deportation or arrest. With Stalin's knowledge and encouragement, the NKVD would fill the prisons and labor camps with millions of political prisoners in the next few years. The so-called purges or terror peaked in 1937 and tapered off but had not ended by the start of World War II.

As the head of the Moscow party committee, Khrushchev preached the Stalinist line on the battle with internal enemies. He publicly welcomed the death sentences pronounced in the show trials. He justified party purges, telling delegates to the Moscow city party conference in May 1937, "This is not an open struggle where bullets come flying from the enemy's side. This is a struggle with the man who sits next to you, who hails our successes and our Party's achievements, while at the same time squeezing the revolver in his pocket, choosing the moment to put a bullet into you the way they did into Sergei Mironovich Kirov."[18] Obviously such hidden traitors had to be rooted out and destroyed. In Moscow and elsewhere the ranks of party officials were decimated. Taubman notes that only three of thirty-eight top Moscow city and region secretaries survived. Khrushchev's assistants, colleagues, coworkers, and friends all disappeared into the city's prisons. And Khrushchev had to authorize the arrests and the sentences lest he too fall under suspicion.[19]

In later years Khrushchev would describe this time as "painful." On the one hand, he felt outraged at the thought he had been duped by people close to him. How had it passed his notice that so many of his closest comrades had been enemies? On the other hand, it seemed incredible that so many old Bolsheviks and young enthusiasts would betray the cause. Stalin showed him transcripts of their confessions, yet even so Khrushchev sometimes doubted. The hardest thing to bear was the increasing power of the secret police. But he could not find the means to argue with it. "I saw things then through the eyes of the Central Committee, that is, Stalin, and I repeated the arguments that I heard from Stalin."[20] Two years later, serving in another important post, he allegedly confided to a friend: "Do you think I understand what's going on in this country? Do you think I understand why I'm sitting here in this office as Ukrainian first secretary rather than in a cell at Lubyanka [prison]? Do you think I can be sure that they won't drag me out of here tomorrow and throw me in prison? Nonetheless, we must work, we must do everything possible . . . for the happiness of the people."[21] For many party members, the only coping mechanism to deal with the fluid line between victim and victimizer was virtuousness: increased professions of loyalty and renewed exhibitions of dedication to the tasks assigned by the party.

Belief in the Communist Party and its leadership and disbelief in some of the wild accusations against loyal officials created a terrible tension among insiders. Tat'iana Rybakova, later the wife of writer Anatoly Rybakov, whose anti-Stalinist novel *Children of the Arbat* was a perestroika era sensation, tells the story of her mother-in-law from her first marriage. A plain woman who earnestly supported the Bolsheviks, her mother-in-law had become a party secretary for one of the districts of Moscow in the 1930s. Around the time of the devastating purge of the Moscow party organization, the poor woman was stricken with paralysis. She spent four of the worst months of the purges in bed, unable to move her legs. When the storm passed, she recovered and returned to work. She never admitted that her paralysis might have been the result of psychological trauma, nor did she change her politics. Nevertheless, in the early 1950s she accepted and treated kindly a daughter-in-law whose father had been executed and whose mother languished in eternal exile.[22]

For most high-ranking party members, however, survival required a certain amount of realism. Consider Khrushchev's treatment of Kseniia Chudinova, an old Bolshevik and one of his subordinates in the Moscow city party organization during the purges. Chudinova later recounted that she had asked an old comrade, Samuil Chudnovskii, then a top judge in Leningrad, to explain the wave of arrests of party people. When he answered, "I myself do not understand," she lit into him. How could he as a judge not know the basis of accusations against the people whose cases he heard? Angrily he informed her that the NKVD rebuffed any inquiries and that all the members of the judiciary felt their own vulnerability. When Chudinova urged him to write to Stalin about the situation, he told her, "Stop being so naive. He knows everything and oversees it all himself via the NKVD and [prosecutor general Andrei] Vyshinsky." Chudinova refused to accept his reasoning. Indeed, learning subsequently that Chudnovskii had been arrested, she wrote a letter to Khrushchev to ask his help in arranging a meeting with the secret police investigators so that she could vouch for her friend. To her chagrin, "Nikita Sergeevich took my letter, read it, tore it into small pieces, and threw them in different wastebaskets. I understood [then] that he himself was afraid."[23]

By 1941 the frenzy of the purges had abated, and for a few years all attention was on the front as the USSR fought for its very survival in World War II. At the cost of huge human sacrifice, Soviet soldiers beat the Nazis. They came home to a country devastated by occupation, warfare, hunger, and deprivation. Veterans carried with them a new self-confidence and, some historians argue, hopes that they had earned the trust of the state. Perhaps now Soviet citizens would be freer to live and work without suspicion from or strict oversight by the party. Yuri Orlov recalled that as he waited with other soldiers and officers to be demobilized in 1946, "For the first time in my twenty-two years I encountered serious political talk." These men had fought their way across Europe, and they were testing out their opinions. Their wishes for a less-fraught atmosphere, however, were not realized. In fact, the late 1940s witnessed new rounds of ideological testing, Stalin-inspired paranoia, and persecution.[24]

In Ukraine at war's end, for instance, Khrushchev was busy overseeing the capture of Ukrainian independence fighters, the Sovietization of newly added territory, and a centrally initiated campaign against "bourgeois nationalism," all while coping with a war-ravaged industry and a devastated countryside. On a national scale, in 1948 many political prisoners who had been freed after completing long camp terms were rearrested and consigned to the newly created punishment of eternal exile in remote parts of the USSR. Central officials also initiated a campaign against "cosmopolitanism." In the Soviet context, *cosmopolitanism* meant the embracing of foreign ideas or practices. For instance, scientists could not praise foreign technology or admit to building on research done overseas. The whole field of genetics was declared alien. Soviet biologists would follow the practical work of native agronomists on plant breeding, not imitate Western colleagues who studied fruit flies in a laboratory. In practice, the anticosmopolitan campaign took on a strong pro-Russian and anti-Semitic character. Jews—"rootless cosmopolitans"—were driven out of universities and high posts of every sort.

Sergei Dmitriev, a historian at Moscow State University, captured the atmosphere of the times in his diary entry for February 20, 1949. On that day, he noted the appearance in a major newspaper of an article, signed under a pseudonym, attacking a textbook he had coauthored for its alleged bourgeois leanings and "objectivism" (that is, not bearing in mind the party's interest in the choice of facts to include). That evening Dmitriev visited a friend where he heard about: "1) the discovery of some "Zionist" organization . . . 2) that [Jewish theater director Solomon] Mikhoels did not die naturally, but was murdered; 3) that some famous figures in medicine—[Sergei] Iudin and Lina Stern—were arrested."[25] Indeed, the secret police had begun arrests in the so-called Doctors' Plot, an alleged conspiracy by Jewish doctors to poison party leaders and Russians. These lurid charges of political terrorism sparked anxiety among the public and raised fear among astute consumers of the Soviet media of a new round of persecutions, this time with a racial focus.

High Stalinism was characterized by mixed economic progress and relative political stability with a constant undercurrent of anxiety.[26] The daughter of two repressed parents, Tat'iana Rybakova, in some respects, was thriving in 1951. After bouncing from one relative's home to another after her parents' arrests in 1938, she had found a haven with her sister-in-law, the widow of her older brother. Rybakova had been admitted to study at an institute, albeit a technical institute and only in the less-prestigious evening courses. Moreover, through connections of her disgraced parents, she had found a job as a receptionist at the Writer's Union. But when a policeman seemed to be following her and her date one evening when they walked out of a movie in the middle—she and poet Evgenii Vinokurov had found *Tarzan* too idiotic to finish watching—she trembled with fear, sure that somehow fate was catching up to her. Her boyfriend won her heart at that moment by reassuring her that he would stand by her no matter what. He swore that he would even follow her into exile.[27]

Now consider the position of the highest Communist Party leaders, Stalin's closest assistants. In his typically colorful manner, Khrushchev tells an apocryphal tale in his memoirs. He begins, "I remember when Stalin took a vacation for the last time at [his state dacha on the Black Sea] Novy Afon. This was in 1951 (I know this because in 1952 Stalin didn't take a vacation. And since Stalin didn't take one, the rest of the leadership didn't either)." Stalin had summoned Khrushchev and fellow presidium member Anastas Mikoyan from their nearby holiday spots. As he met them for dinner, he suddenly blurted out, "I'm a rotten person. I don't trust anybody. I don't even trust myself." Assailed by the truth of this statement, Khrushchev and Mikoyan "were literally struck dumb." After all, Stalin combined his mistrustful nature with "a temperament that [drove] him to destroy everyone he [didn't] trust. That's why the people in his inner circle were there only temporarily," Khrushchev concluded.[28] When Stalin's paranoia got the better of him, the objects of his suspicions would be physically exterminated.

At the time of Stalin's sudden and ultimately fatal stroke in March 1953, his protégés were locked together in a poisonous atmosphere of mutual doubt, fear, and loathing. Not only had each lived in terror of the leader's notorious paranoia, but rivalry for favor had complicated their relations with one another. Stalin's death raised the possibility of breaking free from the situation in which the secret police wielded great power and political competition produced fatalities. But leadership and its limits had to be settled first. As William Taubman notes, "For Khrushchev,

Stalin's death was a decidedly mixed blessing, just as his patronage had been . . . His death freed Khrushchev from physical fear and psychological dependence. But it also exposed him to deadly new dangers—first from his Kremlin colleagues, later from himself, and all the while from the terrible legacy that Stalin's heirs faced and that eventually defeated them all."[29] The members of the presidium had been kept on short leashes by Stalin. Now they would have to take both the initiative and the responsibility for running a multinational, economically challenged, and ideologically hidebound superpower.

Out of Stalin's Shadow

In the moment of uncertainty following the dictator's death, the first to seize the initiative was the former secret police boss Lavrenty Beria. Together with Georgy Malenkov, he reassigned leadership posts and introduced new policies, including dismissal of the latest witch-hunt victims—the Kremlin doctors accused of plotting to poison Stalin—and a declaration of mass amnesty of criminal prisoners. Beria also rushed to lessen the much-resented Russification of the ethnic republics of the USSR and proposed relaxing the Soviet stranglehold on Eastern and Central Europe. Khrushchev and his colleagues later discounted Beria's liberal-sounding plans as an insincere effort to disarm critics and win some quick popularity, but some observers have dubbed this rapid revision of Stalinist policies a first "thaw." Historian Elena Zubkova argues convincingly that the pressing problems of the day—reining in the state security organs, relieving pressure on collective farmers, and bolstering morale among allies—imposed a general policy direction, one in which, for once, "the interests of the ruling stratum coincided with the interest of the people at large." The real question was who would address these issues. The initial answer was anyone but Beria.[30]

The minister of internal affairs, with the secret police at his disposal, inspired such fear among his colleagues that in June 1953 they formed a temporary alliance to rid themselves of Stalin's most powerful heir. Khrushchev organized the other presidium members, including Beria's apparent ally Malenkov, to support a surprise arrest in the Kremlin. The presidium members then dealt with Beria in a semi-Stalinist style. Though they convened the party's central committee in a special plenum to "discuss"—that is, ritualistically denounce—Beria, they ordered him tried in secret by a special military court. Afraid to confront the object of their fears, the presidium members listened to the trial in their individual offices via a special remote broadcast. Beria seems not to have been beaten into making a false confession, but he did face a mix of real and fantastical charges. His rivals found it easier to focus on his womanizing and accuse him of having spied for the British in his youth than to dig too deeply into the actions of the secret police for the last decade. Ultimately, like many of his own victims, Beria was shot while his family suffered arrest and exile.[31]

Beria's defeat marked the beginning of Khrushchev's ascendancy. Khrushchev wrangled with Malenkov over agriculture and worked with others to formulate a new foreign policy that would relieve the USSR of some of the burden of the arms race.[32] Khrushchev also finally gained the leeway to champion some of his own pet projects, most notably the sowing of the so-called Virgin Lands, of Siberia and Kazakhstan. Typical of Khrushchev's later policies, the Virgin Lands campaign was a grand quick-fix scheme that involved mobilizing youth and technology to complete a heroic task. But Khrushchev could not command from on high in quite the way Stalin had. The removal of Beria marked the formation of a collective security pact of sorts for the presidium members, but it did not end the rivalry and mistrust among Stalin's heirs. Political quarrels would not be settled by the secret police. Yet how they would be resolved among the collective remained to be worked out.[33]

As the presidium of the Communist Party, known in other eras as the politburo, met in January 1956, its members addressed many policy issues, ranging from developing atomic energy to finding funds to increase the minimum wage. At that time the presidium consisted of eleven full members and several candidate members. All were men, most were in their fifties and sixties, all had worked for the party and the state in a variety of jobs. Kliment Voroshilov, the eldest and most senior, had taken part in the revolution in Petrograd in 1917 and led Red Army troops into battle in the civil war. He had joined the politburo in 1926 and would turn seventy-five on the eve of the Twentieth Party Congress. The other senior members, Vyacheslav Molotov, Lazar Kaganovich, Anastas Mikoyan, and Nikita Khrushchev, had all been born in the last century and remembered the revolution well. They had served Stalin loyally for decades, all having become members of the high council before World War II. Other longtime members were Georgy Malenkov (b. 1902) and Nikolai Bulganin (b. 1895). In 1952 Stalin showed his disdain for and suspicion of his closest associates by unilaterally increasing the number of full and candidate members. Newcomers included Averkii Aristov, Maksim Saburov, Mikhail Suslov, and Mikhail Pervukhin. Slightly younger, these men had been Stalinists, too, protégés of the dictator.

Now all Stalin's men, still smarting over recent internal power struggles, had to define a new course for the USSR. They had a tough agenda. They wanted to reconfigure relations with the West while promoting the international communist movement, which implied repairing relations with Yugoslavia and reducing discord with China. At home they wanted to win popular support by improving standards of living, but they would not consider altering the basic framework of the planned economy and collectivized agriculture.

Psychological constraints also bound the old guard. As Khrushchev would put it years later, "There were several million people in the prison camps then. Three years had already gone by since Stalin's death. During those years we had not been able to break with the past, couldn't get up the courage, didn't find it an inner necessity to lift the edge of the curtain and take a peek at what had really gone on behind the scenes . . . we ourselves were constrained by our years of activity under Stalin's leadership, and we hadn't yet freed ourselves from the posthumous pressure of his influence . . . The same old policies were being followed, and everything that had been done under Stalin was being approved."[34]

In February Khrushchev would force a break at the cost of stirring up new enmities among his colleagues and disrupting the well-polished narrative of the party's steady and unerring leadership of the Soviet Union along the path to communism.

2 | FEBRUARY

A SUDDEN THAW

On February 1, 1956, all the members of the presidium met in the Kremlin. Ostensibly they gathered to settle details for the Twentieth Congress of the CPSU, which would convene in just two weeks. Party Congresses were huge events requiring careful preparation. Delegates from across the USSR would come to Moscow to hear their leaders give an account of the nation's achievements and lay out the agenda for the future. The new five-year plan for the economy would be outlined, and developments in foreign policy would be explained. Representatives of foreign communist parties would testify to the strength of the international workers' movement and pay their respects to the revolutionary vanguard, the Soviet Communist Party. For Stalin's heirs, this Congress represented an opportunity to reinforce their authority and rally their followers.

Preparations for the Congress had begun back in April 1955, when Khrushchev proposed February 1956 as a date for the event. The CPSU's charter called for holding Congresses at least once every four years, but under Stalin this regimen had fallen by the wayside. The previous Congress, held in 1952, had been the first and only one since the start of World War II. Convening the Twentieth Party Congress in 1956, therefore, would be a step toward restoring procedural regularity as well as a chance for Khrushchev personally to demonstrate his new prominence in the leadership. It would also provide a potential platform for launching a major change in the party's evaluation of Stalin.

Many arrangements had to be made for the Congress to flow smoothly. Representatives had to be "elected" in their regions—one for every five thousand CPSU members. In practice, this meant that local party bosses had to compile a list of appropriate people for approval by regional party committees. A proper roster consisted of party notables, model workers, and farmers, plus some prominent people, such as military officers, factory directors, or renowned scientists; it also included a few women and representatives of any local ethnic minorities. Invitations also had to be issued to carefully vetted foreign communists and left-wing allies. Accommodations, cultural programs, gifts for delegates, even the assortment of books to be offered for sale from a kiosk in the Kremlin conference hall received scrupulous attention from party bureaucrats.[1]

Meanwhile, Khrushchev, Malenkov, and the other presidium members and their staffs toiled over the reports and speeches to be delivered. At leadership sessions, they discussed issues ranging from how to increase agricultural productivity to whether they could afford to reduce the length of the working day. In particular, they argued over the meaning and wisdom of the party's new policy of "peaceful coexistence." Had nuclear weapons undone the inevitability of war between capitalism and socialism? Could socialism spread without armed revolution? Khrushchev had to defend his position that the world communist movement could battle with capitalism by nonmilitary means, such as economic and cultural competition.[2]

Behind the debates about foreign policy, ideology, and economic priorities lurked an even more sensitive question: how to treat Stalin. Commemoration of Stalin's birthday and his death had been steadily muted and reduced in scale in the three years following the dictator's passing. Nevertheless, Stalin's image and teachings remained omnipresent. His portrait graced the walls of every school, factory, museum, and office. His words were cited daily by teachers, journalists, scholars, and politicians.[3] Visitors to Moscow flocked to the renamed "Lenin-Stalin Mausoleum" to pay their respects to the late leader. Indeed, delegates to the Congress would make it a priority to visit the mausoleum. As the representative of the Communist Party from Trieste, Vittorio Vidali recounted in his diary of the Twentieth Congress, "[We] looked at the mausoleum, which is the goal of a constant pilgrimage of Soviet citizens who come to see Lenin and Stalin. There they were, the one next to the other, Lenin wearing a Russian shirt, Stalin in uniform." Vidali found the display "macabre rather than impressive"; others presumably found it more moving.[4] Indeed, reverence for Stalin made it hard for prior policies to be criticized. The question of whether old wrongs could be amended in silence split the leadership.

One man firmly believed that the presidium members needed to take the opportunity provided by the Congress to address the representatives of the whole party. "If they don't dethrone Stalin at this congress, the first after the tyrant's death, if they don't tell of his crimes, then they will go down in history as his willing collaborators," argued Aleksei Snegov, a veteran party member and survivor of seventeen years in the gulag. "Only by revealing Stalin's role, can they convince the Party that they were unwilling participants," he explained to presidium member Anastas Mikoyan's son. By challenging them to think about what they would say if the issue arose at the Twenty-First Congress or the Twenty-Second, Snegov helped to convince Mikoyan and then Khrushchev that the time to act had come.[5]

How did a former prisoner manage to gain the ear of the first secretary of the Communist Party? Snegov's story illustrates the very limited extent to which Stalin's heirs had engaged with the recent history of mass repressions before 1956. After the arrest of Minister of Internal Affairs Lavrenty Beria in June 1953, Aleksei Snegov had smuggled a letter out of the labor camp in Kolyma, where he was serving a long and unjust sentence. He wrote to his old comrades Mikoyan and Khrushchev to tell them of the horrors of the gulag and the many honest people still suffering there. He also volunteered himself as a witness to the misdeeds committed by Beria and his henchmen. Brought directly from camp to Moscow, Snegov appeared before the military tribunal presiding over Beria's closed trial. Beria allegedly reacted angrily upon seeing his former comrade, exclaiming, "What, are you still alive?" To which Snegov responded, "Your organization didn't do its job properly."[6] Few witnesses to Beria's machinations survived the purges, but Snegov had dodged execution and endured the camps.[7]

At the closed trial, Snegov related how Stalin had promoted Beria through the party ranks against the wishes of other old Bolsheviks in the Transcaucasia bureau. He also recounted his personal experience of being tortured in prison in 1938 and told of the terrible, inhumane conditions in Kolyma. Historian Roy Medvedev, who interviewed Snegov in the 1960s, avers that Snegov was automatically remanded back to the labor camps to finish his sentence when Beria's trial ended in late December 1953. Historian Matthew Lenoe contends that Snegov was in fact sent into exile in Komi for the three months leading up to his rehabilitation on March 6, 1954. As Medvedev noted, Snegov preferred not to talk about this setback.[8]

With his March rehabilitation, Snegov became one of the first gulag survivors to be allowed to return to Moscow. There, at the home of his friend Lev Shaumian, the son of one of the famously martyred Baku commissars, he met with Anastas Mikoyan, his former boss and fellow veteran of party work in the Caucasus. According to Mikoyan's son, the Kremlin at that time remained like a fortress. A member of the presidium had to go to more neutral territory to talk to a former political prisoner. Snegov's account of the purges and the camps impressed Mikoyan so strongly that he recommended to Khrushchev that he too consult this firsthand source. And so at some point early in 1954, Khrushchev renewed his acquaintance with Snegov, whom he had known through party work in Ukraine in the 1920s. Shortly thereafter Khrushchev arranged for Snegov to enter the Ministry of Internal Affairs (MVD) as deputy head of the political department of the main administration for camps (gulag), where he worked till 1960.[9]

It is impossible to say with any certainty how much Khrushchev learned from Snegov's tales of torture and imprisonment. All of the senior members of the presidium were well aware of the mass nature of arrests of party cadres in the 1930s. Several of them—most notably Molotov, Kaganovich, and Voroshilov—had signed off on numerous lists confirming death sentences for thousands of people in 1937 and 1938. Khrushchev too had been involved in reviewing lists of his subordinates who had been arrested and certainly knew that many of those purged were loyal Bolsheviks. But, with the exception of the secret police bosses, members of the party elite most likely knew little about what happened inside the walls of the prisons or in the remote Siberian labor camps. Snegov provided invaluable firsthand testimony and a reassuring interpretation of the purges as a deviation from the Leninist path.

Throughout his prison ordeal and through the vagaries of the thaw and stagnation, Snegov remained a steadfast Leninist. Mikoyan's son Sergo describes Snegov in 1954 as "not looking at all like a broken man. On the contrary, he acted like a conqueror. And he was—he had beaten the 'master torturers' in his case and the whole repressive system of the Gulag."[10] Slim and handsome, the dark-haired Snegov bubbled over with energy and ideas, traits that resonated with Khrushchev.

Moreover, Snegov's loyalty to the party in spite of great suffering at the hands of the police made him the perfect person to persuade Khrushchev that denouncing Stalin could redeem and even strengthen the party. As historian Miriam Dobson has suggested, the "stories of heroic self-sacrifice" offered up by loyal victims in their petitions for rehabilitation and readmission to the party provided a new model for dealing with past crimes.[11] Mutual forgiveness could create a strengthened community of reformers. Khrushchev not only adopted Snegov's ideas about de-Stalinization but used the man himself as a pretext to push the idea that the past abuses had to be dealt with at the Congress.

The decision to denounce Stalin could not have been an easy one for Khrushchev. Not only had members of the Communist Party been trained to idolize Stalin, but Khrushchev, like all the senior leaders, had made his career under Stalin. He and his colleagues had begun as admirers of Stalin's confident policy making and dexterous maneuvering. They had advanced by demonstrating extreme devotion. Furthermore, high-ranking party members—and indeed many ordinary Russians as well—could not easily separate out their efforts and the many achievements of the Soviet regime from Stalin's leadership. Stalin had provided both the carrot and the stick—or the lash and the gingerbread, as Russians say—to get his subordinates to give their all for the cause, and they took pride in their nation's military and economic feats.

Khrushchev's explanations of why he felt compelled to make the report denouncing Stalin—all made in the Congress's aftermath—reveal a muddle of conflicting sentiments. Khrushchev resented Stalin's often humiliating treatment of his subordinates, and he recognized many costly mistakes had been made in domestic and foreign policy. Yet he was reluctant to believe the worst of Stalin. Khrushchev's biographer William Taubman succinctly describes the leader's mental state in the months leading up to the Twentieth Congress as "a kind of manic ambivalence, his consciousness streaming wildly from self-justification to guilt to pride."[12] Even after he made the Secret Speech, Khrushchev seemed incapable of reconciling Stalin's cruelty with his commitment to building communism. For instance, one month after the Twentieth Congress, Khrushchev floundered when he tried to explain Stalin's hold on his subordinates: "Was [Stalin] more stupid than we were? No. Smarter than we were? As a Marxist he was stronger. We have to give him his due, comrades, but Stalin was ill, he abused his power . . . He wanted to serve society with all his heart and soul. I'm absolutely convinced of that. The whole question has to do with the ways and means."[13] As for his own culpability, in his memoirs dictated years later, Khrushchev would temporize: "Of course, doubts had crept into my mind as they would into any man's . . . But Stalin, this was Stalin! I had no idea that this man was capable in principle of consciously abusing his power."[14]

In 1953 the party leadership had decided to heap all of the blame for the Doctors' Plot and lapses in collective rule on Beria. But, as Khrushchev admitted, he felt the "falseness of that position" especially when Yugoslav comrades made snide remarks about Beria's responsibility. The presidium's position was bogus, and therefore its proponents felt vulnerable to ridicule. At some point in late 1955, Khrushchev privately decided to support a more complete accounting of what happened. Having confirmed with his prosecutor general that the show trials of the 1930s had been based entirely on forced confessions and having received affirmations of the innocence of some close comrades who had been executed as "enemies of the people," Khrushchev began to plan a way to bring his fellow party bosses around to sanctioning a denunciation of Stalin.[15] Heeding Snegov's warning that any public reevaluation of Stalin had better come sooner rather than later, Khrushchev wanted the party to admit its mistakes at the February Congress.

Others in the leadership were less certain of the need for revelations and more concerned with potential repercussions. Senior presidium members wanted to know: Who was asking for all this? Why risk raising questions of accountability? They were unlikely to be consoled by Khrushchev's pointed reminder: "Even in the case of people who have committed crimes, a moment comes when they can confess, and that brings them, if not acquittal, at least a reduction in sentence."[16] To obtain the consent of his fellow presidium members for the Secret Speech, Khrushchev—with Mikoyan's strong support—chose to shock them with some of the worst facts about the purges, while gradually introducing the topic of Stalin's complicity. He also stood ready to remind the potentially recalcitrant senior members of their own guilt; the top leaders knew that Khrushchev had already parlayed Malenkov's culpability in the postwar purge of the Leningrad party organization against him in the behind-the-scenes struggle for dominance among Stalin's heirs. Khrushchev was not above shaming other members of Stalin's inner circle to block them from curbing his own ambition to be first among equals within the new "collective leadership."[17]

In December 1955 Khrushchev proposed that the presidium form a commission to research the fate of the delegates to the Seventeenth Party Congress and the Central Committee that it had elected. The 1934 "Congress of Victors" had been convened shortly before the assassination of Leningrad party leader Sergei Kirov and the subsequent intensification of the hunt for internal enemies. Khrushchev knew full well that many of the delegates to this Congress had died in the purges—he calculated that exposure of the tragic fates of these top communists would touch the hearts of presidium members.[18] After all, these delegates were their former coworkers, comrades, and friends.

Even before the commission could complete its report, Khrushchev began to introduce the topic of the purges at every session of the presidium. On December 31, 1955, he presented thirdhand testimony from a former political prisoner suggesting that Kirov's assassination had been masterminded by the NKVD, presumably with Stalin's approval. Three weeks later Khrushchev circulated a letter from Snegov asking that he be allowed to attend the Twentieth Congress. Snegov wrote that since the Tenth Congress, he had missed only two "for reasons well-known to you." In light of Snegov's appeal, Khrushchev broached the idea of inviting several rehabilitated old Bolsheviks to attend the Congress, and soon a list of thirteen names was compiled. Here would be living reminders of loyal party members who had suffered but who were now restored to the party's trust.[19]

On February 1 Khrushchev raised the heat by bringing one of the perpetrators of the purges before the presidium. Boris Rodos's name figured prominently in the files of old Bolsheviks being reviewed by the commission looking into the deaths of the delegates to the Seventeenth Congress. Uneducated and tough, Rodos had risen in the ranks of the secret police starting in 1939, when he had demonstrated his ability to extract confessions by force in the case of the former head of the NKVD, Nikolai Yezhov. Now facing charges of violating Soviet law in his methods of investigation, a sullen and defensive Colonel Rodos told the presidium members that he had only followed what he understood to be the party's instructions. Khrushchev related in the Secret Speech that when questioned about his abuse of specific top-ranking communists, "[Rodos] announced: 'I was told that [Stanislav] Kosior and [Vlas] Chubar were enemies of the people, and thus as the investigator I was supposed to wring out of them confessions that they were enemies.'" Rodos expressed no regret for his torture of old Bolsheviks, and the presidium in turn showed him no sympathy, sending his case to the Military Collegium for a closed trial. He would be sentenced to death the day after the Secret Speech.[20]

After listening to Rodos, Averkii Aristov, who had been serving on the new investigative commission, asked the tough but logical question: "Comrade Khrushchev, do we have the courage to tell the truth?" A rough transcript of the ensuing discussion shows confusion and discord about the history of repression and how to judge those who carried it out. Khrushchev first responded to Aristov's question by raising the fate of Rodos's most infamous victim, former secret police chief Nikolai Yezhov. "Yezhov, surely, is not guilty, an honest man." But Mikoyan hastened to remind Khrushchev that the decree on terror used to justify torture was adopted during Yezhov's reign. Stalin, too, had his advocates. When the discussion turned to what might be said in the Congress, Vyacheslav Molotov, one of Stalin's closest assistants, protested, "We must say in the report that Stalin was a great continuer of Lenin's cause. I insist on this." Kaganovich in turn reminded his colleagues that Stalin had been at the helm of the USSR for thirty years. The purges, in other words, ought to be viewed only in the larger context of Stalin's leadership. But the weight of what they had just heard could not be ignored.

A more junior presidium member, Maksim Saburov, daringly interjected: "If these facts are true, then how can this be communism? This cannot be forgiven." To which the older, more experienced Mikoyan could only reply, "Take a look at [our] history—it's enough to drive you mad!"[21]

The presidium's discussion revealed several layers to the problem of revealing the terror. First, what really happened? Second, who was responsible? Third, what should be said about the past? Fourth, what if anything should be done as a result of the revelations? Stalin's old comrades Molotov and Voroshilov defended the dictator. If the truth had to be told, they contended, it should be that under Stalin's leadership socialism had triumphed, albeit with some shameful episodes. Voroshilov specifically warned Khrushchev not to throw out the baby with the bathwater. Reckless words, he worried, could endanger the party. Others, however, supported a more negative evaluation of the past. As Mikhail Suslov put it, "Over the last several months we've learned terrible things. None of this can be justified." Mikhail Pervukhin raised the problem of accountability: "Did we know? We knew, but there was terror. At that time we couldn't do anything." Like Khrushchev, he concluded, "The Party is obliged to explain, to tell at the Congress, and at the plenum."[22]

Khrushchev had the last word at the February 1 session. He noted that the Stalin question had to be decided in the interests of the party. Symptomatic of the difficulty veteran party members would have in reevaluating Stalin and his place in the history of the party, Khrushchev averred: "Stalin was devoted to the cause of socialism, but used all sorts of barbaric means. He destroyed the party. He was not a Marxist. He obliterated all that was holy in a man. Everyone was at the mercy of his whims." The time had come, Khrushchev declared, for stronger measures to be taken against the cult of personality. He did not at this point demand a denunciation of Stalin at the Congress, but he was laying the groundwork.[23]

Eight days later the presidium convened again. With less than a week before the opening session of the Congress, the meeting began with several routine items of current business: a minor change to be made to the party charter, ongoing talks with Mongolian leaders, a report by Marshal Zhukov on military affairs, including such details as the cessation of a special grain levy on collective farms in light of disbandment of the cavalry. Finally, the floor was turned over to Central Committee Secretary Petr Pospelov to report on the findings of the commission formed just two months earlier to look into the fates of delegates to the 1934 "Congress of Victors."[24]

Pospelov, a loyal Stalinist and former editor of *Pravda,* had worked with junior presidium members Averkii Aristov and Nikolai Shvernik and the deputy head of the Party Control Commission Petr Komarov to collect information about the repressions of the prewar period from the NKVD archives. According to Mikoyan, Pospelov read the report with great difficulty, weeping at times.[25] The spectacle of this highly placed official—a man known for his serious demeanor, dedication to Stalin, and propagandistic flair—reporting starkly on the execution of his comrades was calculated to touch the consciences of even the most obdurate presidium members.

Pospelov began with the statistics: between 1935 and 1940 1,920,635 persons were arrested and charged with anti-Soviet activity, of these persons 688,503 were subject to execution by firing squad. Even a cursory study showed that the repressions peaked in the years 1937–1938 and that they disproportionately affected party officials. Of 1,966 delegates to the "Congress of Victors," 1,103 were arrested and of those 848 were shot. From the members and candidate members to the Party's Central Committee elected at the 1934 Congress, 98 of 139 were arrested and all of those arrested were executed.[26]

Next Pospelov described some of the mechanisms of the purges. He started with the passage of a new law in the wake of the December 1934 assassination of Kirov. To speed up prosecution of the state's enemies, appeals in such cases were forbidden, as were petitions for mercy. Then in 1936 a telegram from Stalin accusing the secret police of being "at least four years behind" in uncovering Trotskyite-Zinovievite conspiracies sparked a surge in charges of anti-Soviet activity. Then NKVD head Yezhov began issuing commands to his subordinates to increase arrest totals. For example, in July 1937 he ordered the immediate arrest of all German subjects and immigrants who were working or who had ever worked in Soviet factories producing military goods. Soon he was issuing every region of the country with targets for the arrest of anti-Soviet elements. The Moscow NKVD, for instance, was expected to find and charge thirty-five thousand persons. Progress had to be reported by telegram every five days. Such measures quickly ignited a competition in which regional NKVD bosses rushed to fill their quotas and then asked permission to raise them.

Huge quotas could be fulfilled only by irregular means. Hence, the secret police targeted a whole range of nationalities. In 1938 the NKVD could report having arrested more than 100,000 Poles, nearly 32,000 Germans, and so on, down to 691 Afghans. Fabrication of group cases against alleged anti-Soviet organizations or spy networks also permitted the rapid arrest of large numbers of "spies" and "agents." Hence, the police used torture and false promises to extract spurious testimony implicating ever wider circles of acquaintances. Moreover, the police went after former kulaks, onetime members of prerevolutionary political parties, veterans of the White army and members of their families, all of whom were deemed "capable" of committing anti-Soviet acts. Impure thoughts alone became sufficient grounds for prosecution, and the secret police appointed themselves mind readers.

Pospelov read summaries of the cases of a dozen prominent party figures to his colleagues. The details of each biography blur together: member of the party since 1905, since 1907, since 1909 . . . worker, from a family of fishermen, soldier . . . imprisoned many times under the old regime . . . served in party positions since 1917 . . . veteran of the civil war. All were arrested in 1937 or 1938 and confronted with outlandish charges of treason and terrorism; all died in front of firing squads, except for the two who did not survive the beatings they received from their NKVD interrogators.

Amid the litany of party service, arrest, and torture, Pospelov stressed the brave but futile resistance of many old Bolsheviks. He quoted at length a letter from Robert Eikhe, who wrote to Stalin from his prison cell, confiding, "There is no more bitter sorrow than to sit in jail under the system for which you always fought." Eikhe, a revolutionary since 1905, defended his honor as a truthful man and a loyal communist. His case, he explained to Stalin, was a "model of provocation, slander, and violation of the most basic norms of revolutionary legality."[27] In his note, Eikhe refuted many of the ridiculous accusations against him and explained how he came to sign a false confession: at the end of a sixteen-hour interrogation session, during which he had lost consciousness more than once, the investigator held up a pen and a truncheon and asked Eikhe to choose. He decided to sign the false statement, but his letter to Stalin showed that he had not lost his fighting spirit.

Although not specifically tasked with accounting for why the purges happened, the Pospelov commission nevertheless offered some explanations. The weakening of legal protections in the wake of the Kirov murder created a situation that allowed for "mass violations of socialist legality." Pressured to make ever more arrests, the secret police hierarchy rewarded careerists and sadists like Rodos, while NKVD men who questioned torture and other dubious practices found themselves under arrest. Moreover, the secret police had worked with the compliance and even assistance of the Procuracy. Prosecutors did not complain about arrests without warrants; they rubber-stamped police materials, thereby giving the appearance of legality to fraudulent cases. The courts, too, had mechanically delivered the verdicts already assigned by the NKVD. When defendants tried to tell of torture, judges had looked the other way—even ignoring instances when investigators manhandled defendants out of the courtroom to deliver a "reminder" of the consequences of changing one's story. Lastly, Pospelov deduced, a "psychosis" of spy mania infected law enforcement agencies and the public.

The report also stressed that the terror was not a secret from Stalin. In fact, Stalin used the purges to change the composition of the Central Committee to suit himself. Then he raised the status of the secret police while pushing aside the weakened Central Committee. Meanwhile, the cult of personality that had been allowed to grow up around Stalin had resulted in a horrific situation in which no one dared to challenge the leader's departures from Bolshevik norms. Lenin had been right in his "last testament," Pospelov concluded, to warn that Stalin was crude and dangerous.

After Pospelov's report, the main question in the presidium shifted from whether to disclose the history of the purges at the upcoming Congress to what to say and to whom. Again, more conservative senior members of the presidium urged caution and restraint. They argued that Stalin's achievements should be stressed and that the real danger posed to the party by Trotskyites and other ideological foes in the 1930s not be forgotten. In response, Mikoyan offered up a conciliatory formula in which Stalin's behavior would be divided into two phases—before 1934 and afterward. Thus, Stalin could be credited with industrialization and even the battle against Trotskyites. Such a formula would also preclude criticism of the conduct of collectivization.[28]

Junior members of the presidium took a harsher stance. Averkii Aristov directly challenged conservatives. "I am not in agreement with one thing that is common to the remarks of Molotov, Kaganovich, and Voroshilov—[the refrain] 'we don't need to say.' The [Congress] delegates are sharp people. [To say] 'we didn't know about this' is unworthy of members of the Presidium." Aristov raised the example of Eikhe, who had remained truthful and brave even after the worst torture, and averred that the party would not lose its authority by facing up to the truth that "we wanted to make a god and we ended up with a devil." Saburov also supported a stronger statement. "These are not shortcomings (as comrade Kaganovich says); these are crimes." Dmitrii Shepilov added that by telling the truth, the presidium could explain that it was not the party that needed to imprison millions.

Khrushchev ended the meeting by noting that the presidium could make its own fate. The members of the top leadership had already shown their will by arresting Beria. By debunking the cult of personality, Khrushchev told his fellow leaders, "We can say at the top of our voices that 'We are not ashamed.'" They would have to be careful how they expressed themselves, but if they said nothing in the light of all they had learned about the purges, they would in effect be justifying Stalin's actions. The fact that they had all worked together with Stalin could not constrain them. Echoing his own exchange with Snegov, Khrushchev asked the others what they would say "when the Party learns the truth from former prisoners."[29] After all, they could not in good conscience keep innocent survivors hidden away forever.

On February 13 at a last presidium meeting before the Congress, it was decided that Khrushchev would ask that day's plenary meeting of the Central Committee for permission to give a report on the cult of personality at a closed session. Khrushchev had suggested the Secret Speech be given by Pospelov or even Snegov, but—not accidentally—the job had fallen to him. Pospelov lacked seniority. As for Snegov, Kaganovich, for one, rejected out of hand the idea of having "ex-convicts pass judgment on us."[30] Better that the leadership retain control over any statement and that it come from the first secretary. The plenum approved Khrushchev's request without debate. Though only the inner circle knew it, Khrushchev had set the stage for Stalin's dethroning.

The Congress Convenes

On Tuesday, February 14, the Twentieth Party Congress opened inside the Kremlin, the symbolic heart of the Soviet empire. The delegates and guests crossed Red Square, entered the high fortress walls, passed by the Kremlin's ancient cathedrals, and gathered in what Vittorio Vidali described as a "large and fine" hall. The only known diarist of the Twentieth Congress, Vidali was a professional revolutionary and longtime member of the international communist movement. Born near Trieste in 1900, he had lived and worked in Moscow in the early 1930s, been involved in bloody rivalries in the Mexican Communist Party, killed both fascists and left-wing factionalists during the Spanish Civil War, and now represented the Communist Party of Trieste, a city whose territory was disputed by Italy and Yugoslavia. On that first day of the Congress, Vidali observed, "At one end [of the auditorium], there is a statue of Lenin, which shows him speaking. I looked for a picture of Stalin. One sees these in the squares, in the shops, in the offices. It was strange that there wasn't even one." As the delegates stood to applaud the entrance of the presidium members, Vidali noticed that Khrushchev, Malenkov, and the others looked tired and strained. With some foreboding, he concluded, "In general they have aged; they look like the survivors from a great shipwreck; they represent all that has remained after so many storms."[31]

Although behind the scenes aides scrambled to write Khrushchev's Secret Speech, the leadership gave few hints as to what was to come during the public sessions of the Congress. Khrushchev did not criticize Stalin or his policies in his report delivered on the opening day; he simply failed to quote the great leader's words. Instead Khrushchev boasted about the amount of land newly dedicated to growing grain, extolled the success of new economical housing programs, and promised to lighten housework by providing more technology, such as washing machines.[32]

For the next week the Congress proceeded inexorably according to plan. Select delegates, including members of the presidium, gave speeches complimenting Khrushchev's report on the state of the nation or offering their views on the new five-year plan. The Congress seemed to be "nothing special . . . just like any other party meeting," recalled Aleksandr Iakovlev, the future architect of perestroika. Then a high-ranking but youthful bureaucrat in the Central Committee apparatus, Iakovlev

Fig. 02-01 Nikita Khrushchev, Nikolai Bulganin, and Anastas Mikoyan surrounded by delegates at the Twentieth Party Congress. Courtesy Russian State Film and Photo Archive.

attended several sessions of the Congress. Writing nearly fifty years later, he remembered: "The usual boring words were pronounced, only loudly and with pathos. Everyone boasted of their successes—the productivity of land use, the efficiency of labor, yield of milk cows, percentages of growth, the steady rise of the masses' standard of living. The wisdom of Party leaders was hailed. Imperialism in all its manifestations was condemned."[33] In other words, the conference proceeded mechanically and predictably. Indeed, the biggest excitement on the second day came when a Chinese delegate read greetings from Mao that included praise for Stalin. The rare mention of the late leader roused the delegates to applaud warmly.[34]

Only on the third day of the Congress did delegates hear a speech that leveled some specific criticism at the Stalin period. During the evening session, presidium member Anastas Mikoyan, after offering the customary ritual praise for Khrushchev's opening report, stated that for twenty years the Soviet Communist Party did not have collective leadership, and that this had harmed its work. Without pronouncing Stalin's name, Mikoyan in effect condemned the late dictator's monopoly on power. Yet Mikoyan also carefully stressed recent changes. Couched in jargon, his spin sounded like this: "And now, when in the course of the past three years the collective leadership of the Communist Party has been restored on the basis of Leninist principles and Leninist unity, one can feel the positive influence of Leninist methods of leadership."[35]

He did not directly denounce the cult of personality or explain its mechanisms; however, Mikoyan singled out Marxist theorists, historians, and party propagandists for criticism. Without explaining why historians had worked badly, Mikoyan ripped into the canonical textbook of the day, positing somewhat mysteriously, "If our historians had really deeply studied the facts and events of the history of our Party during the Soviet period, and I don't mean those ones that are illuminated in the *Short Course*, if they had really dug deeply in the archives and historical documents and not only read old newspapers, then they would now be able to cast more light on many facts and events laid out in the *Short Course*." Specifically, he ridiculed historians for scapegoating individuals, namely, purged old Bolsheviks Vladimir Antonov-Ovseenko and Stanislav Kosior, for all sorts of historical ills.[36] By mentioning their names in a positive light from the podium of the Congress, Mikoyan in effect instantaneously rehabilitated the two men, both of whom had been executed in 1938.

Mikoyan concluded his remarks by praising the Central Committee for "bravely revealing the mistakes and shortcomings that had piled up in past years." Without enumerating these mistakes or mentioning the destruction of party cadres, he nonetheless strongly signaled that the Stalin period was to be subject to criticism, albeit in a party way. His speech contained the broadest hint of what was to come, but at that moment it attracted negative attention. At the intermission, his brother Artem, also a delegate, chided him: "Anastas, why did you make that speech? You were correct in essence, but many delegates are upset, are cursing you. Why did you attack Stalin so? Why should you take the initiative on this? After all, Khrushchev did not say anything of the kind."

Mikoyan recalled responding, "You're wrong. And those comrades who didn't like my speech are also wrong. As for Khrushchev, well, he's going to make a report to the closed session and speak of much worse things!"[37] Before that closed session, however, the tone of the Congress remained mostly upbeat.

Ironically, another delegate who dared to make a critical speech was a party historian—the doyenne of the very profession Mikoyan had disparaged. Anna Pankratova, a senior scholar and Central Committee member, was the only other speaker to directly address the cult of personality. Although she, too, avoided mentioning Stalin's name, Pankratova cited the damage done to Soviet historiography by an inappropriate focus on the role of individuals. Marxist historians, she reminded listeners, ought to focus on the masses. Moreover, they ought not to "lacquer" or whitewash events. Omission of the real struggles of the party only made history dull. Though decrying attention to individuals, Pankratova called for more attention to the biographies of Lenin, Marx, and Engels. Again Stalin stood out by his absence. Pankratova finished by presenting a vision of a fundamentally different form of scholarly life from that which had existed under Stalin. Scholars needed to tackle important questions rather than "safe topics." Furthermore, she stated, "Scientific questions cannot be solved by orders or by voting. The Party teaches us that science develops by the free exchange of opinions, through discussions."[38]

The audience listened but was little impressed. Abstract talk about cults of personality and the omission of Stalin's name sent a message, but it was an opaque one. Meanwhile, among well-connected delegates sensational rumors circulated about "rehabilitations" of political and military figures who had disappeared under Stalin. Vidali heard from his old friend and former boss Elena Stasova in whispers during the intermission about how she was busy helping victims or their survivors. Stasova, an old Bolshevik who had worked with Lenin and later with the communist international movement, had a wide circle of acquaintances especially among foreign revolutionaries. She told Vidali about dozens of their mutual friends who had died or who were languishing in exile. The few who had returned, she confided, were "human wrecks."[39]

Vidali reported feeling oppressed by his growing knowledge of the injustices wrought under Stalin and by the hollow pomp of the Con-

Fig. 02-02 Elena Stasova with Hungarian Communist Party leader Mátyás Rákosi at the Twentieth Party Congress. Courtesy Russian State Film and Photo Archive.

gress. Vidali laconically summarized the delegates' routine existence: "The fourth day of the Congress. Now our life consists of getting up at seven; having breakfast at eight-thirty; going to the Congress and remaining there until half-past two; having lunch and attending to any personal matters that may crop up; back to the Congress at four o'clock and staying there until half-past seven; then to the cinema or the theatre if there are any shows that we haven't seen; back to the hotel; supper and then bed." Soviet worker delegates enjoyed the chance to stay in nice hotels, attend the Bolshoi, visit the capital's famous museums, and spend a generous per diem, but Vidali was bored. He complained of feeling isolated from real life. "No contact with the people whom we see strolling or hurrying in the streets . . . no contact with the factories."[40]

Khrushchev, by contrast, was frantically busy. On February 18 Khrushchev received a draft speech based on Pospelov's report to the presidium. As per the Pospelov commission's mandate, it centered on the fate of the delegates to the 1934 Party Congress. The next evening, with a short break to appear at a banquet for foreign delegates in the Kremlin's St. George's Hall, Khrushchev dictated additional text that doubled the length of the report. Now it included a long section on Stalin's wartime and postwar leadership and ascribed some of the blame for the terror to mental illness on Stalin's part. While the first secretary played genial host, his aides hastily polished a final version. Khrushchev did not even confide in his family about the upcoming bombshell.[41]

Finally, Friday, February 24, the last day of the Congress, dawned cold and gray. The skies hinted of more snow to come. Inside the stifling hall, delegates sat through one more long morning of speeches, this time on the new five-year plan for economic development. The agronomist Trofim Lysenko, famous for attacking bourgeois genetics, made an appearance, rambling on about hybrids, soil types, and fertilizers. The Congress also heard short speeches of greeting from the more obscure foreign leftist parties, including representatives from Costa Rica, Bolivia, Paraguay, and Ecuador. Vidali declined to speak in the name of the Trieste Communist Party, and so a written message from his party's Central Committee was read into the proceedings. Finally, delegates voted to approve the proposed changes to the charter and the Congress dragged to a close.[42]

Vidali wrote in his diary on that final day of how wearying the whole ceremonial gathering had become. "I rather envied two Uzbek women who were sitting near me quietly reading short stories," he noted. "They never stopped reading except to express an opinion about the stories." Vidali found their indifference to the proceedings typical and also disheartening. The spirit of the old revolutionary movement to which he had devoted his life was absent here. "The new Soviet citizen," he concluded, "is almost always a good technician, but the only Marxism he knows is taken from books; he doesn't know the world outside his own country and doesn't study it."[43] Meanwhile, the ranks of the old guard of Bolsheviks who might have been able to preserve the revolutionary atmosphere were sorely depleted as a result of the purges.

Late in the afternoon, the foreign visitors were finally dismissed to wrap up their affairs in Moscow. They had heard the announcement of a closed session for the following day, but assumed it was part of the "normal procedure" for the CPSU's election of its Central Committee.[44] Soviet delegates with voting rights did meet in a private session that evening to elect the new leadership bodies of the CPSU. Some anxious members of the presidium had insisted that elections be completed before Khrushchev's report on the cult of personality lest delegates direct their unease or even enmity against the members of Stalin's inner circle. So at 6:00 p.m. the Soviet delegates reconvened and listened as a list of candidates for the Central Committee was read aloud: 133 names for 133 full memberships; 122 names for 122 candidate members. Later that evening, the electoral committee counted all 1,341 ballots. Malenkov garnered the most disfavor; three delegates struck his name from the list. One vote was cast against Khrushchev. The only immediate impact of the election was that new additions to the Central Committee had to be invited to the closed session the following morning.[45]

A Speech to Remember

On Saturday, buses brought the Soviet delegates straight from their hotels through the gates of the Spasskaia tower and into the grounds of the Kremlin. They streamed into the meeting hall of the Supreme Soviet and checked their heavy coats, fur hats, and scarves. Having learned of the extra session just the night before, out-of-towners had interrupted their packing and changed their travel plans. Now, delegates found their seats in the rows of padded leather chairs, each with a swing-armed writing desk. Vladimir Semichastnyi, a young Komsomol leader, had attended the Congress as a guest, but, having been elected the evening before to the Central Committee, he had been instructed to attend the morning's closed session. Semichastnyi, a future head of the KGB, did not know what to expect, though talk of the cult of personality and Mikoyan's veiled attack on Stalin had raised some uneasy suspicions.[46]

Some of the other guests probably had a better idea as to what lay in store—these were the old Bolsheviks who had been rehabilitated, cleared of the "crimes" for which they had suffered in Siberian camps. Thanks to Snegov's advocacy, a dozen former prisoners sat in the balcony to hear the proceedings of the Congress. They awaited Khrushchev's report with painful anticipation. Indeed, so stressful was the prospect that one of their number, former Komsomol boss Aleksandr Mil'chakov, lay in the Kremlin hospital struck down by a heart attack in the night.[47]

Semichastnyi, as befitted a newly minted member of the Central Committee, sat up front, ten or twelve rows from the podium. He watched as Nikolai Bulganin, the portly head of the Council of Ministers, starkly announced: "And now we will hear the report 'On the Cult of Personality and Its Consequences.' The floor is given to Comrade Khrushchev." With the members of the presidium on the stage behind him, Khrushchev began his recital. In a break with his normal extemporaneous style of speechifying, Khrushchev started to read carefully, hardly lifting his eyes from the text.[48]

Khrushchev warned his listeners that they were not about to hear a complete evaluation of Stalin's life and accomplishments. They could find plenty of published materials praising the late leader. His task was to explain how a cult of personality had gradually formed around Stalin and how it had become the "source of a whole series of exceedingly serious and grave perversions of Party principles, of Party democracy, of revolutionary legality." The Central Committee, he noted, had deemed it necessary to fully acquaint delegates with what the cult of personality had meant in practice. To preclude any recurrence, they were to be trusted with the story of Stalin's excesses and charged with alleviating the consequences of his misdeeds.[49]

Not surprisingly, Khrushchev grounded his speech with quotations from Marx and Lenin condemning cults of the individual and lauding collective rule. Khrushchev described Lenin's modesty and collegiality, stressing the great revolutionary's use of persuasion to generate consensus among party leaders. He also cited long-suppressed correspondence from Lenin criticizing Stalin for his erratic and overweening nature. Khrushchev reminded delegates that Lenin had written a letter, presented to the Thirteenth Party Congress after his death, warning against keeping Stalin on as general secretary. Lenin's fears about Stalin came true, Khrushchev lamented. After Lenin's death, Stalin began to chip away at collegial decision making. "Stalin acted not through persuasion, explanation, and patient cooperation with people, but by imposing his concepts and demanding absolute submission to his opinion. Whoever opposed this concept or tried to prove his [own] viewpoint, and the correctness of his position, was doomed to removal from the leading collective and to subsequent moral and physical annihilation."[50]

Khrushchev carefully distinguished between Stalin's capricious and cruel behavior in the late 1930s and the party's real battle against Trotskyite opponents. In line with presidium members' suggestions that Stalin's rule be divided into two periods, Khrushchev justified the prosecution of right-wingers within the revolutionary movement. Without the ideological battle headed by Stalin, "We would not now have a powerful heavy industry, we would not have the collective farms, we would find ourselves disarmed and weak in a capitalist encirclement."[51] Khrushchev conceded that Lenin had endorsed violence, but only against class enemies who resisted Soviet rule. Stalin, by contrast, initiated mass repressions only in the mid-1930s when the opposition had already been completely routed. It was then that Stalin coined the fatal term *enemy of the people*. Whereas Lenin had reformed the wayward, Stalin destroyed them.

Khrushchev then reported the bulk of the evidence collected by Pospelov. He stunned the delegates with the statistics about the executions of their predecessors, the delegates to the Seventeenth Party Congress. He retold the narrative pieced together by the Pospelov commission—the speeding up of trials and ban on appeals in political cases, the green light for use of force in extracting confessions, and the mass arrests of 1937–1938. Here Khrushchev paused to admit the worst. "Now, when the cases of some of these so-called 'spies' and 'saboteurs' were examined, it was found that all their cases were fabricated. Confessions of the guilt of many arrested and charged with enemy activity were gained with the help of cruel and inhuman tortures."[52] Stalin, he charged, knew full well that many defendants recanted their farfetched confessions in court, but he resolutely ignored them. Khrushchev read the pleas to Stalin preserved in Eikhe's case file, described how false group cases were concocted, and told how Stalin had signed off on long lists of death sentences.

For more than four hours, with only a short hushed intermission, Khrushchev bombarded his audience with tales of Stalin's misdeeds.[53] When he finished with the purges, he moved on to the conduct of World War II. Khrushchev charged Stalin with ignoring intelligence reports warning of the German invasion and of bungling military preparedness. Here Khrushchev became more animated and spontaneous as he referred to his own experience at the Ukrainian front. Khrushchev sharply accused Stalin of frequently overriding his generals' advice and claimed that Stalin had followed the course of the war on a globe. Recounting Stalin's unnecessary and cruel deportation of whole ethnic groups from the Caucasus, Khrushchev bitterly joked, "The Ukrainians avoided meeting this fate only because there were too many of them and there was no place to which to deport them."[54]

In the postwar period, Khrushchev explained, Stalin's paranoia had continued to drive policy—the tragic results of which included the execution of numerous party leaders in the so-called Leningrad Affair and the disgraceful persecution of Jewish physicians in the "Doctors' Plot." Here, Khrushchev also reminded the audience of Beria's role in encouraging Stalin's madness. He cited testimony from Snegov, the only survivor of a fateful meeting of the party bureau for the Caucasus, as to how Stalin insisted against opposition that Beria be promoted. Khrushchev went on to explain Beria's role in fabricating cases and persecuting those who tried to protest against the injustices of the secret police.

At several points in his speech, Khrushchev addressed the causes of and responsibility for the cult of personality. In part, he blamed Stalin's mental state, which he described as "sickly suspicious." Beria, he argued, had exploited Stalin's paranoia and the other presidium members had been incapable of stopping him. The terror had persisted because Stalin "possessed unlimited power." One opposed him at the risk of one's life. Moreover, the cult of personality raised Stalin to such a level that any public criticism of the leader would have seemed absurd. Still, the question remained: Why didn't the other high-ranking party leaders somehow block the Stalin cult as it was being formed? Here Khrushchev reminded his audience that Stalin "was one of the strongest Marxists and his logic, his strength and his will greatly influenced the cadres and Party work." Stalin had won many allies in his fight against Trotskyites and other real oppositionists. The problem with Stalin was that his suspiciousness increased even as the number of real threats shrunk.

At the close of his speech, Khrushchev defended Stalin, noting his real dedication to the interests of the working class and the revolution. Stalin, he confirmed, did lead the party to many successes; but he took too much credit for these accomplishments. Now, past mistakes would not be repeated; Stalin did not merit the treatment he gave his famous victims, whose names suddenly vanished from towns, streets, factories, and collective farms. Khrushchev warned delegates that the issue of the Stalin cult was a very sensitive one, hence the closed session. Without being specific, he directed: "We should know the limits; we should not give ammunition to the enemy; we should not wash our dirty linen before their eyes." Concretely, he stated that ideological work had to be carried out to "condemn and eradicate the cult of the individual as alien to Marxism-Leninism and not consonant with the principles of Party leadership and the norms of party life." Undoing the damage of the cult would mean restoring the emphasis on Marxism-Leninism especially in history, literature, and art. New textbooks had to be written. The restored allegiance to party norms and principles would be maintained. Last, Khrushchev charged the delegates with "restor[ing] completely the Leninist principles of Soviet socialist democracy, expressed in the Constitution of the Soviet Union, [and fighting] willfulness of individuals abusing their power." Legality, in other words, must become the new watchword.[55]

Having instructed the leading cadres of the party on their obligations, Khrushchev ended the speech with a rousing cry: "We are absolutely certain that our Party, armed with the historical resolutions of the XXth Congress will lead the Soviet people along the Leninist path to new successes, to new victories." The audience members clapped mechanically as Khrushchev exhorted, "Long live the victorious banner of our Party—Leninism!" Then Bulganin came forward again and read out a short, vague decree committing the Central Committee to "realize measures to guarantee the complete overcoming of the alien to Marxism-Leninism cult of personality, to liquidate its consequences in all spheres of party, state, and ideological life, and to strictly observe the norms of party life and the principles of collective party leadership formulated by the great Lenin."[56] Without any remarks as to how these goals were to be achieved, Bulganin called for and received a unanimous vote. He reminded delegates that neither Khrushchev's report nor the resolution they had just adopted were being published at present, but promised that materials would be sent out later.

Bulganin did not call for questions, and so the stunned members of the audience filed out quietly. As one Leningrad delegate would later recall, "Everyone voted. No one spoke up; no one abstained. In that sense, everything passed as usual."[57] But nothing would be the same.

3 | MARCH

A FLOOD OF QUESTIONS

1956 was a leap year, and on the night of February 29, Vittorio Vidali embarked on the first stage in his long trip home by flying from Moscow to Kiev. The delegate from Trieste had spent the last few days of the month taking nostalgic walks through the streets of Moscow, sampling the capital's cultural wealth—including a performance of *Swan Lake*—visiting a few old friends, and even doing a little shopping. As a final souvenir Vidali received an enormous illustrated album of the Congress, but studying the book's bland ceremonial photos offered no insights into the increasingly common rumors about posthumous rehabilitations of old comrades and a new line toward Stalin. He and the other foreign delegates had heard that Khrushchev had spoken about Stalin for four hours at a special session after the Congress ended, but no one informed them officially. Hoping for some inside information, Vidali sought out Elena Stasova, but Lenin's friend had taken to her bed and barely had the strength to receive him.

On the plane to Kiev, Vidali chanced to sit next to a fellow delegate, a woman history teacher from Ukraine. Vidali wrote that when she politely asked him about his impressions of the Congress, he replied rather acidly that he would have a lot of questions to answer back home. The teacher lamented that the same would be true for her. Everyone, she agreed, was stunned by the turn of events. She confided in him that the most astounding part of Khrushchev's report for her had been his attack on Stalin's conduct of World War II. She felt that Khrushchev's criticism of Stalin's wartime leadership was overblown and unfortunate. Yet, Vidali's new acquaintance accepted the speech's basic message.[1]

As Vidali took notes, the teacher explained to him the lesson she had extracted: "I have learnt at this Congress, that in writing and discussing we must stop continually quoting phrases from leaders in order to give authority to our own opinions. We must avoid confusing our Party with a religious order and transforming a leader into an infallible Pope." She noted that the habit of taking one leader's words as the gospel truth "paralyzes peoples' minds and paralyzes the Party itself. It encourages bureaucracy and passivity; it weakens internal democracy and suppresses collective work, criticism, initiative, the ability to create."[2]

The Ukrainian teacher assured Vidali that when he became acquainted with the contents of the report, he would see that Khrushchev had acted bravely to "cut out the abscess [that] had dangerously contaminated the lives of our people." As to why the cult had not been addressed during Stalin's lifetime, she repeated Khrushchev's explanation that attacking Stalin while he held power could have endangered the revolution, which, after all, had faced so many external enemies. Yet she seemed equally certain that the present discussion of mistakes would strengthen the party and show the correctness of the communist cause.[3]

The more worldly-wise Vidali did not share his Ukrainian acquaintance's apparent confidence in the strength of Khrushchev's accounting for the cult and the terror. As he traveled on by air to Budapest and Vienna and finally by train to Trieste, Vidali met anxious comrades who begged him for information and reassurances that he could not give. As he anticipated, when shared with foreign communist parties over the course of March and April 1956, Khrushchev's report sowed dismay and confusion, a situation that only worsened when a leak from Poland allowed the text to fall into the CIA's hands. On June 5, 1956, the *New York Times* would publish the full report, which would be widely reprinted in the West and broadcast back into the Eastern bloc by anticommunist radio stations.[4]

Although Khrushchev's report "On the Cult of Personality and Its Consequences" would not be published officially in the Soviet Union until 1989, what Western analysts dubbed the "Secret Speech" was not very secret inside the USSR in 1956. Two days after the closed session, Central Committee officials shared the report with those heads of the most important socialist parties who had lingered in Moscow after the Congress. These select foreign leaders initially were allowed to read a copy of the speech, but not to take it home or to share its contents with anyone. Yet, at Khrushchev's urging, on March 5 the presidium decreed that members of the Soviet Communist Party and its youth league, the Komsomol, as well as those who fell into the ill-defined category of "non-party activists" be acquainted with the report.[5] By mid-March, the speech had been specially reproduced and distributed to party leaders in all regions of the USSR. In his diary, historian Sergei Dmitriev meticulously described the booklet containing the report—"printed typographically, thirty-eight pages long, bound in a red cover with the inscription: 'Secret. Subject to return within three months and subject to destruction.'"[6]

Party officials were tasked with reading the report (or supervising its reading) at lower-level meetings.[7] One of those assigned to read it out that spring was Mikhail Gorbachev, then a newly minted Komsomol official in his native region of Stavropol'. Although he had been raised to revere Stalin, the future general secretary of the CPSU remembered that he fully accepted Khrushchev's condemnation of Stalin's cruel practices. But as he crisscrossed his large agricultural province reading the report at local meetings, Gorbachev met officials with less confidence. One grumbled, "We're sitting here and we don't know what to do." When Gorbachev protested, "There are materials, there's the press," he heard, "You go and listen to what people are saying, then you'll see . . . They don't understand . . . And they don't accept it." Indeed, Gorbachev encountered "provocative questions" directed against Stalin, as well as peasants who defended Stalin, believing quite erroneously that the late dictator had used the purges to punish those who carried out collectivization so brutally.[8]

The disgruntled Stavropol' official who did not know how to act was hardly alone. Khrushchev's report came with strict instructions on safeguarding its contents, but no advice for how to deal with the questions that it would surely spark. The resulting difficulties for party activists are captured in the recollections of one self-described "committed Stalinist." Then a graduate student in philosophy and head of the Komsomol at a college in Siberia, this man vividly remembered his shock and instinctive recoil from the controversy: "Having received the text to read out to the [Komsomol], I spent the whole night reading it and copying it out. For me that night was a kind of nightmare. Soon afterwards, the students began to ask questions—questions that we were not accustomed to answer, and didn't know how to answer, and were even afraid to answer. And besides that report, no other information. Only the "enemy voices" [foreign radio broadcasts]." Fifty years later, this man still remembered how he had ducked questions until two young women sarcastically asked, "What are we supposed to do, go to the gym teacher with these questions?" Only then did the young Komsomol leader accept that he had to "think for myself."[9]

Not surprisingly, many party officials followed Khrushchev's lead and simply did not take questions at the meetings where the speech was read. Those who did open the floor had to field bitter remarks and politically incorrect questions. Some classified reports recorded queries from the floor, hence offering a glimpse into the reception of the Secret Speech.[10] To get a sense both of public reactions and of the possible "spin" provided by official spokespersons, we will look at the special case of a historian who tried to answer for the party in March 1956. Responses to her explanations as well as to Khrushchev's report foretell conflicts to come and show that from the very start the party struggled to articulate a persuasive rationale for limited reform.

Answering for the Party

Anna Mikhailovna Pankratova, the party historian who had carefully but lucidly addressed the problem of cults of personality in her speech to the Twentieth Party Congress, became one of the first representatives of the regime to attempt to answer questions about the meaning of Khrushchev's report. As befitting her dual status as a senior scholar and a deputy to the Central Committee of the CPSU, Pankratova had the duty of instructing professional historians. In advance of the Congress, she had been invited to visit Leningrad to lecture on "The Decisions of the XXth Party Congress and the Tasks of Historical Science." When she arrived there in mid-March, frantic local officials begged her to help alleviate the "great agitation and confusion" created in the ongoing process of reading out Khrushchev's report.[11] A supremely conscientious party member, Pankratova did not refuse.

Between March 20 and 23, Pankratova tackled the topic of the cult of personality in nine separate lectures. Her audiences ranged in size from fifty of the city's historians to two thousand members of the Leningrad party organization. She also spoke to archivists, scholars, and school-teachers. Each lecture provoked a flurry of questions. At some, if not all, of her talks, listeners submitted questions in writing; 825 persons out of her combined audience of 5,930 posed such queries.[12] The Soviet custom of writing comments on slips of paper and passing them forward provided relative anonymity for the questioners, removed constraints on the number and length of commentaries that could be accepted, and buffered the speaker against verbal assaults. Still Pankratova found the questions so painful and troubling that she compiled a list and sent it along with a memorandum to Khrushchev and the Central Committee. But she also tried to come up with answers for historians and teachers, lecturers and propagandists—the very people charged with having to speak for the regime. Pankratova shared this responsibility at the highest level; as the author of textbooks on Soviet history, she had to teach the teachers.

In many ways, Pankratova was the ideal person to cope with the difficult task of explaining what ought to be done in light of Khrushchev's report. She had written and lectured on Soviet history for decades. Moreover, she had earned her colleagues' esteem for her dedication to her work and for her calm, warm personality. Pankratova also had been recognized for her loyalty by the party leadership as evident in her invitation to address the Twentieth Party Congress, her inclusion in the Central Committee, and her appointment to head the most powerful journal in her field. Perhaps most importantly, she had experience with contradictions and changes in the party line. A closer look at Pankratova's career shows that it consisted of a ceaseless struggle to reconcile her faith in the party's principles with the shifting demands of political correctness. Her biography reflects both the opportunities bestowed on the revolution's supporters as well as the costs extracted by internecine struggles.

Just three years younger than Khrushchev, Pankratova was born in 1897 to a working-class family in Odessa. Although her surroundings—a busy port city known for its wits and con men—differed greatly from Khrushchev's native village, Pankratova, too, endured a poor childhood

Fig. 03-01 Anna Pankratova. Courtesy International Memorial Society Archive.

and harbored ambitious dreams. Pankratova's father, disabled in the Russo-Japanese War, died when she was only nine years old. Her mother worked at menial jobs to support Pankratova and her two younger sisters. Pankratova helped, too—making wicks for lamps and later as a tutor. She excelled in school, and her teachers helped her enter a private high school. Pankratova went on to study in the University of Odessa's "higher courses for women," and in the revolutionary year 1917 she graduated from a hastily combined program for men and women.[13]

Pankratova had dreamed of furthering her education, but after the October Revolution she postponed her plans so that she could serve the party. As a student, she had been involved in left-wing study groups and had helped teach workers. In 1919 she joined the Bolshevik Party and worked as an agitator in White army–occupied Ukraine. Under the pseudonym Niura Palych, Pankratova participated in dangerous underground activity. She became a full-time party worker with the Soviet victory. Dispatched to the Urals to aid industrial workers, she fought to improve their living conditions and also began to research the history of the labor movement in local factories. After being accepted in 1922 to study at the newly created Institute of Red Professors in Moscow, Pankratova turned her interest in factory strike committees into an important first book.

The demands of party life, however, constantly interrupted Pankratova's academic work. No sooner had she settled in at the Institute in Moscow than the Central Committee sent her to Leningrad to help strengthen the local party organization, which had just expelled a great number of "Trotskyites." With the help of her mentor, the Marxist historian Mikhail Pokrovskii, Pankratova worked to unite the Leningrad historians and teachers around the party line. A pattern had been set for Pankratova's life: combining scholarship and party service. This balancing act was no mere matter of finding time for two demanding activities. It also required making choices based on *partiinost'* (party-mindedness). In Pankratova's case, this included breaking with her husband, a fellow historian, when he sided with Trotsky in the fierce ideological conflicts of the 1920s. Her husband ended up in prison in Tashkent, and Pankratova duly reported to her party organization when she visited him there in 1929 to try one last time to win him over to the Stalinist line. When he did not repent, she broke off contact. In 1933 she even refused to let him correspond with their daughter since he had not renounced his views. Regardless of how much she once cared for him, Pankratova would not consort with someone "hostile" to the party.[14]

Despite her best efforts to be a truly loyal member, Pankratova fell into disgrace in the early 1930s when she defended a comrade from criticism during the inner party purges. She was rebuked for lack of vigilance for not noticing and informing on the many "Trotskyites" and "spies" that had been uncovered among Moscow historians. In 1937, as arrests hit her neighbors, Pankratova was expelled from the party and demoted to a teaching position at Saratov University, which had just created a history department. In difficult times Pankratova, like Khrushchev, found redemption through her work. She labored to build up her new department and continued to work with coauthors on a textbook on Soviet history for middle schools. The resulting book became a huge success, ultimately appearing in twenty-three editions.[15]

By dint of hard work and consistent demonstrations of *partiinost'*—including criticism of her mentor Pokrovskii—Pankratova gradually won back the party's trust and with it her own status and authority. She needed authority to bolster her position in the pitched battles over history and ideology that continued in the postwar years. During a brief evacuation to Alma-Ata during World War II, Pankratova had worked on a textbook on the history of diplomacy, supervised graduate students, delivered propaganda lectures, written popular texts on heroic Russian history, lectured at hospitals, sent food and books to colleagues at the front, and taken care of their families, as well as her own daughter and elderly mother. She also organized and inspired local Kazakh historians to write the first history of their republic. After the war, pro-Russian anticosmopolitan ideologues accused her Kazakh protégés of nationalism, and one was even arrested. Pankratova defended their book, but she lost. She suffered a brief nervous breakdown, and the book was redone to omit criticism of Russian "imperialism" in tsarist times.[16]

By March 1956, however, Pankratova had regained her footing. As the historian Reginald Zelnik aptly noted, "Pankratova truly had nine lives."[17] Despite her failure to protect the Kazakh history project, Pankratova earned honors for her diplomacy textbook. Moreover, she was appointed in 1949 to the board of the new major journal in her field *Voprosy istorii*, becoming its editor in 1954. In the period before Stalin's death,

Pankratova toed the line publicly on the new Russian nationalism, although behind the scenes she defended colleagues who had been attacked as cosmopolitans.[18] Once she took the reins of *Voprosy istorii* after Stalin's demise, however, Pankratova began to publish cautiously revisionist articles. By 1956 the journal no longer sounded like a rehashed version of the infamously Stalin-centric *Short Course of the History of the All-Union Communist Party*.[19]

Stalinist politics, however, had trained historians and other guardians of *partiinost'* to be hypervigilant. Hence, it did not pass unnoticed that after Stalin's death Pankratova had quietly begun to aid victims of the purges.[20] In 1955 some officials complained privately to ideological curators at the Central Committee that Pankratova had published articles by authors who had once been imprisoned—to which Pankratova responded, "I do not consider it reprehensible to select a good article by an author who has been rehabilitated by Soviet and Party organs."[21] Her opponents also accused her of: "over the course of many years, and especially in recent years . . . seeking to offer all kinds of protection and aid to politically questionable persons." They even blamed Pankratova for receiving letters of appeal from sites of imprisonment.[22] Pankratova had dealt with denunciations before, and she knew how to negotiate the minefield of political correctness. But the revelations of the Secret Speech would test her convictions and her skill.

So what happened in March of 1956 when Pankratova met with curious and agitated propagandists and historians in Leningrad? Khrushchev and the other presidium members had not answered any questions in the wake of the Secret Speech, but Pankratova did not allow herself that luxury. Her report about the audiences' reaction to her Leningrad lectures, a transcript of one of those lectures, and one of a talk given later that month in Moscow allow for a reconstruction of this early attempt to make sense of the ramifications of the Secret Speech.[23] Eyewitness testimony of the time and comments in some of the notes from her listeners also convey a sense of how listeners evaluated Pankratova's efforts.

On March 20 Pankratova delivered the first of her Leningrad lectures to a large gathering of educators. A transcript of her talk "On the Most Important Problems of Soviet Historical Science" shows that Pankratova began with a general discourse on the lessons and international significance of the Twentieth Party Congress and then rehashed her speech from the Congress criticizing derivative, unscientific research and calling for new conditions for scientific debate. After an intermission, Pankratova finally turned to the cult of personality. Many listeners had just recently heard Khrushchev's report and likely expected Pankratova to elaborate on revelations about Stalin's misdeeds. However, Pankratova felt more comfortable treating the Stalin cult as a methodological problem for historians.[24] Hence, she discussed the tendency of Soviet textbooks to give undue credit to individual personalities—starting with exaggerated significance being attached to Russian princes of the twelfth and thirteenth centuries. She dwelled on how Stalin's interest in reviving patriotic traditions during World War II resulted in an un-Marxist focus on military heroes ranging from Alexander Nevsky to Mikhail Kutuzov. Pankratova also talked at length about how the *Short Course,* having been endorsed by Stalin, became a text that could not be corrected even though it contained many errors and distortions.[25]

In addressing the flaws of textbooks, Pankratova could not avoid the issue of historians' culpability. She included herself among those who had accepted an exaggerated depiction of Stalin's role (at Lenin's expense) in the revolution. She admitted that historians did so "without thinking, although some knew the facts, the real facts from documents contradicting this." As to why, she explained: "the idea of the cult of personality, the role of Stalin, his infallibility which was expounded by one or another historians in essence shut down all our critical thinking and closed the possibility of raising something that would contradict those facts."[26] Consequently, historians' work was damaged by a striving to show Stalin's role as a creative thinker and leader in all spheres. Now, she counseled her audience, they needed to reevaluate history soberly, from a Marxist perspective with more attention to the masses and the party.

Pankratova tempered her call for change with a warning not to go to the opposite extreme. "Comrades!" she declared. "Stalin's role, his services to the revolutionary movement, in the construction of socialism are well known and from this point of view it does not follow to diminish them, just as it does not follow to exaggerate them, as we have done up until now." Some who had been especially zealous in propagating the cult, she observed, were rushing to remove all citations to his work, to pull his books from circulation, and to take down his portraits. To applause, she insisted, "These people are not looking in the right direction as concerns the interests of our country for the future, of our party and its international authority." Pankratova echoed Khrushchev's praise for Stalin's leadership in building socialism and defending the party line; his mistake had been to postulate that class struggle sharpened as one got closer to socialism. Although she gave no details about the purges or their victims, Pankratova contended: "The tragedy was that Stalin was convinced that all of his actions were necessary to defend socialism and communism, and that to defeat our enemies it was necessary to use methods that violated our revolutionary legality."[27]

Though her immediate concern was to address tasks for historians, Pankratova was anxious that people understand that the party had never faltered in its general line. She noted that Khrushchev pointed out that while the party's victories and achievements would have been greater without the cult, the cult did not sway the party from its course toward socialism. As to the Central Committee's failure to tackle the cult earlier, she again echoed Khrushchev's explanation that Stalin had the unquestioning support of the whole people as a result of his leadership, his influence as a Marxist, and his logic. In other words, his strengths had created an aura of invincibility. Moreover, "much was unknown and was uncovered only later."[28]

Going forward, Pankratova called for new practices in scholarship and preparation of new textbooks. But she warned, "We must, first of all, carry out serious self-criticism. A great psychological *perestroika* [restructuring] faces us." Finally allowing some emotion to show through, she said: "I don't know how it is for those comrades sitting here, but for me and many others this is not easy. Everything that I am saying, all that I am thinking—this is not easily attained. There are some younger people in attendance; maybe it's easier for them. But for me, as a no longer young person who has lived through many restructurings, it seems as if this is the most difficult one." To Pankratova's distress, this confession evoked laughter. It *was* hard, she insisted. Some of the audience's questions were about to make it even harder for her.[29]

Pankratova's listeners, although undoubtedly diverse, had some common queries about the genesis and reception of Khrushchev's report. They wanted to know who had heard it at the Congress and whether the leadership had accepted comments and questions afterward. They were curious about why the leadership had raised the issue of evaluating Stalin at this juncture in time. Certain aspects of the speech also drew special attention: namely, Stalin's activities during the civil war and World War II, the show trials of the 1930s, and the postwar Leningrad affair. For the most part, however, Pankratova's audiences dwelt on the ramifications of the Secret Speech for their professional lives.

Students wanted to know whether degrees would be revoked, whether newly completed theses would have to be rewritten, and whether the period required for graduate training would have to be extended. Scholars were concerned with access to materials, the atmosphere for intellectual disputes, textbook reform, and the fate of academics who had written in the spirit of the cult of personality. Teachers were consumed by a single overriding worry: What should they tell their students about Stalin? By far the most commonly raised issue (fifty-six times) was when new textbooks and examination materials would become available.

Some of the notes concerning the social sciences contained real suggestions for reform. Practicing historians, in particular, lobbied for greater access to classified materials and pressed for guarantees that theoretical issues could be debated without fear of abuse if one ended up in the minority camp.[30] Most inquiries regarding historiography, however, demonstrated a desire to identify the new standards of political correctness. Nearly fifty separate notes asked for evaluations of Stalin's works. Half of them, despite Pankratova's criticism of those who had taken dogmatic approaches to Stalin's writings, inquired in almost identical language whether Stalin's works should be considered "classics of Marxism-Leninism." Others wanted to know which of his works could still be cited.[31] Based on a wider survey of reactions to the Secret Speech, historian Elena Zubkova also observed, "Party workers were most concerned not with analyzing what had occurred but with the external form of its expression. What should be done with portraits of Stalin?"[32]

One explanation for the focus on terminology and appearances is that people believed that their professional and personal survival continued to depend on following every shift in the party line. News of the party's fallibility was upsetting and problematic for those who held jobs that required them to speak with its voice despite having heard Khrushchev's report read aloud only once. In this light one can understand why both those who seemed well disposed toward Stalin and those whose sympathies lay elsewhere wished to know primarily what it meant to say that Trotsky and Bukharin were "ideological opponents" not "enemies" and only secondarily why Bukharin had confessed in court to being a spy.[33] One can also understand the anger that led teachers to shout at Pankratova when she could not give them ready answers about what to tell their students.

Listeners who did try to make sense of Khrushchev's (or Pankratova's) explanations of how the party had overlooked the mass illegalities and the spread of the cult were also dissatisfied. A minority even refused to accept Khrushchev's criticism of Stalin. If he was really so bad, they demanded, "Why did he remain in the leadership for thirty years while people only praised him and no one corrected his mistakes in the Party spirit [po-partiinomu] or removed him from his position in a timely way?" Those who embraced Khrushchev's denunciation of Stalin were equally agitated. After enumerating some of the sharper aspects of Khrushchev's speech, one listener charged, "These are already not mistakes, but crimes." He then asked Pankratova, "How can you suggest the study of Stalin's works after all this?"[34]

Moreover, Pankratova personally was taken to task as "the co-author of a series of falsifications in the history of the USSR" and pointedly asked to "please give the names of honest (from your point of view) historians, their main works, and their location in 1937." She apparently tried to argue in her lecture that "propagandists were always honest in their activity, only there was a lot they didn't understand." Listeners pointed out that this did not mesh with her assertion that historians saw problems with some of Stalin's writings. Apparently, they were not "honest" enough to speak out.[35] As members of the political elite, neither Khrushchev nor Pankratova could escape the dilemma of accountability. Either they knew about the cult but failed to protest, or they were ignorant, or there was no cult. No matter what they professed, they looked bad.

Pankratova's listeners seemed eager to find scapegoats for the cult, and historians who had helped deify Stalin were a natural target. With either remarkable naïveté or bitter sarcasm, audience members probed Pankratova about how the regime coerced conformity. "Was there direct pressure on the historians' collective that was involved with preparing the history of the civil war," one listener inquired, "or was this a manifestation of the fact that the cult of personality had become a habit?"

Another asked disbelievingly whether historians really did not base their work on documents. Or, more bluntly put, "What explains the appearance of a whole generation of cowardly historians, afraid to research the most crucial historical problems of the history of the CPSU and the Soviet society in a Marxist way?"[36] Though not fully understanding how the cult had come about, audience members attacked those, like Pankratova, who seemingly had flourished under Stalin. Was she a victim or a victimizer?

Significantly, though expecting Khrushchev and Pankratova to engage in self-criticism in the wake of revelations about the cult, virtually no one in the audience wished to admit the need to reevaluate his or her own behavior. A grand total of four audience members confessed to having been aware of the Stalin cult. The writer of one of the relatively few signed notes acknowledged the prevalence and necessity of hypocritical behavior: "I don't believe that you didn't understand the harm of the cult of personality, you could not have written otherwise. Respected Academician Pankratova, it could not have been otherwise. Remember [the fate of] seventy percent of the members of the Central Committee of the Seventeenth Congress. You acted correctly in everything."[37] A student argued that some historians in their hearts were both laughing and crying about what was being written about Stalin, but they were afraid to let their feelings show; his conclusion—"historians should be concerned with the question: why were they afraid?"[38]

The young writer Daniil Granin felt sorry for Pankratova. In notes made the day after hearing one of her Leningrad lectures, he wrote: "The first wave of distress broke on her. People are looking for live culprits for these events. Each person, in reality, has dirty hands, for these hands voted, signed, applauded . . . Guilt is [seen as] variable: 'we are ordinary people, what could we do?' They fell on the old lady without mercy— 'You are an academician, you are a historian'—even though they understood the bravery of her speech in such a hot moment."

Less sympathetically, two listeners chided Pankratova for what they perceived as her continuing timidity and naïveté. One complained, "It's embarrassing to listen to you spread your dogmatism, not saying anything about fear before the despot who ruled [*vladel*] you just like all Soviet people." Meanwhile, Granin worried about accepting those answers that Pankratova did give. He noted that she seemed to be making them up as she went along and he was afraid of being made a fool again by parroting a line that would be reversed in the future.[39]

Loyalty to the revolution and the dictates of Marxist theory limited the explanations available to Pankratova for the rise and persistence of the cult. A potentially damaging problem for the party in the long run was the contradiction in Khrushchev's report regarding the power of the individual in Soviet society. Khrushchev simultaneously laid all the blame for the purges at Stalin's feet and argued that the masses not individuals made history. Hence there was no easy answer for the listener who railed: "How many of you academics and scholars are there? 100, 1,000? And what were you doing, tell us, while Stalin (one man!) perverted science and history? In theory you are against exaggerating the role of the individual, but in practice . . . for thirty years, having understood his mistakes, you were all powerless against one individual!!"[40]

Another perceptive audience member observed that by making a scapegoat of Stalin, Khrushchev had created "the cult of personality in reverse." Numerous listeners asked Pankratova for a "more Marxist explanation of the objective reasons for the socio-economic factors behind the appearance of the cult of personality." Or they sought clarification of the distinction between normal leadership and "cults." "Why with Stalin is it considered a cult but not when we honor Marx, Engels, and Lenin?—after all the Party was founded and led by real individuals."[41]

Some of Pankratova's listeners wanted to address the larger issue of how the Soviet system would be altered to prevent a recurrence of despotism. Pankratova hastened to endorse the party's reaffirmation of collective rule and inner-party democracy, yet for some audience members this was not enough. One listener called for glasnost, without which, he or she suggested, no popular control could be exerted over government. Others wanted changes in the electoral system, such as having more high posts be elected positions and having nominees selected at the local level rather than suggested from the center. A few critics broached their own explanations for what had gone wrong. One of Pankratova's questioners tackled the cult in Marxist terms: "Why not explain [Stalin's] behavior as an expression of the interests of a given social class [sloi] arising, let us say, on the ground of Soviet bureaucracy." And another audience member inquired as to whether Pankratova thought that the cult of personality was "facilitated by the one-party system and the almost complete merger of Party and state organs."[42]

Seemingly more willing than Khrushchev to examine the mechanisms of the cult and to shoulder some of the blame, Pankratova was not prepared to seek flaws in the Soviet system. Indeed, signs of what she dubbed "an unhealthy mood" prompted Pankratova to pass on the questions she received to her superiors. In her memorandum to Khrushchev and the Central Committee, she characterized the majority of the questions as "political." The depth of her distress can be seen in a line that she ultimately omitted from the final version of her report: "A torrent of questions requiring more direct answers rained down on me."[43] Meanwhile, she was not allowed to quote Khrushchev's secret report. She had not been instructed how to answer pressing queries such as what ought to be done with portraits of Stalin. She did not know how to deal with outraged demands that Stalin's corpse be removed from the mausoleum on Red Square or what to say to the listener who asked, "Comrade Pankratova, tell us, after all that which you have learned about Stalin, do you preserve in your heart love toward I. V. Stalin?"[44]

Yet despite her uncertainty, Pankratova strove to satisfy her questioners. An aide who accompanied her on her trip later recalled gently that Pankratova had "responded to nearly every note, sometimes saying: 'Now that requires some thought. Let us all think together how it should be.'"[45] Pankratova reasoned with her audiences, urging them not to make hasty judgments. For instance, she tried to finesse the common question of whether to consider Stalin's philosophical works classics of Marxism-Leninism by explaining that many of his reports and speeches were "products of the collective thoughts of the Central Committee" or valuable commentaries on Lenin. She even tried to justify the loyalty of top leaders, arguing, "The Central Committee united around Stalin not as an individual but because they supported the correct line that he introduced."[46]

Even though she did not say so in her report, Pankratova must have known that her attempts to fill the void were not a success. Moscow historian Sergei Dmitriev noted in his diary a friend's account of how Pankratova's comment "that during her lifetime she had already had to refashion [*perestraivat'sia*] her historical views five times" prompted someone in the audience to call out, "And that's the problem." Another heckler had shouted out, "Physician, heal thyself!"[47] Philosopher Igor' Kon heard Pankratova make a similar awkward statement at one of her large lectures and recalled that it produced "unfriendly laughter." When Kon met her at her hotel after she had spoken to Leningrad teachers, he found her distraught to the point of tears. Someone, Kon does not specify who, explained that the teachers had shouted at her: "Stalin made you an academician and now you say that it was all a pack of lies. Who falsified this history? You falsified it. How can you respond to our questions 'I don't know, I need to think' when we have to go into the classroom tomorrow—what will we tell the children?"[48] She had been given a thankless task. Indeed, only one note writer out of hundreds expressed gratitude to Pankratova for her efforts.

Pankratova's perceptions of her own shortcomings motivated her to advise her party superiors as to the dire need for better answers. She did not gloss over the sharpest questions in her report but rather quoted them at length.[49] By passing along many urgent and heartfelt requests that members of the presidium come to Leningrad and explain what had happened under Stalin and what ought to be done now, Pankratova, in effect, challenged the top leaders to do what she had done—face their constituents. Furthermore, Pankratova called for an "explanatory campaign" in the press and for a "deeper, more concrete" explanation of the cult to be given to propagandists, teachers, and members of the intelligentsia to clear up their confusion and to counter "unhealthy moods and (judging by several notes) plainly recidivist Trotskyite-Bukharinist views" held by some individuals. A desire for more academic freedom did not trump Pankratova's ideological vigilance. As she put it sharply in her draft, the leadership ought "to condemn the attempts of some Party members to cast doubt on the socialist essence of the Soviet system and on the correctness of the Party's general line."[50]

Notably absent from Pankratova's report and from the 825 questions recorded were inquiries regarding arrested colleagues or relatives. Although some listeners wondered about the status of famous figures— asking, "Is [Marshal Mikhail] Tukhachevskii rehabilitated?" and "Has the Party reconsidered the verdicts of [Nikolai] Bukharin *et al?*"—no one asked in writing how to find out about the fates of ordinary people. Pankratova must have heard some tales of tragedy, however, because in her report to the Central Committee she observed, "In notes and conversations with Leningraders it became clear that they suffered exceptionally, as in Leningrad there is not one family that did not suffer either in 1937–38, or during the war, or from the 'Leningrad Affair.'"[51] Requests about rehabilitation may have been too sensitive to be aired at public meetings. Pankratova's aide recollected that when they returned to their hotel very late at night, Pankratova, though dropping with exhaustion, met with old comrades who were waiting to try to see her. He observed, "She did not feel she had the right to refuse a hearing to anyone."[52] She, after all, had survived.

Pankratova's difficult task of answering for the party after the Secret Speech and her ever-increasing knowledge of the extent of injustices under Stalin could not help but influence her. Her controversial efforts as editor in chief of *Voprosy istorii* to reform Soviet social sciences are addressed later. But it seems fitting to end this part of her story by noting that Pankratova once again sought refuge in unremitting labor. As one of her biographers observed, after the Twentieth Party Congress, "Her work as a deputy and her participation in rehabilitating those who had been repressed alone took up so much time and caused her such emotional exhaustion, that she ceased to sleep, suffered heart palpitations, and cried a lot." Yet even then Pankratova did not turn her back on her Marxist training: "This was difficult and bitter work, there was a lot she herself did not understand; she tried to make sense of it from the position of historical science."[53]

Chain Reactions

Khrushchev might have done well to heed Pankratova's advice about setting out a more detailed party line in March 1956. For across the country, party meetings where questions or speeches were allowed turned up reams of similar inquiries about the genesis of the speech, the causes of the cult, who was to blame, and what was to be done.[54] Those tasked with speaking for the regime needed answers themselves. "How is a propagandist to act in practice regarding study of the *Short Course of Party History?*" inquired a Murmansk listener. "How should conversations about Stalin be conducted among the workers?" wondered a member in Orlovsk. And in the Stalingrad region, a collective farm chairman worried about how to break the news to his people, noting, "On the day of Stalin's death it fell to me to conduct meetings with the collective farms, and I saw how the farmers, with tears in their eyes, felt this heavy loss. And now we will go to them and we'll say the opposite."[55]

It was easy for party workers to resent the position in which Khrushchev had placed them. As a lieutenant colonel responsible for teaching party history to military cadets admitted to a visiting inspector, "It's very hard for me right now—yesterday I said one thing about Stalin, and today I'm supposed to say something completely different. The students will say I'm just a parrot with no opinions of my own." He suggested, "They should have just fixed the mistakes that had been allowed, and not advertised them."[56]

Khrushchev could dodge taking questions from his constituents, but not the larger consequences of reversing the party line. The Secret Speech did not cause open political unrest in Russia proper, though in Stalin's homeland of Georgia an unsanctioned public demonstration took place on March 5, the anniversary of Stalin's death. Students who felt that Georgia's honor had been maligned by the denunciations of Stalin and Beria led rallies in Tbilisi that drew thousands, spread over several days, and took on a strong nationalist tone, before being dispersed by force.[57] Russia, however, experienced only a few incidents of vandalism against Stalin monuments and markers and a spate of anonymous letters and leaflets, mostly in Stalin's defense.[58] But Pankratova presciently warned of more subtle dangers: the development among some individuals of political views in conflict with the party line and the ill preparedness of propagandists at all levels to deal with such problems.

As discussions of Khrushchev's report took place in party cells across the land, one incident became infamous for revealing both the "dangers" of allowing the intelligentsia to discuss the Stalin cult and the feebleness of propagandists' responses. It became the subject of the first official warning against too much free speech in the wake of the revelations about Stalin. The affair took place at the Thermal-Technical Laboratory, a research institute under the Academy of Sciences, when several young physicists decided that their party organization ought to have a meaningful discussion about overcoming the cult of personality.

Thirty-two-year-old Yuri Orlov, later to become a famous dissident, recollected that he prepared to speak in March 1956 out of a desire to "cleanse himself," to express ideas that he had been pondering since the end of the war. He wanted to expose what he saw as a dictatorship of the bureaucracy prevailing in Russia. Orlov did not question the goals of socialism but rejected the one-party system and planned economy—what Western analysts identified as the very bases of real existing socialism in the Soviet Union. His friends, too, had strong opinions about the Stalin cult and how to prevent any such recurrence. Orlov and two colleagues, all members of their workplace's party committee, prepared comments for the first meeting following their acquaintance with the Secret Speech.[59]

On the afternoon of Friday, March 23, the head of the institute's political department opened the meeting with a detailed and dogmatic account of the work of the Twentieth Congress. The stenographic report of the session laconically notes that he told "how the Congress demonstrated the unbreakable unity of the party's ranks, the convergence of the party around the Leninist Central Committee, and its indestructible bond with the masses." The mood changed abruptly, however, when Robert Avalov, a young physicist from Georgia and a sincere Leninist, took the floor. Avalov expressed his disgust that the Congress had not discussed Khrushchev's report on the consequences of the cult and asked what kind of example that set. The party needed to solicit the opinions of ordinary people, he argued. With excellent logic, Avalov disputed the notion that the cult of personality had caused the problems in the party. Rather it seemed to be the symptom of concentration of power in the hands of a few. To address this, Avalov contended, the most radical solution would be to arm the people so that they could always wrest power away from those who abused it.[60]

Orlov followed with an equally challenging critique of Soviet politics. He argued that the Soviet Union was socialist but not democratic. Property might be in the hands of the people, but power was in the hands of a few careerists. Instead of wasting all their time criticizing capitalist nations' faults, he argued, party members ought to be analyzing their own system's failings. Orlov ended by urging, "We need total democratization in our lives—we'll have socialism [only] when one can live confidently without looking over one's shoulder." He turned then to the head of the institute's security department, its in-house secret policeman, and asked, "Tell us, are they repressing people nowadays for speaking out or not?"[61]

Orlov and his comrades would learn the answer to that question the hard way, but first they finished making their stand. The third young scientist, Vadim Nesterov, decried the horrors of the purges. How could it be that 70 percent of the Central Committee had been wrongly executed? There must have been more Bolsheviks killed in the purges than during the October Revolution itself. Nesterov blamed the press for its blatant misinformation and empty words and called for real political debates and more exchanges of information. The party should not fear opposing views, Nesterov insisted. Why jam the BBC and other foreign stations? Let Soviet citizens judge for themselves. More speakers followed, some of whom criticized the rebels. As the hour grew late, the meeting was finally adjourned for the next day.

As Orlov went home that night to his wife and small sons, his head was full of ideas for how he would elaborate on his remarks. Next time he would lay out his economic ideas. Always interested in philosophy, Orlov had read all the classics of Marxism-Leninism as a teenager. After the war he had discussed the nation's economic woes and political shortcomings relatively freely with some of his fellow officers. At that time he had come up with his own socialist innovation: "I wanted to reorganize society on the basis of Engels's idea that there must be industrial-agricultural units. Factory workers would help agricultural workers with technology and in the fields, and agricultural workers would help out in the factories during the winter." His plan had political ramifications, too: "because the only way to achieve radical social change was by force, according to Marx and Engels, my plans included the creation of a new revolutionary party."[62] In Orlov's scheme, workers would resolve their problems by voting—no need for a bureaucracy. Though none of his ideas found direct expression in Khrushchev's speech, Orlov felt that the denunciation of Stalin's rule had opened up the issue of the nature of the system. Moreover, Khrushchev had implied that the party would tolerate debates again, and Orlov was ready to participate.

Orlov never got the chance to expound on his economic ideas. The bold speeches and disrespectful comments toward the nation's political elite had alarmed the institute's party secretary. Distraught about how to deal with sedition at a top secret research institute connected with the nuclear program, he alerted his superiors. When the meeting reconvened on Monday March 26, Leonid Mezentsev, head of the political directorate for the blandly named Ministry of Medium-Machine Building, which had responsibility for all nuclear-related projects, was in attendance. Under his dour gaze, two senior party members from the institute took the floor with prepared speeches to denounce the three rebels and those who had supported them.

The two assigned speakers charged Orlov and the others with slandering the Soviet leadership and insulting the whole eight-million-strong Communist Party. Echoing Pankratova's concerns, they warned that the violations of legality that occurred in the past had not negated the democratic character of the Soviet political system. Rather than restoring order among the physicists, however, the crude attacks provoked catcalls and more anger about the state of free speech within the party. One person commented that he would know that the cult was over when he heard a real discussion in the Supreme Soviet. More soberly, a senior researcher invoked Khrushchev's reminder that Lenin did not punish those who adopted mistaken points of view. The older members of the party, therefore, needed to educate their youthful opponents, not destroy them. He disagreed with Orlov, the researcher noted, but he judged Orlov as speaking from the heart. Others also praised the rebels' sincerity—a word that had gained special moral weight in the post-Stalin years.[63]

The physicists at the Thermo-Technical Laboratory, some of the nation's finest intellects, were concocting their own explanations for the cult. Whether devout Marxists or not, they felt dissatisfied with and shaken by Khrushchev's report. A lab technician made an emotional speech admitting that he was angry with himself for his own naïveté. Why, he wondered, did Soviet citizens listen to the media passively and never question the authorities? Another person bridled at the perceived hypocrisy of Khrushchev's dodging any accountability. One scientist even cited a widespread rumor that someone had passed Khrushchev a note during the Secret Speech asking him where he had been during the terror. Khrushchev allegedly read the note aloud and then turned on the audience, shouting, "Who wrote this note?" Laughing at the delegates' ashen faces, he supposedly said, "That's where I was." This legend had swept through Moscow in March and was still circulating decades later.[64]

The denouement of the Thermo-Technical Laboratory's meeting showed that a fair number of party members at the lab were ready to shake off fear and subservience. As Mezentsev wrapped up the discussion period by lighting into the rebels and those who failed to condemn them, he faced heckling from the audience. When it came time for the party cell to formulate a resolution as to how to deal with the rebels, four variants were suggested: (1) to condemn Orlov et al. and improve political education in the laboratory; (2) to not offer an evaluation of the rebels' speeches; (3) to condemn both the rebels' statements and the two rehearsed rebuttals; or (4) to condemn specific offensive remarks but not the rebels' whole speeches. Thirty-seven people voted for the first and harshest alternative. Thirty-five endorsed the idea of abstaining from judgment. Thirteen wanted to condemn both sets of speeches, and eight preferred to condemn only the most offensive remarks.

The refusal of nearly one-third of the laboratory's communists to unequivocally censure their colleagues infuriated party higher-ups. Disregarding the results of the meeting, the Ministry saw to it that Avalov, Orlov, Nesterov, and their most vocal defender were expelled from the party, fired from the institute, and blocked from finding suitable employment in Moscow. On the Central Committee's orders the institute's party organization was dissolved and reorganized with new leadership. The lab's director, a renowned scientist and rare nonparty person in a position of power, told the rebels: "I telephoned Khrushchev on your behalf, but he said he was not the only member of the [presidium]. Other members demanded your arrest. He told me, 'They should be glad they got off with dismissals.'"[65] So, the answer to Orlov's question turned out to be that people would still be punished for speaking out, but not as harshly as before. Moreover, the rebels were not shunned. On the contrary, after being featured negatively in a *Pravda* editorial, Orlov and his fellow rebels became martyrs of sorts among the liberal intelligentsia. For several months they lived on donations collected spontaneously by scientists at other institutes from as far away as Siberia.[66]

A Vicious Cycle

The official response to the "seditious" remarks at the Thermal-Technical Laboratory was publication of some guidelines for discussing the consequences of the cult of personality. On April 5, under the upbeat title "The Communist Party Has Triumphed and Will Triumph through

Loyalty to Leninism," *Pravda* published a long editorial lauding the accomplishments of the Twentieth Party Congress. It cited workers' expressions of gratitude for the party's strong Leninist collective leadership and hailed the wisdom of the party's central organs. Halfway through, however, the editorial changed tone. Asserting that the Party welcomed "principled and brave criticism, offered up in the spirit of Bolshevik *partiinost'*," *Pravda* warned that certain "rotten elements" were taking advantage of the party's openness to air "all sorts of slanderous fabrications and anti-Party assertions." Here the editorialists cited the incident at the Thermal-Technical laboratory, singling out the rebellious scientists by name. The editorial mentioned two other outbursts and attributed all three to the influence of "foreign reactionary propaganda." *Pravda* focused not on the content of the critiques—which it dismissed as parroting of foreign slander—but on the failure of party members to immediately correct the misguided speakers. The real danger lay not in the obviously wrongheaded critiques but in inadequate response of supposedly mature party members.[67]

Intended to rein in discussion, the *Pravda* editorial became a mandatory subject for review at party and Komsomol meetings in April. However, it inspired a young Leningrad mathematician with the unusual and apt name "Revolt" to scorn the Secret Speech as merely a weapon in a power struggle among elites, rather than a sign of real political change. Revol't Pimenov's sharp response to this first sign of retreat from the newly proclaimed "Leninist" norms for discussion reveals the danger created by the regime's retrenchment. By initiating and then curbing discussion, the party looked mean and grudging rather than confident and generous.

Like many educated youths, Pimenov had engaged in serious private discussions of the Secret Speech and its underlying intent. Pimenov, his girlfriend, Irena Verblovskaia, and another young mathematician, Ernst Orlovskii, had even taken the more serious step of compiling their own version of the speech by dint of attending as many readings of the speech as possible and combining their notes.[68] The three typed up their own copy of the speech with footnotes by Orlovskii. A bibliophile, amateur historian, and stickler for precision, Orlovskii annotated the speech, explaining the events and identifying the personages mentioned by Khrushchev. By noting omissions, he highlighted the incomplete nature of Khrushchev's coming to terms with past abuses.[69]

In early April, however, provoked by the *Pravda*'s denunciation of the discussion at the Thermal-Technical Laboratory, Pimenov decided to editorialize on the speech's failings. Surviving fragments of Pimenov's "appendix" to the Secret Speech show him to have been a harsh and creative critic. Already concerned that Khrushchev had dodged the key question of accountability, Pimenov interpreted the shaming of the Moscow physicists as the party once again asserting infallibility and shutting down constructive conversation.

"Those who helped Stalin, who surrounded him, who shared his glory," Pimenov wrote, "should also share responsibility with him. They are Stalin's accomplices in crime and therefore the people should condemn them if they condemn Stalin." He went on to ask why the party's rank and file should have to mutely accept the official judgment of the party's past mistakes. It seemed to Pimenov that the outcome of the Twentieth Party Congress was that "the cult of a single personality is being replaced by the cult of 'the collective wisdom of the Central Committee,' put more simply, faith in Stalin is to be traded for faith in our Wise Father-the Central Committee [*TsK-batiushka*]." The CPSU, Pimenov declared, had showed itself to be ideologically bankrupt, and he warned that "the country has arrived at fascism instead of communism." Pimenov ended his essay by rallying his potential readers, "You and I together should be imbued with the idea that the politics of our country is our affair, that the government ought to take us into account, that we do not have the right to entrust the governing of the country to a small group." For Pimenov, civic involvement stood out as the "only guarantee against the repetition of terror and despotism."[70]

Pankratova no doubt would have been horrified by Pimenov's essay. He did exactly what she feared most—made Khrushchev's criticism of Stalin the basis for tearing down the whole system of Soviet rule and discarding the core narrative of party history. But what would she have thought of his concluding plea? Pankratova certainly believed in civic involvement. She had frequently subordinated her personal desires to serve a larger good. But for her, that "small group" at the top included those she judged to be the most committed to the revolution's cause, those who like her had struggled earnestly to do what was best for the cause of socialism. For her, *partiinost'* remained a strict prerequisite for political advocacy.

Pimenov's essay never reached his intended audience. He and his friends couldn't agree on what to do with their bootleg version of Khrushchev's report. Verblovskaia feared that distribution of a secret document would be considered treasonous. Pimenov, by contrast, wanted to sell copies for the price of production. Ultimately, they chose not to circulate copies after one that had been lent to a friend fell into the hands of the secret police. The friend managed to shield them by claiming he had purchased the manuscript from an unknown person in Leningrad's main bookstore. The copy did not have Pimenov's appendix or else it might have prompted a more serious investigation. In summer of 1956 Pimenov and his friends moved on to other interests, but their political awakening could not be undone.

Pimenov was a person of unusual erudition and self-confidence bordering on arrogance. His actions and views in the spring of 1956 were hardly ordinary. Yet, his interest in the Secret Speech and its consequences were typical of educated youth of his generation. Consider the reminiscences of art historian Mikhail German, then a student at Leningrad's Repin Art Academy. When authorities at his institute tried to limit attendance to their reading of Khrushchev's report to members of the Komsomol, students pushed back. As German recalled, "When the crowd [trying to enter the auditorium] was halted once more, the students sang the 'Internationale,' and began to make their way through by force. For the first time I witnessed a rebellion [*bunt*]—a totally childish one, but still for the first time I felt how fear retreats." His fellow students dared to push for admittance but were struck dumb by what they heard. Once the reading began, the giddy crowd fell quiet. At its conclusion the listeners left in silence—"like virtuous family men exiting a whorehouse, as if they didn't recognize each other."[71] The secrecy surrounding its reading made it plain that Khrushchev's report was something to be whispered about, not a proper topic for debate.

March then was a month of questions and silences. Although Khrushchev's report sparked as many questions as it answered, most went unasked in public and those that were posed often went unanswered. Pankratova's personal experience convinced her that it was too much to expect the party's legions of low-level representatives to quickly and independently compose politically correct answers to very hard questions about the cult. She herself could not easily explain how a renunciation of the Stalin cult would be reconciled with a new narrative that did not discard Stalin. But leaders shied away from her challenge to formulate better answers to queries about accountability and reform. Instead April's editorial in *Pravda* just reinforced the old understanding that spontaneity carried risks and drawing incorrect conclusions would be punished.

Reform was to be controlled from above and those who spoke for the party were not to relax their vigilance. Such limitations left little room for initiative, and yet much needed to be done if the damage subsumed under the cult of personality was to be undone.

4 | APRIL

EARLY SPRING

In April 1956 Kseniia Chudinova packed a suitcase to return to the gulag. The sixty-two-year-old had been a Communist Party member for more than four decades, and she was used to tackling tough assignments. As commissar for provisions in a town near Moscow after the revolution, she and her pistol-wielding comrades had seized food from wealthy households. A year later she had crisscrossed Siberia with her infant son in her arms, trying to avoid capture by the Whites while organizing local Bolsheviks. Arrested in 1938, the party loyalist had spent eight years in prisons and labor camps and eight more in exile, but in the summer of 1954, Chudinova had been completely rehabilitated and allowed to return to Moscow. Now she had agreed to serve on a special traveling commission that would review the cases of those sentenced for political and economic crimes and decide on the spot whether to shorten sentences or dismiss charges.[1]

Just two months earlier, on the opening day of the Twentieth Party Congress, Chudinova had sat in the balcony of the Grand Kremlin Palace alongside her old friend Polina Zhemchuzhina, wife of the USSR's foreign minister Vyacheslav Molotov. As Zhemchuzhina wept, Chudinova listened to predictions of the Communist Party's great future and thought about the past. She mourned for her husband and ex-husband, both of whom had died in the purges, and marveled at the turn of fate that had placed her at the Congress. She and Zhemchuzhina had both suffered the disgrace of arrest and pain of exile. Now, thanks to Aleksei Snegov's intercession, they were among a dozen rehabilitated party veterans who had been invited to the Congress.

Although disappointed that Khrushchev did not speak of Stalin's misdeeds on that first day of the Congress, Chudinova felt the honor of having been included. Perhaps it helped compensate for the suffering she had endured since the April day in 1938 when she had been arrested in front of her three youngest children. As secret police agents ransacked her apartment, Chudinova had begged eighteen-year-old Natal'ia to be brave, to believe in her mother's innocence, and to take care of the little ones. There was no one else. Chudinova's husband had already been arrested the year before. In the months that followed, NKVD interrogators questioned Chudinova in long nighttime sessions. They cursed her, called her an "enemy of the people," and threatened to arrest her children. Still, Chudinova refused to confess to false charges and believed to the last moment that she would be freed. She spent sixteen years in prisons, at hard labor, and finally in exile in a poor Siberian village.[2]

Chudinova and her friends had to wait for eleven days from the start of the Congress to the final closed session to hear Khrushchev proclaim the innocence of the many victims of the purges. The great majority of survivors, however, had to wait even longer to learn of the dramatic change in the party line. Their very status as prisoners, exiles, or former convicts disqualified them from admission to those meetings in March and April 1956 where Khrushchev's report was read out.[3] As of spring 1956, few survivors of the terror had been exonerated and fewer still allowed to return home or readmitted to the party. Nothing in Khrushchev's Secret Speech explicitly addressed the plight of current and former political prisoners. How was the party going to do right by its victims without drawing further attention to past mistakes?[4]

In 1956 part of the solution would be the dispatch of traveling commissions to visit every camp and prison across the USSR over the course of six months. Kseniia Chudinova by going from unjust imprisonment to a position of trust would epitomize the heroic arc that Khrushchev imagined for gulag survivors. Transformed from convict to judge, she would become part of the process of shrinking the gulag and restoring "socialist legality." The experiences of Chudinova and a handful of other prominent party veterans in making or implementing policies regarding victims of political persecution illuminate both possibilities for and limits on working inside the system in the post-Stalin period. They also reveal starkly differing opinions among the party elite as to how to address the damage caused by Stalinism.

Special Cases

Before the Secret Speech, release and rehabilitation of political prisoners and exiles had been relatively rare and secretive. Consider the case of perhaps the first to be granted a new life after Stalin's death—Polina Zhemchuzhina, wife, or more accurately former wife, of presidium member Vyacheslav Molotov. Her story is a dramatic but emblematic account of rehabilitation before the Secret Speech. It highlights the initial refusal of Stalin's heirs to systematically address the falsity of convictions during the purges and their expectations that survivors would keep silent about their unjust ordeals.

Zhemchuzhina's woes had begun in the late 1940s when Stalin had become increasingly anti-Semitic in his paranoia. Zhemchuzhina, a senior official of Jewish descent, had been assigned by Stalin to escort Golda Meier when she represented Israel on a state visit to the USSR in 1948. Subsequently, however, Stalin became convinced that Zhemchuzhina harbored Zionist sympathies and ordered Molotov to break with her. According to Molotov, Zhemchuzhina responded by saying, "If the Party needs this then we shall get a divorce." They divorced, but it did not save her from arrest in February 1949.[5] That same year Molotov was removed from his post as foreign minister; he remained a member of the presidium, though he was excluded from its regular activities. Only after Stalin's death would he resume his ministerial position.

When Stalin died on March 5, 1953, Zhemchuzhina happened to be in a Moscow prison cell. She had been transported there from Siberian exile a few months earlier to be interrogated as part of preparations for a new anti-Semitic show trial. Unaware of the dictator's death, Zhemchuzhina was surprised one day to be allowed to bathe and to receive her own civilian clothes and undergarments. Returning to her cell, she found a new blanket on the bunk and a proper dinner set out on a table.

Zhemchuzhina surmised that her execution must be near and guessed that her ex-husband must have asked that she be treated kindly on her final evening. Thus, she was braced for the worst when summoned before Lavrenty Beria, who had called her a "Jewish spy" during interrogations in 1949. To her shock, Beria embraced her and announced that she was a "heroine." Zhemchuzhina promptly fainted. She regained consciousness to find the dapper Molotov on his knees beside her. "Calm down," he implored. "We're going home right now."[6]

Molotov's birthday, March 9, coincided with the date of Stalin's funeral, and one version has it that Zhemchuzhina's freedom was a present from his fellow presidium members. In any event, by the end of the month, the presidium had already moved on to the next step—reversing her expulsion from the party. Although she had been a deputy minister responsible for the textile industry before her arrest, Zhemchuzhina never resumed her career. She did return to her husband and apparently never chided him for continuing to serve Stalin while she suffered in prison. Her husband liked to recall that to the end of her life Zhemchuzhina would brook no criticism of Stalin.[7]

Other survivors did not enjoy such quick and satisfactory recognition of their false imprisonment. Zhemchuzhina's tale offers a reminder, however, that the simplest and fastest way to begin the rehabilitation process was to rely on direct ties to very high officials, a real possibility for many communists. Longtime veterans and their descendants constituted a relatively small but tightly linked group. These men and women had made the revolution and served the regime together in the difficult 1920s. They had socialized, even intermarried, and their children had studied side by side. For instance, Chudinova's son Kim—named after the acronym for the Communist Youth International (*Kommunisticheskii Internatsional Molodezhi*)—studied in the same grade as Vasilii Stalin at Moscow's School 175. The children of Molotov, Mikoyan, and Bulganin also attended this central Moscow school.[8] In Moscow, the party elite even lived cheek by jowl in the new apartment complex known as the "House on the Embankment." Under Stalin, new personnel had been promoted and diluted their ranks and the purges had split their lives asunder, but ties of kinship, histories of patronage, and traces of friendship remained to link prisoners and rulers.

Word of Stalin's death prompted many prisoners to write to their high-placed friends, onetime patrons, or even just acquaintances. The now-famous memoirist of the camps Eugenia Ginzburg remembered addressing her first post-Stalin appeal to presidium member Marshal Voroshilov "because I had once met him in my youth." She recalled, "I included a brief reminder of myself, informed him of my fate and asked him to intervene. He could do so; and *now* he had the opportunity of doing so." Her actual letter, now recovered from the archives, reveals a more tenuous claim to a connection, a recollection of singing "Voroshilov is with us—the first red officer," but it resonates with the sentiment that Ginzburg recalled, that she "had no doubt that the tyrant's death had freed not only us, but all those who had stood behind him in the role of his nearest comrades in arms."[9]

The more skeptical Aleksei Snegov recollected that he acted only after learning of Beria's arrest in June 1953. In his letters to Mikoyan and Khrushchev, he offered to testify against Beria and, as he recounted later, "'I wrote not just about myself—but about how everyone needed to be returned from the camps."[10] Ol'ga Shatunovskaia, who had worked with Khrushchev in Moscow in the 1930s, also at first refused to ask for clemency after Stalin's death. Hard experience had taught her that appeals were useless, but when her fellow exiles literally put pen and paper before her, she relented. As she later told her grandson, "And so on this little square scrap of paper I wrote a few lines to [Khrushchev]. [I wrote] that we worked together and you know, of course, that I'm no enemy of the people. That's all. I didn't write anything more. None of those explanations."[11] Snegov and Shatunovskaia displayed confidence that Mikoyan and Khrushchev would accept their innocence. Other appeals, however, bulged with petitioners' attempts to explain the often inexplicable paths by which the authors landed in camp. Partly such detail may have been intended to aid in the reinvestigation of charges, a necessary step in rehabilitation before the Secret Speech.

Although Khrushchev and Mikoyan had the power to direct the procurator's office to speed the reexamination of specific cases, even they could not sidestep the process. Rehabilitation of political prisoners was a very sensitive topic as those at the top often had played some role in, or had benefited from, the arrests of those now asking for their innocence to be established and for the return of their old homes and positions. Survivors were a reminder of past "mistakes," and their former housing and positions had been redistributed long ago. Hence, in May 1954 the presidium decided to channel requests for rehabilitation by "counter-revolutionaries" through a central commission, and a few regional affiliates, and to make reinvestigation of each case a prerequisite.[12] The operating assumption remained that the majority of prisoners were guilty of something—how else to explain all those confessions and incriminations?

For individuals, the review procedures meant waiting while procuracy officials studied the original case records, interrogated surviving witnesses, examined the files of deceased codefendants, and sought fresh character assessments of the accused. For Eugenia Ginzburg, a former party member, journalist, and spouse of a purged regional party secretary, this involved a reexamination of four witnesses, summations of the cases of four others convicted on related charges, a review of her personal party file, and even an unsuccessful attempt to locate and question the three NKVD men who had interrogated her following her initial arrest. She was rehabilitated on July 5, 1955—more than two years after her first post-Stalin appeal.[13]

By March 1956 the rehabilitation commissions had reviewed cases affecting some 333,183 persons. The commissions amnestied or shortened the sentences of many persons; however, they rehabilitated only some 4 percent (14,338) while leaving intact sentences and punishments for 55 percent (183,681). The miserly rate of legal rehabilitation becomes clearer when one considers that the central review committee was presided over by the procurator general and included the minister of justice and the head of the KGB—all of whom had made their careers in law enforcement under Stalin.[14] Moreover, since revelations of gross use of torture or blatant falsifications sometimes resulted in sanctions against current or former interrogators, those reexamining the cases acted with great caution. Rehabilitations were further slowed by lack of sufficient personnel in the procuracy to even preliminarily sort through all the requests received.[15]

Confusion on the part of petitioners exacerbated prosecutorial inefficiency. Survivors often had not understood who sentenced them in the first place and hence had trouble finding out where their case files were located. The same was even more often true for relatives, many of whom were seeking posthumous rehabilitation for loved ones without knowing the details of their sentences. Since the press carried no information on the procedures for rehabilitations, interested parties had to find their own way through the maze of the procuracy offices, courts, and party institutions. Insiders, however, could provide patronage and technical assistance in these matters.

Old Bolsheviks, longtime party members who retained some of the aura of Leninist purity and dedication to the revolution, took on a special role in helping survivors or families of the repressed. Though largely marginalized (if not actually purged) under Stalin, old Bolsheviks carried a certain weight based on their own past and their advanced age. In the post-Stalin period, old Bolsheviks who had avoided arrest could use their personal standing to demand officials' attention and to vouch for the *partiinost'* of others.[16]

Special Advocates

Perhaps the most famous living old Bolshevik in the 1950s, and the most active advocate for rehabilitation cases, was Vittorio Vidali's friend Elena Stasova. Known as "Comrade Absolute," Stasova had been an active revolutionary since the 1890s. The daughter of a well-to-do, liberal St. Petersburg lawyer, Stasova began her radical career teaching in a night school for women workers. There she met Lenin's wife and other Marxists who drew her into the workers' movement. In 1898 a wave of arrests left the twenty-five-year-old Stasova in charge of the St. Petersburg party cell's archive. From that day onward she devoted herself to the logistics of underground activity and as a result suffered repeated arrests and exile under tsarist rule.[17] After the revolution, she served alongside Lenin as secretary to the Central Committee (of which she was a full-fledged member) and later in the Caucasian bureau of the party. In the 1920s Stasova put her bourgeois education in foreign languages to use in the Communist International movement (Comintern), serving on its Central Committee and heading up the Soviet branch of the International Organization for Aid to Revolutionaries (MOPR), where she met Vidali and many other left-wing foreigners who had sought safe haven in the USSR.

In 1938, apparently at the request of then secret police chief Nikolai Yezhov, Stasova was shunted to a less sensitive position in the foreign literature publishing house, where she worked until retiring in 1946. According to Vidali, who corresponded with Stasova after he left the USSR in 1935 and who renewed his friendship with her at the Twentieth Party Congress, Stasova started to run into political difficulties as early as 1935, when she stood by friends who had been arrested. Vidali cites the example of Osip Piatnitskii, a leading Comintern official. Records now show that Stasova's loyalty consisted of abstaining in the vote to condemn Piatnitskii at the 1937 Central Committee Plenum meeting where Yezhov deemed him undeserving of political trust.[18]

In memoirs written in the late 1950s, Stasova admitted that she had asked awkward questions about those who had been arrested, but she credited this to her sincere confusion. "It seemed to me that I had obviously overlooked something in their behavior and I wanted to know what it was so as not to repeat such mistakes." In other words, she had not been questioning policy or even challenging specific arrests, but rather trying to understand the signs of counterrevolutionary behavior. Stasova caused further offense by naively taking up the question of what to do about wives of arrested foreign communists. She wanted local officials to be ordered to find them some employment, however lowly, lest they turn for aid to their consulates, where, she argued, they might be recruited for espionage work against the USSR. The officials in question had to explain to her that they themselves would be drummed out of the party if they started helping wives of "enemies of the people."[19]

Stasova herself also felt the pain of unjust political accusations. In portions of her autobiography omitted from the published version, she defended herself against accusations of having aided Trotskyites during her work for MOPR. She also recounted her distress at receiving a strict reprimand for "praising Bukharin, slandering Lenin, and distorting party history." This accusation stemmed from a 1947 meeting with Ukrainian journalists during which Stasova answered a question about Lenin's relations with Stalin by observing that Lenin got along well with all the members of the Central Committee and giving the example of Lenin calling Bukharin by the affectionate nickname "Bukharchik." Bukharin, however, had been condemned as a counterrevolutionary in a notorious show trial a decade earlier. Stasova protested the harsh interpretation of her words, but only after Stalin's death did the Party Control Commission (KPK) expunge the black mark from her record.[20]

When Vidali met up with Stasova on the first day of the Twentieth Party Congress, he found her preoccupied with helping victims of the purges from among her wide circle of acquaintances. Stasova had worked out a standard procedure for assisting those who sought rehabilitation. A typical case is that of Sarra Lavarishek, a fifty-five-year-old woman who had once worked with Stasova at MOPR. In 1955 she wrote to Stasova from the far northern region of Komi, explaining that although she had been free for three years under an amnesty (*sudimost' sniata*), she was still deprived of her rights. Lavarishek had written fruitlessly to the Central Committee to ask for a speedy review of her case. Now, she turned to Stasova, who advised her as follows: "First, do not pay any attention to the fact that judgment has been revoked. Do send a petition about your rehabilitation to the Supreme Procuracy of the USSR to the attention of Baranov, First Deputy of the Chief Procurator . . . Second, write a request to the President of the Party Control Committee of the Central Committee of the CPSU, Pavel Timofeevich Komarov asking that you be reinstated in the ranks of the party."[21] Lavarishek quickly replied. She noted that Stasova's response had already lifted her spirits. Something she desperately needed since "here, even if your sentence has been revoked, people look on you as a former prisoner and don't really believe that you can still be of use to the Party or to Soviet power." Upon learning that Lavarishek had followed her counsel, Stasova responded with a slightly warmer note asking who had signed a notice from the Military Procuracy stating that Lavarishek's case was under review. Stasova was ready to phone the investigator to press him to act quickly.[22]

Stasova assisted her correspondents primarily by advising them how to negotiate their way through legal rehabilitation to party reinstatement. She was willing to deploy her strong links with official agencies and to write the all-important character recommendations (*kharakteristiki*). She even offered financial assistance and tried to sort out medical services and housing. When presidium member Otto Kuusinen's estranged ex-wife returned in October 1955, Stasova not only invited her to stay but helped with everything from obtaining good housing to getting a phone installed. Indeed, Stasova's intercession prompted the Moscow telephone office to provide unheard of next-day service.[23]

Stasova's unflagging actions on behalf of survivors show her to have been remarkably generous, helping friends of friends, and answering every letter despite her poor health.[24] For pulling strings, however, Stasova expected something in return—not personal gratitude or favors but political correctness. She was adamant that survivors apply for reinstatement in the party. She implied in her letters that her protégés would naturally take this step to reintegrate themselves into the political fraternity that they shared. She did not ask them how they felt about begging to be readmitted to the CPSU, but she shared the delight of those who rejoiced in their reacceptance.

Stasova also seems to have favored those who were determined to return to productive lives. No doubt petitioners' declarations of eagerness to contribute to Soviet society were to some extent pro forma, but Stasova took them to heart. She responded positively to those who wrote of their ambitions in the workplace and criticized those who gave in to their physical and mental sufferings.[25] Her high expectations mirrored own fortitude in the face of advanced age and blindness and also suggested an expectation that virtuous people would resume their roles as worthy Soviet citizens. Only in this way could the damage of the purges be reversed.

Somewhat jarringly, given her obvious commitment to achieving justice for survivors, Stasova corresponded with her enormous number of acquaintances in a uniformly brusque and businesslike tone. She offered very little in response to highly emotional outpourings. For instance, when her old friend Berta Albert-Ploshanskaia wrote at length about her anger at the interminable delays in her rehabilitation and about her physical and spiritual woes, Stasova replied only with advice on how to speed the processing of her case. She said not a word about her friend's expressions of pain and grief.[26] The written record, confirmed by survivor Galina Voronskaia, who became one of Stasova's voluntary helpers in 1960, shows that Stasova continued to embody not only the high ideals of early revolutionaries, but also their emotional self-discipline.[27]

The Twentieth Party Congress, however, challenged even Stasova's composure. When Vidali met her there on the first day, she drew him aside and "in a low voice, almost a whisper" told him how she had been ostracized and isolated for several years. She had divulged to him in a letter a few years earlier that she often felt lonely and that she struggled not to dwell on her own problems. Now she confided in him about the deaths of dozens of mutual friends in distant labor camps. She explained that her activity at present consisted of two things: helping survivors and lecturing to young people about Lenin.[28]

To her many correspondents, Stasova wrote nothing about the Secret Speech, admitting only that the Congress had been "hard on the nerves."[29] Vidali, however, found her deeply shaken and distressed when he paid her a visit a few days after its end. Vidali himself was in a low mood when he entered Stasova's apartment in the House on the Embankment. Waiting to speak to her, Vidali spotted pictures of Lenin, Kirov, and Stalin among her many photos and souvenirs of a long life. He gazed out of her windows at the Kremlin and imagined, "Probably, when her friends were being arrested and disappeared into some prison never to return, she used to wait calmly for a knock on her own door."[30]

Although feeling ill, Stasova spoke with Vidali that night in February 1956 about her efforts for former prisoners and for the families of victims. "Now," she told him, "everybody is being rehabilitated, but now they are dead." Stasova expressed hatred for Beria and disgust for presidium member Georgy Malenkov, whom she viewed as deeply complicit in the purges. But she did not comment on Stalin directly. And when Vidali began to recount his impressions of the Congress, which he saw as "an assembly of functionaries and bureaucrats," Stasova fell silent. Vidali wanted to discuss what he felt was a dissipation of revolutionary spirit and the problem of extirpating the Stalin cult. For instance, why hadn't the leadership addressed the timing of the critique of Stalin? Why had foreigners been excluded from the closed session? Vidali halted his critical remarks when he realized that Stasova was having trouble breathing. She could not or would not discuss the larger causes of Stalinism or the need for serious remedies.[31]

Stasova recovered from her illness that spring and even turned down the opportunity to recuperate at a sanatorium so that she could press on with her never-ending correspondence on behalf of survivors. Though Stasova diligently pursued aid for individual victims of the terror, she seems never to have addressed higher authorities with demands that policy be changed to make rehabilitation easier. Indeed, historian Barbara Clements observes that despite Stasova's inclusion in the highest political organs after the revolution, she always sought to limit her activity to technical work and professed unsuitability for making policy decisions.[32] She continued this pattern with her unsentimental aid to victims and her resolute avoidance of discussions of what de-Stalinization should entail. When Vidali wrote to her after the Congress with questions about Soviet policy toward the cult of personality, Stasova merely directed him to *Pravda* for answers.[33] Even when frustrated in her efforts in later years to win rehabilitation for Bukharin, Stasova never challenged the system.

Stasova was exceptional in her willingness to help those with whom she had only tenuous links, but she was far from alone in her concern for aiding comrades. Many old Bolsheviks, including camp survivors who had achieved early rehabilitation, wrote appeals to the procuracy and intervened on housing and employment issues.[34] Their influence worked, but only up to a point. Rehabilitation did not guarantee renewal of patronage, reentry to the political elite, or even resumption of personal relations.

From Ignominy to Influence?

Party veterans who expected that rehabilitation would restore them to their old careers were often disappointed. Eugenia Ginzburg describes former Komsomol Secretary Aleksandr Mil'chakov, the first Kolyma exile to be rehabilitated, as one such person: "I have an enduring memory of the day Mil'chakov boarded the plane for Moscow to report back for rehabilitation . . . I was struck by the fact that no one had come along to see Mil'chakov off . . . He had become a 'cat that walks by itself.' Along with his prison clothes he had discarded any relationship with us—all memory of that extra morsel on the bread ration, the horrible propinquity of the plank bunks, the tags fastened to the arms of the dead." Ginzburg felt estranged from her newly energized, ambitious friend. "This was not the same Sasha Mil'chakov who had come to see us to exchange news and conjectures, to complain to [my physician husband] about his digestive disorders, and to laugh at his latest jokes," she concluded. At that moment, he appeared confident that he "had neatly repaired the broken thread of his life. He had knotted the two ends together securely, joined up 1937 and 1954 and thrown away everything in between.[35] In fact, Mil'chakov's experience would show the limitations facing even the best-connected survivors.

Mil'chakov could and did restore his family life. He could and did snub the friends he had made in camp and exile. But, as Ginzburg

Fig. 04-01 Aleksandr Mil'chakov in exile in Kolyma in the 1950s. Courtesy House on the Embankment Museum.

noted, his willingness to set aside the indignities he had suffered was not rewarded as he wished: "After rehabilitation, he was not summoned to stand at the helm of the Ship of State . . . A well-deserved rest? Yes. A personal pension? By all means. Accommodation? It's yours! Publication of memories about his glorious revolutionary past? . . . you go ahead and publish them . . . But that was it."[36] Indeed, shortly after his rehabilitation, Mil'chakov heard from an old friend, the head of the Writers Union Aleksandr Fadeev, that Molotov and Voroshilov had been discussing Mil'chakov's return and remembering him fondly. But according to Fadeev, both men seemed surprised to be asked whether they had contacted their former pal.[37]

In reminiscences written for his family, Mil'chakov laid out the painful limits of his return to the party fold. The party reinstated him, but with a gap in his record and only after he presented fresh character recommendations. He got his Order of Lenin back, a new apartment, and a long rest at a health spa. But when he contacted the Central Committee to discuss work, the options were disappointing. He could not return to his last position in the gold-mining trust, because his old subordinate now in charge did not want him. He could have been a manager in the nickel and cobalt industry, but he refused to work under those who had known him as a prisoner in Noril'sk. Finally, Mil'chakov asked for an assignment dealing with youth. Like Stasova, he felt he could best express his core idealism by investing in the new generation. He was sent to head up an obscure department responsible for political education of the labor reserves—as Fadeev jokingly described it: "working somewhere with trade school pupils and factory apprentices."[38]

Only Khrushchev's decision that the party must acknowledge the worst aspects of the Stalin cult raised the potential influence of veterans who carried the stigma of arrest. On the eve of the Twentieth Party Congress, Mil'chakov finally received the summons for which he had been waiting. Mikoyan invited him to the Kremlin and told him in confidence of the plan for Khrushchev's denunciation of Stalin. He also offered Mil'chakov a chance to serve the state by joining the traveling commissions. A debilitating heart attack on the eve of the Secret Speech prevented Mil'chakov from participating.[39] But other rehabilitated party veterans, including Kseniia Chudinova, took advantage of this opportunity to right some of the wrongs carried out under Stalin. This particular restoration to power came about thanks to Aleksei Snegov and Ol'ga Shatunovskaia, two survivors who had the rare privilege (and hardship) of being brought from disgrace back into responsible positions.

As recounted earlier, Aleksei Snegov became one of Khrushchev's few confidantes on the subject of the purges. Khrushchev arranged for him to enter the Ministry of Internal Affairs (MVD) as deputy head of the political department of the gulag. Even though Khrushchev had appointed a new head of the MVD after Beria's arrest, this ministry remained a hostile environment for a former political prisoner. Snegov, according to Sergo Mikoyan, took the job only reluctantly, saying: "I asked [Khrushchev] to make me secretary of some district Party committee in Moscow. I wanted to work like before, with people, with normal everyday problems and tasks. But now I have to travel around to the camps and see everything that I myself lived with for many years. Trust me, this is all repulsive to see, even as a boss." But, Khrushchev argued, Snegov was needed inside the MVD precisely because he understood the situation and no camp administrator could pull the wool over his eyes.[40]

Despite his past, Snegov had regained clout within the system because he was—as historian Roy Medvedev puts it—an appointee of the Central Committee and of Khrushchev personally" (*stavlennik TsK i lichno Khrushcheva*). In 1954–1955 he visited numerous outposts of the gulag and oversaw some liberalization of conditions for prisoners, such as permitting inmates to organize camp newspapers. But as for getting inmates released and rehabilitated, Snegov could not orchestrate major change. According to Snegov's recollections, when he approached Procurator General Roman Rudenko, another Khrushchev appointee, in 1954 about speeding the pace of liberation of prisoners, he was coldly rebuffed. Only Khrushchev's decision to denounce the purges created an opening for substantive changes in the fates of convicts.[41]

With the approach of the Twentieth Party Congress, Snegov along with Ol'ga Shatunovskaia, another rehabilitated veteran, renewed their pressure on Khrushchev and Mikoyan to abandon the cautious, time-consuming, centralized process of rehabilitation. Having served on the central state rehabilitation commission, Shatunovskaia knew that it could not cope with the demand, especially if victims of wartime ethnic deportations and prewar forced resettlement of "rich" peasants were included. Moreover, she felt that the commission was highly prejudiced. How could those tortured by the secret police expect sympathy when KGB chief Ivan Serov was among the arbiters deciding rehabilitation?

Shatunovskaia had personally felt Serov's hostility. She suspected that he knew that she had urged Khrushchev to hold all the executioners from the NKVD/KGB to account. Although Khrushchev had dismissed her idea out of hand, arguing such a purge would result in another 1937, he did appoint her to the central rehabilitation commission where she could watch over the work of the largely unreformed bureaucracy.[42] Thus, like Snegov, Shatunovskaia had the rare but dubious privilege of serving alongside the very functionaries who had averted their eyes from if not participated in the purges. Shatunovskaia, like Snegov, came back into the party elite after a long absence. Her record, however, was even longer than his for she joined the Bolsheviks as a girl of fifteen.

Born in 1901 to an upper-middle-class Jewish family in Baku, the present-day capital of Azerbaijan, Shatunovskaia joined a radical study group as a high school student. By 1916 she was volunteering in the Bolshevik Party underground and after the revolution, she became the sec-retary to Stepan Shaumian, the charismatic commissar for the Transcau-casus. Shatunovskaia barely escaped execution in September 1918 when the Turks occupied Baku. Her brush with death, however, only rein-forced her commitment to the cause. Against her father's wishes, she left her family home at age seventeen, joined the communist underground full time, and took on dangerous missions including carrying Bolshevik literature across front lines controlled by the White army.[43]

Photographs from the time show a slender young woman with an oval face, dark, wavy hair, and deep-brown eyes. Her serious expression and demure dress—white blouses and long dark skirts—could not hide her high spirits and energy. Known for her principled nature, fearlessness, and generosity, Shatunovskaia attracted many admirers among her com-rades, including Anastas Mikoyan. In later years she liked to tell her children how Mikoyan repeatedly, but unsuccessfully, begged her to marry him. The stubborn and strong-willed Shatunovskaia had her rivals, as well. In 1924 political quarrels in Baku led her to take a temporary assignment in the Russian town of Briansk. There she met her future husband, Iurii Kut'in.

In 1929, after more rifts in the local party organization, Shatunovs-kaia left Baku for good. From April 1931 until the eve of her arrest, Shatunovskaia worked for the Moscow Party Committee, where she met and befriended Khrushchev. He warned her when her old rivals in Baku began to circulate slanderous rumors about her. But neither Khrushchev nor Mikoyan could rescue her when she was arrested as a "counter-revolutionary" in November 1937. Sentenced six months later by an extra-judicial *troika*—a three-person NKVD commission—to eight years of hard labor, Shatunovskaia served out her full term in Kolyma, one of the most distant and harshest outposts of the gulag.

In 1946 Shatunovskaia made her way back to Moscow, where she lived illegally since her passport contained restrictions banning her from settling within one hundred kilometers of the major Soviet cities. She scraped by doing editing work from home and bribing her local policeman, who was tipped off to her presence by the jealous mistress her husband had acquired in her absence. But she left in 1948 after Mikoyan warned her to flee as a new wave of arrests loomed. Hoping to avoid the attention of the secret police, Shatunovskaia traveled to Kyzl-Orda, a backwater town in Kazakhstan where she worked in the office of a dairy-processing plant and frantically searched for a way to avoid arrest. In April 1949 before any of her schemes could succeed—she tried to buy a "clean" passport from a corrupt local official and considered changing her name by eloping with a new admirer—she was apprehended.

Shatunovskaia's new arrest culminated in a sentence of eternal exile, a common fate for those political prisoners who had served out sentences from 1937 to 1938. Thus, in October 1949 she found herself in the Krasnoiarsk region of Siberia. There Shatunovskaia, like Kseniia Chudinova and many other former prisoners, struggled to eke out a living in the town where she was assigned to live. Shatunovskaia worked as an untrained physical therapist and babysat her landlady's child. In October 1953, with Stalin's death seemingly producing no changes in the status of ex-prisoners, she scraped together money to buy a ramshackle hut. It seemed a wise investment in her future.

In 1954, however, Khrushchev responded to the note she sent him from exile. Indeed, so anxious was he to reverse her sentence that he had his aide phone the procuracy daily to check on the progress of her rehabilitation.[44] At their first meeting upon her return from exile, Khrushchev and Shatunovskaia spoke for more than three hours. At that early date, Khrushchev brushed aside Shatunovskaia's ideas about mass rehabilitations. But by December 1954 he placed Shatunovskaia on both the central commission on rehabilitation and at the Party Control Committee (KPK), the institution that screened and disciplined party members.[45]

According Shatunovskaia, she met a rocky reception in both places. In the KPK she heard coworkers gripe, "Why are they all coming here, those rehabilitated? Isn't there any work for them there in Siberia? Let them reestablish themselves [*vosstanavlivaiutsia*] and work there in the local party cells. They shouldn't be allowed in the Central Committee building." Indeed, no one would sit with her the Central Committee cafeteria until one of Khrushchev's closest aides demonstratively joined her. At the central rehabilitation commission, when Serov found out that Shatunovskaia had tried to reverse his denial of rehabilitation to one of her former colleagues, he said in front of everyone, "Aha, Shatunovskaia. She has no business there [in the KPK]. She herself is a counterrevolutionary, and rehabilitated herself." Meanwhile, the chauffeurs assigned to her reported on her activities to the secret police and the list of her visitors at the KPK was transmitted there also. Her work and home telephones were monitored and her mail intercepted. Even for the elite victim, rehabilitation carried no presumption of innocence.[46]

Like other party veterans, Snegov and Shatunovskaia used their insider knowledge to help their friends. Shatunovskaia, for instance, instructed Chudinova's daughter on how to formulate an appeal for rehabilitation.[47] Their rare access to power combined with their first-hand knowledge of the scope and horror of the purges, however, motivated Shatunovskaia and Snegov to persist in trying to get sweeping changes enacted. Finally, a month before the Secret Speech, Khrushchev took up their radical idea of sending out commissions to the camps to review every case indi-

Fig. 04-02 Ol'ga Shatunovskaia in exile in Eniseisk in 1954. Courtesy Olga Shatunovskaya Family Archive.

vidually.[48] Shatunovskaia recalled later that her role consisted of imploring Khrushchev and Mikoyan "that something urgent and extraordinary had to be done. Otherwise people would die, would perish. If this would all drag on for years, then they simply wouldn't survive."[49]

Shatunovskaia also managed to overturn the practice of "eternal exile." Some friendly colleagues in the Military Procuracy alerted her to the fact that the 1948 decree under which she and many others had been remanded to permanent exile was technically illegal because none of the republican criminal codes contained provisions for such a punishment. Shatunovskaia then "wrote a letter to Khrushchev about this. They gave me, so to say, all the coordinates, how to write this, to give it a juridical foundation and so forth."[50] Khrushchev in turn initiated a decree to overturn the 1948 order and to simply release all those condemned to "eternal exile." Without bothering with provisions for reviewing cases or any formal rehabilitation, he simply granted permission for exiles to leave the remote areas to which they had been sentenced. Starting in March 1956, similar sweeping decrees would be used to restore the rights of those who had been deported during World War II as members of "suspect" ethnic minorities.

Yet neither the creation of the traveling commissions nor the undoing of eternal exile went smoothly. In the latter case, Shatunovskaia joyfully wrote to her friends in exile about the presidium's decision. They responded, however, that their status remained unchanged. When Shatunovskaia summoned the MVD official in charge of eternal exiles for an explanation, he wrote up instructions for his local officials, but still nothing happened. Only by summoning the MVD official again did she learn that, contrary to customary practices, the decree had never been issued. Normally decrees were prepared by the presidium, transmitted to the Central Committee for formatting, then passed on to the Supreme Soviet as draft laws with the understanding that they would be acted on the next day. Highly agitated, Shatunovskaia called Mikoyan at home. He at first refused to believe her. But after checking with the duty officer at the Supreme Soviet, he alerted Khrushchev, who also initially scoffed at the notion that such a breach in protocol could happen. It took Khrushchev's angry intercession to get the decree issued. Shatunovskaia blamed the delay on Malenkov and his cronies who could not bear the thought of all these "enemies" on the loose.[51] She, like Snegov, would later reflect that Khrushchev was too trusting regarding the many unreconstructed Stalinists around him.[52]

In the case of the traveling commissions, Shatunovskaia had conceived of them as combining representatives of high judicial and party bodies, local officials, and rehabilitated veterans. Yet she learned by chance when the lists were already circulating to presidium members for their approval that not one of the rehabilitated persons whom she had nominated had been included. When she protested to the Central Committee bureaucrat in charge, he told her that all of those whom she had recommended had refused to serve—a barefaced lie given that she had preliminarily obtained their consent. Shatunovskaia managed to have the lists redone, but even so approximately one third of the commissions did not include rehabilitated persons.[53]

By the middle of April 1956, some ninety commissions had been formed under the auspices of the USSR Supreme Soviet, briefed, and dispatched to the far ends of the USSR. They were assigned to review the cases of all prisoners charged with political or economic crimes or abuse of official position, as well as of all juveniles. They had the authority to shorten sentences or to liberate prisoners whose detention no longer seemed expedient. Though, as historian Marc Elie notes, "by the beginning of 1956 the Gulag had slimmed down to a third of its 1953 level with 781,630 inmates," the size and geographic scope of the prison system meant a tremendous amount of work lay ahead of the commissions.[54]

Written instructions to the members of the commissions echoed some of the revelations of the Secret Speech. Participants were to remember that many political cases had been falsified, built only on confessions extracted by torture. They were also warned to watch out for unjust convictions under Article 58–10. Its provisions against anti-Soviet speech and propaganda had often been wrongly applied to those who "spoke positively of foreign technology or who expressed dissatisfaction with the cult of personality or with some individual instances of material deprivation." However, the commissioners were not to show clemency to spies, war criminals, or those who fought in the nationalist underground movements in Ukraine and the Baltics.[55]

Years later Kseniia Chudinova succinctly described her commission's work at the Kargopol' camp in Arkhangel'sk. Her team reviewed the cases of 383 political prisoners, whose numbers included some genuine Nazi collaborators but consisted mostly of persons who were, in her words, "not in essence enemies of Soviet power." For example, she heard the cases of Lithuanian peasant women arrested for giving food to nationalist partisans who had come begging at their doors. She also recalled a man sentenced as a "counterrevolutionary" because in a laudatory poem about Stalin he had referred to the leader's pipe going out and this turn of phrase had been interpreted as a death threat.[56] Chudinova did not find many political prisoners of her generation in Kargopol' in 1956. Most of those arrested in 1937–1938 had either served out their sentences or perished by then. Instead the numerous juvenile prisoners caught her attention. With a renewed sense of authority, she not only remonstrated with the camp administration about the wisdom of mixing juveniles with hardened criminals but also composed a memo to the Central Committee on the matter.[57]

Writing three decades after her service, Chudinova recounted her experience in a matter-of-fact tone. Like Stasova, she downplayed the emotional aspects of confronting Stalinist injustices. Yet the commissions' work must have been grueling. Given a deadline of October 1 and a huge number of prisoners, each of whom had to be interviewed, commission members worked long hours. Petr Shelest, the only current party official to have written later of his experience on a traveling commission, recalled that his team, which covered Kiev and Vinnitsa in Ukraine, sometimes worked fifteen- or sixteen-hour days to meet its goal of deciding thirty-five to forty cases a day. Even so, they needed an extension to deal with their caseload.[58]

No statistical data has yet emerged from the archives to allow for a thorough comparison of rates of release by different commissions, but the private letters that Shatunovskaia received from her friends in the field show that rehabilitated persons sometimes found themselves pushing their fellow commissioners to be more lenient. Georgii Petrosian, a camp survivor serving on another commission working in the Arkhangel'sk region, for example, complained to Shatunovskaia that the president of his commission, "from your institution" (presumably the KPK) was "lacking in his own opinion, a representative of old thinking." But, Petrosian noted, although members often argued, they all took their work seriously and resolved their disputes by majority votes.[59]

In at least one instance, informal contacts among the rehabilitated party veterans promoted more liberal practices. When Petrosian happened to share a train compartment with Kseniia Chudinova, he learned that her team was working more rapidly and releasing higher numbers than his. With this information, Petrosian convinced his fellow commissioners to increase the percentage of those whom they allowed to leave for home. He also drew on Chudinova's experience to intervene in the question of when inmates should be informed of the commission's results. The Kargopol' team announced its decisions on the spot, whereas his group had been delegating the matter to the camp administration, which often took three weeks to pass the news along. Now, he reported to Shatunovskaia, prisoners would be informed of their fates on the day after their interviews with the commission.[60]

In Vorkuta, one of the most infamous outposts of the gulag, the workload required the dispatch of multiple commissions, not all of which were predisposed to clemency. One of Shatunovskaia's contacts, Ivan Aleksakhin, who like her had labored in the Kolyma camps and later been exiled to Krasnoiarsk, served on a commission in Vorkuta for six months. He wrote to alert her to the "formalistic approach" taken by one of the late arriving commissions. It took an official complaint to Averkii Aristov, the presidium member in charge of the traveling commissions, and a visit from an official from Moscow to remedy the very low rate of releases and no rehabilitations that had issued from the problem group.[61]

At least one prisoner echoed the view that the commissions were dominated by unhappy bureaucrats. Aleksandr Boiarichkov, an admitted Trotskyite, described his encounter in Karaganda, the center of the gulag in Kazakhstan, in a letter to his wife, an exile in Krasnoiarsk: "Yesterday I was in front of the government commission. My heart wanted to burst free like a bird from a cage. From the other side of the table, two dozen unfriendly eyes stared at me. All of these commission members are Stalinist products [*staliniskie vykormyshi*]. They don't approve of the new course, but they obey it out of fear." Even though Boiarichkov defiantly told the president of the commission that he had been arrested "for no reason," he was soon informed that he was free. One week later, he was on his way to Moscow, where he called on the procurator in charge of his wife's case to ask that he expedite its review.[62]

Presidium member Aristov extracted a narrative of unabashed gratitude from the commissions' work. In his monthly report on their progress for June 1956, he recounted at length the case of an Azeri Party member and war veteran who had been convicted of anti-Soviet agitation for having suggested among a group of his friends that the title of Generalissimos ought to have gone to Marshal Georgii Zhukov (instead of to Stalin). While serving a ten-year sentence in a labor camp, he had gotten slapped with an additional twenty-five-year sentence for an unfounded charge of terrorism. Aristov reported to the Central Committee that upon learning of his rehabilitation the man wept and "swore that never in his life had he had any bad intentions toward Soviet power and his own dear party [*rodnoi dlia nego partii*], that he had been turned into an 'enemy' by the real enemies in Beria's gang." He also asked that his deep gratitude be relayed to the Central Committee.[63]

Work on the commissions also had an emotional impact on its members. The rehabilitated persons often could identify with the individuals who came before them and saw their work as "a sacred cause."[64] From Arkhangel'sk in May, Petrosian had shared his first impressions with Shatunovskaia: "The work is very interesting, responsible, and noble—you are deciding the fate of a living person, moreover one who has suffered innocently." Two months later, from the grim coal-mining camps of Vorkuta, however, he would write, "We can't wait to finish. Since arrival, we've been tortured by mosquitoes. There's swamp all around, even the house we're staying in is built on swamp land. Now the rain, cold, and wind don't even allow for a stroll after work. Well, you know what sorts of places they choose for camps and exile."[65] Even when doing honorable work, it was hard to return to such places that one knew all too well.

By contrast, for forty-eight-year-old Petr Shelest, then second secretary of the party organization for the Kiev region, the whole experience was eye-opening. He headed a *troika* additionally composed of another Kiev region official and an MVD colonel. Together they visited prisons and strict regime labor camps and juvenile colonies—all new sights for him. He also learned a lot from the details of the cases he encountered. He recalled years later, "It was distressing work. After all, people's fates are quite varied and many of them were sentenced unjustly, simply for no reason." He concluded, "One felt that often our 'justices' were under definite pressure and handed out sentences according to the principle 'Proof is not absolutely required. Everyone is guilty of something, no one is completely innocent.'"[66]

Shelest looked back at his service decades later with pride also recalling that as party secretary he later participated in readmitting victims to the party as well as in drumming out some who had participated in falsifying cases. The issue of whether reform would extend to holding responsible those who participated in gross miscarriages of justice deeply concerned some of Shatunovskaia's envoys, most of whom would not see their tormentors held to account.[67] As Aleksakhin wrote to Shatunovskaia in June 1956, "For any person of commonsense, the question arises: by whom and when will these criminals who for years destroyed innocent people, be brought to justice?" He suggested that each obviously fabricated case be sent to the procuracy to trigger an investigation of those who had concocted it. Aleksakhin assured Shatunovskaia that he made his suggestion not because he was a troublemaker, but "in the name of Marxist-Leninist justice." After all, he asked, "Where is the *partiinost'* of our commission if for the lack of a directive we formalistically and bureaucratically take up only the issue of results, that is of those who suffered—whom we free and rehabilitate—and shamefully keep quiet about those who are guilty of having committed a crime."[68] Shatunovskaia's reply does not survive. But in retirement, she, too, would admit disappointment in the general failure to even try to prosecute those who fabricated cases.

Highly placed survivors of the purges like Shatunovskaia also faced the dilemma of daily encounters with those who had risen to the top in part because they collaborated in carrying out the mass repressions. For instance, Molotov was put in charge of the initial internal party commission to investigate the show trials of the 1930s and the shooting of Kirov—both issues of great concern to Shatunovskaia. Unlike Molotov, she believed in innocence of the show trial defendants and the alleged involvement of Stalin in Kirov's death. She later refused Polina Zhemchuzhina's private request that she try to persuade Molotov to take a more liberal stance on de-Stalinization—she had seen too many documents in which Molotov signed off on death sentences for purge victims, including one where he changed the fates of hundreds of wives of "enemies of the people" from eight years in camps to execution.[69]

Beyond the personal affronts they suffered in encountering unreformed Stalinists, the rehabilitated veterans worried about what the presence of such persons the party and state bureaucracies might mean for politics. At the very least, they rightly suspected that those who resented the radical about-face regarding Stalin might undermine efforts to ameliorate the harm caused by the purges. Both Mil'chakov and Shatunovskaia warned Mikoyan and Khrushchev of potential "sabotage." To the end of her days, Shatunovskaia would regret that she could never persuade Khrushchev either of the need for even deeper de-Stalinization or of the extent of the threat to him from conservatives in the presidium. She warned him that many in his top circle were "not Leninists"; presumably he learned this hard way when his colleagues turned on him in 1957.[70]

Unfinished Business

According to Aristov's final report of October 1956, the traveling commissions reviewed the cases of 176,325 current prisoners (of whom 81,027 officially had been convicted for political crimes). Of political prisoners, 50,945 (62 percent) were liberated, though only 3,271 (1.8 percent) were fully rehabilitated on the spot.[71] The miniscule numbers of rehabilitations shows that—despite the Secret Speech—commissions feared taking responsibility for judging the nature of Stalin era prosecutions. Moreover, the number of lives affected by the traveling commissions pales beside the overall figures of millions of lives damaged or lost owing to Stalinist policies, including forced resettlement of "rich peasants" and mass executions, as well as the deportation of whole nations during World War II. And, in fact, top-down reform in 1956 allowed many deportees to return home and lessened restrictions on others. The traveling commissions, however, not only had an immediate impact on the lives of prisoners; they also, at least temporarily, put rehabilitated party veterans into powerful positions—a significant achievement at a time when survivors tended to be treated as if they had been amnestied rather than exonerated.

The experience of Snegov, Shatunovskaia, and other high-level survivors reveals that Khrushchev's denunciation of the cult of personality, in part because of its secrecy and in part because it left in place condemnations of "Trotskyites," by no means totally altered attitudes inside the party toward former prisoners or alleviated fear of potential "enemies." Recalling the incident of the greatly delayed decree ending eternal exile, Shatunovskaia recounted: "I corresponded with my friends. I wrote them an exultant letter. That soon you will all be free! And they answered me, that no such thing, no such indications." Recollecting this incident years later, she still sounded embarrassed, as if her touted new powers had turned out to be worthless, as if her job was all a farce, or as if the party had not truly reformed itself.[72]

The image of the party mattered immensely to its veteran members. For old Bolsheviks particularly there was a high value to continuing the Leninist cause. Hence, though Mil'chakov admitted that recalling his past suffering made him feel physically ill, he toiled over his reminiscences driven by thought that "Lenin would not have allowed it, Lenin left us too soon."[73] Mil'chakov accepted the urging of his friends and family to include his camp experiences even though they could not be published. Yet, even for a private audience, he did not try to analyze Stalinism but rather concentrated on his own innocence and that of his comrades in misfortune. Over all, he preferred to recall the romantic days of revolution and building the Komsomol, to inspire, not to depress. Stasova, too, favored young audiences for her reminiscences about Lenin. They embodied hope for the future not a difficult past.

Although their influence was limited both by political reality at the top and by their own loyalty to the party, old Bolsheviks could and did improve the lives of victims of the purges in 1956. In advocating for their friends and former colleagues, they assuaged their own consciences and tried to restore their party's standing. As one survivor reckoned, "Who will listen to [me]? . . . Lenin is no more, but there is Stasova."[74] By their own moral code, old Bolsheviks were obliged to be the Lenins of the present, to continue to serve loyally despite all obstacles and setbacks.[75]

The influence of even the most privileged survivors, however, had serious limitations. By the time the traveling commissions finished in late September, the momentum generated by the Secret Speech would have dissipated. No one called the commission members together to account for their activity. In Shatunovskaia's words, "It wasn't of interest to anyone. Aristov was supposed to do it. He had been tasked by the Central Committee. [But] we gave our statistical report to some third secretary in [the administrative department of the Central Committee] and with that it all ended."[76] The inherent secrecy surrounding Khrushchev's report and around rehabilitations made it difficult to broaden pressure behind the needs of victims.

Snegov and Shatunovskaia used their remarkable access to Khrushchev and Mikoyan to push for sweeping relief for survivors of repression; however, they would struggle throughout the Khrushchev era and beyond to keep victims on the agenda. To undermine myths created around the Stalin cult he would write controversial articles about early Soviet history for Pankratova's journal. She would work on a special KPK commission that investigated aspects of the purges, including the Kirov assassination. Her commission's findings would go unpublished, and Snegov would nearly be expelled from the party in the 1970s for speaking too frankly about Soviet history. In April 1956, however, they had cause to rejoice: their friends were free at last and it seemed as if the party could redeem itself by righting its wrongs.

5 | MAY

FRESH AIR

While on vacation at a sanatorium for coal industry workers in Donetsk, Iulii Dunskii and Valerii Frid received sixteen telegrams. In all but one, friends used Aesopian language to congratulate them on the news that as of May 28, 1956, they had been officially rehabilitated. The two men took the night off from working on their screenplay about life in a northern town—modeled on the place where they had been stuck since their release from the gulag two years earlier—to toast their freedom in the resort's dining hall. The next day, slightly hungover but newly energized, the friends set about finishing their draft. They promised themselves that if their script were accepted, they would make their way back to Moscow at once. If it were rejected, they would stay on longer in the north, where workers earned high salaries. So as not to jinx their luck, Dunskii and Frid kept to plans to enlarge their little wooden house in Inta. But before they could even finish the scaffolding for their addition, their connections reported success. It was time to return to the capital and try to pick up where they had left off a dozen years earlier.[1]

In the aftermath of the Secret Speech many former political prisoners found the legal obstacles to fulfilling their dreams of returning home and restarting careers falling by the wayside. The transition to "normal" life, however, was not easy. As a friend wrote to Ol'ga Shatunovskaia in

1957, "I must confess to you entirely in secret that dreaming about return turned out to be much more interesting than return itself. Few former friends came through unscathed, and those who did survive have become distant." It was hard in middle age to "have to make new friendships."[2] Younger survivors, too, often felt estranged. Returning to Moscow, which he had left as a student, Iulii Dunskii visited a girl whom he had a crush on before his arrest only to encounter a married woman nursing her small son.[3] Normal time had been suspended for him, but not for those on the other side of the barbed wire.

The memoirist Ol'ga Adamova-Sliozberg, survivor of two terms in Stalinist labor camps, described the surprisingly painful aftertaste of rehabilitation: "No one will return the best twenty years of life, no one will resurrect friends who have died. No one will fasten the torn and decayed threads connecting us with loved ones." Moreover, she warned, "and here as never before it is important to calculate your capital: with what did you return? What can you command?" She knew that many former prisoners would find themselves destitute, with no home and no strength. She prophesied, "Your place is occupied, because life doesn't tolerate a vacuum . . . Your parents died, your children grew up without you. You haven't engaged in your work for twenty years."[4] The one thing of value Adamova-Sliozberg felt that she had carried with her from her years in prison and in a labor camp was insight into the true nature of how things were in the Soviet Union. For memoirists and other writers, knowledge of the gulag and understanding of the roots of repression became part of their intellectual capital.

Here I focus on four returnees who had in common the vocation of writer. Anna Barkova was a poet published in the Soviet Union only in the 1920s; Varlam Shalamov, also a poet, became more famous for his unpublishable short stories about the camps written in the 1950s–1960s; the screenwriting duo of Dunskii and Frid starting in 1956 authored scripts for a dozen popular Soviet films. Four individuals cannot represent the breadth of the experience of returnees, nor can the events of a single month capture the long difficult "resurrection" of gulag victims. Hence, I take the liberty of examining these four survivors before and beyond May 1956. Despite the small sample size, the lives of these four illustrate common issues confronting ex-prisoners and offer a window into the choices individuals made to "survive" outside the camps; moreover, their rare proclivities for writing mean that we have evidence of how their intellectual capital proved a problematic resource in the semi-reformed Soviet Union.[5]

The experiences of former prisoners in 1956 illuminate the consequences of the partial and mostly silent policy changes regarding restoration of justice to victims of the purges. I argue that even in this watershed year, exultation over the possibility of restoring a lost life was tempered by the top-down nature of reform. Khrushchev's choice not to publish his report on the consequences of the cult of personality, his near-exclusive focus in that speech on party members as worthy victims, and the lack of publicity regarding procedures for rehabilitation and compensation meant that survivors had to fight to be exonerated, to regain lost property, and to return to professional work. The life stories of Barkova, Shalamov, Dunskii, and Frid testify to the capital and connections necessary to reintegrate; their experiences as writers demonstrate the near impossibility in 1956 of casting light on the past suffering of and present discrimination against those unjustly prosecuted. While Shatunovskaia and Snegov faced direct opposition from Stalinists within the party hierarchy, the four writers confronted indifference or fear from bureaucrats and helpless sympathy from other members of the intelligentsia. The time had not yet come for former prisoners to publically pass judgment on the system that had wronged them.

A Poet Adrift

In January 1956 Anna Barkova left the small zone of a labor camp in Inta for a precarious life in what some wits called "the big zone," the heavily regulated and politically fraught world of "free" Soviet citizens. On the eve of her release, Barkova penned a poem she entitled "Passing By . . . Passing By" (*"Mimo . . . mimo"*). In it she foretold a return to familiar "loneliness and drought," to "Russian misfortune and pestilence." She predicted that once more she would stand on the sidelines, apart from others' happiness, deprived of the comfort of a hearth. These things, she reasoned, did not belong to her and had even become alien notions during her years of deprivation.[6]

Barkova's expectations of what awaited her were shaped by her previous release from imprisonment in 1939. Then, having served out her full five-year term in a labor camp in Kazakhstan, she had emerged penniless and homeless. Like other ex-convicts, Barkova held a passport that forbade her from residing within one hundred kilometers of Moscow and other large cities. She had resorted to begging old friends in Moscow to send her money and advice on where to seek employment and housing outside the capital. Ultimately Barkova had settled in Kaluga approximately 180 kilometers southwest of Moscow and worked as a janitor, a night watchman, and once—miraculously—as a bookkeeper. She rented corners of rooms in tumbledown houses, where she suffered from cold, noise, and lack of privacy. In the eight years she spent in Kaluga, Barkova managed the short train journey to Moscow only twice—once in the spring of 1941 and again in the summer of 1947. She nearly had to forgo the latter trip because she literally had nothing to wear. Barkova had nearly starved in Kaluga under German occupation, and her clothing had been worn to tatters.[7]

In 1956 Barkova once again faced leaving a labor camp with virtually no "capital." Her health had seriously deteriorated during the eight years she had served near the Arctic Circle. She had no savings and no property other than her camp clothing and certificates attesting to her amnesty and her status as an invalid. No family awaited her. An only child, her parents long dead, Barkova had never married, never had children. Though she had once lived inside the Kremlin, she had no home to which to return.

To understand Barkova's utterly bereft situation in 1956, one must start with her meteoric rise and catastrophic fall from grace. Born in 1901 in the working-class city of Ivanovo-Voznesensk—the "Russian Manchester"—Barkova came of age with the revolution. In 1917 she was finishing her education as a charity student at a private girls' high school. Intense, studious, and unhappy, Barkova spent her youth reading widely and composing poetry. In 1918 she began as a journalist at the new local newspaper, *Rabochii Krai* (The Workers' Realm). Central authorities had sent a well-educated Muscovite, Aleksandr Voronskii, to edit the paper and nurture proletarian writers. Barkova, who hungered for fame and a creative life, found a vehicle for her poetic aspirations in the writers' group he founded.[8]

In turning the political and social order topsy-turvy, the events of 1917 opened the way for Barkova to break conventions and pursue her own goals. The intensity and feverish mood of the times found a reflection in her strong, often harsh, poetic voice and in her personal style. An acquaintance who bumped into Barkova in the summer of 1920 later recollected that she hardly recognized her former schoolmate. Barkova had traded her sober green wool gymnasium uniform for a plain black dress of the sort favored by women workers. To this costume Barkova ostentatiously had added a traditional flowered peasant shawl, which she pinned over a long braid of her flaming red-gold hair. She looked "genuinely democratic," averred her more genteel observer.[9] Barkova had invented her own sort of Bolshevik chic to fit her new persona as a revolutionary poetess. But it was her poetry, not her looks, that caught the attention of Lenin's minister of culture and education, Anatolii Lunacharskii.

Barkova made no impression on the Bolshevik leader when he visited Ivanovo and its newspaper in 1919, but she won Lunacharskii's favor two years later when she sent him a draft of her first collection of poetry. In her early poems, Barkova cast herself alternately as a Red Army fighter, an Amazon, even a "criminal" who dared to blow up monastery walls and trample sacred books. Barkova's love poems were tender but also fiercely intense. Lunacharskii recognized Barkova as a novel sort of woman writer, one free of bourgeois delicacy and piety and he counterpoised her work to that of St. Petersburg's Anna Akhmatova. Lunacharskii even cautioned Barkova that, "The less you resemble Akhmatova, the better for you."[10] He saw the value of a young woman from a humble background whose poetry reflected the rapid tempo of revolution. In the preface to *Woman*, Lunacharskii praised Barkova's thematic diversity, which surged "from bursts of purely proletarian harmony to revolutionary tempestuousness and concentrated cataclysm, from acutely painful insight into the future to intimate lyrics of noble and scorned love."[11]

At Lunacharskii's invitation, Barkova moved to Soviet capital in 1922 and took up a post as one of his personal secretaries. Due to the severe housing shortages of the time, she lived with his family in their Kremlin apartment. Lunacharskii's patronage gained Barkova a foothold in Moscow's literary world. The young poet wrote exultantly to friends back home, "I want to be famous, rich, and splendiferous so that on one crazy day for a new heroic and agonizing game I can burn all of that wealth and splendor."[12] Apocalyptic visions often appear in Barkova's poetry, and Barkova seems to have felt uncomfortable both in the rarefied quarters of the Kremlin and in the rancorous and masculine literary circles of the time. She disliked what she saw as the hypocritical lifestyle of the Bolshevik elite and resented the increasingly stifling atmosphere for free expression as well as the clerical work that left her little time to write.

Before long Barkova's sharp tongue and irrepressible spirit triggered an end to her Moscow idyll. In 1923 a catty letter Barkova had written to a friend back home fell into Lunacharskii's hands—one version has the secret police delivering it to him, another has Barkova putting her letters in the wrong envelopes. Whatever she wrote about the lifestyle of the inhabitants of the Kremlin's apartments so angered Lunacharskii that he fired her on the spot and ordered her to leave his household. With the help of Lenin's sister Mariia Ul'ianova, Barkova found a job freelancing for *Pravda* and other more obscure editions. She eked out a living, sometimes resorting to secretarial work, for which she admitted she was quite unsuited. More important to her, without Lunacharskii's patronage, her second volume of verse languished at the publishing house.

Verbal indiscretions tripped Barkova up again in late 1934. This time bitter comments about the country's leadership, including a flip remark that it was too bad Sergei Kirov's assassin had shot the wrong person, landed Barkova in serious trouble. In December 1934 the NKVD arrested Barkova, confiscated her manuscripts, and questioned her friends. Judging by police records, Barkova seems to have tried to answer her interrogator honestly. Yes, she had sympathized with the Trotskyite opposition in the late 1920s. She had disapproved of collectivization as hasty and premature. She had criticized the Bolshevik leadership for not allowing its opponents to express themselves. Barkova even admitted that some of her unpublished poems could be interpreted as "counterrevolutionary."

The catastrophic consequences of her arrest seem to have dawned on Barkova slowly—as if she could not believe that the police could really consider her a danger to Stalin or to the state. On the day that she signed the testimony in her case, Barkova wrote despairingly to the minister of internal affairs Genrikh Yagoda, asking to be sentenced to execution. A political conviction meant that "it would be impossible to work quietly and to return to my profession, writer, which is for me the most important thing in life." At the same time, she cited her insignificance before

Fig. 05-01 Anna Barkova's 1934 mug shot. Courtesy Museum of the History of the Criminal Justice System of Kuzbass.

the powerful Soviet state and repented her poor judgment, pouring out a list of extenuating circumstances—she was in poor health, she had been discouraged by her lack of literary employment, and she had shared her critical thoughts only in private discussions. Although Yagoda scrawled on her letter: "Exile not too far away," Barkova spent the next five years in a women's labor camp in Kazakhstan.[13]

As for her second "tour," which ended in 1956, Barkova explained it as a result of the first. The local secret policemen who interrogated her in Kaluga in 1947 seemed most interested in her prior conviction—had she really admitted to anti-Soviet sentiments? This obviously made her a suspicious character. A few negative phrases in her private notebooks, testimony extracted from her landlords, and her own terse admission that she had expressed her bitterness toward the Soviet regime in her diary completed the new case against her. In February 1948 Barkova was sentenced to ten years in a labor camp and restriction of civil rights for another five.

Although her health worsened significantly during her second sentence, Barkova found both a measure of happiness and the impulse to write. Her pleasure came from falling in love with another prisoner, an educated Jewish woman from Moscow. Barkova's feelings for Valentina Makotinskaia inspired her to write love poems and then laments at their separation when the other woman was released. When Barkova was amnestied in January 1956, she did not dare try to follow her camp love to Moscow. Barkova's "restriction of rights" barred her from living in major cities. Instead she moved in with another ex-prisoner friend, who was living in exile in a small town in the coal-mining Kemerovo region. There, though Valentina Sanagina charged her no rent, Barkova struggled to make ends meet. Moreover, she found Anzhero-Sudzhensk bleak and brutal. The store shelves were empty and the people discontented and wary.

In "Droplet of Love" written in February 1956, Barkova compared the Inta camps favorably to the provinces:

> There was there a droplet of timid love,
> Of spring more like a gentle winter.
> Here the town is half asleep from drunkenness
> And struck dumb from hard labor.

She claimed that "love" was an unfamiliar word for Anzhero-Sudzhensk's lumpen denizens. "Here they make children and sleep together." By contrast, "My friend, forgive me . . . with you in dark captivity I was happy."[14]

Barkova's ironic nostalgia for life in the "small zone" was fueled by more than longing for her lover. For Barkova, release marked the start of an infinitely frustrating and protracted struggle with state bureaucracy. She had been freed under an amnesty, but release was not the same as rehabilitation.[15] In a petition composed in February or March 1956 to the prosecutor general asking that her two cases be reconsidered, Barkova explained why amnesty was hardly a gesture of benevolence—in her town, she explained, it took intervention by the local KGB boss for one amnestied woman to get hired on as a cleaning lady, and Barkova's health and age precluded such heavy work.

Unlike typical appeals, Barkova's draft letter featured neither a detailed refutation of the charges against her nor an obsequious plea for mercy. Instead the poet vented her philosophical differences with the Stalinist punitive system and griped about conditions in the "big zone." Averring that both of her cases boiled down to the same thing—

criminalization of her thoughts—Barkova argued that she had never conducted "anti-Soviet agitation," merely entertained critical ideas. If private thoughts could still be held criminal in 1956, she reasoned, they should never have released her. "How can I guarantee that in the future not a single 'heretical' thought will spring to mind and that I won't accidently transmit it to someone else and that that someone in a fit of subservience wouldn't run and report that: 'Some citizen thinks thus and such.'" Barely containing her sarcasm, Barkova noted that the new "epoch of the dawn of socialist legality" gave her hope; therefore, she wrote, "I ask that you rehabilitate me in both cases or return me to my previous situation." She bitterly concluded, "In camp everything was simpler and clearer. And if I sat in jail in vain all in all for more than 13 years, I could certainly go on doing so."[16]

Tragically, Barkova would be arrested in November 1957 and serve a third term for anti-Soviet propaganda. But in 1956 she held out hope that she might resurrect a peaceful writing life. In March of that year, she learned that her second sentence had been reduced to five years without a five-year restriction of rights. She left for the capital as soon as she could organize the train fare. Yet from Barkova's meager writings of the summer of 1956—draft letters to various authorities, a poem, a few entries in her notebook—one can glimpse how a morass of regulations, a slew of truculent officials, and persistent fear among ordinary Russians made Moscow a living hell for Barkova. Her problems began and ended with housing and the rules that governed it. Although Barkova's newly reduced sentence meant that she no longer had to live 101 kilometers outside of Moscow, it neither restored her previous housing nor authorized her presence in the capital while she tried to unravel the red tape surrounding her legal status.

To be a legal resident in any Soviet city or town, one needed a *propiska*, a stamp in one's passport certifying registration at a fixed address. There were three main ways for an adult lacking a *propiska* to obtain one. Most simply, a friend or relative could allow registration of an additional person in their living space. Granting a *propiska*, however, was a serious matter in that it gave the bearer permanent rights to that living space. Alternatively an employer could allocate a room or apartment out of its housing stock or municipal authorities could grant a person housing in one of the buildings they controlled, but they were loath to offer such a scarce and valuable resource to unknown tenants. The *prop-iska* system had urban planning and security rationales—it prevented a spontaneous influx of low-skilled migrants and allowed exclusion of undesirable individuals. If found in Moscow without a *propiska*, a visitor would be given twenty-four hours to quit the city and could be fined or even jailed.

Barkova apparently arrived in Moscow with hopes that Valentina Makotinskaia would allow her to register in the room she had rented. Somehow this was not to be. Barkova alludes to cowardice on Makotins-kaia's part—perhaps she feared officials would frown on her associating with a person who had not been rehabilitated.[17] Little is known about their relationship, but the two women did not live together in 1956. Possibly their free selves were simply too different to facilitate the resumption of the relationship they had forged in the camps. A mutual acquaintance would later describe Makotinskaia as "a former camp inmate [*lagernitsa*], turned fashionable Moscow lady." Barkova, by contrast, always lived modestly. In the 1970s, she subsisted on bread, cheese, and strong tea, spending the rest of her pension on books. When someone gave her a tiny refrigerator, she turned it into an additional bookshelf.[18]

In 1956, with no family member or friend willing to register her in their living space, Barkova pinned her hopes on reclaiming her rights based on the apartment she lost upon arrest in 1934. In this task, she faced significant obstacles. Her status as a person released under amnesty meant that officials did not treat her as an innocent victim of the cult of personality. Over and over again she was advised to concentrate on getting rehabilitated, and she tried, but the system was awash in petitions. In the meantime, Barkova was told that she would need signed statements from fellow residents at her old address to prove she had lived there. When she managed to collect statements from her former neighbors and get a document certifying she had been registered from 1927 to 1934 at number 8 Skariatinskii Alley, apartment 5, bureaucrats threw up more obstacles.

The ultimate blow for Barkova came in an encounter with a female inspector at the city housing department. In a conversation that left her more dumbfounded than any exchange with her NKVD interrogators, this bureaucrat challenged her: "And how can you prove that you were arrested in December 1934 and that you spent five years in prisons. You don't have a certificate attesting to that." Barkova lamented, "So it turns out that I am slandering myself by ascribing to myself a fake arrest so that I can get registered in Moscow. Soon, no doubt, I'll need proof that I exist in this world. And perhaps my existence is only a 'criminal masquerade.'"[19] As she wrote in an autobiographical tale a year later, "The fresh, fragile liberalism quickly eroded. I remained in bondage. I was converted from a prisoner into a problematic person . . . neither on the lists of the living nor of the dead. And yet I exist."[20]

Not a day went by in the summer and fall of 1956 that Barkova did not feel her legal and physical limbo. Knowing that she was violating passport laws, Barkova developed an extreme fear of the militia, yet she forced herself act calm so as not to frighten her hosts. As months passed, she began to wear out her welcome. In her private jottings in December 1956, Barkova reviewed her options for spending the night indoors. One friend's elderly mother complained if her daughter slept in her room, so there was no space for Barkova there. Another protested that she was used to living alone. Two otherwise kindly sisters panicked at the thought that neighbors might notice and report an unregistered guest. Another friend had a large apartment but ruled out hosting Barkova lest the reputation of her estranged and absent husband, a well-known cultural figure, somehow be tainted. Her choices boiled down to an elderly schizophrenic or a "normal" woman who kept five cats.[21]

Homelessness hurt Barkova in other ways. Without a proper address, she could not seek work or try to collect a disability pension. Once again Barkova fell back on handouts from old colleagues from the 1920s and childhood friends. Zinaida Stepanishcheva, a scientist who shared a communal apartment with one of Barkova's childhood friends, helped by inviting her own friends to drink tea and hear Barkova read her poetry. After the reading, the guests would leave small donations. Such readings allowed Barkova at least temporarily to reclaim her identity as a writer— for another of the hardships of her homeless existence was an inability to concentrate. "To go into one's corner and write. But I've no corner," Barkova lamented.[22] She did not even have a place to store her manuscripts.

In her one poem that survives from the summer of 1956, Barkova depicts a homeless ex-prisoner who sleeps rough and solicits alms. When the timid narrator forces himself to approach a well-groomed citizen in the street, however, he is met with a diatribe about laziness and drink. The narrator flees as the object of his entreaty shouts for the police. At the end of the long poem, the former prisoner goes mad, convinced that a giant statue—"a cement idol"—is pursuing him, trying to crush him underfoot. The fictional gulag survivor ends his misery by throwing himself under the wheels of a dump truck.[23]

Barkova struggled on in Moscow until early 1957, when, heeding warnings that the police were going to cleanse the city of suspicious types before the International Youth Festival, she returned to live with her loyal camp friend, this time in the village of Shterovka in Ukraine. Her attempt at "resurrection" had come to naught.

A Living Witness

Moscow was also the goal for the writer Varlam Shalamov. Even though he had more human "capital" and physical strength than Barkova, his journey also proved long and difficult. The year 1956 found the forty-eight-year-old Shalamov living in a village just outside the one-hundred-kilometer limit from Moscow. After his release from the harsh Kolyma camps, he had toiled for two more years in the Russian Far East to save up funds. In late 1953 he had settled in the factory settlement of Turkmen, where he found employment as a supply agent. Although his job was poorly paid, Shalamov liked Turkmen for its proximity to Moscow and its simple residents. "There was not a single family in Russia," Shalamov opined, "that wasn't affected by arrests between 1937 and 1953. All of the residents of the peat cutting village had relatives who had died in prisons or camps—and they understood perfectly what 'criminality' was involved!"[24]

Shalamov had made his way back to the environs of Moscow with the hope of restoring ties with his family and of reviving his fledgling literary career. In the brief period between his two camp terms (he "sat" from 1929 to 1932 and again from 1937 to 1951). Shalamov had worked in the editorial offices of some technical journals and begun to build a reputation as a writer of short stories. During his short interval of freedom, he had married Galina Gudz', the daughter of a Bolshevik education specialist; fathered his only child, Elena; and made plans for publishing a volume of short stories and then a book of poetry, his true love. But his second arrest disrupted everything. He would not see his daughter or his wife for sixteen years. And conditions in Kolyma were at times so brutal, as he recalled, that at one point four years passed in which he never held a book or newspaper.[25]

In Turkmen Shalamov found a refuge of sorts. He rented a small wooden house, which gave him privacy to write, and visited his family in Moscow every other weekend. The rest of the time he literally burned the midnight oil, reading and writing by the light of a kerosene lamp late into the night. In March 1955 he had already amassed seven hundred to eight hundred poems and a dozen short stories.[26] Yet by the time of the Twentieth Party Congress, Turkmen had become less of a haven and more of a prison for Shalamov. He had been marooned there for more than two years while his dreams of rebuilding his family and nurturing his friendship with Boris Pasternak had gone awry. His correspondence with the ever-busy Pasternak had dwindled, and his marriage had frayed. The prospect of rehabilitation brought by the Secret Speech, however, emboldened Shalamov; by the end of 1956 he would have severed his old relationships and struck out in new directions. The story of his rocky return demonstrates the difficulties involved in sustaining personal ties in an atmosphere of secrecy and fear.

Shalamov's initial foray into post-Stalin Moscow encapsulated the frustrations and pleasures that would dog him over the next three years as he "resurrected" himself. Shalamov arrived by train in the capital on November 12, 1953. He expected to have to continue on to some more remote place of unofficial exile, but risked venturing into the capital for two days and one night. For the first time in over a decade he saw his wife, who also arranged for him to meet Pasternak. Gudz' brought the welcome news that former prisoners were successfully settling in towns just beyond the hundred kilometer mark from Moscow, but the rest of the encounter was disappointing.

Shalamov would later describe to a friend the difficulty of renewing an emotional bond with his spouse when they talked only in "snatched moments on the street, in the metro, or with company." His wife was afraid to let him into the family apartment, fearing trouble from her brother, a former counterintelligence officer, who had lost his NKVD career in part because of his sister's connection with Shalamov. According to Shalamov, the brother had made the denunciation that triggered Shalamov's second arrest and ultimately tarred his family.[27]

Shalamov later reconstructed a painfully curt account of his first conversation with his wife. He asked a question that had weighed on him ever since 1937 when his interrogator told him that Galina had testified that he was "an active oppositionist, who hid and masked himself":

> *"What did you write in your statement? What superfluous words could you have said in such a year as 1937?"*

> "My testimony was this: that I of course couldn't say what you did in my absence, but that in my presence you had not engaged in any Trotskyite activity."

She wanted to speak of the future, suggesting: "You will meet once a month with Pasternak, and you will come here, well, say once a week." Moreover, she asked: "Give me your word that you will leave [our daughter] Lenochka in peace, that you won't destroy her ideals. She has been brought up by me personally . . . in accord with conventional ways, and I do not want any other path for her." Shalamov acceded to this, but not to her entreaty that he "forget it all" and "return to normal life."[28]

Shalamov would later openly condemn his wife's actions in 1937. She had pushed him down into the abyss even though she must have known that it would not save her. He also dismissed her frequent justification of her choices about how to live as having been made for the sake of their daughter's future. Shalamov regarded ethical compromises in the name of an unpredictable future to be self-serving and hypocritical. Moreover, he could not respect people who remained blind to the nature of Stalinism, but at that point Elena was a stranger to him. He had left behind a toddler and returned to a Komsomol member and student of construction engineering. He hoped to find in her soulmate; instead he encountered a callow Soviet girl.[29]

The looming clash of ideals between Shalamov and his family can be seen in another episode during that first reunion. Galina Gudz' had arranged for him to spend the night at the apartment of a family friend, an old Bolshevik who recently had been rehabilitated. Presumably, his hostess's party credentials would lessen the chances that someone might suspect her of harboring an illegal overnight guest; also, having been unfairly convicted herself, she could empathize with Shalamov's plight.

But, when this woman expressed her hope that he would sincerely strive to demonstrate his loyalty to the Soviet state, Shalamov was taken aback. When she proudly recalled how she had worked unstintingly as a seamstress during her term in the gulag, he was disgusted. Shalamov considered all forced labor to be immoral. In a temper, Shalamov declared that he had different ideas about civic duty, announced that he was not going to spend the night under the roof of such a prison lackey, and stormed out.[30]

Gudz' meanwhile saw herself as already having suffered and sacrificed mightily for her husband's sake. His conviction as a counterrevolutionary led to a sentence for her of ten years in exile in Turkmenistan. In 1947 she had managed to get permission to return to Moscow, where their daughter could receive a good education. It seems to have been at this time that she formally divorced Shalamov so that she could prove she had severed all ties with an "enemy of the people." Shalamov had given Galina his blessing to file for divorce in 1937 and again in 1943 when he got ten years added to his term. Despite their formal break, however, Gudz' had corresponded with him and still considered him as her husband.

In 1953 Shalamov and his wife clearly retained some feelings of admiration for each other. Shalamov compared Gudz' to the Decembrists' wives who had followed their husbands into exile. But misgivings abounded. She fretted about his unsociable nature and resented his unwillingness to let go of the past. He questioned her decision to raise their daughter as a believer in the Soviet system and her continued sacrifice of her (and his) personal interests in favor of a conventional life for Elena. In fact, unlike the Decembrists' wives, Galina did not join him in the Far North or even in Turkmen. As she saw him off on the train in November 1953, she promised that she would write to him constantly—hardly the romantic gesture he might have been expecting. Shalamov respected her fierce maternal instincts, but he sensed that he might have to rethink his plans. As he wrote to a friend back in Kolyma, "Time, after all, has flowed and flowed. She has battled with life alone, unaided, to the limits of her strength, not with the strength you or I possess. What she takes pride in may not be something that makes me proud."[31]

Moscow, however, held another attraction for Shalamov—the prospect of a friendship with Pasternak. On Shalamov's second day in the city, Gudz' escorted him to meet his idol. As noted earlier, Shalamov had initiated a relationship with Pasternak in the spring of 1952 by sending him his own unpublished poetry. Pasternak, who had himself fallen out of political favor, responded with a message of humility and a heartfelt if lopsided correspondence had ensued. Pasternak's kindness made Shalamov feel like an insider of sorts, though by other measures he was firmly an outsider.[32]

Khrushchev's Secret Speech, however, struck Shalamov as a potential game changer. When he got wind of it in March 1956, he puzzled over its implications—why hadn't Stalin been dubbed an "enemy of the people"? Perhaps the leadership was planning to gradually deepen the critique as they reinvestigated the Kirov assassination and other specific offenses?[33] Skeptical about what changes might ensue in publishing, Shalamov nevertheless understood that the Secret Speech would have practical repercussions for former prisoners. From the unpleasant source of an informer—who reported on their conversations to the local secret police over the course of three years—we know that in the summer of 1956 Shalamov was "rushing to restore his literary contacts" because he was counting on moving to Moscow and finding appropriate work as soon as he was rehabilitated.[34]

One of the first steps Shalamov took to change his fate after the Secret Speech was to write to Ol'ga Ivinskaia. Shalamov had met the beautiful blonde in the 1930s, when she had been a novice editor at a journal where Shalamov worked. On March 20, addressing her formally, he wrote, "Dear Ol'ga Vsevolodovna. If you remember me and if you still are interested in poetry—then I ask you to write to me." He offered to share his new work but admitted that even without the pretext of literature he would like to see her. Without explaining his tangled legal and family status, he informed Ivinskaia of his habit of spending every other weekend in Moscow and suggested a date that they might meet. Shalamov closed his letter with a dose of pessimism, writing, "If (for any reason at all) you consider our meeting unnecessary—without any pang of conscience, simply do not answer me."[35]

When Ivinskaia responded warmly to his cautious letter, he was over the moon. He replied immediately, already addressing her familiarly as "Liusia" and apologizing for his previous silence. He explained that he had been afraid to write to her, not just because twenty years had passed since their last meeting but because his post-camp visits to Moscow had "aroused a hidden anxiety" even among his relatives.[36] Most likely Ivinskaia told him in her first letter that she too had served an unjust sentence from 1949 to 1953. She did not tell him that her "crime" had been associating with Pasternak, though she teased him with the news that they had a "common friend" whose identity he would not be able to guess.[37]

Ivinskaia's daughter Irina Emel'ianova remembers clearly Shalamov's first appearance on their doorstep on a rainy night in April 1956. Her mother impatiently awaited the visitor and finally, late in the evening, he came straight from the train. Clad in a dripping canvas jacket, dark pants, and a plaid shirt and carrying a rough knapsack, Shalamov impressed Emel'ianova as being "vigorous, powerful, energetic, and quite young." He reminded her of one of Jack London's rugged gold prospectors. She noted that despite the happy atmosphere of the evening, "Even the shadow of a smile did not appear on his dark, permanently windblown . . . face." Eighteen-year-old Irina saw him as the prototype of the survivor— tough, weather-beaten, and intense.[38] He must have seemed quite the contrast to her own mother, who had retained her soft good looks and lighthearted character.

A spark of romance immediately sprung up between the normally reticent Shalamov and the vivacious Ivinskaia. In April and May their letters flew back and forth between Turkmen, Moscow, and Izmalkovo, where Ivinskaia rented a cottage near the writer's colony where Pasternak lived with his wife. Ivinskaia and Pasternak had been lovers for two years before her arrest in 1949, and he had supported her family during her prison term. Upon Ivinskaia's release in 1953, Pasternak had asked Emel'ianova to gently warn her mother that he did not intend to resume the affair. Irina could not bring herself to deliver the message, and after several months her mother and Pasternak became lovers once more.[39]

By 1956 Pasternak's wife had unhappily accepted the writer's dual life. He lived with her and their son in a large comfortable dacha, but walked over to Ivinskaia's modest rented cabin nearly every day to spend several hours in her presence. Ivinskaia had become his muse and one of his sounding boards for *Doctor Zhivago*. She was the first to learn that on May 20, 1956, he had impulsively given the typescript of his novel to a visiting Italian journalist to share with a communist publisher in Milan.[40]

Shalamov seems to have been unaware of Ivinskaia's history with Pasternak—their own interrupted friendship predated her intimacy with the poet. That spring the usually introverted Shalamov entered into Ivinskaia's circle of male and female friends, including other newly returned camp survivors. Emel'ianova remembers him arriving on Saturday evenings in Izmalkovo and joining Ivinskaia and her company of writers and artists by the lake. They would build a campfire to keep away the insects, and Shalamov would read his poems by its flickering light. The women, Emel'ianova recalled, would look at Shalamov with tremendous sympathy and respect as he sternly delivered his poems, beating out the rhythm with one powerful hand. Pasternak visited during the day, and, hence, it appears Shalamov did not at first know of Ivinskaia's long-standing affair with his idol.[41]

Shalamov seems to have been totally smitten with Ivinskaia and clearly had hopes that she reciprocated. On May 24, in the first of two letters written to her that evening, he addressed the tricky question of their relationship, one that they seem to have been discussing only obliquely. Now he told her, "My plans, that is, my desires, are your plans." He confessed, "For the first time in twenty odd years I am breathing freely again, taking pleasure in the powerlessness of time." Whereas he had earlier thought of quitting the Moscow region as soon as he got his rehabilitation, now: "I want to see you as much as and as long as you want to see me." Beyond that, Shalamov expressed only two goals: first, to write one hundred stories about Kolyma, despite Ivinskaia's evaluation of his output so far as "not good and not bad, [but] simply strange"; second, to find work that involved publishing but that did not require him to "go against my conscience." It was no sacrifice to leave his wife, he told Ivinskaia. "For a long time I have not wanted to live among alien people, amidst mistrust, enmity, and pity."[42]

Shalamov's euphoria lasted for another month. In June 1956 Pasternak invited Shalamov to one of his famous Sunday dinners. Partly to allow his wife to enjoy her status as hostess, Pasternak regularly entertained family friends and interesting artists. He would often read from his work in progress before the meal, and afterward one or more guest might perform.[43] In a letter of thanks Shalamov would admit to Pasternak that he had fantasized for years about someday reciting his poetry in his home, perhaps with Anna Akhmatova in attendance.[44] Though a different Leningrad poetess, Ol'ga Berggolts, numbered among the guests, Shalamov did realize his dream. In the company of Pasternak's close family friends, pianists Genrikh and Stanislav Neigauz and their wives, and other literary guests, Shalamov had listened to Pasternak read his new autobiographical essay before dinner. Shalamov later recalled that during the meal, "The sensation of some falseness did not leave me. Maybe because over dinner much attention was given to cognac and I hate alcohol. [Moreover] it seems that [Pasternak's] wife and the Neigauzs—in essence his closest circle—treat him like a child prodigy."[45]

When it finally came his moment to perform, Shalamov was acutely aware of his small audience's reaction. For an author who had been deprived of the traditional markers of success, this was both a jubilant and frightening moment. To Shalamov it seemed that Zinaida Pasternak "listened approvingly, poems from the north should be approved, and also Boris Leonidovich likes them." Indeed, he felt that Pasternak with a gaze was daring his guests not to like them.[46] So perhaps Shalamov, too, ended by feeling like a child being humored by the grown-ups. Undoubtedly, the experience left him somewhat unnerved—his fairy-tale vision would not have included awkward small talk at the dinner table or arriving too soon and having to wait on the veranda while the great writer finished bathing and changing for dinner.

At some point over the next week, Shalamov learned more about Ivinskaia's relationship with Pasternak. Did she let it slip after listening to Shalamov's description of Pasternak's salon, a place from which she was excluded? Did Shalamov offend her with either fawning or critical comments on his visit to the Pasternaks? One friend of Ivinskaia's in later years says she told him that Shalamov became angry with Pasternak for not either marrying Ivinskaia or relinquishing her. Meanwhile, Pasternak allegedly felt sorry that he had added to Shalamov's misfortune but would not contemplate giving up Ivinskaia. Neither Shalamov nor Ivinskaia included an account of their brief romance in their memoirs, but Ivinskaia's daughter disclosed the moment of their breakup—a letter from Shalamov that began: "I consider it better if I don't visit Izmalkovo anymore." From that day forward, Emel'ianova regretfully observed, he left their lives. "And already it was not us, but other people, another woman, who helped him to return to Moscow, to acquire a home, and to begin his path to the reader." In fall of 1956, he married Ol'ga Nekliudova, an author of children's books, whom he had met through Ivinskaia.[47]

Nekliudova and Shalamov conducted an intense courtship in July 1956. He lectured her on her the mediocrity of her personal library and criticized her reliance on sleeping pills, but he complimented her young son. She wrote him breathless letters and took on the task of promoting his poetry among her literary contacts. On July 24 she reported to him that Ivinskaia had told Pasternak about Nekliudova and Shalamov's relationship.[48] But as the liaison between Shalamov and Ivinskaia foundered, so, too, did Shalamov's connection to Pasternak. On August 12 Shalamov penned a final letter to Pasternak. Without mentioning his messy private life, Shalamov reiterated his admiration for Pasternak and his confidence that Pasternak would weather the looming crisis over *Doctor Zhivago* with honor.[49] After that, Shalamov stopped trying to insert himself in Pasternak's life.

Later that month Shalamov took another fateful step. On August 28, 1956, he wrote bluntly to his wife:

> Galina. I don't think there's any point in us living together. The past three years have clearly shown us both that our paths have diverged too much and that there is no hope for their convergence.
>
> I don't want to put any blame on you—you, by your own judgment, always strived for the best. But that best is bad [*durnoe*] for me. (And I felt this from the first hour of our reunion).

He instructed her to bundle up whatever of his things that she had and added that he would not bother to inform Elena separately. "For three years I haven't had the chance to speak to her heart to heart. Therefore I've nothing to say to her at present."[50]

Shalamov's cavalier attitude toward Gudz' sparked a letter from his daughter, who was angry at his seeming indifference to those people, like her mother, who had supported him and helped him. She could not understand why his bad experiences had not heightened his sense of appreciation for what was good in people, for their sacrifices on his behalf. She reproached him for his apparent inability to express gratitude or warmth to those closest friends and relatives. Why couldn't he ever congratulate his wife on New Year's or her birthday? Why couldn't he send holiday greetings to his one surviving sibling?[51] She wanted a conventional father, while he wanted an unconventional daughter. Thanks to her mother's protectiveness, she had no understanding of what he

Fig. 05-02 Narlam Shalamov, 1956. Courtesy Russian State Archive of Literature and the Arts and Shalamov.ru.

had suffered in Kolyma. Thanks to his long ordeal, he had no patience with her callowness.

In September Shalamov received notice of rehabilitation for his 1937 and 1943 convictions, and on October 11, 1956, he married Nekliudova and took up legal residence in Moscow with her and her young son. His camp friend Arkadii Dobrovol'skii admitted to being rather shocked at the rapid developments: "After all, in the present times fate—otherwise known as politics—rarely creates scenarios with a 'happy ending' [*s happy end'om*] such as yours."[52] In fact, Shalamov paid a high price for his "happy ending." He destroyed his relationship with Pasternak. He so offended his family that neither Galina Gudz' nor Elena would visit him during his last illness.[53] But, even though their relationship would also founder in time, that fall he found a companion who did not chide him for living in the past and who shared his desire for literary success. Shalamov ended the year with a fresh chance at marital happiness, a new job as a contributor for the journal *Moskva*, and prospects of having several poems published.[54]

Aiming at the Big Screen

Shalamov and Barkova found listeners for their poetry even in the labor camps. Aspiring screenwriters had a harder time imagining their work would ever reach an audience. In October 1954 Iulii Dunskii wrote despairingly from Inta to his childhood friend and "co-conspirator" Mikhail Levin that Frid wanted to quit trying. "He says that we cannot write anything of genius or even anything nice, so why should we bother to try . . . I asked him: 'So, what does this mean? Are you going to live out the rest of the century as a bookkeeper?' 'Well, yes.' 'Don't you have any inner need to write?' 'Well, no.'"[55] Levin, who had known Dunskii and Frid since they had met as schoolboys, understood the gravity of the problem.

The two aspiring screenwriters had been writing together since they met in eighth grade when a mutual friend engaged them both in an argument about the newly released movie *The Children of Captain Grant*. Passionate fans of Jules Verne's classic tale, each deplored the film's departures from the text. Each went home that night and wrote a parody of the story; the next day, having laughed heartily over each other's versions, they wrote a joint script. From then until Iulii's death in 1982, they wrote together.[56]

Their love of the movies led Dunskii and Frid to enroll at the All-Union State Institute for Cinematography (VGIK) in 1940, but their education had been disrupted first by wartime evacuation to Alma-Ata and then by arrest in 1944. Falsely convicted of having plotted with other young people to assassinate Stalin, Dunskii and Frid had spent the second halves of their terms in the same northern camp and had been released simultaneously into "eternal exile" in January 1954.

In some ways Dunskii and Frid's lives in exile were tolerable. In the small northern settlements that arose around labor camps the need for workers tempered discrimination against ex-convicts, and upon release in Inta the two men found white-collar jobs. They borrowed money to purchase a dilapidated wooden cottage, and Dunskii's elderly mother came from Moscow to keep house for them. They had each other's company as well as many friends among the city's ex-prisoner and civilian communities. Dunskii and Frid also kept in touch via frequent and witty letters with friends old and new. The latter included Aleksei Kapler, a famous screenwriter they had met in the camps. Kapler had been imprisoned on Stalin's direct orders after the dictator learned that his daughter Svetlana had become enamored of the much older Jewish bon vivant.[57]

Yet in other ways life in Inta was unbearable. Arrested at ages twenty-one, Dunskii and Frid had lost the prime years for establishing themselves professionally and finding spouses. How were two intellectual Jews to find suitable wives in a rough and isolated town with a mostly male population? Indeed, it was Frid's infatuation with a local beauty that temporarily derailed their writing partnership in 1954. The problem of brides—a demographic rarity in postwar Soviet society—remained unresolved during their northern years, but, with the encouragement of friends, the two did resume their writing, sustaining the dream that selling a script might be the first step back to a cultured existence.

From the very first days of their release from prison through their full reestablishment in Moscow in 1956–1957, Dunskii and Frid benefited from their "capital" investment in strong friendships. First of all, their comradeship made life in Inta significantly easier. Second, their childhood compatriots, most especially Levin, kept their spirits up during their exile. Levin, an aspiring professor of physics, had served three years in a camp where prisoners worked on specific defense-related projects. Now he wrote cheerful letters, sent books and other tokens of civilization, and encouraged them to keep writing.[58] Lastly, Kapler, with his unparalleled contacts in the film world, took up the task of promoting their scenarios.

When the two young men sat down in their hut in Inta to try composing a script after a decade of penning only letters, they emphatically eschewed any camp themes. They first attempted a lightweight comedy, but their hearts were not in it. When Frid agreed to get back to work after his 1954 outburst, he and Dunskii chose to adapt a short story by a noted Russian writer. The 1881 satire "The Tale of Cross-Eyed Lefty from Tula and the Steel Flea" by Nikolai Leskov was regarded as a classic work on relations between Russia and the West, and Dunskii and Frid appreciated the story's funny colloquial language and its English scenes. In 1955, however, Kapler tried in vain to find a director of live action or animated films to take on their version. Rehabilitated in 1954, Kapler had returned to writing for the prestigious Mosfilm studio. Although he could not deliver good news about "Lefty," he passed along compliments from those who had read it. Moreover, Kapler assured Dunskii and Frid that changes were afoot and lectured them on the need to keep petitioning for reconsideration of their cases. "Let it become a habit, like brushing your teeth or washing your face . . . Every morning: you should wake up—and write an appeal. It doesn't matter to whom [it is addressed]: to the procuracy, the ministry of shipping . . . The main thing is to write!"[59]

The boys were skeptical, however, that the thaw would extend to them. Kapler, after all, was a Stalin prize laureate and the author of the first Soviet two films about Lenin. Nevertheless, even Inta gradually felt some warming trends. In 1955 Dunskii and Frid learned that the punishment for attempt to escape from eternal exile had been reduced from twelve years of hard labor to three years of prison, and they decided to risk a brief visit to Moscow. Since, like all exiles, they had to report in person at the local commandant's office twice a month, they planned a short trip to fall between those dates. Like Shalamov's first foray into Moscow, theirs foreshadowed the future, but one marked by high spirits, a taste of real work, and a warm reception.[60]

To avoid trouble on their illegal journey, Dunskii and Frid took all possible preparations in October 1955. They bought first-class tickets on the train to Moscow so that they would be in with the more elite passengers and hence less likely to attract the scrutiny of railroad guards. Indeed, their traveling companions proved to be an important railroad bureaucrat and a uniformed colonel, whose presence deterred close inspection. Once ensconced in their compartment, Dunskii and Frid donned newly purchased striped pajamas—typical loungewear of privileged Soviet men. They wanted to look respectable, not like ex-convicts. Once in Moscow they exercised great caution, even crossing only at crosswalks lest some policeman decide to ask to see their documents. Their large network of close friends also ensured that they could change accommodations frequently so as to avoid attracting unwarranted attention.[61]

In Moscow the experience of relative autonomy, leisure, and, perhaps most important, interaction with free, lively, and interesting people, made it easier for Dunskii and Frid to think about writing. In a letter thanking Levin for facilitating their visit, Frid wrote, "There, we understood and believed that we might be able to write screenplays (though there's no guarantee that they'll be good ones); we felt the joy of real, beloved work and the pleasure of being able to choose one's own style of living." As a consequence, however, Inta seemed drearier than ever. Frid observed that though he had never before cried over his life in exile, upon his return he had wept shamelessly. Dunskii added, "Now it's all mixed up together: a sense of distance from you, from our dear ones, from work (because for a week we created the illusion that we were screenwriters who could sit and write as long as they wished)." The memories of their brief idyll would have to fade before they could "restore our usual *modus vivendi*."[62]

As spring 1956 arrived, Dunskii and Frid still had no news of rehabilitation, but they benefited from the next stage in the liberalization of the regime for exiles. With new passports, albeit with a ban on residing in thirty-eight major cities and all border towns, Dunskii and Frid began to plan a legal vacation. Moscow was out of the question and the resort towns of Crimea or the Caucuses counted as border zones, so they settled for vouchers offered through their trade union for a holiday at a modest coal miners' sanatorium in Ukraine reasoning that they could at least pass through Moscow on their way. Much to their surprise, Dunskii and Frid discovered that they liked the Donbass "resort." They had wonderful weather and a lovely river for swimming. More important, they gained the mental freedom to tackle their new script about something they knew well—the clash of generations in a northern mining town. They were deep into the draft of what would become their first successful screenplay when news came of their rehabilitation.[63]

Buoyed by the news of their May rehabilitation, Kapler and the boys' mentor from VGIK, Leonid Trauberg, lobbied the head of Mosfilm on their behalf. Kapler later recounted that when they approached the autocratic Ivan Pyr'ev and explained that they were interceding for two young writers who had spent ten years in the camps, Pyr'ev had scornfully replied that it was hardly his fault; he hadn't put them there. But he read the screenplay and liked it. He gave it the green light, and another of the boys' former VGIK teachers recruited a young, up-and-coming director to take on the project.[64] Dunskii and Frid returned to Moscow triumphant in June 1956.

Dunskii and Frid were quickly registered and living in central Moscow, though their housing situation was not ideal. They both squeezed into Frid's mother's one-room apartment. She had swapped her three rooms for one in a neighboring building after her husband's death in 1946 because she was afraid of "condensation" (*uplotneniia*)—a process whereby city officials maximized the use of living space by turning "under-occupied" apartments into communal ones. Better, she reasoned, to maintain some privacy than to have to share a larger space with strangers who might be hostile toward the mother of a "counterrevolutionary." In the summer of 1956, using shelves as dividers, Dunskii and Frid camped in one corner of her room.[65]

Even overcrowded conditions could not stand in the way of life. By the end of 1956, Frid had married Evgeniia Guseva. Awkwardly, he fell in love with Marina Romanovskaia the very next year. In short order, he fathered a son with one and daughter with the other. When his disapproving mother insisted his legal wife and infant son remain with her, Dunskii and Frid rented a dacha for themselves, Marina, and little Iuliia. They would live there for the next three years until they could buy neighboring flats in a new cooperative apartment building for writers. Dunskii would marry only later in life.[66]

Domestic turmoil in 1956–1957 did not hamper Dunskii and Frid's professional takeoff. Their classmates had spent the twelve years of Dunskii and Frid's absence advancing in various niches of the film

Fig. 05-03 Iulii Dunskii (far right) and Valerii Frid (third from right) parting with friends on the train platform in Inta as they depart for Moscow in 1956. Courtesy Zoya B. Osipova.

world. Perhaps pricked by pangs of conscience for having put Stalin's victims out of mind, their friends leaped into action. They arranged jobs writing scripts for science films, judging a screenwriting contest, and doctoring other writers' problematic scripts. Their mentors also interceded at VGIK so that the two writers—who had been arrested during their final year of studies—could submit the screenplay for *The Incident at Mine 8* as their required senior project; though, to be safe, the rector insisted it be graded "good" not "excellent." Dunskii and Frid took their final exams with the next graduating class in late spring 1957. At the examinations the other students speculated intensely as to the presence of these two unknown and unusual-looking fellows. As one recalled later, "To us twenty-three or twenty-four-year-olds, they seemed really old, and they looked ancient, gaunt, balding, with missing teeth."

Dunskii and Frid were only thirty-five, but the gulag had taken a physical toll.[67]

Writing a Return to Life

For survivors, return was filled with joy and stress. The passive stance of the prisoner seeking to avoid notice had to be replaced with the active role of seeker. As Kapler put it, "Paradoxically, my existence now [after rehabilitation] is more anxiety filled."[68] He had to put himself forward to regain housing, to promote his career, and so forth. Many returnees compared the multiple steps involved in restoring justice, housing, and career to the Stations of the Cross (*khozhdenie po mukam*). They used the verb *khlopotat'*, meaning to make a fuss about or to lobby to describe their endless pleas for help to their acquaintances, to their deputies in the Supreme Soviet, to the Central Committee, to Khrushchev himself. Even well-connected returnees were in the position of beggars long after the Secret Speech. There was no proactive policy of assistance regarding rehabilitation, housing, or employment, and no guarantee of a friendly reception from officials. In the "big zone," one had to fight for one's rights, and capital counted.

Dunskii and Frid benefited from their personal and professional networks in reentering the film world. However, their attitude toward the past and (the present) may have been even more important in achieving conventional success in their native country during their lifetimes. Since their scenarios could only fully come to life on the big screen, they strove to find topics that would please the public, attract directors, pass review at the film studio and with censors, and yet also meet their ethical standards. As Frid explained to a young interviewer in 1998: "Dunskii and I never wrote directly about our camp experience. It was impossible to do so truthfully and we didn't want to lie. And from half-truths we'd most likely have been nauseated. But recollections about that life—some concrete observations, encounters, fates, characters—of course did help us to write. For us, this was a secret trunk from which we were always pulling something out."[69] They set two scenarios in Inta: *The Incident at Mine 8* and *There Once Lived an Old Man and an Old Woman* (directed by G. Chukhrai, 1965).[70] But in 1956 and afterward Dunskii and Frid did not share Shalamov's and Barkova's compulsions to write about the camps. Perhaps because they could share their experience with each other—and friends noted they recalled their camp lives every day—they did not feel the same drive to record it on paper. Certainly, too, their general outlooks on life also played a role. Arrest and incarceration introduced them to a dark side of Soviet life but did not destroy their senses of humor.

Shalamov, by contrast, wrote only serious works, most famously short stories on the theme of the brutality of life in the gulag. In 1956 he composed several of his "Kolyma tales," ranging in subject matter from a stark account of how prisoners made roads by wading through the chest-high snow to a complex tale of a prison doctor exposing fakery among his exhausted patients. Each story is a snapshot of inhumanity—Shalamov referred to them as "slaps in the face of Stalinism."[71] Yet the man who refused to heed his wife's edict to live in the present also rejected the idea that he had gained something from his incarceration. In reminiscences written in 1964, Shalamov famously contended: "In essence, I am not an old man yet, time stops at the threshold of that world where I spent twenty years. The experience of living under the earth does not add to one's general knowledge of life—there the dimensions are distorted and knowledge gained there is not useful in the free world."[72] Despite his own documentary prose, Shalamov averred that no literary work could truly convey the experience because it had to be written in the language possessed by the free writer; whereas, "Never once in those years did I take delight in the landscape—if I noticed something, I only remembered it later. Never once did I find in myself strength for some strong emotions."[73]

Although he recovered his literary sensibilities, Shalamov lost whatever lightheartedness and camaraderie he had possessed as a young student. He developed a solitary streak and judged people harshly. Though he had no hope of publishing his stories at home and little interest in foreign audiences, Shalamov wrote compulsively about his camp experience. His past shaped every contour of his life—where he could live, what he would write about, whom he could trust, and who would trust him. Hence his difficulty in dealing with his wife and daughter, who wanted him to act as if he had returned from a routine business trip and not from "hell."[74]

Homeless for most of 1956, Barkova appears to have written only a few poems and petitions that year. Personal lyrics would comprise the bulk of her later work, yet during her self-exile to the Ukrainian town of Shterovka in 1957, Barkova penned three bitingly sarcastic anti-utopian tales, one of which dealt with housing. In it, an old man is finally awarded a room of his own. He laments that it has come too late for him to marry. A coworker comforts him that at least he will be able to die in comfort. Alas, he does not even manage that—he suffers a heart attack after the speech of gratitude he is required to make goes off track and unwittingly disparages socialism's provisions for the people. In "Seven Scenes of Insanity," the narrator meets the devil who grants her glimpses into a terrifying future marked by atomic war. In the third story, she is a camp survivor drawn into high political intrigue.[75]

Barkova's stories reflect her preoccupation with the absurd, surrealistic side of Soviet life. Her bitter life experience, sharp sense of irony, and apocalyptic visions made her a natural writer of grotesque parodies. But such writing was dangerous and her short stories would figure in new charges of anti-Soviet agitation and propaganda in late 1957. When asked then by the investigator why she wrote stuff that clearly could never be published, Barkova explained, "I wrote for myself, to take the measure of my own thoughts. Moreover, I hoped that with time there would be a more democratic regime in the Soviet Union and that then my works in a somewhat edited form would be published." She never had another publication in her lifetime.[76]

For Barkova, 1956 had brought fleeting physical liberty, but not greater freedom of expression. Camp themes remained taboo in the press and in polite conversation. Meanwhile, the state devoted few resources to helping survivors negotiate a return to "normal" life. Barkova with her meager human capital, tiny network of friends, and no certificate of rehabilitation could not gain a foothold in Moscow. Writing no doubt served a therapeutic function for all four survivors profiled here, but the limited nature of reform stunted their literary output, most sharply for Barkova, who could not even find space to work.

Khrushchev had granted himself permission to address the purges, but he did not extend that privilege to others. Hence, in 1956 Shalamov "wrote for the drawer," Dunskii and Frid set aside certain topics, and Barkova poured out her frustration in petitions for mercy.

6 JUNE

FIRST FLUSH OF YOUTH

In contrast to the rehabilitated writers who pined for Moscow, twenty-year-old Anatoly Gladilin abandoned the capital in the summer of 1956 to work on a Siberian building site. At the very moment that many of his peers were assiduously preparing for entrance exams, Gladilin was happy to temporarily take leave of the Literary Institute where he had just finished his second year. His first novel, *The Chronicle of the Times of Victor Podgursky*, was about to be published in the most fashionable journal for young people, *Iunost'* (Youth). Anxious about critics' reception of his tale of a boy who had flunked his university admissions exam, Gladilin hoped to labor in anonymity while collecting material for a new book about young people who had forgone the studious life. Gladilin's interest in working construction looks less startling in light of the mixed messages about citizenship sent by communist authorities to the generation that came of age in the 1950s. Postwar Soviet youth got conflicting signals about how best to prove themselves—by conscientious study and pursuit of white-collar jobs or by emulating the early Komsomol and throwing themselves into the physical work of building a better society. In 1956 Anatoly Gladilin would experiment with both paths.

Though the "youth prose" movement in the USSR—represented most famously by the novelists Vasily Aksyonov, Anatolii Kuznetsov, and Georgii Vladimov—gained notoriety in the 1960s, Gladilin had the honor of being the youngest and first practitioner of this new style to break into print. Gladilin's novel published in August 1956 captured the experience of pursuing higher education. His second would be based on his toil in the summer of 1956 alongside Komsomol recruits building a secret defense plant. In both, Gladilin deliberately set out to "mirror" the life of his contemporaries; in both he ended up recording disappointment with false promises of opportunities for all.[1] Exploring the officially propagated notion that service and sacrifice could mesh with self-fulfillment and achievement, Gladilin would reveal the dreams of his generation and their brushes with reality.

Gladilin's first novella about an unsuccessful college applicant serves as the jumping-off point for an examination of the socialization of youth under Stalin and of university system in the USSR and its place in the popular imagination. I draw on both Gladilin's rich psychological portraits of Soviet youth and accounts of the ambitions and problems facing real students—including Gladilin—in the spring and summer of 1956. I argue that higher education, which was held out as a duty for all capable youth, often proved hard to access. Moreover, while schools tasked young people with managing their own affairs, self-government had many limits. Soviet young people craved genuine collectives and real self-rule, but when their initiatives brought them into conflict with university authorities—as increasingly became the case in 1956—the threat of exclusion proved a powerful tool to suppress non-conformism. Students clamoring for change found themselves hostage to their own ambitions.

Soviet Childhoods

Gladilin belonged to a cohort born in the mid-1930s. These were Soviet children who had missed the revolution, civil war, and the building of a new state, but who were brought up on romantic legends of those eras. They grew up entirely under Stalin, and, while not of an age to understand the purges, they inherited a conviction that the Communist Party had to be vigilant against its many enemies. Too young to fight in World

War II, they nonetheless suffered as part of the civilian population and took pride in victory. Many of them grew up fatherless, orphaned by the war or some vague circumstances—they were raised not to ask "indiscreet questions."[2] While they lived in poor housing and ate badly, especially in the lean years following the war's end, they boasted of their state's accomplishments. They compared their circumstances favorably to those of their parents' generation—owing to an information blockade by the government they did not really know how people lived in other countries.

Those brought up in the 1930s and 1940s participated in a myriad of socialist and patriotic rituals. They joined the young pioneers and then the Komsomol, marched in May Day parades, and sang songs praising Stalin. Their schoolteachers stuffed them with moralizing stories about brave pioneers, like the martyred Pavlik Morozov, allegedly murdered by his *kulak* relatives because he had revealed his father's hoard of grain. In science classes, they learned about the work of Soviet agronomist Trofim Lysenko, who was finding ways to grow crops that would withstand cold and heat and feed the nation. At play they reenacted the adventures of Komsomol partisans from *Young Guard*, Aleksandr Fadeev's fictionalized account of real anti-Nazi resistance on occupied Soviet territory. In school, they wrote essays about the young worker hero of Nikolai Ostrovskii's civil war era novel *How Steel Was Tempered*. They were expected to model themselves after Fadeev's partisans and Ostrovskii's fervent socialists, to be honest, stoic, self-sacrificing, socially conscious members of the collective of Soviet citizens.

Schools formed an important site for socialization for this generation. The war left many orphaned or half-orphaned children; others had parents who worked very long hours as the Soviet Union struggled to restore its economy. Parents were expected to nurture their children's interests or talents, but many lacked the time, energy, or know-how to do so.[3] Schools helped fill this vacuum. Soviet teachers had traditionally been charged with their young charges' *vospitanie*—often translated as "upbringing," this term includes character education and cultural edification. Values were a matter of public interest and therefore, as historian Larry Holmes observes, "The [Stalin era] school served as a second home for its pupils, blending child with school and school with society, its children living almost always in the public realm."[4]

Assigned the vital task of nurturing good citizens and productive members of society, Soviet teachers often organized extracurricular activities, and overcrowded housing conditions contributed to the popularity of such programs. Children wanted a place where they were welcome, and parents were pleased to have their children involved in some supervised activity rather than hanging out in the street. One participant in the Moscow planetarium's large children's club admitted that although few of the one-hundred-plus members in any given year went on to become astronomers, the circle "left its imprint" on all of them by keeping them out of trouble.[5]

Children in rural villages had few options for organized extra study; however, those living in provincial towns often had access to well-educated teachers and after-school programs. Budding scientists, for instance, could often study chemistry, botany, entomology, zoology, or small-animal husbandry. Some urban schools created sizable gardens—a few even built their own greenhouses—as a way to engage pupils in practical science and to foster respect for labor.[6] In cities, newspapers, theaters, museums, and clubs also hosted special circles (kruzhki) for young people to learn to write, act, perform, and so forth. Such extracurricular activities helped many pupils whose own parents were poorly educated to aspire to higher things.[7] Gladilin benefited from such circles. So too did Boris Vail', who grew up in the city of Kursk. He joined a club for aspiring writers sponsored by the local newspaper and soon was sending his poems to the central children's newspaper, Pionerskaia pravda. Although he did not get his work published in Moscow, the experience inspired him to aim high when it came time to think about getting a university education.[8]

The schools and the mass media framed programs for schoolchildren as patriotic as well as educational. As part of a concerted effort to mold young people, they connected self-improvement with citizenship and service to the nation. Decades later biologist Margarita Monakhova could still list a range of activities, local and national, in which she and her Moscow classmates participated—everything from working in their own greenhouse to collecting seeds for planting protective forest zones and joining in a campaign to turn one kilogram of potatoes into one hundred. Behind all their projects, she avowed, lay a "spirit of patriotism, a desire to be helpful."[9] To a large extent, children internalized the expectations and definitions of virtue presented by teachers and the media and sometimes reinforced in the home, as well. Patriotism was inextricably linked to hard work, modesty, and respect for the Communist Party and its leaders. At the outer range of this generational cohort, Mikhail Gorbachev, born in 1931, for instance, called himself a "hereditary Stalinist," because "for my grandfather and for my father, Stalin was an ideal, even though in his time grandfather had been arrested, sentenced to execution, interrogated with bias, and miraculously released. He swore (as did the whole family): this wasn't Stalin, this was our local wreckers."[10]

Loyalty to Stalin and to the party was cultivated from an early age. Boris Vail', who was applying to colleges in the summer of 1956, for example, remembered agonizing as a boy of ten as to whether he ought to follow the example of Pavlik Morozov, who reported his father for hoarding grain during collectivization. His own father worked in a bakery and brought home cakes and butter. These foodstuffs were an enjoyable and important part of the family's food budget, but Vail' was tortured by the knowledge that they were in effect stolen. He could not quite bring himself to inform on his father. However, hoping to shame him into changing his ways, Vail' finally asked: "How can you take those pastries from the factory without paying?" His father exploded: "What are you, stupid? I take those for you!" He warned: "Don't even think about telling anyone."[11] It was a common practice throughout the Soviet period to exploit privileges or goods available through the workplace. But young idealists did not know what to think about such divergences from the public norms or what to make of special stores for the party elite, wage inequalities, and discrimination against Jews. Their teachers stressed deference over critical thinking in political matters and discouraged "provocative" questions. Indeed, a more cynical Vail' got in trouble when after Khrushchev's report he began to torment his history teacher with deliberately difficult questions.[12]

Like young people everywhere, however, those who came of age in 1956 had their own concerns. They competed at sports, swapped books, and spent their summers outdoors. In Kursk, Vail' and his male friends "spent hours kicking around a dirty glass jar (we called this 'hockey')." They fished in the local stream and hunted for unexploded German grenades to blow up. As teens, they whiled away many evenings strolling up and down the town's main avenue—Lenin Street—chatting idly and flirting with their female classmates who were engaged in the same ritual promenade.[13]

As they grew older, those born in the 1930s absorbed more of the news of the day. Describing a typical boy of his generation, Gladilin would later write: "Petya Ivanov . . . knew he lived in the capitalist encirclement and sincerely sympathized with the bitter fate of foreign workers, especially the Blacks in America . . . Petya believed in the newspapers, but in the newspapers one found miracles time and again: today's chairman of a fraternal Communist Party turns out to be a vile bourgeois hireling. But then, Petya Ivanov primarily read the fourth page, where the sports column was."[14] Many who came of age in the 1950s recall Cold War rhetoric and domestic politics as background noise akin to the constant blare of the radio receivers transmitting the state channel. Vail' noted that in his home the radio hung high on the wall and was never turned off—its transmissions flowed from six in the morning until midnight, when broadcasts stopped for the night. Yet he only really needed to know the news when he had to cram for the oral exam to become a Komsomol at age fourteen.[15]

For the youth of 1956, Stalin's death in March 1953 formed their most vivid political memory. Then a Moscow high school student, future biologist Gennadii Simkin later wrote: "I remember the tears in teachers' eyes and the deathly, terrible silence in classrooms and corridors." The burning desire to see Stalin's body lying in state led him and his friends to try to squeeze through the crowds, "leaping and clambering over fences and along roofs and ducking under [police] horses' bellies to get up to the building." He remembered "a man with a bloodied face and head; under the pressure of the crowd he had broken the plate glass window of a shop with his head" and people crying "in the half dark hall alongside the coffin that rested on a high pedestal, in a sea of flowers."[16] Twenty-four-year-old poet Yevgenii Yevtushenko was caught up in same the crush and saw people trampled and suffocated when the police refused to move the barriers positioned at the ends of the alleyways leading off Gorky Street. The policemen's fear of acting without orders became a symbol for him of the negative side of the Stalinist system, which rewarded obedience and punished initiative.[17] The dominant emotions of the day, however, were grief and anxiety about the future. Gorbachev, for instance, remembers a university classmate turning to him and worriedly asking, "Misha, whatever will become of us now?"[18]

Gladilin and his contemporaries mourned Stalin's death and puzzled at Beria's arrest. As young adults, they learned from Khrushchev's report about the purges and other Stalinist misdeeds. Responses to revelations about Stalin varied widely. Even before the details of the Secret Speech were known, journalism student Lidiia Kliatsko was unsettled by talk of the cult of personality. Disturbed by her classmates' arguments about its causes, she wished for a simpler time, lamenting to her diary that it was too bad that Lenin was no more.[19] Some young people could not accept what they saw as Khrushchev's self-serving attack on a dead man. Others felt that the analysis of Stalin's "crimes" needed to be deeper and more detailed. The strongest impression left by the Secret Speech, as recalled by a former literature student at Moscow State University, was "shock, disappointment, and pain." She noted, "Internally something collapsed, was broken, and so began the first reevaluation of values." She added, "In this, as always, our writers and poets, our literature and history occupied far from the last place."[20]

For Soviet adolescents and young adults, books served as important sources of insight into how to deal with personal as well as existential questions. Soviet youth in 1956 had much to ponder in the wake of the revelations about Stalin and the purges. At the same time, like their peers everywhere, they were also preoccupied with more egotistical worries: how to prove themselves to their friends and parents, how to find satisfying careers, how to be fashionable, and where to find love. In this regard, Gladilin's fictional heroes modeled some of the choices and trade-offs faced by the generation that came of age with the thaw.

Youthful Ambitions

Gladilin entered Moscow's Gorky Institute of Literature in the autumn of 1954 at the precocious age of nineteen. The Literary Institute, like all Soviet universities, gave preference to blue-collar workers, though ironically education would transform such people into white-collar workers. Yet Soviet authorities and educators also recognized the benefits of rewarding young people who had already displayed talent and hard work; such youth were ready for rigorous study and had the potential for long and productive careers. Moreover, their own children did not generally qualify as workers or peasants. Therefore, by the 1950s class background had lost priority in admissions. Instead applicants needed to demonstrate solid preparation and good performance on exams, even though such criteria favored children from privileged backgrounds.

In Gladilin's case, the admissions committee at the Literary Institute interviewed him alongside a thirty-year-old army captain and a construction engineer with ten years of experience under his belt. Gladilin observed that the other two easily passed the oral examination, but that the interviewers eyed him with suspicion. What could he write about, they asked doubtfully, when he was too young to know anything of life?[21] In truth, Gladilin had little to show for himself. At nineteen, he had graduated high school only the year before. Dreaming of glory, he had signed up for a specialized academy for training fighter pilots. A few weeks of drilling on a hot, dusty air base in Kazakhstan had shattered his romantic illusions about military life, especially when he learned he would have to train for five years before being able to fly a real jet. When offered the chance to change his mind at the end of orientation, Gladilin withdrew.[22] However, upon his return to Moscow, Gladilin found himself at loose ends since his friends were busy at their new colleges. Gladilin drifted into a dull job as a lab assistant and channeled his loneliness into writing stories.[23] The results evidently displayed sufficient promise to counterbalance his meager labor experience because he made it into the Literary Institute.

As luck would have it, Gladilin's immaturity nearly derailed his writing career, before proving its salvation. The very restlessness and sense of dissatisfaction that troubled Gladilin since his disillusionment with the military continued to plague him in his first year at the Literary Institute. He largely devoted the fall of 1954 and spring of 1955 to wooing back the girl who had thrown him over the year before when she had started university and he did not. Hence when it came his turn to present his work to the creative writing seminar that formed the core of the Literary Institute's training, he quickly cobbled something together. Disgusted with his feeble effort, his classmates unanimously urged that Gladilin be expelled for "total lack of talent." However, the seminar leader persuaded them that Gladilin should be granted a trial period to prove himself.

With a stern warning that he had one semester to demonstrate his merit, Gladilin was forced to revisit the admission committee's question of whether he could in fact write anything of significance.[24]

As he trudged home from the institute that spring evening in 1955, stunned at the extent of his classmates' rancor, Gladilin heard in his head the first lines of a novel: "The wind drove scraps of old newspaper along the street. Dust from the boulevard drifted up from the pavement. Suddenly it darkened. Black spots appeared on the sidewalk." As the other pedestrians take shelter, Gladilin's "hero," Viktor Podgursky, stalks bitterly through the rain. He has just learned that he failed the entrance exams at the Aviation Institute. Now he has to wait a whole year before reapplying or trying his luck elsewhere. *The Chronicle of the Times of Viktor Podgursky* would be a cri de coeur of an unlucky youth, shut out of higher education, with all its trappings of status and success. The novel's hero would reflect Gladilin's ambivalent feelings about the elite status and exclusive camaraderie available to university students and about the middle-class presumption that study was the only path to happiness and fulfillment. By looking at student life from the perspective of one left out, Gladilin explored what it meant to be an ordinary young person in the 1950s and what higher education offered besides preparation for a career.

In January 1956 Soviet newspapers boasted of 1,865,000 full-time students in various types of colleges and universities with another 727,000 persons registered in evening or correspondence divisions.[25] The most prestigious places of higher education were located in Moscow and Leningrad. They included Moscow and Leningrad State Universities, which offered degrees in the humanities and sciences, and dedicated institutes for training architects, mining engineers, filmmakers, aviation specialists, translators, diplomats, actors, and so forth. Republican and regional capitals—like Kiev, Minsk, Saratov, and Kazan—also hosted universities as well as technical colleges; smaller cities or towns might boast teacher-training institutes and specialized schools related to local industries.

The most ambitious students aspired to attend famous universities or institutes connected with attractive professions, such as the Gorky Literary Institute, where Gladilin studied, or the All-Union State Institute for Cinematography, from which Dunskii and Frid graduated. Since

Fig. 06-01 Anatoly Gladilin's debut publication in *Iunost'*.

Soviet education was in essence free, it seemed a feasible dream for intelligent youngsters from all economic backgrounds. Students did not pay tuition, but they had to maintain excellent grades to receive a stipend, which afforded the bare minimum for survival. However, many schools lacked sufficient dormitory rooms to house all out-of-town students and, although sometimes students could get an additional stipend to compensate for the cost of renting a room or more often a corner of a room, the scarcity of affordable housing, the cost of travel to take entrance exams, along with the higher academic standards of central universities, meant that the majority of students stayed in their home regions.[26]

Nevertheless, prestigious colleges and universities attracted many candidates for an applications process that was largely based on merit. A very few schools, such as the Institute of International Relations, took only those specially recommended by party authorities—as Boris Vail' discovered when he inquired in vain about admission there in the summer of 1956.[27] The majority of higher educational establishments, however, relied on written and oral exams administered by the department to which a student had applied. In the 1950s preference went to high school graduates who had earned gold or silver medals. The brochure for would-be applicants to Moscow State University (MGU) in 1956 explained that 25 percent of spots were reserved for gold medalists, who only had to undergo interviews with the admissions committee. Silver medalists and other applicants had to sit written and oral exams in the subject deemed most relevant to their department.[28] Officials did not admit it, but scarcity of spaces in top schools meant that a certain number of qualified applicants had to be rejected. Vail', normally an A student, was shocked to receive a C in composition when he sat the exam for admission to the Spanish department at Leningrad State University (LGU). When he asked to see his graded essay, he was refused. Only later did he recognize that the popular department was looking for excuses to disqualify applicants.[29]

Work records, military service, or party membership could also help sway admissions committees toward a positive outcome. Mikhail Gorbachev, for instance, won a place at MGU's law department in 1950 partly because he had earned the Order of the Red Banner of Labor for participating in a record-setting harvesting team in his native Stavropol'. Unlike his future wife, Raisa Titarenko, who had a gold medal, Gorbachev, having received four out of five in German, had only a silver medal and thus had to make the case for his admission.[30]

Overall, urban youth had an advantage in university admissions. They benefited from having had better educated teachers, greater exposure to high culture, and more opportunity to participate in high-quality enrichment programs. Children of white-collar workers, especially, tended to have parents who steered them into the best high schools and who could afford special tutoring. Gorbachev's parents, by contrast, had to arrange for him to live in a nearby town to finish high school—his village school went only as far as seventh grade.[31] By 1955 only 24 percent of the overall student base were workers or came from blue-collar families, while only 13 percent could claim collective farm backgrounds.[32]

While family background could be a positive factor for admission in the case of children of workers and peasants, it could also harm a student's chances. Jews faced discrimination as did those who had lived under German occupation or whose parents had been convicted of political crimes. Despite Stalin's famous adage that "the son doesn't answer for the father," a political conviction in the family pretty much guaranteed that the doors to higher education would be closed. Boris Vail' considered himself lucky in this regard because his father had been imprisoned only for an ordinary crime—the senior Vail', a store manager, had served a five-year term in the Russian Far East for mishandling funds. Vail' included his father's conviction on two unsuccessful applications in the summer of 1956. Taking his father's advice, Vail' omitted this fact on his final, successful attempt. When careful examiners nonetheless questioned him as to why his father was in the Far East during the war—Vail' lied that he had worked there as a free laborer on a railway project. The Leningrad Library Institute, eager for more male students, accepted his answer, and Vail' dodged having to return home a failure.[33]

Gladilin's Viktor Podgursky represented the unheralded category of unemployed or underemployed high school graduates who had failed in their quest for higher education. In his memoirs, Gorbachev would recall trying to find jobs for school-leavers as one of the problems of "disorganized life" that he faced as a Komsomol official in Stavropol' in 1956. Overall, party authorities preferred not to mention that the university system could not accommodate all those who desired to enter. Nor did they have a special policy at the time for finding appropriate work for high school graduates who were often greeted without enthusiasm by potential employers. "You don't know how to do anything," the head of the personnel department at a factory tells Gladilin's hero when he applies for work. "Why should we teach you, when you'll go into the army [there was a draft for men who were not students] in the spring?"[34]

In a subsequent fan letter, a girl from Kazakhstan thanked Gladilin for conveying the anxious idleness that gripped Viktor after his botched entrance exam. She and her friend had experienced the same sensation after failing to get into the local teacher training institute. Unable to find work, the two young women had seized an opportunity to train as salesgirls—"We went joyfully—we didn't care about anything, just to not sit at home." Having embraced the low-prestige job, the letter writer now proudly reported that she had enrolled in the All-Union Evening Institute for Soviet Trade. Meanwhile, her friend had worked a year, retaken entrance exams, and become a full-time student.[35]

In the sarcastically titled *The Chronicle of the Times of Viktor Podgursky*, Gladilin poured out the bitterness of would-be students. In particular, he was disgusted with the media's portrayal of the lives of his contemporaries as uniformly easy and relentlessly joyful. He bridled at newsreel footage of happy high school graduates celebrating in Red Square. Although admissions policies left many capable youths outside the university system, the propagandists acted as if each school-leaver was automatically going on to higher achievement.[36]

Urban parents echoed the expectation that any reasonably smart youth ought to go study, if not in the university, then at a technical college, which could pave the way to a clean, safe white-collar, job. Young people entertained their own romantic aspirations–to learn to be film actresses, writers, or nuclear physicists—all of which could be pursued though specialized training. Although his parents urged him to apply to a local technical college, Valerii Ronkin from the northern port city of Murmansk imagined himself wearing a white lab coat and working on important tasks; hence, Ronkin set the goal of getting into the Leningrad Institute of Technology (LTI), where there were eight candidates for each place and one had to score high on exams in composition, literature, mathematics, physics, chemistry, and German.[37] For the Literary Institute, the competition was even tougher. Gladilin remembered six hundred applicants for thirty spaces in his freshman class.[38]

Ronkin and Gladilin passed their real-life exams, but Viktor Podgursky flunks the mathematics exam for the Moscow Institute of Aviation and Technology. Even though he knows he is partly to blame for mooning around after a girl instead of cramming, the fictional Viktor resents the competition in which only fifteen of sixty in his group can pass. In retelling the story of his defeat to Nina, the girl of his dreams, Viktor tries to inject some wit: "My turn arrives. I'm up at the blackboard. I need to find the angle of the pyramid. I'm sitting in that corner and looking at the examiner and he's looking at me, not like at an ordinary student from whom one needs to extract evidence of how much he knows, but like at a person who ought to have some weak points. They must be found." His attempt at self-deprecating humor falls flat when a friend of Nina's father's, a young engineer just a few years Viktor's elder, condescendingly remarks: "I don't think there's anything difficult about entrance exams for a clever fellow. You must not have approached them seriously."[39]

Viktor's failure not only depresses him and dismays his friends but prompts a fight with his mother. She regrets that she boasted about his intelligence to all her coworkers and she laments, "I dreamed that my Viktor, the son of a waitress in a dining hall would become an engineer, would become a man." He has ruined her Soviet dream. Now she's supporting him financially and expecting that he spend all his new "free time" cramming for next year's exams. When she learns he has been goofing off with a similarly unemployed pal, she explodes. She—and the Soviet reader—expect penitence. As Gladilin phrased it, "The son should weep bitter tears of reawakened conscience, should make a thousand impassioned promises, and hit the books with renewed effort." Instead, Viktor shouts back: "Enough! Have you got anything new to say? Anything?" He announces, "I'll come back when you're done." With deliberately realistic dialogue, Gladilin shocked older readers and delighted his peers.

For Viktor, however, the worst is seeing his girlfriend and other former classmates go off to their new institutes. Before, school had been the natural source of activity and friends. As neither a student nor a worker, Viktor Podgursky loses status and membership in a collective. Nina becomes busy with her coursework and college activities, while Viktor has no new interesting acquaintances of whom to boast. She can invite him to a dance at her institute; he has to beg a loan from a friend just to buy tickets to a concert. Even when they meet in her apartment and he manages to steer the conversation to pleasant reminiscences about their senior year of high school, he notices that Nina looks older, as if she has grown up overnight whereas he has remained a boy to be tolerated but not respected. Real-life MGU student Lidiia Kliatsko similarly observed that the tremendous disappointment of failing entry exams and being relegated to a menial job made her boyfriend rude, self-centered, and childish.[40]

Gladilin's Viktor Podgursky starts to throw off his depression only after he finds a job in a factory laboratory. Gladilin doesn't spare his hero the agony of idleness and loneliness—the story is more than halfway through before Viktor is allowed to end his downward drift and to exult to the object of his affection: "Nina, I didn't want to visit you until I was totally sure . . . You know what, I've got a job. You don't believe me? It's the truth! My uncle set me up [*ustroil*] at a factory . . . He's the main engineer there. In the personnel department they made me sign a statement that I was obliged to work at least two years. But uncle promised that they'd give me time off during [next year's] entrance exams and if I pass, they'll let me go. Congratulate me, I'm a worker."[41] The centrality of connections in obtaining even a lowly job adds to the novella's realism. Rather than being rescued by his own efforts or saved by the party, Viktor has been pulled up by a well-placed relative.

Relieved to have a purpose to his days, Viktor does not, however, immediately become a cheerful, productive worker. Indeed, Nina dumps him on the very evening that he tells her of his new job. His subsequent gloomy introspection and general ineptness do not make him popular at work. He is redeemed finally by inclusion in the workplace Komsomol organization, which he joins as a matter of course. Party membership was a privilege, but Komsomol membership was expected in high schools and colleges. At its best, the Komsomol coordinated all sorts of recreational and educational activities; at its worst, it consisted of dull, pro forma meetings.

Gladilin's hero only becomes deeply involved in his new organization when he acts on impulse to try to impress the pretty Komsomol leader at the factory. When her most troublesome member rebuffs her plea to attend the meeting, Viktor commands the young slacker to take off his Komsomol badge and challenges the teen to explain why they should have to beg him to participate. The young man struggles to come up with an excuse and finally stammers, "But it's boring there. All talk." "That's a different story," Viktor responds. "There it depends on you. Suggest something interesting." Soon the two are planning a cross-country skiing outing for the whole group, and Viktor has a new sense of accomplishment. But Gladilin is careful to give Viktor realistically base motivations—a desire to impress a girl and nostalgia for being at the center of activity.

Whereas those young people who entered higher education found themselves in a rich environment for social activity, those who went to work faced a more varied picture. Young people who worked in retail, agriculture, or small organizations often had to make do without workplace-based organizations. Big factories and institutions had Komsomol and party cells and sometimes their own clubs. Gladilin's Viktor finds a place in the Komsomol and gains fame inside the factory by almost winning the after-hours chess competition organized by a popular engineer. Through the chess matches, Viktor meets older members of his new collective and forges a new identity for himself. Viktor does not suddenly conquer his immaturity—with each chess piece he captures, he childishly says to himself, "Take that, Nina." But as he becomes part of the community his daydreams turn away from student life per se to the endpoint, a career that includes the respect of his peers.[42]

That said, Gladilin himself realized the dream of entering a prestigious college, studying at Moscow's Gorky Literary Institute from 1954 to 1958. His experience of near expulsion followed by fame once *Iunost'* published *The Chronicle of the Times of Viktor Podgursky* was hardly typical, however. Indeed, since Gladilin sought to represent the interests and values of ordinary youth, life in the rarefied atmosphere of the literary institute–with just 150 students total—did not suit as a source of material. Instead, Gladilin made Viktor's erstwhile girlfriend, Nina, a student at a prestigious technical college, the Bauman Moscow Higher Technological University (MVTU).

Nina is not a fully developed character, but she possesses two important traits common to students of the time: first, she seeks a field that will challenge her; second, she is an idealist of sorts, wanting people to improve themselves and to make life better. When a fellow student suggests that she will likely drop out after she marries a successful, older engineer, Nina discloses that she already has rejected such a proposal. Moreover, she hotly protests: "A husband—the head of the family! That's not what I want, I don't need that. I need to study. I should become an engineer. Do you know why I chose MVTU? Because everyone warned me: 'Oh, MVTU—that's a nightmarish institute with a mass of drafting work. There's no place for girls there. Don't even think about going there—you'll squander your youth.'"[43] Nina wants to achieve for its own sake and for her self-esteem. She enjoys her successes and wants to be treated as an equal.

For real students at the country's best institutions, 1956 was also a time to follow their ambitions, to form deep friendships, to pursue independence, and to put their ideals to the test—sometimes at the cost of conflict with authorities. Soviet universities and institutes of higher education channeled young people into groups to facilitate organization and control, but some student collectives—especially in 1956—pursued their values under the radar of or even at cross purposes with higher authorities.[44]

Student Solidarities

From the moment Soviet students entered higher education, they were organized into various groups. The primary purpose of the university was to provide specialized education—therefore, students applied to specific programs or departments and their academic, and often social, lives would be organized around those divisions. For instance, the Film Institute admitted students separately to sections for directors, cinematographers, screenwriters, and actors. At MGU's popular Department of Philology or *filfak* as its members affectionately abbreviated it, first-year students were immediately assigned to groups based on their concentrations in languages, literature, or linguistics. Even fifty years later, its alumni would identify themselves by their group tag, such as "tenth (German) group of the Russian division."[45]

Division into smaller units had organizational and disciplinary benefits. Academic groups had an "elder" (*starosta*)—chosen by the dean's office—who monitored attendance, kept an eye out for students in trouble, chastised those guilty of carousing, and spoke for the group if there was an issue with a professor. Each academic group also functioned as a primary Komsomol cell, which carried out social work, such as giving political education talks in workers' barracks, performing concerts, or volunteering labor, which for MGU students in 1956 often meant working on the construction of the Luzhniki stadium. The departmental Komsomol also chose a leader for each year (*Komsorg kursa*) and enforced discipline.[46] For instance, when Venedikt Erofeev—later author of the infamous drunken odyssey *Moscow-Petushki*—stopped attending classes during his second semester in the MGU *filfak* in the spring of 1956, his *Komsorg* led a student delegation to confront him in his dorm room and try to persuade him to mend his ways.[47]

Besides organizing student activities, Komsomol meetings were used to transmit and reinforce party policy. They could also be convened to punish political incorrectness, a serious issue as no academic field could remain above politics. Every student had to pass courses in Marxism-Leninism and the history of the Communist Party and politics also circumscribed research. Literature students in 1956, for instance, were discouraged from researching Dostoevsky because his politics were considered reactionary.[48]

The moralizing strand inherent in Komsomol work sometimes impeded the efforts of enthusiasts to form tight, friendly groups. MGU *filfak* student Igor' Kochetkov recalled his first-year *Komsorg* as an idealistic young woman full of aspirations to weld her fellow freshmen into a strong collective dedicated to noble and lofty pursuits. Hence, "At one meeting [she] bravely accused several girls of being distracted by fashions and boys to the detriment of their spiritual lives and their studies." When she organized an evening for the class, it featured classical music—to the dismay of those who hoped for dancing and food. Although the members of the group became friends over time, he recalled, it was silly pranks, jokes, and shared songs that knit them together more than admonitions and high culture.[49] Indeed, many students preferred easygoing "elders" who would help cover for those who skipped class.[50]

Although created in part to punish those who strayed, academic collectives and Komsomol groups could also defend their members against the administration, often preferring to solve their own problems. Consider the case of Valerii Ronkin, whose trouble began when he made a sharp speech to the Komsomol meeting of his course at LTI hectoring more students to volunteer at construction sites and to join in the anti-hooligan "raid" patrols, which he led to the admitted detriment of his grades. One girl resisted his chiding, asking: "If the raiders want to hold themselves up as examples, then how come Ronkin himself plays cards during mathematics lectures." Not noticing a representative of the dean's office in attendance, Ronkin rashly counterattacked—touting card playing as developing one's skills at probabilities, naming Marx as someone who enjoyed cards, and noting that he'd only played during

Marxism-Leninism classes. Ronkin's sarcastic riposte in front of the deputy dean elevated the students' bickering into an actionable offense. When the dean gave Ronkin the choice of naming his card partner or being expelled, Ronkin's buddies gathered their academic group and decided to offer up their least vulnerable member, with his consent, as a scapegoat. The son of the head of an important national scientific research center turned himself in to the dean and, as predicted, his father's status shielded him from any immediate consequences.[51]

Collectives also formed within the universities to meet special interests—everything from extramural sports to ballroom dancing, from choirs to literary clubs. Students, not surprisingly, looked primarily for fun and fellow thinkers.[52] In some cases, however, groups officially endorsed by the Komsomol or approved up by the university took on directions of their own. Notable examples include the voluntary "Komsomol Patrols" or "Raid Brigades," organized to fight hooliganism and petty crime, and "tourist" groups. Students also came together around "wall newspapers"—handmade, illustrated broadsheets created by courses and even by academic groups within a course and pasted up in university corridors. Here the Komsomol Patrol at the LTI and hiking groups at LTI and MGU are examined as examples of student-run collectives that allowed participants to put their ideals into practice in somewhat independent ways.[53]

Valerii Ronkin, who came from Murmansk to study at LTI in the fall of 1954, became both an avid "tourist" and a devoted "raider." Both of these activities require some explanation. With international borders essentially closed to them, adventurous Soviet young people had to make do with internal travel. In the 1950s postwar reconstruction of roads and railways opened up possibilities for exploring the mountains of the Caucuses and the beaches of Crimea. During the academic year, however, student "tourists" hiked or cross-country skied in nearby rural areas in coed groups, camping in tents or seeking shelter with villagers overnight. This form of travel as filled "some sort of spiritual need" to learn about their own country on their own schedule. For others, it allowed participants to prove their mettle. To gather the strength to keep going on a subzero ski expedition in February 1956, for instance, MGU journalism students imagined themselves in wartime conditions.[54]

"Komsomol Patrols" or "Raid Brigades" were voluntary groups to help the militia. Created in the wake of a crime wave unleashed by the 1953 amnesty, they helped prevent street crime by patrolling at night and policed dances.[55]

Ronkin discovered the "Raid Brigade" during his second semester at LTI. He found a sense of purpose and camaraderie among the self-appointed guardians of order. The "raiders" saw themselves as defending safety and morals and scorned those whom they saw as "debauched" for showing an ardor for stylish clothes or Western music. Ronkin also enjoyed the physical aspect of chasing down those trying to smuggle in drinks to dances and breaking up brawls. But his fondest recollections concerned the ties forged during the long hours that he and his fellow activists spent together. These bonds expanded to dominate the patrol members' university lives. The raiders hung out together between classes, celebrated holidays jointly, went hiking as a group, tended to volunteer together for social obligations, and even performed together. As Ronkin later recounted, "It was the custom then to sing a lot at Komsomol events. Raiders would stand in a circle, put their arms around each other's shoulders and sing." The raiders also resolved their own ethical questions and resisted efforts from above to have a leader appointed by the Komsomol. It violated their ethos to have an outsider "dropped in from above"; they preferred to let all active members have a say, with the most reliable and enthusiastic taking the lead.[56]

For other students, "tourism" played a similar role in ordering their student experiences and fostering a sort of collective independence. Igor' Kochetkov from the MGU *filfak* remembers the vital role that tourism played in his maturation. He arrived in the fall of 1953 from the Suvorov military academy, where he'd been sent at age eight by his widowed mother, who could scarcely afford to feed and clothe him. He felt a bit at sea with his assigned academic group at MGU; "We sat together at lectures, but then each person went off to his own life." With hard-core hiking enthusiasts he found a new lifestyle. The "tourists"—both boys and girls—would hang out together after lectures and plan the week's excursion. They hiked every Sunday and made three-day trips during the November and May holidays. They even set out with skis and tents to celebrate the New Year.

Looking back, Kochetkov asked, "Where did such a passion come from?" He answered, "For me tourism wasn't just walking about in the fresh air; it was a means to enter a new life. On hikes, I really learned to communicate [*obshchat'sia*], there appeared the spirit of camaraderie that had been instilled in me at the Suvorov Military Academy." Indeed, Lidiia Kliatsko complimented a fellow tourist precisely because he proved to be "companionable" (*kompanicheskii*) in the sense of building up the group spirit. Sharing and composing "student songs"—humorous and serious—added to the bonding experience, as did the rare chance for young men and women to share close quarters.[57]

Hikers also had their own internal norms and rudimentary self-government. "Tourists" chose their own leaders and made their own rules—for instance, testing themselves by refusing to use any means of transportation or choosing to follow a compass course rather than existing paths. At MGU, though the university sports committee supplied some equipment, groups did not depend on official structures for guidance or permission. And since their activities took place off university grounds, tourists escaped supervision.

Besides offering some independence, student-run collectives offered the possibility of realizing shared values. As Kochetkov recalled, "On hikes everything was shared, there was a common cause, a passion, a natural form of social intercourse [*V pokhodakh vse byli svoi, bylo obshchee delo, uvlechenie, estestvennaia forma obshcheniia*]." Ronkin similarly cited the sharing of burdens, equipment, and food as part of the appeal of tourism. For idealistic Soviet youth, he argued, such collectivism was the opposite not of individualism, but of egotism.[58] In many ways, the hikers created the sort of democratic collective of equals to which the Komsomol paid lip service. Furthermore, historian Juliane Fürst adds, "Escapism into the privacy of nature and select company was . . . to no small extent infiltrated by a belief in a better Soviet society than that existing in the reality of the tourists' urban homes."[59] In their self-governing groups, students could practice the complementary virtues of self-reliance and mutual support that had been held up to them as ideals since childhood but that eluded them in official institutions. They could also practice a utopian egalitarianism.

Though Soviet institutions were meant to be free of class distinctions, socioeconomic divisions among students existed. Kaluga native and *filfak* student Ruf' Ageeva recalled that she and the one other provincial student in her group stuck out not only for their dress but also

Fig. 06-02 Students in the School of Biology and Soil Sciences—from left to right, a demobilized sailor, a girl from Belorussia, and a boy from Bashkiriia—awaiting the first lecture, Moscow State University, 1956. Photograph by D. Sholomovich. Courtesy Moscow Central Archive of Audiovisual Documents.

for their backgrounds. The daughter of a collective farm president, Ageeva had not gone to a special elite high school that had advanced foreign-language classes. Marina Remneva, later dean of the MGU philology department, added: "In our [academic] group, we did not achieve friendship. It sort of split into two parts. In one were our local stars, all knowing, self-confident, haughty Moscow 'A' students . . . in the other, were quiet, frightened girls who had come from the provinces." Remneva, who grew up in Podol'sk, a small city just south of Moscow, considered herself somewhere in the middle. She described herself as "shy, naive, [and] childishly immature"; however, as the child of teachers she was extremely well versed in the Russian classics and more confident academically than her provincial friends.[60]

At MGU many of the Muscovites were so-called professors' sons, that is, they came from intelligentsia backgrounds and often had prior connections to the university. Besides their confidence in the academic setting, in some cases they brought special knowledge. In the biology and soil sciences department, it meant being aware of the subterranean battle against Lysenko and his denial of the gene. In the humanities, it meant familiarity with out of favor writers such as Boris Pasternak, Osip Mandelstam, Anna Akhmatova, and Marina Tsvetaeva. By contrast, consider the young man from a town in the Kaluga region who had to admit to the admissions committee for the MGU's *filfak* that he could not tell them anything about the Stanislavski method and indeed that he had never been to the theater.[61]

With out-of-town students crowded together into the dormitories and Muscovites living with their parents, two different social groups emerged at MGU. Those who lived in the dorms ate, studied, and explored the capital together, whereas the Muscovites tended to retain their old social networks. Out-of-town students may have lacked sophistication, but they formed their own powerful bonds of friendship and demonstrated allegiance to the shared value system that glorified honesty and fairness. An incident from MGU in the spring of 1956 demonstrates the potency of youthful idealism and the potential ramifications of a clash with unspoken official norms. In this case, students frustrated with hollow promises from the Komsomol, trade union, and party took an unorthodox action to draw attention.

"In our cafeteria, they steal a lot and feed us badly and expensively," read a homemade sign placed by the door of the dining hall at the Stromynka dormitory complex early one morning in May 1956. "Appeals on this subject to higher instances have produced no results," its anonymous authors wrote. "We suggest a last resort: a boycott." To the immense consternation of university and municipal party officials, students successfully organized a three-day action. Students from the philology, history, and law departments—students were clustered in the dorms by academic specialization—organized temporary pickets, and on the first morning of the boycott the dining room was empty, with the initial exception of Chinese exchange students. Word of the boycott spread like wildfire around the campus, garnering sympathy and a certain degree of awe. Students from another dormitory even sent a telegram of support.[62]

Many concrete reasons lay behind the students' anger with their dining facilities. As university authorities had long been aware, the campus cafeterias and buffets offered few of the items listed on their menus, frequently ran out of food, and featured slow service and poor sanitation. One even lacked hot water—so its workers merely rinsed the dishes and silverware in cold water before putting them back out. Cafeteria workers stole food and sometimes resold it. In the buffets, according to students, scales were set to cheat customers. In short, many of the common flaws of the planned economy could be seen in the microcosm of student services, where cheap prices failed to compensate for low quality. Despite repeated complaints to Komsomol and party bureaus and to the university administration, despite negative articles in the university newspaper and bad reports by inspection commissions, the dining halls continued to be poorly managed. The final straw for students in May 1956 seems to have been a scandal over sausages, although its particulars remain unclear. According to some, the cafeteria was selling spoiled meat. Others cite the absence of sausages for sale that witnesses had seen being delivered.[63]

According to later accounts, the cafeteria dispute escalated on the evening of May 23 when the internal radio station at the Stromynka dorm broadcast a complaint about food services and cited a disparaging response from the head of the dining hall. Frustrated students began to meet spontaneously in the dorms to discuss how to press the issue. When the university administration learned that the word *boycott* had been bandied about, they dispatched the secretary of the MGU Party Committee and the president of the MGU Trade Union to discourage students. According to eyewitnesses, the two men actually inflamed the gathering by denigrating the young people and defending the cafeteria boss. They refused the students' suggestion that the dining room be closed until state inspectors could be summoned to examine its books. They also criticized the notion of a boycott but could not suggest any new alternatives to past complaints. At that point the young people shouted that they would decide for themselves whether they wanted to eat in the dining hall or not.[64] That night students prepared the leaflet calling for the strike, and they made their own rhyming propaganda poster that read: "If you don't want / To dine like cattle / Declare a boycott!" (*Esli ne khochesh' / Pitat'sia kak skot, / Ob"iavliai boikot!*[65]) The next morning, the protest began.

Some five thousand Soviet and foreign students dwelled at Stromynka 32 in a quadrangle formed of large four-story buildings. They lived eight to fourteen to a room with a restroom and kitchen on each floor. Bathing had to be done at a separate bathhouse on the grounds of the complex; it served female students one day and males the next.[66] Students slept on metal beds and each got a footlocker for storing personal belongings. The other furniture consisted of a single wardrobe and one large table per room. Lights went out at 11:00 p.m., and rooms were checked frequently for tidiness—some MGU students remember future Soviet First Lady Raisa Titarenko as an especially strict inspector.[67] Small stipends and lack of time for shopping and meal preparation meant that the majority of dormitory residents relied on the cafeteria for at least some of their meals. Students later insisted—when accused of being spoiled—that they did not expect fancy food, just decent meals at a fair price. How could they be expected to concentrate on their studies if they could not rely on the promised provision of subsidized edible meals? They were at the finest university in the land and yet behind the scenes lurked corruption and incompetence.

The Stromynka students succeeded beyond their wildest imaginations in attracting attention. MGU officials and Moscow city party bosses descended on the dormitory en masse after rumors spread of "unrest." To the apparent chagrin of all involved, word of the boycott even leaked out (no doubt via foreign students) to the BBC. After the BBC broadcast a "hyperbolic" account, delegations from various embassies arrived to check up on their exchange students. They most likely found no traces of unrest as it seems the picket dispersed almost immediately. Nonetheless, repercussions followed.

On May 29 an extraordinary session of the University Party Committee met and resolved: "To condemn the attempt at organization of a boycott as a manifestation of petty bourgeois dissipation, anarchism, and political immaturity on behalf of a certain portion of the students residing in the Stromynka dormitory." The form of the action even more than the content alarmed university authorities. Strikes were seen as the tool of oppressed workers in capitalist countries—what role could they serve when deployed by the privileged beneficiaries of a socialist education? One senior party member even blamed the strike on the foreign students. He did not think Soviet students capable of conceiving of a boycott.[68]

Participants in the strike, however, categorically rejected the ideological characterization of their actions. A transcript of a party meeting in the philology department in early June reveals students shielding the identity of organizers and defending the action. Resisting pressure to identify "ringleaders" and "provocateurs," the students insisted that their boycott was spontaneous and carried out by a mass of young people without formal leaders. One young woman challenged being tagged as a "ringleader," saying the head of the dormitory management only remembered her because she had been brave enough to accuse him of covering up for thieves. She also countered the image of the students as pawns in a political game. "Where," she asked, "did he get evidence to say that I was a 'weapon in the hands of provocateurs'?" She even took the offensive, castigating another party representative who had grossly insulted her by accusing her of "selling out [her] motherland for a piece of bread."[69] Thus, even in the face of serious criticism and potential expulsion from the Komsomol and university, in 1956 the student activists dared to defend the content of their complaint and, indirectly, the form. After all, they had not made any political demands during their strike and they had resorted to the boycott only after "legal" methods had failed.[70]

At the party meeting in the philology department, a few adults defended the students as naive and immature rather than politically hostile. Activism needed to be welcomed, but directed in a constructive fashion, one opined. After all, the whole problem might have been avoided had the young people's complaints been taken seriously from the start. One attendee even located the root problem in the authorities' arrogance. Having begun to battle against the cult of personality, one party member suggested, they now needed to deal with "another cult, the cult of the party."[71] More liberal, or at least more lenient, faculty members invoked Khrushchev's revival of Leninist norms as implying the need for more humility on the part of political leadership and perhaps more room for frank exchanges of opinion. Spring 1956 was a relatively good moment for protest, but still some adults described the students' behavior as "indecent" and "disgraceful." At a meeting of the party bureau for the biology and soil science department, one member angrily exclaimed: "The students are spoiled. They've never experienced any hardships in life, not like what we lived through and the hard conditions under which we studied in previous times."[72]

The boycott, hence, served as a lightning rod for expression of generational differences. Students conceived of themselves as full-fledged citizens with the right to be heard on matters relevant to their studies. As idealists, many expected that administrators once aware of the extent of their problems would sincerely empathize and hasten to fix them. The young people did not, it seems, imagine that their actions would be interpreted as anti-Soviet or subversive. The older generation, by contrast, expected more realism both in expectations of what the economic system could deliver and in cognizance of the unwritten limits on free expression. The boycott reinforced the older generation's suspicions that the youth of 1956 were a pampered generation. They thought students ought to have been more grateful for their free education, whereas students felt they were earning their places by hard work.[73]

Idealists and Realists

The generation that came of age in 1956 had been encouraged by teachers, parents, and the media to have high standards for their own behavior and high expectations for their careers. They were taught to see themselves as the fortunate citizens of the first ever socialist society and told they had a moral duty to strive not only for individual success but to join the collective effort to improve conditions for everyone. Higher education in its many forms offered a venue for achieving individual goals—"we needed feats in life, nothing less," as Ruf' Ageeva confided to her diary—while acquiring skills that would be useful to the national economy.[74] The lure of student life, however, extended beyond the career possibilities. The university setting promised a chance to form lasting friendships with likeminded age mates.

The youth of 1956 eagerly participated in groups, especially those that offered some independence. Students wanted to prove themselves individually and in collectives of their own making. "Tourists" in particular created small societies of equals and temporarily escaped the pedagogical and moral *vospitanie* of their elders. Such groups were not in opposition to official institutions, but they intentionally sought autonomy. They were not always internally harmonious—Lidiia Kliatsko, for instance, recorded numerous quarrels among student participants on a frigid expedition in February 1956—but they governed themselves.[75]

The tension between self-help and *vospitanie* stands out in the reactions to Gladilin's *The Chronicle of the Times of Viktor Podgursky*. His work succeeded with young people because he depicted a sort of youth subculture with its own norms and slang. Teachers and others in charge of the "upbringing" of Soviet youth, however, disliked the novella because its hero did not seek counsel from his elders. A high school teacher wrote to *Iunost'* to question why Viktor was so sarcastic and rude to his mother. Why was he depicted as being at sea initially in his new workplace? She accepted that fiction for young people was not supposed to "whitewash" reality any longer, but she did not care for such an egotistical "hero." Younger readers, by contrast, were more struck by the fact that Viktor's friends did not help him more. How could Nina, for instance, not share in Viktor's joy at finding a job?[76] Gladilin, however, wrote from life, drawing on his own feelings of loneliness when all his school friends went off to their new institutes without him and reflecting on his Literary Institute classmates' readiness to expel him.

Students themselves could be harsh critics of their peers. Ronkin and his fellow raiders despised those who caroused or aped Western fashions. Others scorned those who did not take their studies seriously or behaved promiscuously. The high ideals practiced by Soviet students also sometimes led to overly optimistic expectations in dealing with official institutions. The cafeteria boycott shows one clash between idealists grappling with messy economic conditions and adults committed to prioritizing political order.

1956 would be a hard year for idealists. Lidiia Kliatsko, for example, did not know what to think when her classmates began to quarrel over the causes of the cult of personality. She found the disparagement of Stalin unpleasant and disliked the noisy contention among her peers. That year, however, she would be drawn into public disputes in the MGU journalism department over the nature of Stalinism, the Komsomol, and her chosen profession. Moreover, she would find solidarity among young people further challenged that fall when political discussions spread dramatically.[77] When some young people took Khrushchev's promises of a return to free discussion to heart, their friends would have to choose sides.

The clashes between students and university and party authorities that swelled in 1956 were both emboldening and frightening for participants. Svetlana Angelina, daughter of the famous "shock worker" female tractor driver Pasha Angelina, recalls almost being sucked into a strike in fall of 1956. She and some fifty other fellow classmates from the MGU *filfak* had been dispatched to the countryside for two weeks to help with the potato harvest. Such agricultural interruptions were neither unusual nor totally unwelcome. Students knew they would live in rough conditions and do manual labor, but they also would have break from their studies and a chance for fun all together. However, in September 1956 the *filfak* students ended up in execrable conditions helping harvest potatoes on a state farm (*sovkhoz*) near Mozhaisk, a town west of Moscow. They were housed in a barn that had recently held pigs, and their meals consisted of small portions of potatoes, brown bread, and milk. Water was in scarce supply and could not be spared for bathing. Worst of all, the farm was poorly run. "Our potato harvesting combine is constantly breaking and being repaired. We could dig potatoes by hand with spades, but there aren't any shovels at the *sovkhoz*. So we sit on our upturned buckets and sing our favorite student songs, joke and laugh."[78]

The students' laughter ceased when a commission of bigwigs from the department, Party Committee, Komsomol, and dean's office visited only to announce that the students had to prolong their stay for another two weeks because they had accomplished so little. Although ostensibly responsible for the students' well-being, the commission refused to listen to their concerns about missing more classes or their complaints about their living and working conditions. After the inspectors departed, the angry students voted to go on strike. They debated how they might escape by walking a very long way to Mozhaisk, where they could catch a suburban train into Moscow. Without a real leader, however, their bluster soon gave way to resignation. They stayed and starved and dug.

To risk being excluded from the exclusive circles of higher learning was too terrible to contemplate. Angelina observed with hindsight: "In those days, such self-government/initiative [*samoupravstvo*], disobeying directives from the leadership, was punished very harshly—expulsion from the Komsomol and University, of which there were many examples during our years of study. Our whole futures and careers hung by a thread. In all likelihood, we were swayed not only by reason, but also by fear, which always lived in us."[79] It was easier in this case to suffer nobly together than to fight to be heard by the obviously unsympathetic university authorities. After all, Soviet youth were supposed to be willing to sacrifice for the state that educated and nurtured them.

7 | JULY

INTELLECTUAL HEAT

In July 1956 Nina Balandina, a mathematics student at Moscow State University, packed for her summer vacation. She equipped herself with a volume of Blok's poetry, a sewing kit, a travel chess set, and a collapsible kayak. Then she joined the Liapunovs, long-time family friends, for a journey to Lake Miassovo in the Urals. The mathematician Aleksei Liapunov, his wife, and two of his daughters planned to spend the summer in the middle of a nature preserve in the company of biologists working at a field station there. As Balandina would recall decades later, the elder Liapunov set off for Miassovo with the intent of discussing "principles of evolution and mathematical genetics" with their hosts. His youngest daughter, Natal'ia, proposed to carry out research for her biology coursework at MGU, while his wife would "tend to their daily cares and beautify their lives." Daughter Alla and her husband planned to enjoy the natural setting. Nina looked forward to relaxing, but she brought the boat to help Natal'ia collect zooplankton for her project. Nina's job would be to row to the center of the lake and to hold the boat still while Natal'ia filled her collecting jars.[1]

These idyllic-sounding plans masked the length and the difficulty—both in geographic and existential terms—of the journey that would bring the guests and their hosts to Miassovo. In the most prosaic sense, the Muscovites would have to take a nine-hundred-mile train trip to the East through the Ural Mountains, where European Russia ends and Asia begins, then travel by jeep over twenty miles of horribly rough road. In fact, the research center's host, Nikolai Timofeev-Resovskii, loved to joke that when a man stumbled (or was poured) out of the station's truck after several hours of bouncing over the rugged track, he generally needed some time to figure out the location of his liver in relation to his spleen. That summer Timofeev-Resovskii had a shorter trip to reach Miassovo—some 150 miles—from Sverdlovsk (formerly and currently Ekaterinburg), where he had been living for the past year. His larger journey to the Urals, however, had been more circuitous; he had traveled from Moscow to Berlin in 1925 and returned at the end of World War II only to be shunted via the gulag to a secret laboratory deep in the forests of the southern Urals.

Existentially, the young travelers from Moscow would be stepping out of the highly structured and politicized world of Soviet academe into an oasis of free speech, casual good humor, and creative thinking. They would do so at the risk of associating with a scientist who been convicted of treason for having worked in Nazi Germany and whose area of expertise—genetics—had been effectively banned during his absence and incarceration. In 1948 the agronomist Trofim Lysenko had gotten the Soviet Communist Party to endorse his denial of the existence of the gene, but in Miassovo in the summer of 1956 Lysenko's teachings would hold no sway. As a prisoner working for the Soviet atomic project, Timofeev-Resovskii had continued his work on radiation and mutation and now he was ready to offer training in genetic research. Natal'ia Liapunova, having just faced censure at MGU for her "unhealthy interest" in Western theories of genetics, would become the first of many to learn the theoretical and practical fundamentals of the field in Miassovo.[2]

Although theories of evolution and heredity have often sparked controversy, the battle over genetics in the Soviet Union has earned well-deserved notoriety for its passion, politics, and impact. The dramatic tale of Lysenko's rout of genetics, however, has overshadowed the equally important if less histrionic process of Lysenkoism's gradual rollback.[3] Lysenko and his theories about heredity were not fully defeated until the mid-1960s; however, 1956 witnessed several key moments as scientists from different generations came together to undermine Lysenko's dominance and to chip away at the USSR's isolation from the international scientific community.[4] In 1956 genetics became one of the arenas in which dogma and pluralism clashed. Those who gathered at Miassovo did not see themselves as "dissidents" or categorize their actions as anti-Soviet, but their efforts to pursue their professional calling challenged the monopolistic state and its politicization of every sphere.

One Road to Miassovo

The Miassovo biostation came into existence in the spring of 1956, as part of a bargain between Timofeev-Resovskii and the Urals branch of the Soviet Academy of Sciences. He would bring his laboratory for the study of biophysics to the Institute of Biology in Sverdlovsk in exchange for housing for his staff and support for creating a research station in the middle of the Il'mensk nature preserve.[5] In explaining the genesis of this deal, Timofeev-Resovskii later described himself as a "rich bride." He had spent seven years running a well-funded top secret laboratory dedicated to studying the effects of radiation. When this particular part of the atomic project was slated to be dissolved in 1955, Timofeev-Resovskii was given some leeway to select a new host for his lab and its valuable equipment—so valuable indeed that some of it was still in use in his son Andrei's laboratory in Ekaterinburg in the 1990s. Timofeev-Resovskii's tarnished past put Moscow off-limits, but he had the choice of several provincial suitors. The prospect of summers at Miassovo tipped the balance in favor of Sverdlovsk.[6]

How had Timofeev-Resovskii, a world-famous scientist, wound up splitting his time between a provincial city and a cabin in the woods? How could a former prisoner be in a position to bargain with the Academy of Sciences? How did he become a valuable mentor for a new generation of biologists? And why did would-be geneticists have to seek out a tutor in the midst of a remote nature preserve? Timofeev-Resovskii's life story is so fantastical as to make the stuff of great fiction—and indeed has inspired more than one novel.[7] His biography also demonstrates the very real influences of Stalinism on the conduct and notion of science, as well as the possibility for an individual to ameliorate some of these effects. In Miassovo Timofeev-Resovskii began to teach genetics to a new generation and revived a collaborative, avowedly apolitical, and worldly model of intellectual inquiry—no trivial task after the anticosmopolitan campaign.

Timofeev-Resovskii's scientific worldview reflected his education and experiences in pre- and postrevolutionary Russia. Born at the turn of the century into an educated family, Timofeev-Resovskii, like many biologists, became a devoted naturalist at a young age. He interrupted his studies at Moscow State University in 1919 to fight in the civil war on the side of the Red Army. An injury at the front, however, soon led to a return to Moscow, where he continued his scientific education as best he could at that turbulent time. While eking out a living by teaching in a school for workers and lecturing for the Red Army's literacy program, Timofeev-Resovskii apprenticed himself to the illustrious zoologist Nikolai Kol'tsov. In 1922, without having finished his degree, he joined the scientific staff of Kol'tsov's Institute of Experimental Biology. There he met and married fellow student Elena Fidler and joined a freewheeling seminar on fruit flies. Here the elements of his future career came together: a constant collaborator in his wife, a habit of lively scientific exchange, and practice in conducting genetic experiments.[8]

The young Bolshevik regime had an interest in promoting science for the economic benefits it might generate and to demonstrate the superiority of the socialist system. Fresh channels of funding were welcomed by scientists and engineers, many of whom sympathized with the regime's goals even if few were party members in the years following the revolution.[9] Historian Nikolai Krementsov observes, "Despite the trauma and shock of the revolutions and the civil war, Russian science in the 1920s was actually an expanded, slightly modified version of the science system that had existed in Russia under the tsar: a diversified network of scientific institutions and an essentially autonomous scientific community with well-developed foreign contacts." However, he adds that the 1920s also witnessed distinctive investments in science—"the creation of a single state patron for science, the lavish privileges and support it afforded, the takeover and transformation of the educational system"—all of which made science dependent on the state and its ideology.[10]

Timofeev-Resovskii, however, stepped outside the Soviet scientific system in 1925 when with the backing of Kol'tsov and the Soviet Min-

Fig. 07-01 Nikolai Timofeev-Resovskii and his wife, Elena, at the Miassovo biostation during the summer of 1956. Courtesy Natalya Lyapunova-Yurii Bogdanov Family Archive.

ister of Health Nikolai Semashko, he accepted an invitation to work at the German Institute of the Brain outside Berlin. There he and his wife experimented on radioisotopes and mutation and he soon became head of the department of genetics and biophysics. Timofeev-Resovskii also quickly became integrated into the international scientific community. He traveled to Denmark to participate in seminars with the physicist Niels Bohr; attended the Sixth International Congress of Geneticists in Ithaca, New York; entertained foreign visitors; and published his findings in an array of journals. Timofeev-Resovskii also tirelessly promoted contacts between Russian and Western scientists, often overseeing the translation and publication of research done in the USSR.[11]

While Timofeev-Resovskii was pursuing research in genetics that reflected the new paradigm in the West—one grounded in Mendel's core discovery of mathematically based laws of inheritance and identifying the chromosome as a unit of heredity—his closest colleagues in the Soviet Union found themselves attacked in the press. The campaign against fundamental research on genetics was led by Trofim Lysenko, an agricultural specialist with a grudge against laboratory scientists, especially those who carried out what seemed to him to be frivolous experiments on fruit flies. Lysenko's rise must be briefly examined here because it reflects the changes in the institutional setting and in the intellectual atmosphere for doing science that took place in the Stalin era and because in 1956 and years afterward Lysenko played a major role in polarizing the profession.

A Detour

Based on his notoriously political pronouncements and his failure to produce convincing proof of his own theories, Lysenko has frequently been presented as an outright charlatan who propagandized out-of-date notions about the inheritability of acquired characteristics. A recent reassessment of Lysenko's work has drawn attention to the persistence of debates about heredity outside of the Soviet Union at the time and has credited his ambitious ideas of transforming agriculture to the overall utopian thinking of his era. The new field of epigenetics has also revived an interest in environmental influences on heredity. Nevertheless, Lysenko's views on inheritance were roundly challenged during his lifetime by experimental research that he refused to credit. Moreover, when his own ideas failed in practice, Lysenko relentlessly promoted new often far-fetched recommendations always with great haste and fanfare. Hence, his success has been linked to the appeal his views on agronomy had for some in the ruling political party.[12]

Born in 1898 into a peasant family, Trofim Lysenko, like Khrushchev, only began his real education as an adult after the revolution. Lysenko studied agronomy with a specialization in plant physiology at the Kiev Agricultural Institute and initially researched seasonal crops. Most notably, Lysenko subjected seeds to cold temperatures and moisture to try to speed plant growth as a shorter growing cycle could improve farmers' chances of reaping a harvest ahead of bad weather. Lysenko's early "innovations"—including soaking seeds before sowing and allowing potatoes to sprout before planting—drew on existing practices, but were promoted by Lysenko with claims of spectacular results. Lysenko's bravado and confidence held great appeal in the context of upheaval and demoralization in the countryside wrought by collectivization. Here was a real man of the people, a "barefoot professor" lifted up by Soviet power, who was working on the pressing problem of feeding the masses.[13]

Lysenko attracted followers by promising immediate improvements in crop yields and by disparaging rivals. With the help of friendly journalists and the patronage of government officials, Lysenko gained positive press and access to scientific and political forums. In a 1935 speech that earned Stalin's applause, Lysenko adopted the leader's line on class warfare and asserted, "You know, comrades, wreckers and kulaks are located not only in your collective farms . . . They are just as dangerous, just as resolute in science . . . And whether he is in the academic world or not in the academic world, a class enemy is always a class enemy."[14] Lysenko heaped scorn on plant scientists whose works did not have immediate applications or who protested that long years of testing ought to be conducted before promoting new varieties of grain.

Lysenko has not been directly implicated in the arrest of the famous botanist Nikolai Vavilov or other biologists, but he endangered individual researchers by tarring them as saboteurs and Trotskyites. Although the persecution of geneticists dampened scientists' willingness to openly attack Lysenko, throughout the 1930s and into the 1940s many Soviet scientists persisted in defending the utility of Mendelian genetics. Lysenko, however, strengthened his position by promoting the notion that Western-generated theories could not be objective because they reflected the ideology of the capitalist society in which they were developed. Moreover, Lysenko exploited Stalin's antiforeign bias by tracing his own intellectual roots back to the work of the Russian plant breeder Ivan Michurin (1855–1935), a serious amateur horticulturalist praised by Lenin.[15]

Lysenko and Michurin did have in common their rejection of Mendel's "laws" of inheritance. Whereas Timofeev-Resovskii embraced the notion of the gene as a transmitter of inheritance and worked in concert with foreign scientists to study variability and mutation by experimenting on rapidly reproducing fruit flies, Michurin and Lysenko favored traditional, intuitive methods of plant breeding. In practice, as David Joravsky explains, this meant pitting the "gardener's conviction of the *immeasurable* diversity and plasticity of living things" against the geneticist's "proof of their *measurable* diversity and plasticity."[16] The first approach highlighted the possibility for controlled change; the second stressed the role of probability. Lysenko leaned toward the Lamarckian idea that changes in the parent organism would be replicated in the next generation and he postulated that heredity was the property of the entire living organism, rather than being confined to some special particle.[17]

In another system the clash of scientific theories might have worked itself out gradually and civilly though competition among scientists for funding, jobs, and publications and as farmers tested the advice of rival experts. In the USSR centralized financing, publishing, and decisions about what to plant empowered party officials. The plain-speaking and forceful Lysenko proved adept at maneuvering within this system, promoting his own candidacy for high posts within the Lenin All-Union Academy of Agricultural Science (VASKhNIL) and the Academy of Sciences and placing his supporters in research and academe. Although the geneticists gained occasional support against Lysenko's monopolistic tactics, their immediate postwar efforts to get party higher-ups to weigh in on the side of internationally recognized work on the gene backfired. At a special session of the VASKhNIL in July 1948, Lysenko revealed that the Central Committee had endorsed his position, which was based on a total repudiation of bourgeois "Weismannist-Morganist-Mendelist" genetics.[18]

With the party's official seal of approval, Lysenko routed his opponents. In the wake of the VASKhNIL conference, the minister of higher education denounced "home-grown Weismannists" and ordered their firing from universities. At Leningrad State University (LGU), the dean of the School of Biology (*biofak*) was fired, and his department for the study of animal genetics was abolished. Kol'tsov student and renowned zoologist Mikhail Zavadovskii lost his job at MGU and saw the section he headed disbanded. The Academy of Sciences shut several research centers and laboratories destroyed their specially bred populations of fruit flies while research geneticists scrambled to find inconspicuous niches where they might work on economically acceptable topics such as breeding silkworms.[19] Meanwhile, Lysenko's adherents took the places of fired geneticists in the universities and rewrote textbooks. At LGU the entire teaching staff of the School of Biology had to attend study sessions devoted to Lysenko's collected works, and MGU stopped teaching mathematics to its biology students lest they fall under the influence of Mendel's statistical model of heredity.[20]

Back on the Road to Miassovo

Timofeev-Resovskii's career also was affected by the upsurge in hostility toward capitalist countries and their scientists. In the 1930s Soviet authorities made a concentrated effort to recall Russian scientists working in the West. In 1934, for instance, the physicist Pyotr Kapitsa had to abandon his laboratory in Cambridge, England, when the Soviet government revoked his passport while he was vacationing in Russia. Appointed head of a Soviet institute, Kapitsa could no longer travel abroad. In 1937 Timofeev-Resovskii was also summoned to return. However, he and Elena heeded their mentor Kol'tsov, who passed a cautionary letter from through Swedish colleagues. As Timofeev-Resovskii explained in the 1970s: "We really wanted to return. And though we knew what was going on there, we still somewhat underestimated it. But our friends wrote us that return from overseas was presently possible only by going directly to the other world or, if one were really lucky, by going then straight to Magadan [a far eastern city home to many labor camps]."[21] Indeed, in 1937 the purges were raging—two of Timofeev-Resovskii's brothers had already fallen afoul of Soviet authorities—and Lysenko's attack on genetics was in full swing.[22]

When Timofeev-Resovskii politely declined the offer of repatriation, citing his desire to continue uninterrupted with his highly productive research, the Soviet consul responded by withholding the Timofeev-Resovskiis' passports. The family, including two sons, had to get German documents certifying them as legal foreign residents. Though offered German citizenship, Timofeev-Resovskii claims he begged off because he considered himself a Russian for better or for worse.

The German invasion of the USSR in 1941 mooted any question of Timofeev-Resovskii's return. Reportedly, he and Elena privately condemned the German attack, but they continued their work. The Institute of the Brain was a private foundation and it attempted to keep its independence in the face of Nazi suspicion—mistrust that arose in large part because of its long-standing ties with the USSR. Despite allegations to the contrary, Timofeev-Resovskii did not work on eugenics and no evidence has been found to suggest that he supported Nazi racial theories or engaged in defense related work. Despite the fact that his elder son Dmitrii (Foma) was arrested for belonging to a small underground left-wing group that propagandized among POWs and slave laborers from the East and disappeared into the Mauthausen concentration camp, the mere fact of having lived freely in Nazi Germany cast a permanent taint on Timofeev-Resovskii's reputation.[23]

At war's end Timofeev-Resovskii tried to salvage his laboratory and protect his coworkers by taking over directorship of the remnants of the Institute of the Brain and offering its services to the Soviet government. Timofeev-Resovskii recognized that his own work on radiation and mutations had the potential to be of use in the new atomic era—especially in the USSR, where study of heredity and mutation had been hampered by Lysenkoism. Yet even as the directorate in charge of the Soviet atomic bomb project began to inquire about Timofeev-Resovskii, other intelligence agents identified him as a dangerous traitor. In September 1945 Soviet secret police arrested Timofeev-Resovskii and quietly removed him to Moscow's Butyrka prison.[24]

Newly published documents from Timofeev-Resovskii's KGB file show that even under duress the scientist gave his interrogator calm and consistent accounts of his life and work abroad. Admitting that he had not complied with the order to return to the USSR, Timofeev-Resovskii denied charges of conspiring with White émigrés against the Soviet Union and of making anti-Soviet remarks. He hoped that a court would take into account his many scientific achievements, but his refusal to return in 1937 was categorized as treason and he was sentenced to ten years' incarceration plus five years' deprivation of civil rights. Sent to the massive Karaganda labor camp in Kazakhstan, he was nearly dead from starvation and pellagra when the atomic project's overseers finally accounted for him. Having realized that he could lead a team of Russian and German scientists in investigating the effects of radiation on plant and animal life, the Soviets now wanted to put him to work as soon as possible.[25] Hence, spring 1947 found Timofeev-Resovskii being nursed back to health in a special hospital. The biologist would later recall that his illness had progressed so far that he could remember only his first name and that of his wife. In time Timofeev-Resovskii recovered his memory, but his already poor eyesight was permanently impaired. His future writings would all have to be dictated to others.

Before he was even able to walk unaided, Timofeev-Resovskii was transferred to a new secret facility in the village of Sungul' in the Urals, where a former sanatorium had been converted into a laboratory. Together with some of his former German colleagues who had been "recruited" from the eastern zone, some young "free" Soviet scientists, a motley staff of local people, and other captive scientists—both German POWs and Russian prisoners—Timofeev-Resovskii began to work in earnest.[26] But first he wrote to his wife in Germany. Elena had not heard from him for a year and a half since his arrest. Now she read: "After a series of misadventures [*peripetii*], I am living at present as if in paradise, in lovely countryside, on the shore of a marvelous lake (full of fish), in a delightful house, with nice people." Assuring her that they would be able to continue their research, he asked her to send his personal items and copies of his publications and to pack their household and laboratory for the move.[27]

Villagers in Cheliabinsk Province greeted the arrival of German academics and Russian prisoner-scientists with suspicion. They were mystified to see such odd types housed in materially luxurious but otherwise prisonlike conditions. By local standards the scientists lived very well. The laboratory campus got electricity in 1949, two years before it arrived in the nearest town, Kasli. Moreover, scientists received daily allotments of meat, fish, oil, dairy products, barley, and even chocolate—whereas workers in Kasli made do with ration cards that guaranteed only 450 grams of bread per day. The scientists and their families also made an impression with their talents and hobbies. Their numbers included avid botanists and stamp collectors, pianists and chess players, a yachtsman, and even a figure skater. Depending on the season, the Sungul' families filled their leisure time with skiing, fishing, volleyball, and nature walks. They organized a choir, staged amateur theatricals, and even held ice hockey matches. But mostly they concentrated on science.[28]

The lab's status as part of the atomic project assured its workers access to resources necessary for their research. Isolation from the regular Soviet shortage economy even had its positive side, though at a price. As Elena would explain in a letter to a Moscow friend in 1954: "We have a separate cottage with five rooms, a bathroom and central heating, all just a five minute walk from work. We eat at home, but we pick up our meals from the dining hall. Three times a week a woman comes and cleans the whole place . . . but for 7 1/2 years I haven't attended a concert—frequently in my dreams I see myself entering a large concert hall and beholding [Sviatoslav] Richter sitting at the piano."[29] No one could enter or leave the compound encircling the laboratory, its offices, and staff housing without permission. Those who came to work there took an oath to keep state secrets, including the exact location of the lab. When Timofeev-Resovskii was "freed" early as reward for his "great successes in scientific research work" in 1951, he and family had to stay on in Sungul' in a sort of never-ending exile. Four years later, he would get a passport that allowed him to live in urban areas, but not rehabilitation.[30]

Only a decision from above to dissolve the Sungul' lab brought the Timofeev-Resovskiis the chance to relocate outside the cloak of secrecy. For nearly a decade after World War II, no one outside Sungul' and the offices of the Soviet atomic project knew of the family's fate. In spring 1954 the Timofeev-Resovskiis started corresponding with relatives and old friends, and in 1955 they settled in Sverdlovsk, where Elena had to accustom herself to standing in lines at the stores. Finally, in late November 1955, after sorting out housing, starting the process of publishing some results of their hidden work, and receiving new passports, Timofeev-Resovskii and his wife ventured to Moscow for the first time in thirty years. They were unsure of their reception given that most of their peers had no idea that they were alive, let alone in Russia.[31] To their great pleasure, they received a warm welcome from several prominent scholars, including their new acquaintances, the Liapunovs.

Mathematician and amateur geologist Aleksei Liapunov and his wife had been traveling near Miassovo in the summer of 1955 when they had heard from locals about the laboratory being set up there by Timofeev-Resovskii. Recognizing the biologist's double-barreled surname, Liapunov had sought an introduction through the geneticist Nikolai Dubinin, who himself had recently returned to Moscow after having spent the six years after VASKhNIL working as an ornithologist for the Institute of Forestry. An immediate friendship arose between the gregarious biologist and the curious mathematician. Indeed, Aleksei Liapunov hastened to invite Timofeev-Resovskii to speak at an informal seminar devoted to genetics that he and his daughters had been running from their apartment. Hence, on December 9, 1955, a group of about fifty persons, students as well as a few friends of the senior Liapunovs, squeezed in to hear Timofeev-Resovskii lecture on "biophysical analysis of the molecular size of genes."[32]

Another Road to Miassovo

Unbeknownst to the participants, the gathering at the Liapunovs' home was about to spark off a new clash in the battle with Lysenkoism. Stalin's death had not displaced his protégé. On the contrary, Khrushchev empathized with Lysenko and supported him till the end of his own reign in 1964. Nevertheless, as specialists in other disciplines maneuvered to "rehabilitate" topics or viewpoints taboo under Stalin, those frustrated with Lysenko's monopoly also acted. Most notably, in late autumn 1955, a group of Leningrad scientists composed a collective letter to the Central Committee sharply critiquing the development of a Lysenko "cult" and detailing how it had stunted the Soviet Union's agricultural productivity, damaged its overall scientific progress, and harmed its reputation in the world. The "Letter of 300"—whose signatories included biologists, mathematicians, chemists, and leading nuclear physicists—requested a change of leadership in the most important institutions of biology including VASKhNIL. The signatories further called on the party's ideological arbiters to withdraw their endorsement of Lysenko's views and to permit resumption of the study and teaching of genetics and cell development.[33]

In the letter's wake, in January 1956 the Academy of Sciences replaced the head of its section for biology—a Lysenko supporter—with an esteemed biochemist, who was interested in the workings of the cell. Yet February found Lysenko giving a speech at the Twentieth Party Congress. Moreover, in high schools and universities the curriculum for studying genetics remained a puree of Lysenko's statements.[34] While some researchers had found refuge under the wing of physicists and chemists, professors of biology continued to face intense pressure to conform to Lysenkoist doctrines in their classrooms.

Lysenkoism profoundly affected the training of biologists in the 1950s. Fifty-five years later, a student from the MGU entering class of

1954 could still vividly describe an experiment that he and other first year students had to conduct. They were meant to prove the inheritance of acquired characteristics by exchanging the whites from eggs belonging to a white hen and a speckled hen. According to Lysenko, the embryo (contained in the yolk) would be affected by the fluid surrounding it, and the resulting chick would no longer bear the coloring of its mother. None of the fifteen lab sections produced living chicks, and the instructor gave students a variety of explanations for their failure. Since there was no time to repeat the experiment, he told students to write down what the correct results should have been. "This is how Lysenkoists-Michurinists taught us how to falsify scientific results," Lev Kiselev reminisced. Many students entered MGU without the knowledge, tools, or confidence to question what they had been taught in school, but as the son of an eminent expert in viruses, Kiselev knew about Lysenko's detractors and recognized the deception.[35]

Mathematician Aleksei Liapunov's youngest daughters—Elena and Natal'ia—also entered the School of Biology at MGU with some idea of how ideological dictates had affected the study of science. Having grown up in an intellectual milieu of rare intensity with a father who was passionate about informal colloquia, the girls were accustomed questioning and testing hypotheses. They had formed their first study circle (kruzhok) as fourth and fifth graders. In their homegrown club, Natal'ia, Elena, and their friends had conducted elaborate experiments in biology and physics and had taken turns giving reports. As teens the sisters took part in formal circles for schoolchildren at Moscow's Darwin Museum and Moscow State University. Here the girls met other serious young scientists including Nikolai Vorontsov, Elena's future husband and later Gorbachev's minister of ecology.[36]

When the sisters decided to apply to the biology department at MGU, their father did not object despite his disdain for Lysenkoism. Like many other well-educated people, he was convinced that Lysenkoism was a temporary aberration given the value the party placed on scientific progress.[37] Although not a biologist, Aleksei Liapunov (1911–1973) was well placed to assess the state of Soviet science. A descendant of an intelligentsia family, Liapunov had a doctoral degree in mathematics and deep interests in geology and physics. In 1956 he was affiliated with the Academy of Sciences Applied Mathematics division, was teaching mathematics at MGU, and had begun to play a major role in developing the new field of cybernetics. He had also had acquaintances among Kol'tsov students. Hence Liapunov did not oppose his daughters' decision to study biology but rather sought to address the gaps in their education. As Natal'ia later recounted, however, "It soon became evident that he could not even explain Mendel's laws to us because we didn't know the principles of statistics. That's when the Liapunovs' home seminars were born."[38]

Starting in 1954 the girls invited fellow biology enthusiasts to form a new *kruzhok* that met in the Liapunov apartment. Aleksei Liapunov taught the students statistics and the basic principles of genetics. He also hit upon the idea of inviting out-of-favor geneticists of the Kol'tsov school to speak. Once a month or so the aspiring biologists would gather; one of them would give a report or a senior scientist would talk about his research, then all would have tea together. The study group expanded that fall when the girls made friends with other first-year biology students at MGU. At its largest—and last meeting—some fifty people gathered to hear Timofeev-Resovskii. The buzz among students about this unusual guest, however, came to the attention of vigilant Lysenkoists in the MGU *biofak,* and they initiated a departmental investigation of the sisters. Two months after Timofeev-Resovskii's talk on the gene, on the evening of the very day on which Nikita Khrushchev made his Secret Speech, Natal'ia and Elena found themselves in front of their classmates at a disciplinary meeting convened by the Komsomol.[39]

The girls faced three serious charges: creation of a secret organization, dissemination of "alien" approaches to genetics, and instigation of a split among the second-year class. The Liapunov sisters' acquaintance with Timofeev-Resovskii might not have had any open repercussions if it had taken the form of a personal visit—association with former political prisoners was perhaps unwise but not illegal. However, some campus authorities were incensed that a formal lesson had taken place within the context of an informal organization, a group that had carried on for over a year unbeknownst to university authorities. The department leadership referred to the *kruzhok* as an "underground" (*podpol'naia*) organization and accused the sisters of having "recruited" (*verbovali*) participants. In retrospect, the application of espionage terms sounds awkward, to wit the testimony of one repentant participant that he had been "seduced by the meals."[40] But the language of enemies and spies was familiar to those raised under Stalinism and was calculated to evoke alarm and revulsion.

The Liapunov sisters recall being shocked by the characterization of their domestic club as a subversive secret organization. Their father, a professor and party member (he had joined at the front during World War II), had always been involved in multiple study groups, several of which met at their home. Moreover, their *kruzhok* had been exploring mathematical and scientific topics—not conspiring. As Elena recounted many years later, the charges stung particularly because she and Natal'ia had led sheltered, "rosy" lives; they were used to being praised for their seriousness and diligence, not publicly rebuked. Natal'ia in particular had become accustomed to respect for her Komsomol activism. Freshman year she had been named organizer (*komsorg*) for their class; as a sophomore she served on the leadership bureau for her year and ran the newly restarted student science club.[41]

The department's party stalwarts, however, were outraged by the *kruzhok*'s study of Mendelian genetics. Here was a direct repudiation of strictures against practicing or propagating "bourgeois science." Moreover, as the sisters' Marxism-Leninism teacher observed, "They did not trust us, Soviet teachers, that we would teach them everything that is necessary, but wanted to find out something for themselves."[42] Indeed, the sisters wanted to learn about "normal" genetics, a subject so taboo that some wits in the Academy of Sciences jokingly dubbed the sisters' disciplinary hearing "a new monkey trial."[43]

While the Liapunovs could challenge the characterization of their group as an "underground organization," they could not honestly deny that they had promoted knowledge of classical genetics in knowing contradiction of the party's official line. When the department higher-ups initially summoned the sisters for questioning about the *kruzhok*, their father and his friends urged the girls to be diplomatic, even conformist, so as not to spoil their futures. Perhaps they could get off lightly by emphasizing the mathematical part of their activities. Study of statistics might have been deemed irrelevant for biology students, but it was not forbidden. Natal'ia did her best to stick to this line. But when asked outright if she disagreed with the VASKhNIL resolutions of 1948, Elena lost her temper and answered that she did. In so doing, she not only openly repudiated party doctrine but violated the standard practice of expressing repentance in the face of the official criticism.

In light of the sisters' obduracy, the Komsomol bureau summoned a meeting of the second-year class to hear charges against Elena and Natal'ia. By exposing the subterranean struggle against Lysenkoism, however, the school's leadership ended up spreading information about "normal" genetics. At the February 25 assembly, Elena's fiancé, recent MGU *biofak* graduate Nikolai Vorontsov, delivered a pithy description of the nature of modern genetics and an explanation of why proper understanding of the gene was essential in all areas of biology. For some students, this was the first time they had ever heard Western genetics expounded. To the even greater shock of the audience, a graduate student in mathematics dismissed the party's endorsement of the VASKhNIL resolution, declaring: "Who doesn't make mistakes? Even the Central Committee makes mistakes." This heresy so upset the attending deans and professors that they cleared the hall and readmitted only those who could show by their Komsomol cards that they were second-year biology students, some three hundred persons out of an estimated initial audience of five hundred. Those turned away included graduate students in biology as well as curious students from other fields.[44]

Natal'ia and Elena's fellow biology students were not unaware that Lysenko had detractors. Many disliked Lysenko's crude manner of speaking and his vituperative style. Moreover, since Stalin's death they had witnessed the unmasking of several pseudoscientists once hailed by the Soviet press.[45] Personal dislike for Lysenko, however, by no means equated to a disbelief in official teachings or rejection of party discipline over curriculum. Notes passed from the audience during the stormy meeting showed the sisters' critics to be upset by the apparent unorthodoxy of the *kruzhok* and the perceived secrecy surrounding its existence. In particular, Natal'ia's role as a Komsomol leader exacerbated students' anger. Clearly, she had said one thing at official meetings and another at home.[46]

By largely limiting their heretical studies of genetics to the private sphere, however, the Liapunovs consciously or unconsciously had chosen a nonconfrontational strategy for pursuing their scientific goals. They did not force their views on their classmates; they shared them with those they found sympathetic. They did not petition for a change in the curriculum—as some graduate students in the biology department had done that same spring.[47] Nor did they harass their teachers with politically sensitive questions. In fact, the sisters prized their reputations as serious students and devoted members of their course. At the hearing, however, the sisters' good deportment worked against them—it made their betrayal of political orthodoxy seem sinister.

Unmentioned at the meeting, however, was the dilemma that by party standards there were no acceptable means for young people to challenge Lysenkoism. Even the graduate students' unpublicized petition to change the curriculum had been judged unacceptable: "A letter—this is a form of hidden battle," the head of the School of Biology, Leonid Voronin, had charged at a closed party meeting. "Repressions, of course, shouldn't follow for this," he had added, "but it is necessary to renounce such a form of criticism."[48]

The final charge against the Liapunov sisters, that they had caused a "highly damaging . . . split in the collective of the course," makes sense only within the Soviet educational system. As we have seen, student collectives functioned as a means of mutual aid and supervision. The university authorities assumed that the selective nature of the Liapunovs' "secret society" had generated a faction within that year's course. But arguably a tacit divide already existed between those who knew science only from official discourse and those primarily from intelligentsia families who disregarded Lysenkoism. The "monkey trial" brought this split to the surface and worsened relations by forcing students to take sides. At the end of the meeting participants had to vote on the prepared resolution to expel Natal'ia and Elena from the Komsomol, an action that would have meant the sisters being forced out of the university as well.

By a majority vote, however, the more moderate sanctions—a reprimand to be noted in her personal file and removal of Natal'ia from the Komsomol bureau, a strict reprimand with notation for Elena, and a reprimand without notation for second-year *komsorg* Lev Kiselev—won out. The girls' peers had deemed their "crimes" insufficient to merit expulsion. Kiselev, though accused of "political shortsightedness and sheltering the members of the *kruzhok*, which is incompatible with the role model [*oblik*] of the Komsomol leader" was merely removed from the post of secretary.[49] The "professors' children" had received the benefit of the doubt as to their political reliability. The girls and Kiselev felt hostility from a vocal group of students, mainly from the less academic soil studies division, but as a professor of Marxism-Leninism angrily reported, thirty-two speakers had defended the *kruzhok* at the meeting and received "extraordinarily enthusiastic applause." The vote also may have reflected tolerance toward the idea of investigating the existence of the gene; after all, these students had chosen science as a profession. Several classmates later approached Natal'ia quietly and asked what they could read to learn about "real" genetics.[50]

The department's party bureau recognized that the "trial" had not united the students around Lysenkoism. At its meeting on March 20, 1956, the secretary of the *biofak* Komsomol, Sergei Ianushkevich, reported: "The discussion did little. It seems to me that the students have split even more."[51] Yet, in the wake of the Secret Speech, likely in combination with behind-the-scenes efforts by Aleksei Liapunov, the issue of the Liapunov home seminar was dropped that spring. The public dunning of the sisters, however, left lingering hard feelings among the second-year students. It also put the sisters in a difficult spot in terms of finishing their studies while under scrutiny from department conservatives. Elena sidestepped this unpleasantness by transferring to Leningrad State University that fall after marrying Vorontsov. Natal'ia stayed at MGU but found a mentor outside of its walls. She made the journey to Miassovo.

A Haven, Not a Retreat

Timofeev-Resovskii awaited his guests in Miassovo in the summer of 1956 in good spirits, though he, too, had spent an eventful spring. Timofeev-Resovskii's visit to Moscow in December of 1955 had not only triggered the case against the Liapunov sisters; it also exposed the biologist himself to opportunities and risks. Bolstered by their success in renewing contacts with friendly scientists, Timofeev-Resovskii and his wife had thrown themselves into raising the profile of their laboratory. To this end, Timofeev-Resovskii made a second trip to the capital in early February 1956 to take part in a conference on medical radiobiology. He also took up a request from the nuclear physicist Pyotr Kapitsa to speak at one of his famous biweekly seminars at the Institute of Physics Problems.[52]

Kapitsa asked Timofeev-Resovskii and prominent physicist Igor' Tamm to report on developments in genetics. Timofeev-Resovskii proposed to discuss the use of radiation dosages to stimulate the mutagenic process and a theory for predicting the size of genes.[53] Tamm offered to describe recent work in the West on modeling the chromosome. Watson and Crick had published their discovery of the double helix structure of DNA in April 1953, but their findings had passed without comment in the Soviet press. As Kapitsa's son Sergei would recall decades later, "Now, this is all written up in biology textbooks, but we were effectively learning about it for the first time." Sergei, himself a physicist, was in charge of organizing the Wednesday seminars and hence found himself at the center of the furor aroused by Timofeev-Resovskii's official thaw debut.[54]

According to Sergei Kapitsa, on the morning of the lecture, the institute switchboard was flooded with calls from various scientific institutions across the city inquiring about the seminar. He rushed to rearrange the hall to hold as many extra chairs as possible and to set up a relay so that the speakers could be heard in the building's foyer. Then: "One hour before the seminar I was stopped in the corridor by the Institute's Party organizer, V. Khoziainov, who said that great difficulties had arisen in connection with this session of the seminar and that N. S. Khrushchev himself was against it." Ascertaining that the "news" of Khrushchev's opposition had come from the local Moscow City Party Committee, Pyotr Kapitsa dialed the first secretary—as befit his position on the atomic project he had access to the Kremlin. Sergei listened as his father inquired as to whether Khrushchev had some objection to his having invited Timofeev-Resovskii to speak on "the problems of biology." According to Sergei, "Khrushchev fairly sharply retorted to the effect that you are the director of the institute, and you are conducting the seminar, why are you asking me?" Chastened, the institute's party representative hastened away, and Kapitsa convened the event.[55]

Kapitsa tried to defuse potential political conflict by giving a laudatory introduction that focused on the speakers' scientific achievements and allotting no time for questions. According to witnesses, Timofeev-Resovskii did not seem worried about possible attacks on his character or his work.[56] Lysenkoists, however, found his poise and his appearance among the elite nuclear physicists threatening. Several attendees complained afterward about what they perceived as the scientist's self-promotion. The archive of the Central Committee preserves a letter charging the following: "I saw [Timofeev-Resovskii] close-up after his report at the Institute. His face and eyes burned with spite. My impression is that he is not only not a friend, but an enemy [*nedrug*], who could turn out to be a dangerous traitor if allowed to settle in Moscow in the Academy of Sciences, close to atomic affairs."[57] The Central Committee's department for science responded by sending an inspection team to Sverdlovsk in the spring of 1956. With some help from powerful friends inside the Academy of Sciences, however, Timofeev-Resovskii's lab survived that scrutiny.[58]

Timofeev-Resovskii had witnessed several positive developments in the erosion of Lysenko's dominance in the spring of 1956, but he was well aware of the Liapunov sisters' troubles. The scandal at MGU highlighted the continued strength of ideological constraints in the universities. Scientists in the USSR, as Loren Graham explains, were "distributed in three gigantic pyramids, which for the sake of convenience can be called the 'university system,' the 'industrial and defense ministry system,' and the 'Academy of Sciences system.'" Lysenkoists were weakest in the industrial and defense sectors and strongest in the universities. (Though at the peak of Lysenkoism the order had come even at Sungul' to arrange special seminars devoted to Lysenko's ideas.) In 1956 Timofeev-Resovskii could not influence hiring in academe, but he could share what he knew. Hence he urged Aleksei Liapunov to come to Miassovo and to bring "all your young people."[59]

The extroverted Timofeev-Resovskii hailed the arrival of Moscow guests that July. His exuberant personality shone through in his reception of his visitors, especially Nina Balandina. The daughter of a prominent industrial chemist who twice had been imprisoned under Stalin, Balandina was studying mathematics at MGU in 1956. The Liapunovs had invited her to Miassovo in part to repay the hospitality her family had offered to Elena and Natal'ia, who had stayed at the Balandins' dacha earlier in the summer while doing practical work at MGU's field station outside Moscow. When Aleksei Liapunov introduced her as Aleksei Balandin's daughter, Timofeev-Resovskii happily exclaimed, "Oh, he is one of ours, a labor camp veteran [*O, eto zhe nash, lagernik*]." He sat Nina next to him at dinner, teased her about her choice of mathematics, and generally put her at ease.[60]

Fig. 07-02 Nina Balandina at Miassovo, summer of 1956. Courtesy Natalya Lyapunova-Yurii Bogdanov Family Archive.

In fact, Timofeev-Resovskii opened wide the doors to Miassovo. He wanted to foster communication across disciplines and he also saw each new acquaintance as a potential source of interest. Indeed, Aleksandr Solzhenitsyn in *The Gulag Archipelago* recalled the "most brilliant cell" in his prison odyssey as the one at Moscow's Butyrka where he was met by "a man who was middle-aged, broad-shouldered, yet very skinny, with a slightly aquiline nose"—this was Timofeev-Resovskii. He invited Solzhenitsyn to join "the Scientific and Technical Society of Cell 75" and inquired what sort of report he might be able to offer. The following morning, using a cigarette pack for a blackboard and writing with a contraband fragment of pencil lead, Solzhenitsyn gave an impromptu talk to a dozen inmates on the recently revealed details of the American atom bomb program.[61]

At Miassovo that first summer, Timofeev-Resovskii organized frequent colloquiums at which staff and guests alike presented their research. Looking back at her notebooks, Natal'ia Liapunova counted thirty such seminars—sometimes featuring two reports—from mid-July to early September. Her father spoke nine times on cybernetics, computer programming, and even theories of the formation of the earth. Geneticist Raisa Berg visited from Leningrad and gave several talks on her work on population genetics. Nina Balandina spoke about mathematical programming.[62]

For the scientifically curious, the Miassovo biostation was a small paradise despite the relatively primitive living conditions. The base consisted of a small two-story laboratory building, a house for the Timofeev-Resovskii family and their guests, and five cottages for the staff. As a matter of priority, the laboratory had already set up equipment to allow for testing of radioactive and chemical traces in water and soil. During the day everyone worked at their science, but in the evenings they came together through sports, seminars, or music, and at dinner. Given the distance from proper stores, meals at Miassovo were plain. That first summer, they dined mainly on potatoes, cucumbers, and tomatoes grown at the biostation, fish from the lake, and wild cherries or strawberries—a repast that inspired Timofeev-Resovskii to comment, "Silage. This is food for botanists, but I'm a zoologist, I need some real food."[63] The real treat at Miassovo was the conversation.

Fig. 07-03 Nikolai Timofeev-Resovskii (left) gestures to Anastasia Liapunova (center) and Natal'ia Liapunova (right) in the woods near Miassovo. Courtesy Natalya Lyapunova-Yurii Bogdanov Family Archive.

Address and dress at the biostation were polite and democratic. Casual dress went along with informality absent in Soviet academic institutions. Despite Marxist disdain for "class," rank played an important role in Soviet institutions. At Sungul', for instance, films had been shown in two sessions—the first reserved for officers, foreign scientists, and specialists. Timofeev-Resovskii, however, placed little stock in degrees and titles and eschewed bureaucracy.[64] Iurii Novozhenov, who came to the nature preserve in 1956 as a field biologist upon graduating from the Urals University, noted that the preserve's administrative center, where he was based, typified provincial life—"full of grumblings and petty intrigues." By contrast, at the biostation "everywhere reigned the spirit of freedom and creativity, the cult of science and knowledge, foreign languages, mathematics, physics, world culture, art, and much, much, more that makes a person an individual."[65]

Moreover, Novozhenov watched and learned from the style of discourse at Miassovo, which differed greatly from highly ritualistic public discussions. Novozhenov recalled: "N. V. Timofeev-Resovskii, like a rooster, pecked away at Liapunov, smashing his arguments, and the mathematician, who knew genetics quite well, would intelligently beat him back."[66] No angel, Timofeev-Resovskii could be brutally dismissive or brusque with those he considered frivolous or who made specious leaps of logic, but he never shrank from debate.[67]

Timofeev-Resovskii also assumed that science should know no borders. Less than a decade had passed since the campaign against those who "bowed down before the West." However, Timofeev-Resovskii blithely "propagandized" the names of other scientists regardless of their national origins or political standing. At Miassovo he often reminisced about Niels Bohr's international colloquiums, and in his study he hung his "iconostasis," a gallery of portraits of his favorite scientists, including Bohr, Kol'tsov, Vavilov, and Thomas Hunt Morgan—a collection of foreigners and apostates.[68]

New Kinds of Semifreedom

Miassovo proved to be a haven for those interested in genetics. Participants returned to their places of work and study that fall with a renewed energy and commitment to promoting what they saw as good science. Aleksei Liapunov expanded his study group in cybernetics and touted its promise in private and public. He also accepted invitations to speak about genetics and "biological mathematics" and prided himself on parrying questions from "Lysenkoids." Moreover, he played a driving role in the creation of a new Siberian science city, Akademgorodok, which would include an institute devoted to genetics.[69] Raisa Berg, who would later work there, spent the fall of 1956 promoting genetics in Leningrad. She arranged for Timofeev-Resovskii to lecture and aided biology students at LGU in securing permission for a course in proper genetics.[70]

Everywhere that he went, Timofeev-Resovskii let students know that they were welcome to come to Miassovo the next summer. Some could not believe a simple oral invitation was enough, but Miassovo did not require advance documentation or permission from some higher administration. One simply wrote to Timofeev-Resovskii and then showed up with camping gear. Already in 1957 forty-four persons, including a dozen MGU students, as well as young researchers from as far off as the Komi branch of the Academy of Sciences, came to hear short courses by Timofeev-Resovskii on the basics of biophysics and ionizing rays, an introduction to experimental and radiation genetics, and the fundamentals of microevolutionary processes, and to listen to Aleksei Liapunov on mathematics and biology. They also got practical training in radiation chemistry. By the time unfriendly officials shut the biostation to outsiders in 1963, up to one hundred persons were arriving each summer.[71]

In the fall of 1956, however, Natal'ia returned to a difficult environment at MGU. Indeed, when she sought to extend her summer stay at Miassovo for a few weeks to finish her experiments using the new technique of atom tracing to measure the accumulation of certain chemical elements in zooplankton, her adviser responded by telegram that she of all people ought not to risk giving anyone grounds to criticize her academic discipline. While some of her classmates would return from a long summer in the Virgin Lands with a greater sense of independence and a desire to reopen the case of the Liapunov home seminars with an eye toward reversing the vote of censure, many on the faculty remained hostile or frightened.[72]

Overall, the situation in biology in the fall of 1956 reflected the incomplete nature of the break with ideological monopolies. Khrushchev had won favor from scientists for loosening norms about secrecy and exchange of information with foreign experts. Moreover, Slava Gerovich argues persuasively that even Stalin in 1948 was leaning away from a "Criticize and Destroy" approach toward Western science toward the call to "Overtake and Surpass." Military foes had come to seem more dangerous than class enemies, and nuclear physicists, in particular, had made a case for the practical merits of building on the work of foreign scientists.[73]

While Timofeev-Resovskii and his pupils embraced such universal notions of science, however, Khrushchev stood with one foot in each camp. He desperately wanted to close the arms gap and reduce the divergence in standards of living between socialist and capitalist countries, but he also believed in the superiority of the Soviet ideology. Focused on increasing harvests, Khrushchev naturally gravitated toward Lysenko and his optimistic view of the possibility of transforming nature. "In a sense," Ethan Pollock argues, "both Lysenko and Khrushchev were anachronistic holdovers from the 1930s, when Marxism-Leninism had more to do with passion than logic."[74]

In 1959 Lysenko would persuade Khrushchev to approve personnel changes in his favor at scientific institutes and journals. In 1961 Khrushchev even restored Lysenko to the presidency of the VASKhNIL, from which Lysenko had stepped down in April 1956.[75] Yet Lysenko's resurgence did not resemble his victory in 1948. After 1956 work on genetics was never again cut off. Indeed, Mark Adams identifies a pattern that lasted through the thaw: "Initiatives originating within the Academy [of Sciences] tended to oppose Lysenko and support the development of molecular biology: when they became too critical or threatened the security of Lysenko's position, political forces intervened and the result was compromise." At the heart of the new compromise, however, lay a delinking of "Michurinist biology" and "physico-chemical biology"—each could develop separately.[76]

Although the negative impact of Lysenkoism on the advancement of genetics as a field of study and on the intellectual climate for science in general is evident, historian Loren Graham recommends that one consider the many ways in which science, nonetheless flourished in the Soviet Union. He concludes that the power of funding seems to have outweighed the lack of freedom and that frightening political times may have actually concentrated minds on science: "If one is trying to live through a whirlwind of violence while retaining some sense of integrity, science (especially the more abstract areas in which Russians excelled) provides a refuge . . . Science was the one activity that made sense of [many researchers'] lives, the one area where they could serve truth without automatically coming into conflict with the system."[77] Timofeev-Resovskii certainly embraced science as a constant and welcome distraction amid frightening political moments, but his area of study did not spare him from conflict with the system. On the contrary, the experience of geneticists in 1956 suggests that it was the collective reclamation of science from ideology that had a positive effect on motivation and determination.

The Liapunova sisters and many of their *kruzhok* friends would go on to outstanding careers in the sciences. Natal'ia and Elena both earned their PhDs and rose to head research programs in cellular genetics. Moreover, among specialists, association with the Liapunovs' *kruzhok* became a badge of honor. Eza Kaliaeva recalled interviewing for a position at the Institute of Atomic Energy. When her future boss learned that she was part of the Liapunovs' circle, he hired her on the spot.[78] Both the Liapunov *kruzhok* and the Miassovo summer school connected a new generation into powerful somewhat hidden networks without which it is impossible to understand how the Lysenkoist stranglehold on the discipline of biology was broken.[79]

Timofeev-Resovskii was key in bringing people together and modeling apolitical behavior. As Inna Molchanova, who went to work with Timofeev-Resovskii in 1957, recalled: "Timofeev-Resovskii didn't recruit [*ne verboval*] supporters; he didn't call on us to spit on our idiot-teachers, adherents of Michurinist biology. He simply suggested a different viewpoint on biological problems in his lectures and collaborative research clearly proved: it was he who was right."[80] Some of Timofeev-Resovskii's protégés were disappointed that their mentor did not attack Lysenko directly or spar with him. But Timofeev-Resovskii demurred, noting: "What can a surgeon armed with modern knowledge discuss with an old medicine woman?! They simply haven't got a common language."[81] He preferred to concentrate on doing science.

At Miassovo starting in 1956, Nikolai Timofeev-Resovskii and Aleksei Liapunov brought generations and disciplines together. For the next six years aspiring scientists would follow in Natal'ia's footsteps to soak up the atmosphere of intellectual freedom and internationalism created in the woods of the Il'mensk nature preserve. They would gain practical knowledge of laboratory techniques for working with fruit flies and using radioisotopes, as well as theoretical knowledge of genetics and evolution. Visitors also found role models for doing science. Timofeev-Resovskii's pupils would later compare themselves to pilgrims and even joke that in the beginning there was "the Word" and they heard the Word in Miassovo.[82] Here a decidedly unorthodox authority figure had revived a tradition of depoliticized inquiry and experimentation.

8 | AUGUST

BY THE SWEAT OF THEIR BROWS

Anatoly Gladilin also headed east beyond the Ural Mountains in the summer of 1956. "The press blared on about the glorious deeds of our youth at the building sites of communism," he later explained. "How could I, a young writer, not go to Siberia?" The administrators at the Literary Institute agreed. That summer they supplied willing students with third-class train tickets and a little money for the road. Gladilin set off with a press pass from the journal *Iunost'* to smooth his path and the outline of a novel already in his head. He wanted to follow up on his tale of the thwarted student with a story of another urban ne'er-do-well who would find his place on one of the heroic construction projects taken on by the Komsomol.[1]

Iulii Dunskii and Valerii Frid, meanwhile, had happily exchanged Inta and its mines for Moscow. Yet their debut project featured a raw engineering graduate sent to work in the Russian far north. In the opening scene, their hero, a young man, lightly dressed, rides on the back of a heavily loaded truck. In the distance, the shafts of coal mines can be seen jutting out from the muddy tundra. From the cabin of the truck a voice calls out, "Hey, Leningrad! Are you frozen? Didn't you know where you were going?" Sheepishly, the young man answers, "I thought—September, it will still be warm." The driver chides him,

"Here, for September they pay the northern bonus."[2] Though Dunskii and Frid had arrived in Inta involuntarily, they understood that for many Soviet moviegoers, especially young ones, the sparsely settled far reaches of the Soviet Union conjured up adventure and opportunity. With foreign travel a near-impossible dream, young Soviet citizens looked to the outskirts of their own civilization for undomesticated landscapes and the possibility to test their mettle.

The hinterlands also mattered to Communist Party planners, who sought to extract the nation's natural resources regardless of their locations, and military leaders, who saw a security rationale for building defense plants in remote spots. The goals of harnessing the Soviet Union's latent economic assets gave the party a strong incentive to invest in rallying young people to set out for challenging places. Throughout its existence, the Soviet regime had called on its citizens, and especially its youth, to tackle special tasks, whether to fight in the civil war, carry out collectivization, build industrial centers like Magnitogorsk, or defeat the Nazis. The prewar generations had responded. In 1937, for instance, young people by the tens of thousands had answered the summons from army wife and Komsomol activist Valentina Khetagurova directed especially at women to come to the Russian Far East to civilize and defend that Soviet border. Although many departed after only a few months because of the extreme shortage of housing, lack of ready work, and absences of basic goods, "Khetagurovaites" became the subjects of a romantic myth about patriotic young settlers.[3]

The generation that came of age in 1956 had been too young to really participate in either the war or recovery, but now their yearning for adventure dovetailed with Khrushchev's dream of rapid development. Khrushchev's confident view of socialism's economic potential, his penchant for large scale experiments, and the prosaic need to replace draft labor made him a fan of schemes to activate young people.[4] He also needed a signature project to help him consolidate his desired position as first among equals in the allegedly "revived" but in fact untested collective form of leadership. Hence, in the mid-1950s the party summoned youth foremost to cultivate the steppes, but also to harness wild rivers and build new industry. Starting in 1956 many who were preparing for professional careers took up the challenge of working in the Virgin Lands for a summer.

Here I examine the attraction and reality of working on the grand youth-oriented projects of the 1950s. Individual decisions to participate are hard to parse. As a woman who set off for Noril'sk in 1956 at age seventeen reminisced: "Some went for the mists, some for romance, and some for the money."[5] Yet historian Elena Shulman suggests that the collective responsiveness of those called on to make sacrifices indicates some depth of support and patriotism in the USSR.[6] I argue that the state-supported narrative—which in 1956 was not about combatting enemies but rather about building a bright future—matched with values inculcated in the young generation. Soviet youth received competing messages about the virtues of physical labor and white-collar success. Khrushchev's proposals for Komsomols to build hydroelectric stations in Siberia and settle the wild steppes promised young people a chance to prove themselves and to construct their ideal communities. Clean, modern settlements, volunteers imagined, could be created from scratch by their future inhabitants, who would mature alongside their towns and cities. Honest labor would lead them to ever more skilled jobs and higher standards of living.

Propaganda and popular culture contributed to high expectations of the periphery as a land of opportunity. Young people's experiences at far-flung outposts of the planned economy, however, would challenge their idealistic optimism. They would learn to rely on one another out of necessity as the state proved unready to provide the resources and management to maximize their labor or support basic needs. Problems with coordination of labor and supplies were inherent in the centrally planned Soviet economy, and in this regard 1956 was just one year of many. However, in 1956 encounters with the raw edges of agriculture and industry would be magnified as the party ramped up construction projects and responded to a bumper crop in the Virgin Lands by mobilizing hundreds of thousands of students, soldiers, and workers to help with the harvest and hundreds of journalists, writers, and artists to capture the heroic moments. The mass nature of participation and the high-profile propaganda campaign heightened the impact of contradictions between rhetoric and practices.

In outlining approaches to the study of Soviet culture of the Stalin era, literary scholar Eric Naiman has noted that one could profitably concentrate on "material remnants" of the time, or on the production of ideology, or on its consumption.[7] Here I incorporate all three—by looking at a film and a novel, the creative processes behind them, and some recipients of their messages. Triangulating between reflection, creation, and consumption can help capture what Naiman calls "ideological space," meaning "discourse in three dimensions, discourse through which the subject *moves*." "One might define ideological space," he contends, "as language (broadly conceived) that seeks to transform life on a poster into life on the skin." Yet he cautions, "Discourse can transform life into a poster, producing subjects all too aware of the ideological inadequacy of sham three-dimensionality."[8] Indeed, readers approached travel to new places with expectations shaped by ideological discourse and yet also with often unarticulated awareness that gaps between rhetoric and reality were common in the USSR.

In Anatoly Gladilin's second novel, *The Brigantine Raises Sail,* the author once again tackled the experience of an ordinary young person, this time a construction recruit. The novel's hero explicitly comments on variances between myth and reality in management of the economy, hence offering a glimpse into divergences between posters and life, so to speak, in 1956. Moreover, Gladilin subsequently revealed the problems he encountered in crafting a publishable text. The second cultural artifact was produced by Dunskii and Frid. At the age of thirty-four, they injected a more jaded view of grand economic projects into their film *The Incident at Mine 8* and mixed inspiration from life with their perceptions of what audiences and studio gatekeepers wanted. Last I turn to the difficult task of assessing young people's perceptions of the grand experiments before, during, and after their own encounters with them. To access student experiences in harvesting the Virgin Lands, I rely on post-Soviet memoirs, especially those based on diaries; archival materials; media coverage of the time; and a short documentary film made in 1956 by students from the Moscow Aviation Institute.

Young People in New Places

In the 1930s a popular theme in film and fiction involved a person from the periphery making his or her way to Moscow and achieving renown in the capital. Moscow represented the height of modernity, a magical place where all sorts of wonders of technology and consumption could be seen.[9] For Anatoly Gladilin in 1956, however, Moscow seemed staid and confining. His heroes—boys and girls alike—feel smothered by the weight of parental care and control. Even marriage offers no escape since housing shortages usually meant moving in with one set of parents. Independence requires radical steps. Hence *The Brigantine Raises Sail* starts with eighteen-year-old Vovka Andrianov chucking in his factory job in Moscow to go toil on a big construction project (*stroika*) sponsored by the Komsomol.

Frustration not patriotism motivates Vovka to cast aside a stable urban existence for the promise of a hard job in a tough place. Tired of the cramped communal apartment, where his girlfriend, Liusia, shares a single room with her mother, and the courtyard of his own building, where neighbors scrutinize his every action, Vovka sees the *stroika* as an opportunity to start an independent life, preferably with Liusia. Her horrified mother, however, exclaims, "He must have been thieving. Why else would he run away from Moscow?" After all, in past decades, Russians had left cities mostly under duress—hunger, arrest, deportation, or the proximity of battle. She certainly is not dreaming of life on the fringes of society, and she pressures Liusia not to go.[10]

As he travels eastward by train over the course of several days, Vovka has time to mull his choice. On the one hand, he's angry and heartsick that Liusia's mother persuaded her to wait and see how Vovka gets settled. On the other hand, he is full of bravado about his resolution to swap his routine existence for the unknown. He sings to himself a popular song from the 1930s, "The Brigantine Raises Sail," about swashbucklers heading off to sea. Not for him a suit and tie to start his grown-up life. Although Vovka thinks he is wise to the romantic myths trumpeted by writers, he still expects to be building an ideal community with like-minded boys and girls. Moreover, he imagines himself earning a lot of money and carrying out some noteworthy feats.

Being surrounded by other young people in an unsettled place is an important part of Vovka's vision of his new life. At the *stroika*, he is sure, young people will organize things their own way, and toughness will earn him respect. Recruiters for the grand building schemes, whether for hydroelectric dams in Siberia, smelters in Noril'sk, or the untilled grasslands of Kazakhstan, purposely emphasized both the youth composition of the workforce and the novelty of the projects. To this end, as

historian Michaela Pohl has observed, the party created a false image of the "Virgin Lands" as empty spaces when often they were used by Kazakh herders or dairy farmers. Similarly, many of the Komsomol *stroiki* had their own Stalinist pasts. The polar mining town of Noril'sk, for instance, arose in the 1930s as an extractive labor camp, and construction of the Irkutsk Hydroelectric Station started in the early 1950s using forced labor.[11]

Biisk, Gladilin's destination in the summer of 1956, had been identified in the early 1950s as a good site for a weapons complex. Construction of chemical factories and facilities for an influx of workers had begun there in the summer of 1953 with battalions of draftees followed by prisoner labor. Meanwhile, similar workforces were building the secret outposts of the USSR's nuclear program. The bosses on these hush-hush projects were not Komsomol idealists, but experienced military and party veterans who had supervised military conversion of industry during the war and built northern railroads with prison labor. The remote locations for the new secret defense plants meant planners relied heavily on soldiers and convicts who could be moved where needed. Only in 1956 did the mass mobilization of young people fill a significant gap left by reductions in the use of these labor forces.[12]

For the Virgin Lands campaign launched in 1954, as well as in the later recruitment drive for the *stroiki*, the Komsomol invited and screened applicants. The ceremonial awarding of the *komsomol'skaia putevka*, a special travel voucher, created a sense of exclusivity. It certified the party-state's faith in the ability and commitment of the applicant and conveyed authorization to relocate—key for peasants who at the time did not have passports and hence could not register to live in towns or cities.[13] In turn, recruits put themselves in the party's hands. One Leningrader assigned to the secret Biisk chemical plant remembered her excitement in October 1956: "In the morning, we, who were just schoolgirls the day before, got our first money. Of course, we ran around to the stores buying everything—felt boots, pots and pans, galoshes, cereal, guitars. We acquired things in such quantities as if we were planning to

Fig. 08-01 Young Muscovites recruited by the Komsomol on their way to build the artic city of Noril'sk, 1956. Photograph by M. Red'kin. Courtesy Moscow Central Archive of Audiovisual Documents.

move to a deserted island."[14] The remoteness of the destination was part of the thrill, and the party relied on writers, especially those working for youth publications, to stir up excitement.

The journal *Iunost'*, which published Gladilin's first novel, printed many stories and sketches from the Virgin Lands and the new construction sites. The November 1956 issue, for instance, featured a selection of letters home from Muscovites who had gone off to work in Magadan, Krasnoiarsk, Komsomol'sk-na-Amur, and other distant locales. Letter writers assured their friends, families, and former workmates that that they were living well, getting their bearings, and beginning to earn. They averred that they were inspired rather than frightened by the prospect of building everything themselves. One girl recounted quitting a post as a secretary to work in a group of female painters on the building sites. She wanted camaraderie and the promised challenge of mastering new skills.[15] The myth of the *stroiki* made hard labor a coveted privilege, at least in theory.

Gladilin, however, tried from the start to establish that Vovka's tale would not match the rosy stereotypes propagated by the press. He subtitled his story "the history of an unlucky guy [*neudachnik*]" and made Vovka self-pitying and prickly. From the first moments of his trip, he finds signs of his "bad luck" at every turn. Traveling east without Liusia, he grumbles: "All respectable people are going to Noril'sk, to Magadan, to the Far East."[16] Vovka's destination—Biisk—was an unprepossessing small city in the Altai region. Founded as a garrison town in the time of Peter I, Biisk was a regional transportation hub with a rail connection to Moscow and a road link to Mongolia. However, the city had little infrastructure to accommodate a population influx. In 1956 it had no trams and only limited bus service. Enterprises used open trucks to transport people and supplies along mostly unpaved roads. Workers at the chemical plant slept in barracks and ate in canteens. Large apartment blocks had yet to make an appearance, and the city's housing stock was already severely overtaxed.[17] Gladilin's hero notices shabby buildings, drunks in the streets, and a ludicrously irrelevant poster advising people to save their money for a trip to a resort.[18]

Amenities, or more accurately the lack thereof, figure large in Vovka's first impressions of the *stroika*. He gets off on the wrong foot with the overworked local Komsomol boss, who shames Vovka and his roommates when they grouse about the lack of an electric kettle. They should be grateful that they have a more or less regular supply of electricity and that they are not living in tents like the first arrivals did. He makes the malcontents feel like spoiled children, exactly the mold they are trying to escape. Vovka, however, strikes back. He grabs an old issue of a newspaper and declaims a pathos-filled poem about young people packing for the road ready to achieve great feats (*podvigi*). Now it is the Komsomol organizer's turn to feel defensive—he hesitates to criticize a published work, but he recognizes the falsity of its exalted tone given the truly mundane nature of the work on offer.[19]

By drawing a contrast between official rhetoric and the blunt talk of local bosses, Gladilin strikes one of his main themes. He wants his heroes to be ordinary, but not "typical"—to resemble the author and his friends and not the allegedly perfect average Soviet youth depicted in propaganda. His characters are moody, self-interested, and always sensitive to trite phrases. Liusia, for instance, laughs when her mother wants to know why Vovka did not come to her explain that he was setting off "out of patriotic motivations."[20] Vovka scorns the official youth leadership on the site largely for their clichéd talk. Yet when his workmates choose him to be their new brigadier, he finds himself relying on the same hackneyed language to motivate others. His role shifts, but he is trapped in the same ideological space—an uncomfortable, flawed poster boy.[21]

The Brigantine Raises Sail displays the anxieties as well as the aspirations of young urban settlers. On one of his first nights in the Altai, Vovka is struck with fear when a rumor spreads that hooligans are going to storm the girls' dormitory because one of the Moscow belles has refused to dance with a local lad. He and his new acquaintances panic at first, cursing the Komsomol bosses off in their safe apartments, but then rally and keep watch over the girls' barrack until the wee hours of the morning. After the night passes without incident, Vovka morosely wishes there had been a clash—he imagines himself heroically wounded, with Liusia flying to his side. With his characteristic mocking humor, Gladilin shows the urban adventurers juggling feelings of neglect and aspirations to be self-reliant. The young men are united and invigorated by their brush with hardship, but it is not the kind of adversity that the party wanted to advertise.

In all seriousness, the Muscovites' first reaction to the specter of an angry gang of "locals" reveals something about the new settlements. When Vovka tries to rally his friends by repeating the familiar trope about having known about the hardships when they signed up, one guy retorts, "I'm ready to work, just let them get rid of the locals," by which he means those who arrived at the construction site before the Komsomol began to issue *putevki*. The "free workers" (so called to distinguish them from prison laborers) also tended to be young but came from nearby villages or were ex-cons or demobilized soldiers. The urbanites considered the "locals" to be uncultured and violence-prone.[22] Gladilin may have also drawn on stories about brawling by special contingents of soldiers mobilized for construction. Such units had become very popular with planners as the availability of gulag labor declined, but often served as dumping grounds for draftees with criminal records, physical ailments, or behavioral issues as well as those from non-Slavic republics. Historian Vladimir Kozlov has documented numerous cases in which such units created violent disturbances, including one in Biisk in December 1955 that resulted in some five hundred soldiers being removed from the city.[23]

In contrast to draft labor, Komsomol recruits if treated decently might see themselves as heroic founders of new cities, not exploited labor. Urban youth especially were meant to be a civilizing force on the periphery. The influx of builders and specialists at the various *stroiki* did provide the stimulus and the volunteer labor for construction of clubhouses, libraries, sports fields, and theaters.[24] In the short term, however, familiar Komsomol remedies for addressing boredom, promiscuity, and hooliganism—shipments of musical instruments, chess sets, and sports equipment—did little to distract from drinking and card playing. Gladilin does not denigrate spontaneous fun for the urban youth—Vovka enjoys playing DJ with a record player propped up on the windowsill so that couples can dance on the rough dirt square outside the dorm. But for Zina, a village girl, he provides a drama club so that once she tires of empty flirtations she can improve herself in readiness for being part of a new community of enlightened workers.

Work, of course, lay at the center of Gladilin's coming-of-age story. Vovka expects it to be strenuous but fulfilling. He assumes he will be damming a river or building an important factory. Unlucky Vovka, however, is assigned to unload trucks at a wood-processing plant. He understands that the mill's lumber will be used to build houses, furniture, and so forth, but he struggles to find anything romantic about the tedious job. Moreover, being a loader turns out to be poorly paid and contingent on the supply chain. If the trucks don't arrive with logs to be processed, the workers' pay is docked for lack of productivity. The director tries to console the angry Muscovites: "A shortage of lumber means a shortage of work. Next month, please God, it'll be better." He reassures them, "If it's possible—gradually, we'll fix you guys up to work by specialty or send you off to more interesting work, or for training."[25] Vovka subsequently has a dream in which God shouts into a phone about needing supplies urgently. Humor aside, the director was the highest authority in the locale with tremendous responsibilities and enormous power over his subordinates. Vovka knows it is wise to steer clear of conflict with management, yet he ends up in the middle of a scandal.

Vovka's trouble starts on one of his early days at the site when he learns that the girls in the plasterers' brigade are kicking in ten rubles a month to their brigadier, who "looks out for them." The girls sheepishly admit that their boss originally said it was for treats for the collective, but in reality it lines his pocket. They do not protest because they know he could make their lives miserable. Vovka asks Zina, "Why have you kept silent?" But when she challenges him to confront the offender, he chickens out. An older youth, Losev, later extracts the story from Vovka and shames him and Zina, the girl who spilled the secret. Doesn't Zina know that "besides your brigadier, there's also Soviet power"? Zina defensively retorts, "Well, so they say. But where is it?" Losev whistles and replies, "I can't believe I lived to see this day. Soviet power has gone missing. By the way, you know what it is. It's you, Vovka, [and the lads], and me, and [the Komsomol organizer]—all of us together."[26] With this atypically trite line, Gladilin provokes Vovka into revealing the wrongdoing and unleashing a scandal.

A standard story of the day might have concluded on a high note with Vovka having become a leader on the site. However, Gladilin ends his tale with Vovka receiving a letter from Liusia explaining that she's not coming to join him, she's marrying someone else. Vovka reads her missive while traveling by truck on a supply expedition. He absorbs the emotional blow by concentrating on the dangerous road. At that moment snowcapped mountains come into sight, and he thinks about how they look like the white sails of a huge ship. As in *The Chronicle of the Times of Viktor Podgursky,* the ending is very ambiguous. Does the vision of sails refer to the title and imply Vovka is just starting his adventure? The reader is left in the middle of a lonely road near the Mongolian border wondering what Vovka will do next. Moreover, the tale of the *stroika* also remains incomplete. The loaders are still just wrangling logs and the reader has not seen any objects built as a result of their labor.

The unusual nature of Gladilin's plot can best be seen in contrast with a novella written by another Literary Institute student who spent the summer of 1956 on a *stroika.* Published in *Iunost'* in July 1957, *The Continuation of a Legend: Notes of a Young Man* by Gladilin's slightly older classmate Anatolii Kuznetsov also featured an unsure youth. Drawing on a summer spent working at the site of the Irkutsk Hydroelectric Station, Kuznetsov as well started with a journey, strove for realism and took self-discovery as his theme. His more traditional hero, however, is appropriately awed by the Siberian landscape, the tremendous activity on the construction site, and the energy to be generated by the wild rivers. Kuznetsov's protagonist gets into the top brigade of cement workers, struggles to master physical tasks, but witnesses the release of the penned up Angara river to run through the works. At the end, he is dreaming of the next construction site and contemplating a correspondence course in engineering.[27] Although he is not making revolution, he is following in the footsteps of early Komsomols by adopting the party's new mission.

Kuznetsov's book has no plot lines about conflict with Komsomol leaders or site bosses. A vivid paean to the hardiness of Soviet people, it mentions shortages but has a powerful image of success. For Gladilin, the *stroika* could not be the star of his story given the secret nature of the object where he worked—most likely the Biisk Chemical Complex, which produced fuel and explosives for the Soviet army. In retrospect, he wished he had followed Kuznetsov's tactic of toiling the whole summer as an ordinary worker instead of leveraging his correspondent's credentials to roam the site and ride along with long-distance truckers. Still, Gladilin did not regret his choice of harsh material. As he later wrote: "In the clash with actual reality, all romance was completely shattered. I saw that the guys from Moscow and Leningrad had come to Biisk with the best of intentions . . . They sought a truly worthy life. They were ready for primitive surroundings. But they got the dirty work, they were cheated on their pay, and the press, instead of helping the Komsomol volunteers, lied shamelessly." He admitted, "The 'Altai material' wouldn't listen and led me off in completely the wrong direction."[28]

The difficulties of presenting a realistic but upbeat portrait of *stroiki* can be better understood with an examination of three documents from 1956 preserved in the Komsomol archives—a collective letter from 216 disgruntled "patriots" at the Bratsk Hydroelectric Station, a subsequent inspection report, as well as a report from a commission that visited several *stroiki* in eastern Kazakhstan, just south of Biisk. Complaints from young workers at the lumber-processing section of the Bratsk project in December 1956 included: unwinterized barracks, frequent power outages, lack of newspapers and journals, low wages, and expensive meals. The recruits reported that at every turn they were met with incompetence, corruption, and price gouging. Moreover, they lived in fear of prisoners from a nearby camp who had permission to move about without guards. The letter writers admitted that hungry recruits often refused to turn out to work, but the situation, they argued, was exacerbated by local authorities, who responded to their complaints by asking: "Why did you come here? We didn't summon you! You were driven out of Moscow and turned up here."[29]

An investigation of the letter turned up rampant disorganization in Bratsk. Inspectors confirmed instances of low wages and improper deductions. They reported having shamed the site's bosses into getting heating for the dormitories, subsidizing the cafeteria food, and firing a crooked bookkeeper. However, having found that among 259 workers in the lumber unit, 59 had worked fewer than ten days in the month of October, they chastised the youth for "a parasitic lifestyle." They also rebuked girls who had formed relationships with prisoners, and listed by name some young men who drank and refused to work unless they got higher wages.[30]

Commissioners who toured five major projects in eastern Kazakhstan in August 1956 found even worse conditions. None of the construction trusts were meeting their plan, and workers often stood idle for lack of materials. Given problems with supplies and organization, local bosses had no interest in taking in new recruits. As a result, they sometimes took upward of two weeks to process the paperwork for new arrivals. A paucity of opportunities to learn higher paying skills and catastrophically poor housing conditions led to considerable turnover. At one construction trust, 4,721 workers had arrived over the course of the year, but 4,288 had left for various reasons.[31]

In Bratsk the inspectors issued party reprimands to site bosses and sent in extra Komsomol workers to get the young people to bring order to the dormitories and organize constructive leisure activities. They offered no solutions for the underlying problems created by poor planning, scant resources, and lack of mechanisms for accountability. Nor did the other oversight team reflect (at least in writing) on the costs and benefits of the policy of shipping large numbers of untrained youth to distant worksites where they could not easily be housed, fed, trained, or efficiently deployed. Clubs and sporting equipment were not going to solve the problems with this centrally run distribution of labor. And the cost of such mismanagement came not just in rubles lost or construction delays but in the morale of a generation of enthusiasts.

In the Footsteps of Prisoners

Dunskii and Frid also targeted a youth audience with *The Incident at Mine 8*, but they started out well aware that they could not tell the full story of polar projects. Nevertheless, they introduced a definite political message into their tale of generational conflict. *The Incident at Mine 8* revolves around the experiences of a graduate of Leningrad's prestigious Mining Institute who has been assigned to work in a coal town in the arctic north.

Having hitched a ride on the back of a supply truck, Volodia Batanin arrives at his new posting as an enormous sinkhole has opened up with mud and water flooding into a mine tunnel. A black sedan pulls up and disgorges a man wearing a suit and fedora. As Batanin watches, the well-dressed mine director storms into the crowd, summons the elderly geologist responsible for the site, and fires him. Then, looking about for some lumber with which to try to stem the collapse, he orders the demolition of a nearby house. As workers rush to pull down the ramshackle cabin—to the mute dismay of its residents—Batanin pushes forward to suggest dumping flour to thicken the mud and stop its flow. When asked where they're to get flour from, he announces, "I just rode in on it." To the distress of the driver, who has his own boss to report to, all the men form a chain to unload the sacks of flour and dump them into the sinkhole.[32] It seems the protagonist is off to a fine start, yet the seeds of conflict have already been laid.

Batanin disagrees with how the mine director, Kraev, has treated the old geologist—in the screenplay it is clear he is an ex-prisoner who has stayed on in the north. Moreover, eager to publicize the success of the experiment with the flour, Batanin writes an account of the accident's resolution for a local newspaper. The article puts Kraev in an awkward position—he had not reported the sinkhole, preferring not to invite outside scrutiny of his fiefdom. Finally, conflict looms in attitudes toward work and reporting. The young engineer is a fan of new methods of planning that are supposed to allow a steadier tempo of production and predictable work schedules, rather than the lulls and frenzies common as socialist enterprises gathered materials and then stormed to meet their quotas. The mine has adopted the new method only on paper and, despite his developing romance with Kraev's daughter, Batanin refuses to certify otherwise.

Originally titled *The Commissar of the Mines,* the screenplay centers on the conflict between the autocratic mine director and the egalitarian young engineer. Kraev cares deeply about "his" mine; he wants it to fulfill its quotas and in the process to earn bonuses for the workers. But he does not want to admit to any mistakes. His management style is evident in the clash over the article about the sinkhole. Kraev rationalizes that news of an accident will discourage young workers from wanting to come north, while Batanin insists Soviet youth do not need fake advertisements. But when he begins, "I personally think . . ." Kraev cuts him off. "Ha! You 'personally think.' I think for the state [*Ia po-gosudarstvennomu dumaiu*]. Not about myself, but about everyone!"

Kraev is not presented as entirely bad. Though he now lives in a luxurious cottage, the townspeople remember how he lived with his family in a tent while they built the first structures. Older workers assure Batanin that Kraev used to be more open and compassionate. Dunskii and Frid imply that Kraev, like Stalin, had his head turned by the weight of his responsibility.[33] They illustrate his evolution in a melodramatic scene in which Kraev's daughter Alla points out how he has changed by noting that there are no recent photos of them together in the family scrapbook. Kraev snatches the album from her and slowly turns the pages. But she is right. In the early days, he was always with family and friends; now each image shows him alone, standing on a tribune, or receiving an award.

The character of Kraev had roots not only in national politics but in Dunskii's and Frid's lives. They modeled their "little Stalin" on the NKVD colonel who headed up the coal enterprise in Inta where they served out the final years of their sentences. "Such a boss, in practice, was not subordinate to the *raikom* or the *obkom* [local or regional party committees]— he was tsar and god in the purest form," Frid recalled. When the film was shot on location, Dunskii and Frid had the exterior of their former colonel's villa serve as Kraev's house. It and another similar one, both belonging to NKVD officers, were famous among the locals who mostly lived in barracks and shanties.[34] To become a proper heroine, Kraev's daughter has to acknowledge her privileged home and abandon it.

The film also depicted a generational division regarding idealism that was bound to resonate with Soviet youth. Batanin and Alla, Kraev's daughter, both feel sorry for the fired geologist. But when Alla asks her father if he is sure the geologist is to blame for the cave-in, she hears: "There are not accidents without guilty parties. And everyone should know that young lady. I have to think about everyone, and not just your geologist." Here, Kraev makes excuses for his hasty cruelty and repeats a common sentiment of the Stalin era that justified arrests. Batanin, by contrast, questions and pushes back against drastic punishments. After admitting, "Well, perhaps the geologist permitted some carelessness [*khalatnost'*]," Batanin asks, "Should he be buried alive for that?" He answers his own question: "If a person wants to work—let him work. And that's how it's written in the Constitution." In 1956 Dunskii and Frid could remind people about their rights and authorities about young workers' expectations of fairness.

Dunskii and Frid modeled the kindhearted Batanin on their friend Mikhail Shvarts, who arrived at "Inta Coal" in 1951 to find a hybrid institution—a mining enterprise combined with a camp for "especially dangerous state criminals." The recent graduate was to head up the planning department of one of the mines where the personnel consisted of eleven hundred prisoners and two hundred "free workers," the majority of whom were former prisoners. For Shvarts, acquaintance with Frid and Dunskii was eye-opening—he had been warned that the inmates consisted largely of murderers and wartime collaborators. In turn, Dunskii and Frid admired Shvarts's goodhearted nature. For the film, they used the character of the geologist to allude to the gulag roots of northern towns and imagined how Shvarts's arrival in a post-Stalin Inta might have raised uncomfortable questions about the past and the present.[35]

In *The Incident at Mine 8* Dunskii and Frid drew out the differences between old-style Stalinists and new thinkers. For instance, whereas Kraev will not make time to deal with the people whose house he ordered destroyed during the attempt to stem the sinkhole, Batanin insists that the fired geologist stay in and share the apartment that has just been reassigned to the young engineer. Yet in resolving the clash of generations, Dunskii and Frid were careful not to have the young hero get full credit for changing the management of the mine. The party secretary plays a key intermediary role, including parrying Kraev's scornful question about how long he has been in the party by asking "Don't you think, dear comrade, that it's important not just when you became a Communist, but to what year you remained a Communist?" And the turning point is set at an open party meeting when a worker stands up and asks why Kraev, who arrived late, automatically took a seat on stage in the meeting's presidium. Another adds, "Who elected him? That doesn't seem right [*Ne krasivo poluchaetsia*]." Kraev wordlessly rises and leaves the stage, and at that moment it is clear that his undemocratic tendencies are no longer wanted in the modernizing city.

In a discussion after a screening of the first cut of the movie in September 1957, members of Mosfilm's Artistic Council disagreed sharply about the merits of the film as a whole and the final scene in particular. The experienced director Mikhail Kalatozov objected to the depiction of party members as "human wolves, eating one another." But for the screenwriters, as well as the film's director, the meeting scene contained the picture's moral heart. Indeed, those who liked the film admired the tension that it created and its resolution. Director Mikhail Romm defended the film precisely because "[it] presents a sharp theme in essence about the battle with the remnants of the cult of personality in everyday practices."[36] By subjecting a "little Stalin" to the will of the collective, Dunskii and Frid had drawn a line between old ways and new. They had cleared the frontier for the new generation of idealists that was moving to the periphery.

Sowing the Steppe (with Wild Oats)

Hundreds of thousands of young people really were on the move in the summer of 1956—including students and young workers who flocked to the Altai and Kazakhstan to help bring in a record harvest of grain that resulted from Khrushchev's ambitious project to address the Soviet Union's chronic shortages of bread. Khrushchev had decided in 1954 that it would be easier to mobilize new resources than to try to make existing kolkhozes more efficient and so he pulled together young people and new equipment for large scale agriculture in previously untilled places.[37] Given that the Virgin Lands project ultimately produced a very uneven record in terms of harvests and had a negative impact on the environment, its merits remain a subject of debate.[38] In 1956, however, the big problem was how to collect, transport, and store the bounty generated by the confluence of good topsoil, excellent weather, and huge inputs of machinery and once-fallow land.

Between 1954 and 1956 the Komsomol sent more than three hundred thousand settlers to the Virgin Lands. Not all the recruits stayed, but the expansion of old farms and creation of new ones meant the acreage of sown land increased tremendously, more than doubling Khrushchev's initial target of thirty-two million acres by the end of 1956 and requiring for the first time that temporary harvest workers be assembled to augment the inflow of settlers. The call went out for volunteers to pack: "a pillowcase, light blanket, sheets, warm clothing . . . sturdy work shoes, a raincoat, knife, spoon, mug, a brush, razor and whatever other toiletries they think necessary," and by mid-July the Komsomol could report that 150,000 persons had arrived to bolster the local workforce.[39] The Komsomol liked to deploy students because they had long summer vacations and, though few university students were attracted by the long-term prospects of agricultural life, many were enthusiastic about a brief trip with a worthy goal. Unlike trips to local state farms to help dig potatoes, here students could see new places and even earn some money.[40]

At MGU and other institutes, there were more volunteers than spots in 1956. As philologist Irina Matveeva recalled, even the language reflected the desirability of the trip; people spoke of "obtaining" a *putevka*.[41] Both documents from the time and reminiscences invoke a spirit of gaiety. A documentary made by students at the Moscow Aviation Institute in the summer of 1956 shows travelers gathering with bed rolls and backpacks. One smiling youth wears strings of *bubliki*—a sort of hard, dry bagel—looped around his neck. At MGU train cars were pulled up to the Lenin Hills using a special spur that had been built to transport building supplies for the construction of the new campus. Matveeva notes that students were not daunted by the sight of the converted goods wagons that would carry them to Kazakhstan. "Many of us were acquainted with such train cars from wartime (many had been in evacuation) and hence we were not that surprised by the lack of comfort, and quickly tossing our rucksacks up on the bunks," she recalled. "The whole philology crowd spilled out onto the platform to listen to our farewell speeches and to sing."[42]

Popular songs of the day included rousing numbers touting the policy of sending youth off to settle new places. Viktor Lamm, a chemistry student at Moscow's Mendeleev Institute, even remembers singing about how "and just like the hero in a novel, we're off to raise the Virgin Lands." Along the way students composed and shared new own ditties. Matveeva reproduces the MGU historians' ode:

> Along the long and boring road,
> Along a long and boring road,
> Ten days we shook on the bunks
> And we sang to the accordion
> And drank just a little
> And strummed on guitars.[43]

Such songs helped pass the time as the young people traveled slowly since their trains had to yield to scheduled passenger and freight trains.

On the way east, students subsisted on canned goods and meals at soldiers' canteens in stations along the way. "July 6. Life on the road is

Fig. 08-02 MGU students setting off to work in the Virgin Lands, July 1956. Courtesy Russian State Film and Photo Archive.

becoming a habit," Matveeva observed. "We even sleep quite nicely on the boards with four thin layers of blankets. In the mornings you get a mug full of water to wash with. We manage to wash and clean our teeth. At the stations they pour you as much water as you want while the train is stopped." Provision of water was a major concern, in fact, since the converted freight wagons had no infrastructure for storing water. Komsomol authorities also struggled to get students fed as their trains often arrived at those stations with canteens at unpredictable times and odd hours.[44]

The students journeyed thousands of kilometers, passing through many small stations and scruffy towns without electricity before they saw the Kazakh "sea of wheat." "It ripples like the ocean, only without white caps," one young man noted in his diary.[45] The stalks stood as high as a man's chest and the fields stretched out to the horizons. Indeed, the MGU students were astounded to learn that their host farm "covered a territory the size of Belgium."[46]

The MGU students arrived in Kazakhstan with the expectation of austere living conditions, and they were not disappointed. In 1956 the philologists slept on straw-filled sacks in a single long tentlike building that housed some 150 from their university. Groups from other institutes lived in small tents, schools, clubs, or even caravans without proper roofs. In Altai, where farms covered smaller territories, students often bunked with families. The philologists did not mind being housed all together, but they hated the dust that seeped in through every crack and the masses of flies that descended as they dined on endless bowls of macaroni.

Based in the midst of a large farm, the MGU students encountered few locals—with the exception of the traveling combine drivers, who memorably swiped the students' mugs and bowls, which when recovered stank of "Triple Cologne," popular for its alcoholic content. Other students noticed some villages with distinctive architecture and reticent dwellers, but did not always recognize "special settlers" from Slavic borderlands as such. Chechen and Ingush deportees stood out, but students were generally unaware of the significant presence of ex-convicts among state farm employees—though Valery Soyfer learned his farm's boss had formerly managed a prison camp. More commonly, students encountered other temporary laborers and native Kazakhs. Galia Osipova and her fellow students from the Moscow State Pedagogical Institute made friends with the Kazakh children in whose school they lodged and with the soldiers assigned to the harvest—even though the latter teased them for their conscientious approach to work.[47]

The philologists initially cut hay for animal fodder and prepared the threshing floor, while MGU biology students worked without gloves to pull chest-high weeds from beet fields. When the harvest began in earnest, students drove combines or rode atop the threshers, worked at threshing points, and transferred grain to the elevators, which often meant loading and unloading trucks by hand. Ironically, the hardest physical work—loading grain using shovels or small conveyer belts—often went to the girls, while the boys operated the heavy machinery. In the course of a day a single student might load or unload tons of grain. Work on the machinery could be painful too. Matveeva describes how riding on the threshing apparatus, where she had to fork the grain into stacks, left her black and blue.[48]

Despite the grind, students found a little time for recreation. The philologists formed a club called "BURT." A play on the word for *haystack,* the acronym stood for "We will Attain Reason, Comrades." Its "events" included fellow students lecturing on ballet and the works of Prokofiev, the latter accompanied by a whistling rendition of themes from the composer's works. More commonly, students played soccer or volleyball on courts they made themselves and if they had windup record players, they held dances right in the fields, putting on the same few records over and over. Lamm recalled, "Once we held an 'evening of reminiscences about the cult of personality'" which ended "with the choral rendition of songs about Stalin, which many then still remembered."[49]

The respite from adult supervision allowed for more frank conversation, but it meant students had minimal support to address the many problems that arose. For the MGU contingent, the first serious issue was the "threat of hunger." After a few days, the state farm (*sovkhoz*) authorities announced that the students would have to pay for food; only tea would be served for free. Students, however, arrived with little spending money—indeed, given the unpredictable length of the journey, some student brigades ran short before they even reached their destinations. Only after sending a telegram to the university authorities asking for help did the MGU Komsomol representative get farm authorities to

Fig. 08-03 Student volunteers working on a state farm in the Kostanai region of Kazakhstan in the summer of 1956. Photograph by Semyon Fridlyand. Courtesy Dalbey Photographic Collection at the University of Denver.

agree to feed the students against their future earnings. In a similar conflict, Leningrad student Aleksandr Genkin's group briefly and effectively went on strike. Other groups kept costs down by purchasing provisions and cooking for themselves over open fires.[50] Once again lack of planning and shortages made young volunteers feel unwelcome, but students with their preexisting bonds and confidence found ways to cooperate and maneuver to address their problems.

Like the young recruits to the *stroiki*, Virgin Lands' volunteers also faced disappointment regarding wages. Authorities sometimes cheated students in calculating how much work had been done and some labor was valued very low. According to historian Ol'ga Gerasimova, the wage for loading fifteen tons of grain by hand was only 80 kopecks.[51] Those working on the harvesting machines or driving trucks earned significantly more. Given the gender division in assignment of tasks, this meant

that men typically outearned women. Here one can find students deciding how to arrange their affairs in a "just" fashion: Matveeva's group,
which had few boys, organized themselves so that the girl scholarship
students were the ones to work on the harvesting machines, while a
group from the Mendeleev Institute pooled their earnings. A student
from this institute recalled that as a result, after paying for food, he had
640 rubles left, the equivalent of two months' worth of his student
stipend—enough that "one could buy a good suit, or two pairs of very nice
boots, or a decent radio or bicycle."[52]

Students also confronted worn, unreliable equipment. Since 1954 the
Virgin Lands had gotten the majority of tractors and combines produced in the USSR, but by 1956 much of the machinery was in bad
shape. Future geneticist Valery Soyfer recalls that he and a friend who
had been a mechanic in the army accepted the challenge of assembling
a working tractor from the remains of dozens of combines and tractors
that had been broken in the past year. Given the high value put on
mechanization as key to realizing large-scale farming, they were shocked
by the neglect. However, Khrushchev had not considered how technology would be preserved given that the new farms often lacked barns
or garages. Moreover, the equipment was employed intensively on the
massive farms—harvesters often worked two shifts, reaping late into
the night by the headlights of their vehicles. Wear and tear led to frequent breakdowns and the lack of skilled mechanics meant that often
the settlers simply abandoned machines. Locals, Soyfer noted, covered
up the situation by making junkyards "in spots far from the roads and
invisible from them. . . . the bosses never delved into the depths of the
endless fields; from the windows of their cars they could see only the
array of crops."[53]

Students were also often bedeviled by inefficiency and idleness. Many
arrived in mid-July, when the academic calendar freed them up, only to
find nothing ready for harvest. The first scene of student labor in the
MAI documentary, not coincidentally, shows young women working on
some sort of construction project with the narrator cheerfully noting
that though these women are preparing to be aeronautical engineers,
they will always remember their first work experience as plasterers in the
Virgin Lands. Out of boredom, Soyfer and his friends designed and built
an irrigation system to make possible a vegetable garden for their farm.

Other groups painted schools and built outbuildings, though often farm leaders did not want to trust them with the supplies necessary to tackle big projects.[54]

The most distressing aspect of the 1956 harvest in the Virgin Lands, however, was the enormous waste. Authorities were unprepared to reap, transport, and store a record grain harvest—which outstripped the previous year by 20 percent overall, with much of the increase due to the Virgin Lands. In 1957, owing to drought conditions, grain totals for the Virgin Lands would drop by 40 percent.[55] Yet in 1956, even two hundred thousand temporary workers were not enough to harvest all the fields. In places, farmers simply plowed under corn and wheat.[56] Students' awe at seeing mountains of grain—especially after hungry years of wartime and reconstruction—turned to dismay as they witnessed the wheat they had collected begin to spoil as it sat exposed to damp air or watched it blow away from the back of open trucks. Although they did not know it, the poor storage of grain along the way would also reduce its usefulness for making bread.[57]

The new settlers and the squads of soldiers on loan witnessed the worst of the waste in 1956 as they stayed on after the student volunteers went home. Witnesses recall the heat that radiated from shoulder-high heaps of decomposing grain. Fifty years after the opening of the Virgin Lands, writer Anatolii Strelyani, who went as a settler in 1956 and worked in a brigade of tractor drivers, admitted that not only was it agonizing to watch the grain rot but humiliating to dump it in ravines so that higher authorities would not see it. He recalled, "This is a serious suffering, and anger grows in you, despair." He blamed officials all the way up to Khrushchev himself.[58]

Student harvesters for the most part ended their adventures on a lighter note. For the MGU philologists, there was an outing to Lake Issyk and an excursion to Alma-Ata, where students bought exotic melons and crates of apples to take home. For MGU history students, however, the trip back from Lake Issyk was marred by a road accident in which three were killed and many seriously injured. The philologists returned to Moscow by regular passenger train, trying not to spend what was left of their meager earnings. Matveeva notes, "Moscow met us like heroes. And honestly, we felt ourselves to be heroes, though we did not want to admit it."[59] This pride in their own ability to labor intensively and cooperatively partially negated their disappointment with the uncivilized economy and poor management rampant in the new settlements.

For those who went to the Virgin Lands in 1956 as temporary visitors, feelings of achievement and adventure could assuage memories of waste and disarray. The students recalled the hardships but laughed at themselves. In a skit at MGU that fall the philologists performed a comic song about struggling to start up a tractor and had their audience in stitches with a display of "Virgin Lands Fashion"—a fellow wearing an unbuttoned plaid shirt, long johns for pants, and rubber boots. In truth, they had worn their clothes to rags. Perhaps the most often retold anecdote among the MGU group came from an encounter with a young reporter from the central Kazakh press, who went into raptures over the philologists' "multinational" brigade, which included students from Lithuania, Belarus, and Georgia. When she asked one female student: "Do you have romanticism?" she heard in response: "No, we have diarrhea."[60] Students suffered tremendously from stomach ailments caused by brackish water and conjunctivitis due to the dust, but they took pride in their nonchalance.

Optimism, however, had in fact taken a beating on the steppes as evident in the lessons derived by Komsomol organizers from the first Virgin Lands summer. At a postmortem conducted by the Bureau of Propaganda and Agitation that fall, leaders of brigades from Moscow factories, institutes, and universities listed common problems concerning living conditions. More troubling to the young people, however, was the poor organization of work, with some farm directors "insuring" themselves by taking more people than they needed and others unprepared for an influx of helpers. Moreover, they reported encountering rampant corruption, especially in the dining halls. One activist bemoaned that the local prosecutor would not receive him when he tried to complain about "barbaric theft." Komsomol superiors back in Moscow had also failed to respond to grievances about pay disputes. Finally, the hands-on leaders denounced "whitewashing" by the media and the creation of "Potemkin villages." One participant scornfully noted that local shops put out all sorts of scarce goods for the visit of the Minister of State Farms, while oil and sugar that were supposed to go to the students were diverted to local bigwigs. Injustices were rampant and the young activists had learned that they had little leverage when it came to advocating for their charges.[61]

Tarnished Romanticism

The official press heralded Soviet youth as hardy, cheerful patriots, while depicting their far-flung destinations as romantic. What did romanticism mean in the USSR in 1956? In response to a letter complaining about the dullness of Komsomol activities in schools, the editors of *Iunost'* answered: "And what is *romantika*? Is it necessarily some kind of underground activity? Or a distant path? Or sleeping in the woods? Or shadowing an enemy agent on the border? What about the feat of those who founded Komsomol'sk-na-Amur? Or the lives of the Virgin Land settlers? Or what's happening right now with the youth movement to the construction sites of the North, East and Donbass? This is also romanticism . . . So, the essence of our revolutionary romanticism lies in selfless service to the people and in brave and stubborn overcoming of difficulties on the path to communism." Romanticism, then, lay in one's attitude toward labor. The state provided the opportunity for modern day youth to serve the revolution, but the nature of the experience depended on participants.[62]

For young people, however, the setting and conditions for service also affected its appeal. The high school students who wrote to *Iunost'* did not want to do community projects in their neighborhoods. Thanks in no large part to journalists and creative writers, work seemed more attractive when connected to some distant and grand project that had been specifically entrusted to youth. Enthusiastic volunteers were part of Khrushchev's scheme to revitalize the party. However, firsthand views of massive waste and inefficiency sparked questions about the projects themselves. The 1957 MGU student brigade would be stunned by the half-meter layer of rotten grain mixed with dirt that remained on the threshing floor at their Virgin Lands farm. Konstantin Levykin, a graduate student sent by the history department to supervise, dutifully attributed the spoilage to problems with technology and transport; but his explanation only aroused more queries, culminating with an inquiry as to why it was even necessary to expend so much effort sowing the Virgin Lands if the resultant harvest would just be wasted. Alarmed that the conversation was turning into an inappropriate debate, Levykin instructed the students: "The local authorities saw the faults in the current situation, were taking necessary steps, while vigorously seeking radical measures from the central leadership in support of the Virgin Lands so to meet the country's demand for bread."[63]

The 1956 student pioneers had happily traveled without supervision. Indeed, the very idea that by leaving the parental nest and journeying to remote places youngsters would grow into weighty responsibility had inspired Gladilin. His heroes wanted to conquer obstacles and build a more just society. On the *stroiki* and in the Virgin Lands, youth did have to improvise as they looked for solutions to their various problems with living conditions and organization of work. But, as Gladilin's sojourn in Biisk revealed, such hardships were not the only hindrances. Gladilin knew there would be a gap between propaganda materials and the conditions on the ground, but he did not anticipate the corruption and callousness from the project's leaders, nor the poverty and crassness of the local populations.

The frontiers of Soviet society turned out not to be a blank slate for the Komsomol to write on, but rather the rough edges of Soviet society. The grand construction sites were run with standard practices of the planned economy—including demands for speed and disregard for workers' safety and comfort. Political campaigns to send masses of new recruits clashed with the economic reality of enterprises unready to employ them efficiently, let alone house and feed them properly. Corruption and bureaucracy characterized big projects and bosses were likely to be cut from Stalinist cloth, used to dealing with prison labor. Hence, Gladilin's hero had to grow up in unexpected ways—Vovka's feat of strength turned out to be moral, not physical. The author too faced an unexpected challenge—how to make his disillusionment palpable to his target audience and yet palatable to publishers and censors.

Gladilin left Biisk with his sense of himself as a savvy operator shaken. In the spring of 1957, his confidence would take another blow when the major literary journals all rejected *The Brigantine Raises Sail*. Some of the reviewers asserted that the novel was full of ideological errors, and an experienced editor warned Gladilin that it was too "dreary." When Gladilin retorted that it was grim because life in Biisk had been that way, the veteran editor urged: "Take my advice, I'm trying to help you.

Go ahead, leave your favorite pages, but you've got to 'interleave' them with brighter episodes. Draw us a zebra—black stripe, bright stripe, black stripe, bright stripe . . . Step back—and you've got an objective picture."[64] Gladilin's hope to once again act as a mirror for his generation clashed with the establishment's commitment to depicting life as it ought to be.

Gladilin had no qualms about letting his hero struggle to envision the city of the future when around him he could only see "dirty streets, drunks and brawls."[65] His writing fit the newly emerging genre of youth prose in which, as literary scholar Richard Borden notes, "Gone was the 'objective' narrative of socialist realism, replaced by the subjectivity of first-person narrators, unsure of themselves, but unwilling to rely on external authority to validate their impressions . . . Without their parents' fixed 'truths' . . . space was cleared for doubt and puzzlement, leading to epistemological ambiguity and relativity."[66] Gladilin's intended audience approved. A soldier sent to help with the harvest in the Virgin Lands in 1956 recalled decades later that while his platoon waited to be redeployed he read out loud *The Chronicle of the Times of Viktor Podgursky*. "We were all different, but still this was about us."[67] It would take another burst of liberalism in 1959, however, to get Gladilin's "dreary" tale about the construction site to readers.

Dunskii and Frid were also well aware of the need to tread carefully with the studio's ideologically vigilant review board. Taking a more traditional approach to storytelling, they wrote *The Incident at Mine 8* with little ambiguity in the characters or the plot. Their goal was to use a conventionally idealistic young hero to point out the painful persistence of "little Stalins." While the plot may have been melodramatic and somewhat trite, Dunskii and Frid took pride in the democratizing tone of the film's ending and in the inclusion of details from their years in Inta. By alluding to the important role of forced labor in the city's history and shooting it in Inta, Dunskii and Frid grounded the film in reality and exercised power over their own past.

Frid later noted that there were several "freethinking" pictures in the works at the Moscow Film studio in 1957, but most of them were derailed by the Hungarian events. He and Dunskii were lucky that their screenplay had been accepted in 1956 and that their director was a speedy worker. He managed to finish shooting before the backlash could endanger production. As it was, they had to edit and maneuver to get the film launched successfully.[68] Gladilin, too, ultimately decided: "I really got very lucky with *The Chronicle of the Times*. It was published in September and two months later—after the Hungarian events— would most likely not have been published at all. And I was even luckier that . . . the so-called 'serious critics' simply didn't take note of it. And for that reason there was no rout [*razgrom*] as with another novel that also had huge success with the readers and 'success' with the critics—*Not by Bread Alone* by Dudintsev."[69] The thaw had its own ambiguity, as writers and young people alike would find out in the fall of 1956.

9 | SEPTEMBER

OCEAN BREEZES

In fall 1956 the writer Konstantin Paustovskii sat in a small wooden cottage on the banks of the river Oka in the village of Tarusa and thought about Paris. He and his wife had sought out a country home so that the writer could retreat from the hubbub and interruptions of Moscow life, and Paustovskii was using the respite to try to capture some lessons from what had been for him an extraordinary month. From September 4 to the end of the month he had sailed around Europe along with several hundred other handpicked representatives of Soviet society on the cruise ship *Pobeda* (Victory). For the sixty-four-year-old Paustovskii, a best-selling novelist and short story writer known for his lyrical writing about nature and travel, this was his first real encounter with Europe.

Although his novels and his memoir *Story of a Life* had been translated into many languages, Paustovskii had no firsthand experience of the wider world. Now he exhorted his fellow citizens: "If you want to be true sons of your country and the whole earth, people of knowledge and spiritual freedom, people of bravery and humanity, of labor and struggle, people creating spiritual values, then you must be true to the muse of distant journeys and you must travel to the extent of your strength and free time. For every journey is an entry into the realm of the meaningful and the beautiful."[1] The notion that travel can be enriching is hardly original. But for Soviet citizens in 1956, the concept of seeking out other cultures as a civic and moral duty was novel. In the USSR journeys abroad had long been a rarity, and not just for curious intellectuals.

Under Stalin, Nikita Khrushchev had been stymied in his desire to see more of the world, but 1956 found him on the move. Khrushchev's schedule that year included a flurry of unplanned foreign trips starting with a visit to Warsaw in March for the funeral of the first secretary of the Polish communist party, who had died in Moscow following the Secret Speech, and ending with a round of frantic shuttle diplomacy in Eastern Europe in October and November as he to tried to hold the socialist alliance together. In between, however, Khrushchev made a much anticipated trip to Great Britain, his first prolonged foray into the capitalist world. Khrushchev toured Britain with verve tempered by anxiety as he strove to promulgate a fresh image of a competitive, confident, and more open Soviet Union. He went to London to promote conciliation based on a position of perceived strength. After all, the Soviet Union now had socialist allies, including China, while Western countries faced mounting anticolonialism. More important than his diplomatic efforts, I argue, was his eagerness to engage friends and foes alike. Khrushchev's barnstorming approach to travel reflected his mounting self-assurance, innate inquisitiveness, and his acquisitiveness regarding technological advancements—all traits that supported an opening in the so-called Iron Curtain.[2]

Both Soviet delegations and tourist groups followed on Khrushchev's heels that summer. Such trips reflected a propaganda barrage aimed at Western audiences but also testified to a genuine shift in attitude and policy toward the merits of overseas travel. Indeed, in January 1956 the Central Committee had decreed: "Soviet tourists should be sent abroad not only for recreation but to acquaint themselves with the lives of other peoples and with the accomplishments of foreign science and technology." Given that a just few years prior Soviets were arrested for praising foreign technology and barred from marrying foreigners, such an admission of the practical benefits of contact with other societies marked a sharp about-face and one that could be implemented quickly. In 1955 outgoing tourism was planned for 1,500 persons visiting other socialist countries; 1956 saw some 561,000 Soviets traveling abroad with a small percentage able to visit noncommunist countries. Paustovskii and the some 1,500 others who sailed that year on four voyages by the steamship *Pobeda* to visit Bulgaria, Turkey, Greece, Italy, France, the Netherlands, and Sweden were among that lucky minority.[3]

While the fortunate few cruised on the *Pobeda,* back at home, jazz musician Leonid Utesov offered a series of concerts entitled "Around Europe for 3.80 [3 rubles and 80 kopeks]." The price referred to the average cost of a ticket to listen to Utesov as he performed foreign melodies and his own compositions—a cheap thrill compared with a trip to Paris. Utesov's jest captured a relaxation of official hostility toward Western artistic products, one that allowed a large number of Soviet citizens to learn about and connect with other cultures without leaving home. Soviets had long enjoyed a small selection of Western "trophy films" acquired during World War II, but in 1956 urbanites could stand in line to see exhibitions of Western art and vie for tickets to shows by the touring American Everyman Opera or the Boston Symphony. Owners of televisions—a new luxury available only in some cities—could catch first time broadcasts by foreign ambassadors.[4]

The possibilities of meeting foreigners also rose as the number of incoming travelers increased. 1956 saw 487,000 foreign tourists arriving in the USSR—more than quadruple the number from 1955, while in May alone Khrushchev received delegations from France, Indonesia, Britain, and Denmark.[5] Most Soviet citizens, however, encountered the outside world via media representations. Indeed, I argue that an important part of the deal that allowed a fortunate few to visit Europe was the unwritten rule that they would "pay" for the privilege by acting as informal ambassadors while abroad and by conveying carefully curated impressions to domestic audiences. The curtain on the West was not to be flung open willy-nilly; trusted and influential persons would mediate the exposure for the mass audience. An examination of travelers, therefore, can capture elite reactions and the message presented for public consumption.

Two notable encounters took place between Soviets and the West in 1956: Khrushchev's maiden trip to Great Britain in April and the four *Pobeda* cruises that took place from June to October. The first secretary himself was testing the waters to see how Stalin's heirs could manage in front of sophisticated and potentially antagonistic audiences. I argue that while the Khrushchev vacillated between confident openness and churlish defensiveness, his innate optimism not only propelled him forward but led to the experiment in trusting mature socialist citizens to resist ideological and consumerist temptations. The tourists were guinea pigs testing the wisdom of a partial and controlled opening up to the outside world. In three weeks of cruising, they would learn a lot about other ways of life and about themselves. After all, the experience of being a traveler is one of constant comparison between here and there. The Soviet creative intelligentsia would fulfil its assignment of filtering impressions of the West in their subsequent travelogues. Paustovskii, for one, however, would return envious of others' freedom of movement and deeply critical of the pro-Soviet chauvinism displayed by some of his countrymen.

Khrushchev on the Loose

The number one Soviet traveler in 1956 was Nikita Khrushchev. Before Stalin's death, Khrushchev had seen little of the world. The only exception was an incognito visit in 1946 to Soviet-occupied Germany, Czecho-slovakia, Hungary, and Austria to inspect technology that might be adapted for use at home. Then Khrushchev had hustled to examine everything from paving brick production to mechanized laundries. The frustrated engineer-turned-party-boss had found intriguing potential imports at every turn.[6] Yearnings to venture further afield, however, were disappointed. While Stalin valued Khrushchev's loyalty and managerial prowess, he chose more polished and less impulsive members of his inner circle to represent the Soviet state in rare dealings that involved travel to the West.

Stalin's death and Khrushchev's subsequent maneuvering to become first among equals in the new collective leadership, however, placed the curious and energetic new first secretary in a position to make up for lost time. By 1956 he had visited many of the USSR's socialist allies, including Yugoslavia and China, as well as the developing nations of India, Burma, and Afghanistan. In July 1955 Khrushchev also got his first taste of representing the USSR in negotiations with its capitalist counterparts as a member of the Soviet delegation for talks with the United States, Great Britain, and France in Geneva.

Khrushchev fretted over his reception in Geneva not only because of his inexperience in diplomacy but also because as head of the Communist Party he technically lacked standing among Western heads of state. As a matter of protocol, he had to defer to Nikolai Bulganin, who, as chairman of the USSR Council of Ministers, was formally the head of state. Though little of substance was accomplished at the four-power talks, they left Khrushchev feeling as if he had passed an exam. He did not speak at the negotiating sessions, but in the afterhours socializing his status as a leader was recognized. He came away relieved that the delegation had avoided major gaffes and guardedly optimistic that cooperation might be possible. The "mutual probing," he believed, had shown his former wartime allies that "we were worthy representatives of our country, that we were prepared to defend the gains of our revolution and defend the agreements made as a result of the defeat of Germany."[7]

Khrushchev's fear of embarrassment and of being deceived by foreigners can be attributed to more than lack of experience and Cold War tensions. Stalin had habitually denigrated his associates' foreign policy skills. Khrushchev recalled being invited to dinners for visiting dignitaries where—like a child—he was allowed to observe but not speak. Moreover, Stalin frequently chided his subordinates for their alleged lack of vigilance and savvy. As Khrushchev admitted in an off-the-cuff speech in Poland in March 1956, "[Stalin] sincerely told us when he was feeling weak, that . . . 'You're blind kittens. You're not able to see the enemy. I'll die and the State will die, because of you.'"[8] In 1956, coming off the successful organization of the Twentieth Party Congress, Khrushchev felt more confident about stepping out from Stalin's still-long shadow. Yet his curiosity about the West remained tempered with fear. According to his son, having received an invitation to visit Britain, Khrushchev was excited but uncertain of his reception. Concerned to avoid any humiliation, Khrushchev sent his fellow presidium member and sometimes rival Georgy Malenkov to tour Britain first.

Malenkov, who had initially assumed the important role of chairman of the Council of Ministers after Stalin's demise, had been shunted in 1955 into a lesser office—minister of electric power generation. In this capacity, Malenkov took up an invitation from his British counterparts March 1956 to learn about energy production in England. The *Times* of London noted with some amusement that Malenkov detoured from his official program for an impromptu visit to the home of a worker whom he met while touring a power plant in Fleetwood. It also recounted that he stopped to examine a caravan being pulled by a car, commenting: "We have not seen anything like that in Russia." Here one can see an effort not to be duped by officially arranged itineraries as well as a sincere interest in the lives of English workers and a genuine curiosity about "foreign marvels." As Khrushchev's son later noted, for the Soviet leaders in the 1950s visits abroad were as much about making discoveries of how others solved common problems as they were about official negotiations.[9]

When Malenkov reported that he had been greeted warmly by both officials and common people, Khrushchev was reassured. He also took seriously Malenkov's news about British efforts to develop nuclear power. Khrushchev aimed to impress. If the British were interested in nuclear research, Khrushchev would bring one of the Soviet experts of the day. He also included leading Soviet aviation designer Andrei Tupolev, who had addressed an embarrassing memory of the 1955 Geneva trip when Khrushchev had been aghast to realize that the Soviet delegation's two-engine plane looked puny on the tarmac next to the four-engine aircraft used by the Americans, French, and British. Tupolev had since engineered a passenger jet of impressive size and power. Unfortunately, the new TU-104 jet had not undergone sufficient testing to be deemed safe for the leadership to use in April 1956. But it would make several flights back and forth between Moscow and London during the course of the visit ostensibly to carry mail and the queen would delight her guests when she mentioned the jet admiringly.[10]

Rather than fly to Britain on a less prestigious aircraft, Khrushchev chose to transport his delegation on a new naval cruiser. The sea voyage also gave Khrushchev time to bone up on preparations, including protocol, which bedeviled the Soviets at every stage of planning. For instance, the British Embassy asked to send a naval attaché along on the sea leg of Khrushchev's journey. When inquiries revealed that this was a common practice, Khrushchev acquiesced—to the horror of the naval brasses who did not want to allow prying eyes onto a base or their new cruiser. The question of what to wear for the royal audience also vexed Khrushchev who neither owned nor wished to wear a tailcoat—the traditional garb of the bourgeoisie in Soviet caricatures. When told a dark suit would be acceptable, Khrushchev happily ordered a new jacket. Khrushchev also responded eagerly to Mikoyan's remark that etiquette allowed the heads of delegations to travel with family members. He invited his twenty-year-old son Sergei to accompany him.[11]

Sergei later recalled his amazement and delight at this unexpected treat. "To go to England—no one dreamed of it in those days. The whole household was envious. With the exception of [his sister] Rada's husband, [journalist] Aleksei [Adzhubei], none of them had ever been out of the country." Sergei was instructed strictly by his father to be on guard, and decades later he still remembered his shame at having made a gaffe by answering a dinner companion's query about reactions to the Secret Speech. He had forgotten that the USSR had not confirmed the existence of the speech. Moreover, his father did not allow him to take up the invitation to tour Oxford in the company of young Britons. Khrushchev fretted that Sergei might get in trouble, even be kidnapped—a level of fear that would have totally dissipated by the time of their 1959 trip to the United States, but one that underscores the leader's perception of being in unknown territory.[12]

Upon their arrival in Britain, the Soviet delegation encountered new tests—everything from the unheard of "delicacy" turtle soup to frank questions about Soviet military might and human rights in Eastern Europe. The thin soup garnered scornful comparisons to hearty Russian fare, while impolitic complaints about persecution of social democrats in the East infuriated Khrushchev. Alternatively defensive and belligerent, Khrushchev brushed back what he saw as challenges. In one notable exchange, Khrushchev responded to a question over the dinner table from Prime Minister Anthony Eden's wife about Soviet missiles with a sharp retort that they had plenty of capacity to reach Britain. As his son would later note, the success of Soviet missile tests that spring had given him a "club" that he could brandish to put foreign skeptics in their places. While Mrs. Eden perhaps was not the most appropriate target, Khrushchev wanted British audiences to know that he understood warfare in the atomic age.[13]

Khrushchev's sometimes obnoxious remarks stemmed in part from his sense that his important message about the rationale for peaceful coexistence in a nuclear age was being greeted skeptically. Khrushchev had already been hectoring his own military leaders with mixed success

Fig. 09-01 Nikita Khrushchev and Nikolai Bulganin touring Oxford, April 1956. Courtesy Russian State Film and Photo Archive.

about the need to rethink the future of war in a time of intercontinental missiles and hydrogen bombs. Reliance on nuclear weapons provided Khrushchev a vital justification for cutting conventional forces, a reform that carried significant potential cost savings and freed up labor for more productive use. In Britain he and Bulganin steadily made the case that peace was in the interests of the peoples of Britain and the USSR, but he felt that the English leadership's response was rather tepid. While they, too, praised improved relations, they seemed to be firmly attached to NATO and mistrustful Cold War thinking.

For the Soviets, the proffering of peaceful coexistence marked a major ideological shift. After all, the Bolsheviks had historically called for world revolution and had maintained that such revolution would inevitably be violent. Now, in effect, Khrushchev was assuring Britons (and looking for reassurance in turn) of non-intervention. In his speech at a luncheon hosted at the Soviet embassy, Khrushchev in his typically frank fashion opined: "You gentlemen do not like communism. We know it. Nor do we conceal the fact that we do not like capitalism. But we must live in peace. Of course, we do not demand of you some kind of love for us. But there is no denying the fact that such a great country as the Soviet Union exists, and that this country wants peace, not war. As the people say, you have to live with the neighbors God sent you and not only with the neighbor you would like to have."[14]

Khrushchev's call for peace drew on an assertion that the Soviet Union had already achieved a competitive level in the new arms race. He reasoned: "Today, as a result of the fact that technology has reached such a high degree of development, our planet is shrinking . . . formerly many days were required to travel from our country to Britain, now aircraft designers have developed planes that cover this distance in several hours."[15] As he got more tired and frustrated with cool responses from British leaders, Khrushchev got testier and cruder. In unscripted remarks, Khrushchev responded to continued Western export controls on technology by blustering, "I am quite sure that we will have a guided missile with a hydrogen bomb that can fall anywhere in the world."[16]

The domestic Soviet audience, however, received only images of calm, confident leaders. For instance, a big pictorial spread in the popular magazine *Ogonek* reassured Soviet readers that Bulganin and Khrushchev were met officially with the pomp and ceremony due representatives of a superpower and greeted warmly by ordinary Britons. One picture showed Khrushchev in conversation with the ornately garbed Lord Mayor of London, while photographs of Oxford students clambering to get a view of the first secretary and large crowds on the sidewalks outside Buckingham Palace created the impression that Westerners had pent-up curiosity about the Soviets.[17]

Western journalists, however, disputed the reports of a warm reception. The *New York Times* observed that crowds were notably cool and remarked that "there were as many boos as cheers" during the leaders' trips to Harwell and Oxford. Moreover, East European émigrés organized protests, including a march of some sixteen thousand through the center of London that coincided with Khrushchev and Bulganin's visit to the queen.[18] Indeed, though in their initial speeches the Soviet leaders remarked on the cordiality of their welcome, Khrushchev's discomfort grew, especially when a British Labor Party representative pressed on Bulganin a list of some 150 social democrats imprisoned in central Europe. Bulganin tried to finesse the situation by silently pocketing the list, but Khrushchev could not let the insult pass and exchanged sharp remarks that brought the evening to an early close.[19]

Although Khrushchev had rebuffed the Laborite petition on the spot, his remarks the next day in Birmingham showed a preoccupation with the perceived offense. At a reception hosted by the local city council, Khrushchev raised the topic of a spectator who had allegedly waved his fist at them. In his characteristically folksy and tough manner, the first secretary went on the offensive, averring: "Every family has its freak." Then he added, "And maybe these freaks aren't even from your family"—hinting that those who were stirring up discord were unhappy émigrés who had chosen to abandon their native lands. Khrushchev went on to instruct the locals that anti-Soviet demonstrators were bound to fail, just like English, American, and Japanese interventionists had failed to reverse the Bolshevik takeover in 1917, and just as Hitler had not succeeded in subjugating the Soviet people.[20]

Khrushchev wanted to impress upon Westerners that they had to reckon with the Soviet Union. To that end he not only cultivated an image of toughness but eagerly showcased Soviet scientific and military achievements. Khrushchev's show-and-tell tactics, however, required him to overcome worries at home about opening up to the West. Whereas in the 1930s Stalin had blocked star physicist Pyotr Kapitsa from returning to his laboratory in Britain, Khrushchev included atomic physicist Igor Kurchatov in his delegation. This move required challenging his head of the secret police to give cause as to why he should not trust the scientist and overruling those who hesitated to allow Kurchatov to accept an invitation to speak at the Atomic Energy Research Centre at Harwell, which would necessitate some sort of reciprocal offer.[21] As Khrushchev later reasoned, "Of course there was much that was correct in that [fearful] point of view. But to take things to an absurd length, to frighten your very own self, and to absolutely lose faith in your own people, who were fighting to build communism, who had their own national pride and self-respect, their own sense of self-worth—that was inadmissible." He was breaking sharply with Stalin, who "only [had] faith in police measures to keep people locked up and not let them go . . . any exchange of experience was considered theft."[22] Khrushchev liked to check out things for himself and he felt confident that Soviet experts and politicians could hold their own in direct contacts.

The Soviets came to see as well as to be seen. On the very evening of their arrival in London, Khrushchev and Bulganin spent two hours quickly touring Westminster, Festival Hall, St. Paul's, and the Tower of London. Even the sailors from the naval cruiser Ordzhonikidze were bussed into London for a day of sightseeing that started with a visit to Karl Marx's grave in Highgate Cemetery. As their stay wore on, however, the increasingly weary Soviet leaders tried to limit the touristic portion of the trip, only grudgingly acceding to the British prime minister's insistence that they visit Scotland as planned. Khrushchev would later complain that their itinerary had not included factories or chances to meet ordinary people, activities de rigueur for Soviet delegations. When Bulganin had briefly visited London in 1936 as part of a group of city managers, for instance, he had gone to a building exhibition, where he viewed labor-saving technology and got a sense of workers' attitudes. By contrast, in 1956 Khrushchev grumbled that crowds at the technical exhibition in Birmingham had prevented him from examining the displays properly.[23]

Khrushchev found much to criticize in Britain. In his memoirs recorded some dozen years after his visit, Khrushchev commented disparagingly on the "rather dilapidated and sorry looking" brickwork of the prime ministerial residence on Downing Street and judged the queen's dress unspectacular. Khrushchev even expressed disdain for Winston Churchill, whom he found to have aged poorly. He reported that he did not respond to Churchill's proffered sentiment that he had been impressed by Stalin during the war and only agreed politely when the former prime minister counseled him that people did not like change and that in the case of criticizing the cult of personality it would be wise to act "very cautiously and gradually."[24] Khrushchev had gone to London not for advice but to showcase Soviet strength. Though he professed disdain for ceremony and the trappings of high office, Khrushchev sought to impress, as can be seen in the luxurious gifts brought by the Soviet delegation (but as the British press noted, not mentioned in Soviet coverage). The presents ranged from a white sable stole for Prime Minister Eden's wife to horses for the royal stables.[25] The USSR was to be understood as a rich country by anyone's standards.

On the last day of their trip, Bulganin and Eden made final statements, and Khrushchev and Bulganin took turns answering queries from the press. Soviet initiated changes to the schedule limited the duration of the press conference, and Khrushchev managed to keep his cool while hammering home the message that the USSR and Britain had advanced the cause of peace. While little concrete business had been transacted—indeed, the American press was pleased that the Soviets had not driven a wedge between Western allies on trade—Khrushchev felt he had proven he could hold his own.[26] He replied cavalierly to a question about issue of visiting America, asking, "Who wouldn't like to visit, if he had business there?" and in the same breath criticizing the US government for denying visas to a group of Soviet chefs.[27]

The British had not exactly welcomed the Soviet leaders with open arms, but they had been correct and generally constructive. Khrushchev had basked in demonstrations of warmth and had happily given back as good as he got when he saw the need. To him peaceful coexistence did not mean admitting one's own faults and he did not mind defending Soviet-style socialism. Moreover, he recognized the merits of gathering fresh ideas.

In 1956 Khrushchev was ready to send his people to extract the best from Western culture and technology and to open the USSR to return visits. That summer British electrical power specialists and atomic scientists would travel to the USSR while historian and Supreme Soviet member Anna Pankratova visited London as part of a delegation of fifteen "parliamentarians." Soviet transport workers, tennis players, cultural workers, and others were also allowed to form tour groups to Great Britain in 1956.[28] The most widely publicized tourists that year, however, were the four boat loads of specially vetted Soviets who represented their country in a deluxe European tour, and then translated their findings for mass domestic audiences.

Fig. 09-02 Anna Pankratova (center) watches as Ekaterina Furtseva, the head of the delegation of Soviet parliamentarians, shakes hands in Cambridge, England, July 1956. Courtesy Archive of the Russian Academy of Sciences.

Around Europe in Three Weeks

The cruises on the *Pobeda* in summer and fall 1956 embodied the new policy toward extending leisure travel beyond the socialist bloc. The unprecedented opportunity to visit capitalist countries as private individuals, however, was open to only a select few and was both regimented and monitored. The travelers had little choice in itinerary and were constrained both by strict collective discipline and strong norms of behavior. Yet no filter stood between the tourists and the West—they were unavoidably exposed to a welter of sights and an unpredictable mix of people. Although much of their time was spent on organized excursions, the tourists felt like explorers. All tourists feel some uncertainty in new settings, but the Soviet travelers were mostly novices at interacting with foreigners. With varying degrees of open-mindedness, they pushed themselves to see as much as possible, especially so they could repay their privilege by sharing their new knowledge with those back home.

Analysis of Paustovskii's voyage—one shared by approximately fifteen hundred others between June and October—illustrates the partial nature of the opening up in 1956 as well as how travel by a few could be repackaged for the education of the many. The social composition of passengers on the initial cruises demonstrates who was thought to benefit from exposure to Europe, who was deemed a proper representative of the USSR, as well as who had the clout to obtain a spot. The restrictions and expectations placed on travelers reveal the limits of trust, while passengers' spontaneous and redacted responses to the officially planned itinerary and to glimpses of the ordinary lives of foreigners shed light on levels of knowledge of the outside world. Finally, the propagandizing of the tourist trips as an achievement of Soviet civilization shows how the elite thought an experience of rare luxury could gainfully be shared with a mass audience. From a jumble of impressions, the Soviet intelligentsia was to distill and convey appropriate lessons that offered a cultural education while highlighting the negatives of life under capitalism.

The *Pobeda*'s four trips in 1956 received significant coverage within the USSR. Film and radio crews sailed with the first cruise to collect material for documentaries. *Izvestiia* columnist Tat'iana Tess and *Pravda* special correspondent and Stalin Prize–winning novelist Boris Polevoi sent dispatches from ports of call along the route of the first sailing. Polevoi, who had recently published a popular account of his 1955 trip to the United States, also gathered materials for a new travelogue, as did Paustovskii's fellow passenger Leningrad novelist Elena Katerli. At least three other full-length books for armchair or future tourists resulted from the initial *Pobeda* sailings.[29] The fourth trip in October received the least coverage, perhaps owing to a worsening international situation or perhaps to oversaturation of the media as regards the cruises.

Paustovskii kept a personal diary of travel impressions and talked about his trip in two speeches in the fall of 1956, but he published only a few stories and sketches based on the trip. However, posthumous publication of his European journal prompted fellow passenger and younger novelist Daniil Granin to compose a frank account of their cruise together. Writer Leonid Rakhmanov also left reminiscences of the voyage with Paustovskii.[30] Hence a wealth of contemporaneous and a few key retrospective accounts allow for reconstruction and analysis of the experience of the pioneering "tourists" and the third cruise in particular.

Who were the lucky few who got to see Europe in 1956? The Soviet media stressed the diverse social makeup of the passenger list. The hour-long documentary film of the first trip lists those tourists appearing in its opening footage by profession as (in order) a mechanic in a factory, an engineer, a scientific worker, a factory worker, a mining engineer, a sculptor, an artist, a factory director, another scientific worker, and a worker.[31] Members of large delegations from Moscow's Kauchuk Factory made frequent cameos in Soviet accounts and were put in front of Western reporters as proof that Soviet cruises were not reserved for the elite. That said, the *Times* estimated the average age of passengers to be about fifty and noted that they seemed to be drawn largely from "what in the west would be called the professional classes, or from those connected with the arts." Indeed, alongside a smattering of exemplary workers, large numbers of their bosses and other regional and national VIPs made up the tourists' ranks.[32]

The intelligentsia was well represented—with members of the Academy of Sciences, award-winning artists and writers, and successful performers—as well as engineers, doctors, teachers, judges, and other white-collar professionals. Paustovskii's group included the aforementioned writers Elena Katerli and Daniil Granin as well as three poets, a dramatist, and a literary critic.[33] However, as Paustovskii later asserted in a controversial speech about an antibureaucratic novel—Vladimir Dudintsev's *Not by Bread Alone*—"half of the passengers were from our intelligentsia—artists, writers, scholars, workers, actors. This was one layer, which for the most part traveled second and third class. The other layer was composed of important [*krupnye*], so-called *nomenklatura* workers. With them there was no conversation. And there could not be." Paustovskii described the political bigwigs and high-ranking managers as boors, claiming: "They were absolutely indifferent to everything—and I would say even hostile toward everything, except their positions and the chance to display their own arrogance."[34]

The creative writers, artists, and workers mostly traveled solo. They obtained their berths through their professional unions as rewards for service and accomplishments.[35] Political and regional elites, however, seem to have been permitted to travel en famille as revealed in Granin's account of what happened when he tried to intercede to get Paustovskii better lodgings. The elderly Paustovskii had been assigned a tiny second-class cabin—"airless as a coffin," as he wrote in his diary—right above the noisy engine room. Concerned that their senior colleague would have his trip spoiled by poor sleep, the other writers tasked Granin with approaching "the boss of the cruise" (*nachal'nik kruiza*). Granin later recalled: "What a 'cruise' [*kruiz*] was I didn't know . . . But I recognized the boss of the cruise, although he rarely appeared and few glimpsed him. As with any big boss, his presence was more often invoked than seen. There were 450 tourists on the ship and we were on the open sea, outside our borders, he was everything—power, law, justice." Regarding Paustovskii, the commandant heard Granin out, looked him over appraisingly, and responded: "I need to move the first deputy minister to another cabin; I need a deluxe berth for the wife of the deputy president and for her son as well, and you are here about Paustovskii?" As for the racket, he suggested, "Let him drink a cognac every night. Writers do indulge, am I right?" Rank mattered and the desires of *nomenklatura* passengers trumped those of everyone else.[36] That said, all the passengers were privileged.

Travel to the "bourgeois" West was extremely expensive and required vetting so as to ensure that only politically mature and well-disciplined persons would represent the USSR. All potential overseas travelers had to present character references and health certificates and fill out forms documenting their personal and work histories. Those seeking to visit non-socialist countries had to answer extra questions—to list any relatives who lived overseas and to account for any family members who had been convicted of crimes or lived under occupation during World War II.[37] The amount of vacation days required and cost also limited the number of potential participants. Though a few chosen workers received subsidized or free vouchers from their trade unions, others paid in full for the privilege with the cheapest berth costing four times the average monthly wage.[38]

All passengers, however, had equal access to entertainment on board and shared the same excursions by coach and set meals in restaurants

Fig. 09-03 Tourists on the deck of the *Pobeda*. Courtesy Parkhomenko family archive.

booked by the local tour operators. From the Soviet tourists' perspective, the ship itself was luxuriously outfitted. A reconditioned German liner, the fourteen ton *Pobeda* had three decks and many amenities. Paustovskii joked that the crowded swimming pool looked like a kettle of fish, but travelers' accounts brim with excitement about it, as well as about the volleyball court, music salon, and solarium. Moreover, an American correspondent who sailed from Yalta to Sukhumi on the *Pobeda* in the winter of 1956 observed, "We had a bathroom done in blue-green tile, the only modern bathroom I saw in the USSR, and the toilet paper was non-state."[39]

Given the plethora of well-placed civil servants and factory directors, as well as a fair number of celebrities aboard the third sailing of the *Pobeda*—including the popular comedy duo Tarapun'ka and Shtepsel', young soprano Tamara Miansarova, and composer Rodion Schedrin—

Paustovskii did not stand out in the eyes of the organizers. However, though his works are little known outside Russia today, his novels were popular in translation in Europe in the 1950s. After reporters in Turkey, Greece, and then Italy sought him out, Paustovskii found himself moved to a better cabin. When asked about his change of mind, the commandant reportedly replied, "We must take into account the opinion of foreigners!" When Elena Katerli asked why he had not taken note of their opinions—after all, they had told him Paustovskii was a famous writer—he replied, "Your opinions? Why they'll remain with you [*Vashi mnenie? Tak ono zhe pri vas i ostantetsia*]."[40]

Discomforts and slights aside, Paustovskii's mood was buoyant. Although he had roamed the length and breadth of the Soviet Union, famously writing about the far-flung, mysterious bay of Kara Bugaz in Central Asia, he knew Western Europe only from literature and art. This was the author's first significant experience of traveling abroad.[41] Katerli, in her subsequent travelogue, created the character of "Grandpa," who embodied the enthusiastic, mature, novice traveler. Grandpa promised his grandson that he would swim in every sea and ocean through which the ship passed, just as the boy would do if he could make the trip. Katerli's older people swore not to go to bed early or to stay in the cozy lounges reading newspapers, but to use their binoculars and to explore the ship and land. And indeed, Paustovskii was constantly on deck, taking in the sights and sounds of the voyage. Despite tiredness, he and Katerli both pushed themselves to go out into nighttime Paris and to rise early to visit sights not on the official itinerary.[42]

Journalists depicted the good tourist as dutifully active and attentive at all times—each ready to convey his or her experiences to friends, family, and even larger audiences. At the send-off for the tourists from the Moscow train station (from which they traveled by special train to the port of Odessa), *Pravda* special correspondent Polevoi, for instance, observed that he overheard travelers from the Kauchuk factory being admonished to take note of everything. "'Don't forget your factory newspaper,' one well-wisher implored—'We'll expect a whole series of essays.'"[43] Indeed, the tourists armed themselves with notebooks, binoculars, and cameras to record their impressions. Every stage of the trip inspired a frenzy of photography. Katerli described her companions as snapping away before they even departed Leningrad for Odessa and then trying to capture the Russian landscape from the moving train. Her group leader constantly intoned, "Conserve your strength, conserve your film," as he shepherded the travelers onward. Paustovskii himself later reported having developed five hundred photos from the cruise.[44]

Historian A. N. Chistikov examined two personal albums from cruises around Europe—one from 1956 by an engineer and another from 1957 by an architect containing 185 and 92 photos, respectively. He found that their contents fit into three general types: images of historical and cultural sites, photos of themselves and of fellow passengers, and pictures of daily life that showed ordinary but to the photographer unusual things. Objects of material interest included Western automobiles, advertisements, a folding wheelchair, and American tourists in shorts. Notable activities included traffic jams and masses of bicycle commuters. Nikolai Krivenko selected similar images from the photos he took on the first cruise to illustrate his subsequent travel guide. His photographs are apolitical with the exception of one of a poorly dressed man toting a large advertising signboard, who, according to the caption, is working "for a pittance."[45]

The zeal to document everything, however, later caused Granin some remorse. In Athens the tourists had been granted a few rare free hours: "Free from programmed time. Most importantly, free from the crowds of one's own people, from the guide's explanations, from questions, from the commands of the group leader." For Granin, "These were the blessed, sacred, most precious hours when we could feel our selves to be travelers." Anxious about exploring alone—they had been lectured about the dangers of "gangsters, spies, intelligence agents, and so forth"—Granin invited Paustovskii to join him, but the older man chose to spend the afternoon in an open-air café. At home, however, Granin needed his guidebook to identify a statue that he had snapped from several angles. "I didn't see that monument myself, I only photographed it," he concluded. As Paustovskii gradually shared stories of the couple he had observed in the café and of his conversations with an American tourist who had emigrated from Russia and with the waiter who had once worked in the Russian orthodox monastery at Mount Athos, Granin realized that Paustovskii by sitting still had seen the most.[46]

The tourists had an enormous number of sights, sounds, and tastes to take in as they visited Bulgaria, Greece, Italy, France, the Netherlands, and Sweden with the second, third, and fourth cruises stopping in Turkey, as well. To process the experience, the writers drew on their familiarity with artistic renderings of the various sites. As Paustovskii explained to a gathering of students: "[In touring Rome] you suddenly recall all the great people who lived there . . . I went around under the influence of Stendhal the whole time while my traveling companions recalled Goethe, Byron, and Gogol." Katerli noted that the whole group of tourists gasped upon first glimpse of the Acropolis. She later tried to convey the mix of wonder and familiarity: "A strange sensation seizes you; it seems you've seen this hill crowned with columns long, long ago, that from childhood you've known it exists, that you are accustomed to thinking that it belongs to you no less than to those who live alongside it."[47] The one-dimensional representation had given way to a full sensory experience. But by asserting an old, if secondhand, acquaintance, the Soviet writers claimed the foreign monuments and works of art as their own.

Demonstrations of familiarity with classical Western art and architecture also confirmed the cultured nature of Soviet people. One of the few public complaints by the lucky tourists, in fact, concerned the absence of guidebooks in Russian with which they could have prepared themselves ahead of time. The author of the complaint nonetheless bragged that guides had praised the Soviet visitors for their curiosity and excellent questions. Polevoi similarly boasted: "You had to see with what I would say was tremulous excitement Soviet people—workers, engineers, doctors, scholars, writers, performers, people of various professions and ages—walked through the halls [of the Vatican galleries], accustomed by the whole structure of our lives to value and understand true art. Moreover, many of us who had never been here before could distinguish the real from the second rate at first glance."[48] The visitors might be newcomers from the periphery of Europe, but they were worthy heirs to the traditions of Western civilization.

Stories of unwitting faux pas, crude behavior, or ignorance on the part of some tourists had no place in the official narrative, yet such incidents stuck in the minds of the truly cultured travelers. Paustovskii in his antibureaucratic diatribe in October would recount the ignorance of a bigwig who asked if Michelangelo's fresco *The Last Judgment* was about a trial of Mussolini and recall another who asked: "How did the proletariat permit the construction of the Acropolis?" Some of the uneducated queries were amusing—Rakhmanov and Paustovskii later reminisced about the woman tourist who said: "So, I guess the Italian government doesn't have the resources to repair the coliseum." But others were disturbing, such as when one writer standing on deck praised the beauty of the sea, prompting a fellow traveler to retort: "What? Does the sea look worse back home?" and another bigwig to remark: "That comrade should be investigated."[49] In short, some of the elite retained a reflexive nationalism that interpreted any admiration of foreign ways as treachery.

For both cruise organizers and the majority of participants, however, patriotism mandated trying to make a good impression on European audiences, an idea that encompassed behavior and ideological correctness. As historian Anne Gorsuch has argued, Soviet tourists in the 1950s and 1960s were very aware that they were representing their country. Hence, like Khrushchev, the travelers worried about being perceived as uncouth or ignorant. Excessive drink, informal attire, and interest in trinkets were all abjured. The 1956 documentary *Around Europe . . .* shows Soviet passengers dressed formally for touring, with women in dresses and men generally wearing suits or shirts with ties. Granin recognized that Soviet men stood out for their out-of-date fashions, but he considered their efforts superior to casually clad Americans. Indeed, American tourists were frequently reviled for their skimpy outfits, loud haggling over souvenirs, and apparent condescension toward the natives. Soviet travelers singled out with special horror the wealthy visitors who chose to be carried through the ruins at Pompeii on special stretcher chairs. They empathized with the men who had the job of human mules and made a point of letting locals know that they were from the homeland of workers.[50]

Good behavior also included discipline. Soviet tourists were expected to report on time, keep up with their groups, be attentive to cultural programs, and to behave with dignity. Each group had a *starosta* (elder) to keep the schedule and monitor behavior, which no doubt included writing confidential reports for the security services. When Granin and poet Sergei Orlov were late reboarding the *Pobeda* at the first port of call in Bulgaria, cruise organizers wanted to send them home by train. They even tried to persuade Paustovskii to sign a letter in the name of all the writers supporting such a punishment, but he demurred noting that they were on a tourist trip, not a military exercise. After Paustovskii's objection, a security officer told Granin and Orlov they could stay on board but not disembark at any other ports. Only by invoking their status as frontline war veterans did the two writers get this sanction lifted. Dagestani poet Rasul Gamzatov also got in trouble for going off by himself. When questioned as to where he had been, Gamzatov coolly explained that he had sought out a mosque and acquired a copy of the Koran.[51]

Freethinking poets, however, were not the most common source of problems on tourist cruises. A debriefing conducted for the Molotov (Perm') regional Party Committee in 1956 included criticism of travelers who "frequented restaurants and bars and carried on conversations and took photographs with incidental persons." Paris nightclubs seemed a special source of tension—they were part of the city's fame, but their shows were deemed vulgar. Limited spending money also caused problems. Each expenditure required evoked anxious deliberation as tourists were allowed to purchase only a set number of dollars to serve as spending money.[52]

The writers seem to have spent a good portion of their cash on orangeade—a novel drink that they greatly preferred to Coca-Cola, which Katerli described as "a brown, overly sweet drink that smells of camphor." Granin spent his money extravagantly on a snorkeling kit—which he tried out rather unsuccessfully in the shipboard pool—and a music box in the shape of a windmill. Paustovskii bought and immediately crashed a toy helicopter. Katerli's fictional Grandpa, however, collected chestnuts in Paris and other "free" mementos. Soviets were not supposed to be acquisitive, though both amateur photographers and the documentary film crew lingered over French shop windows.[53]

Embarrassing behavior by Soviet tourists did not merit mention in published travelogues. Instead the only disappointing moments suitable for print related to occasional hostile receptions by the foreign press and difficulties in communication created by lack of knowledge of foreign languages. On the first cruise, a tourist got lost at Pompeii, and the Neapolitan press turned it into a sensational story about a potential defection. The "slanderous story" hurt the tourists' pride, but it did spread the word of their presence and helped attract a big crowd of communist sympathizers to see them off.[54] Polevoi preferred to cite the Italian paper that noted, "Soviet tourists could easily be mistaken for German,

Dutch, or Austrians. The women are interesting enough and elegantly dressed. The men readily enter into conversation though unfortunately few of them know foreign languages." The comments provoked him to sarcastically opine, "Yes, it seems, the very fact that we turned out to be similar to all other people on the earth was a disappointment to some of the inhabitants of Rome."[55]

Katerli and others, however, did bemoan their "lack of languages." It was easy enough to communicate with a woman selling cold drinks, but hard to have the meaningful conversations that Soviet tourists desired. When they wanted to learn about the lives of ordinary workers, they had to rely on their guides—often unsympathetic émigrés—to translate. Journalist Iosif Osipov lamented later that it would have been nice to have pocket phrasebooks. Yet he hastened to assure readers that the travelers found a "common language" with ordinary people during their trips. "When the dockhands in Havre, the workers at the Renault factory or the fishermen on the island of Capri raised their fists shoulder high, we understood them perfectly: they were expressing their readiness to fight for world peace."[56] Other tourists turned necessity into a virtue. Tat'iana Tess, who made her living as a newspaper columnist, ironically celebrated the joys of wordless communication such as when an elderly Italian worker reverently kissed the pin depicting Moscow that she had given him—a better outcome than another journalist's conversation with an Italian who asked if a postcard of Moscow's main street was real because he did not know Russia had such big buildings.[57]

Russian émigrés provided an opportunity for real conversation but aroused mistrust. Nevertheless, one journalist used an encounter with a son of émigrés, who was among those carrying tourists on palanquins through Pompeii, to evoke pity. She described for readers how he and his friends, all in their twenties, could not find proper work and noted that he had received only a fifth-grade education. She left it to Soviet readers to imagine how different his opportunities would have been had his parents stayed in Russia.[58] By contrast, some of the Russian-speaking guides recruited by local tour firms boasted of how well they lived in their new countries. Katerli actively disliked the woman guide in Pompeii, who disdained the tourists' interest in ordinary Italians. She and Paustovskii, however, were both touched by an encounter with a very elderly woman in Paris who wept because she had lost her ability to

Fig. 09-04 Soviet writers with Lydia Delectorskaya in Paris, September 1956. Left to right: Daniil Granin, Delectorskaya, Paustovskii, Elena Katerli, and Leonid Rakhmanov. Courtesy Moscow K. G. Paustovskii Literary Museum-Center.

speak Russian. Paustovskii also befriended Lydia Delectorskaya, Matisse's last muse and companion, whom he met when he stopped in at his French publisher's to see if he could collect any royalties directly.[59]

Based on their subsequent travelogues and recollections, the Soviet passengers seem to have been remarkably attentive to their reception in each city, hoping for approval and friendly curiosity but fearing hostility. Rakhmanov and Katerli both commented on the substantial police presence in Turkey, where police cars and jeeps escorted the tour buses everywhere and seemed bent on protecting locals from contact with communist visitors. Katerli was particularly upset when a man in a suit stopped children from accepting pins and postcards. Falling back on her trope of the "grandpa," Katerli had him imagine how his grandson back in Leningrad would react if someone tried to stop him from exchanging souvenirs with a foreign tourist. The suspicion and hostility were disgraceful.[60]

Yet just as Khrushchev feared dirty tricks against his son in Britain, Granin admits that he, too, was instinctively fearful of Western deceits. When a Russian-speaking priest approached him outside the Vatican to inquire if he was one of Soviet tourists that the press had written of and to ask whether there were any writers among them, he was taken aback. He refused the priest's request to enter the building and to meet with the ailing sister of an émigré writer, the late symbolist poet Viacheslav Ivanov, who allegedly wished to return his archive to Russia. Granin prevaricated that they had no time. He recollected: "I thought what if it is true and I ought to go—but then I imagined how the heavy gates would bang behind us, imagined the stone tunnels of the Vatican, a labyrinth, guards, a dungeon." As a man who had fought through the whole war, he felt ashamed of having turned away in fear, but he could not overcome the gut reaction that this was a provocation.[61]

For Paustovskii the primary emotional impact of the journey went far beyond the anger he later admitted feeling toward the boorishly behaved *nomenklatura* passengers. In a speech to literature students on December 13, 1956, Paustovskii spoke eloquently of having forsaken a youthful fascination with exoticism and exploration. "But exoticism in that time was declared if not a mortal then a great sin. All of people's thoughts were directed toward the earth, to the construction of new social relations. Exotica was rejected and died in me." Although he had remained a romantic, Paustovskii had taken up writing about the reality of the Soviet experiment. But over the course of his trip to Europe he had been stunned by the sights, which were "much more interesting than I had understood from books and from the depths of my own imagination." He described entering the Bosporus and "coming to meet you are whole flotillas of feluccas, little sailboats, painted with the colors of Van Gogh—white, black, green—so colorful under enormous white sails."[62] The overlap of the fantastic and real created for him the sensation of being in a dream, and perhaps awakened thoughts of what he might have written without the pressures of socialist realism.

Upon his return, Paustovskii urged his fellow citizens to roam as much as possible. In his travel diary after a day in Sorrento he had written: "I make it my wish [*zaveshaiu*] for [the children] Galia and Aleshka that they absolutely must see all this." Perhaps his conscience bothered him that his family had not been able to share his good fortune. Or he may have been conscious of how such a journey could have affected his career if it had come earlier in his lifetime.[63] The door to the West ought to stay open if only a crack.

Journalists writing for mass audiences offered more pedantic lessons about the *Pobeda*'s new route. Polevoi, for instance, posited that all the tourists came away with a new sense of mutual understanding with the peoples who shared their desire for peace. Yet as the *Pobeda* approached Leningrad, he concluded reassuringly: "When I think about the most important thing that this trip gave us, I am not mistaken, if I answer for all my traveling comrades that the main thing is that having sailed through strange seas, wandered through strange lands, we have come to love our dear motherland even more."[64] In other words, the correct conclusion in comparisons with foreign countries was that the USSR had come out on top. Urban poverty, crass commercialism, class distinctions, prostitution, and peep shows were all phenomena that lowered the West in the eyes of Soviet visitors. Ancient culture did not compensate for present failings. Some Europeans might have access to luxury goods, but the USSR was the land of the future.

At Home

Upon the conclusion of the Geneva talks in November 1955, historian Sergei Dmitriev had noted in his diary: "It's hard to seriously refute the Western participants' conclusion: 'The leaders of the Soviet Union have tried to isolate their own people from contact with the outside world.' They really have tried." Dmitriev predicted such attempts would continue because they were based on "the mistrust of the Soviet leaders toward their own people."[65] In traveling to Britain, however, Khrushchev battled the fear of being duped instilled in him by Stalin and partially defused the atmosphere of paranoia surrounding contacts between Soviets and foreigners.

The *Pobeda* tourists were living proof of change—and they were everywhere in the Soviet media in the summer of 1956. They featured in newsreels and in articles in publications ranging from the topical *Vokrug sveta* (Around the World) to the woman's magazine *Krestianka* (Peasant Woman). Schoolchildren and rural women alike were expected to be impressed by the intrepid tourists who raced through museums, viewed monuments, and shook the hands of workers across Europe. At the local level, trade union officials tasked with filling quotas set from above wanted to drum up interest in expensive package trips. But for the center, the practice of publicizing the travels of Soviet people, especially workers, refuted the Western notion of an "Iron Curtain" and highlighted the perks enjoyed by those who lived under socialism. Indeed, the returning tourists reported that thousands of friendly European workers longed to visit the Soviet Union, but lacked the means. In 1956, Soviet authorities began to offer subsidies for ordinary Britons to visit and to encourage foreign tourists by publishing multilingual guidebooks. Yet for Soviet citizens, overseas travel remained a perk rationed by the state and strictly monitored in practice. Although most *Pobeda* passengers paid large sums for their berths, travel was not simply a commodity to be purchased by anyone or to be enjoyed outside the confines of the collective.[66]

Anne Gorsuch has noted that "tourism as a form of cold war diplomacy differed from other forms of cultural contest in that it required relatively ordinary citizens—in contrast to the more usual delegates, artists, and scientists—to perform Soviet identity on the basis of modest training." As pioneers in opening up Europe, the "first" Soviet tourists in 1956 were elites, who were acutely aware of their status and the need to prove that trust had not been misplaced. Conscious of having been vetted and found worthy, they policed their own and each other's behavior.[67] Attuned to scrutiny from the Soviet side as well as to the gaze of Western media and citizens alike, the tourists resolutely declared their solidarity with the working class and spoke of peace. Many also treated sightseeing like a job, taking extensive notes, photographing important landmarks, and observing the ways of the locals. They were preparing for the second part of the tourist bargain—the reporting of their experiences to domestic audiences.

The Soviet cultural figures included in the tourist cruises understood that they had signed on for a busman's holiday. Abroad they were demonstrating the achievements of Soviet civilization; at home they were conveying appropriate impressions of Europe. The task was not unpleasant. Katerli, for instance, despite mounting health problems enjoyed composing a thorough, gently humorous narrative of the places she had seen and people she had met. With evident sincerity, she presented the Soviet tourists as being like her—sensitive and attentive, open and curious, with pity for those who lived poorly and respect for the creators of cultural treasures. In a final entry in her occasional journal on March 9, 1957, Katerli wrote, "I keep meaning to take stock of my accomplishments for 1956, but they are so insignificant that I don't want to write them down. There was one month of the year—September, unlike any other month of my whole life—this was the trip around Europe on the *Pobeda*." A little over a year later, she would be dead of lung cancer, but first she finished her chronicle of the voyage.[68]

Both Khrushchev and Paustovskii appreciated seeing things for themselves and expected contact with other cultures to have a human-izing effect, including countering negative stereotypes about the Soviet Union. A Soviet pamphlet for the British introduced Khrushchev and Bulganin as *vydviyzhentsy* ("promoted from the rank and file") and ex-plained that this term "impl[ied] not only their working class origin but also their political activities which are closely related to the widest sec-tions of the country's population."[69] They embodied the advancement possible in the USSR. Paustovskii, however, found that closer acquain-tance with the "new class" of Soviet managerial elites diminished his sat-isfaction with the Soviet system. He saw in the dismissive even hostile attitudes of some Soviet bigwigs toward foreign cultures a smug, unques-tioning superiority fostered by the cult of personality and postwar great power nationalism. Khrushchev's memoirs suggest that his aggressive-ness abroad may have stemmed from a deep seated insecurity; Paustovskii, however, had no sympathy for rudeness and chauvinism.

Paustovskii and his friends among the touring intelligentsia repre-sented a different Soviet achievement—the elevation of the arts. Valuing broad-mindedness and curiosity, they embraced the chance to see Eu-rope as a precious gift of access to world culture, admittedly one made possible by the proletarian know-it-all Khrushchev. Paustovskii would later dare to complain that such boorish *nomenklatura* types as he en-countered among the first-class passengers on the *Pobeda* should never be allowed outside the USSR as they had "entirely different understand-ings of the prestige of the country."[70] His judgment may have been tinged with bitterness that he—a travel writer—had been denied so long and that he had to travel in a group, cut off from contact with his Euro-pean peers. In the 1960s he would get the chance visit Europe again, including a private stay on Capri. In 1956, however, group tourism provided a more controlled environment that fit with the conditional trust placed on untested Soviet travelers.

Despite restrictions on free time and pressure not to have informal contacts with locals, the overwhelming mood among the returning *Pobeda* tourists seems to have been gratitude for what had seemed impossible—the chance to see Europe with their own eyes. Having stumbled across the posthumous publication of Paustovskii's travel diary in 1982, Daniil Granin was overwhelmed with memories of their cruise. But he admitted, "If it hadn't been for the diary in the magazine, I wouldn't have recalled that trip. There were so many trips after it, so many countries and cities that that which I had seen the first time lost its value. But this diary . . . it reads like a document from a different epoch, from a former life, with feelings that are hard to understand today."[71]

In 1956 overseas travel was extraordinary. Even armchair travelers who could only read ecstatic accounts of visiting the Blue Grotto in Capri or touring the Louvre gained a feeling of possibility, a sensation of expanding horizons, and an impression that the gap between the East and West had narrowed. Moreover, if Paustovskii had his way, his countrymen would embrace a previously little-touted civic duty—following "the muse of distant wanderings" so as to become empathetic across all borders.

10 OCTOBER

STORM CLOUDS

In October 1956 lines formed in libraries. Readers impatiently sought the latest issue of the literary journal *Novyi mir* (New World), where they could find the third and final installment of a novel about a frustrated inventor of a machine for casting pipes. Before any reviews appeared, word of mouth had made Vladimir Dudintsev's *Not by Bread Alone* a hot commodity. Writing in his diary at the end of the month, historian Sergei Dmitriev observed: "From an artistic-literary perspective, it's a commonplace work of Soviet literature." Its appeal, he reasoned, lay in its "socio-political mood and bias." In Dmitriev's words, "The Party and Soviet leadership (ministerial) *apparat,* as well as the scientific-technical world, are shown as degenerate people, completely absorbed only in the battle for their personal interests."[1] Dmitriev captured in a nutshell the ambiguity that made Dudintsev's novel acceptable in one light and radical in another. The industrial setting and realistic style made the story of the inventor feel familiar to consumers (and censors) of Soviet literature, but the tone of moral outrage combined with a depiction of a lopsided struggle by a talented individual against entrenched bureaucrats made it potentially subversive.

Dudintsev's portraits of self-aggrandizing managers and vain obstructionist academicians would become the talk of the town among readers—from ordinary engineers to eminent critics—in the autumn of 1956. Many Soviet citizens embraced and championed the antibureaucratic message at the heart of *Not by Bread Alone*. Indeed, progressive intellectuals sought to frame its targeting of careerists as deeply pro-Soviet. As the writer Nikolai Atarov told a large audience that fall, "The appearance of this novel in the year of the Twentieth Party Congress is no accident. The history of Soviet literature is full of wonderful examples of how works most needed by the people appear at the necessary moment." Constructive criticism, after all, was crucial for reform. But critiques of party or state institutions had to be tactful; hence, at that same discussion, writer Sergei Mikhalkov hopefully averred: "I am certain that today, in the year 1956, we can allow ourselves not to be frightened if someone recognizes himself in Shutikov or Drozhdov [the bureaucratic characters from the novel]."[2] But the novel, and even more so its reception, did cause alarm.

In autumn 1956 Dudintsev's novel would become a litmus test of sorts with attitudes toward *Not by Bread Alone* standing in for opinions regarding the need for deeper political and moral transformations in the post-Stalin era. In front of packed halls, the young Leningrad mathematician Revol't Pimenov used *Not by Bread Alone* as a pretext to voice a variety of complaints with the Soviet system, while Konstantin Paustovskii expanded on the novel's message of damage done by monopolistic, self-serving, crude apparatchiks. The story of the novel's creation and its polarizing reception reveals festering, but usually unspoken dissatisfaction with Soviet economic policies and administrative practices, areas not addressed by the Secret Speech per se, but also of concern to party reformers.

In 1956 Khrushchev's report "On the Cult of Personality and Its Consequences" had created a rupture in the official narrative of perfect progress that opened the way for challenging the status quo with critiques of political practices and the people behind them. I argue that the timing and content of *Not by Bread Alone* combined to make it a powerful platform for raising ideas about better governance. For both young and old, but especially for idealistic youth, who often took seriously the regime's moral rhetoric, discussion of the novel evoked strong feelings and often inchoate desires for change from within the system. Dudintsev's intentions, his editor's maneuverings, and reactions by book lovers—

including his fellow authors—illuminate the complicated context for political feedback in a moment of disequilibrium and uncertainty. Under socialism, writers and readers had long been engaged in a deliberate, carefully phrased pas de deux in which literary critique served as a surrogate for public policy debate. *Not by Bread Alone* painted a picture of an insular and defensive Soviet bureaucracy in need of oversight, a pressing question given Khrushchev's account of the Stalin cult as having flourished without restraint for two decades. As a student at MGU would proclaim in November, *Not by Bread Alone* persuaded him that more "social control from below" needed to be exerted over the state.[3] A novel about experimental pipe casting would unleash the kind of challenging speech Khrushchev had thus far dodged.

The Literary Arena

Historian Karl Loewenstein, who explored the emergence of a public sphere during the thaw, has concluded, "September and October 1956 were the two months of the most open and uncontrolled criticism of the Soviet regime that occurred in the Soviet Union between Lenin and Gorbachev."[4] Skirmishes over values and ideology centered on literary works. Ilya Ehrenburg's novel *The Thaw* had given the post-Stalin era a hopeful metaphor already in 1954. Two years later new journals had opened, once-forbidden names reappeared in print, as did the work of progressive foreign artists, and liberal writers began to reimagine the fate of sensitive works. In May 1956 Boris Pasternak had quietly passed the manuscript of *Doctor Zhivago* to the representative of a leftist Italian publishing house. Pasternak would win the Nobel Prize in 1958. His decision to send the novel abroad, however, would lead to censure and ignominy at home and deprive the domestic audience of the chance to read his saga.[5] Dudintsev found a Soviet publisher for *Not by Bread Alone* but nonetheless also ended up in hot water.

To understand how a lengthy novel about industrial innovation catalyzed an emotional political debate of national significance, one must bear in mind the special role that literature played in Soviet society. The Bolshevik government heavily promoted literacy in part to make the citizenry able to read political tracts, public health pamphlets, and technical materials. Yet the party also relied on fiction as a less direct but often powerful way to advance official policies and approved norms. Fiction, after all, had entertainment value, and, as literary scholar Vera Dunham noted in her analysis of Soviet mores, "After the war, there was neither bread nor circuses. There were no cafés for the bohemian youth, nor beaches, spas or travel for the majority . . . reading took on new importance, partly because there was nothing else." By 1956 the Soviet film industry had begun turning out more movies and television was beginning to develop, but literature still held a central place. Moreover, being widely read and having opinions on literature denoted being cultured. As Dunham observed, "Reading was more than a leisure activity. To a vast number of Soviet citizens, reading meant not only being *au courant*, it meant participation."[6]

Soviet people were expected to read serious works—indeed frivolous topics got short shrift from Soviet publishing houses—and to read them attentively. Contemporary Soviet fiction was meant to be taken as a source of self-improvement, including in regard to political literacy.[7] Moreover, topical novels regularly provided fodder for press reviews and discussions. In a system where genuine public opinion was rarely solicited, readers' conferences and letters to the editor gave consumers of culture a chance to engage in a limited but important dialogue with the authorities. Indeed, should a newspaper or journal choose to publish a reader's letter, individual sentiments could reach a wide audience. Editors in turn often sought out letters that expressed themes they wished to develop or that provided a pretext for offering guidance. In other words, although literature often served as a transmitter of official ideals, its analysis provided a forum for clarifying or disputing values and positions.[8]

The literary model of "socialist realism" endorsed by the Soviet Communist Party informed readers' expectations and created powerful norms for writers. As "engineers of the human soul," in Stalin's apt turn of phrase, Soviet writers were to help forge new socialist men and women. Indeed, in the infamous 1946 Central Committee decree regarding the journals *Zvezda* and *Leningrad*, they were instructed that "any preaching of ideological neutrality, of political neutrality, of 'art for art's sake' is alien to Soviet literature and harmful to the interests of the Soviet people and the Soviet state."[9] In such a political context, "realism" did not imply authenticity. Too much gritty detail could even be considered as detracting from obligatory optimism. Writers had the responsibility to show life as it ought to be and to raise only those shortcomings in Soviet society that were already being overcome.

Readers in turn internalized the expectation that contemporary literature ought to inspire and instruct. They understood imaginary characters as representing real types and in their role as readers—a dual role that required them to engage with literature from the perspective of socialist citizens and simultaneously to be the objects of further edification—they stood ready to judge the writer and his fictions from the perspectives of doctrine and credibility. Since *Not by Bread Alone* revolved around the travails of a solo inventor, the author received many letters from real-life inventors and engineers. However, readers from many walks of life—including soldiers, workers, teachers, doctors, and students—would respond to Dudintsev's broader themes of the individual and bureaucracy. In his study of *Novyi mir,* the most influential "thick" literary journal in the Soviet Union, historian Denis Kozlov found that *Not by Bread Alone* apparently sparked more letters than any of the journal's other thaw sensations, including Aleksandr Solzhenitsyn's 1962 gulag tale, *One Day in the Life of Ivan Denisovich.* Moreover, the public interest in *Not by Bread Alone,* Kozlov concluded, "quickly developed into a collective examination of the economic and administrative problems, political challenges, past legacies, and ethical dilemmas that confronted the country at the time."[10]

Timing played a key role in *Not by Bread Alone*'s rapid burst of popularity. As the ramifications of the Secret Speech's revelations about the Stalin cult sank in, a vocal minority of writers invoked the "spirit of the Twentieth Party Congress" to suggest their profession needed to address the dereliction of its historical role of civic conscience. "Continuing the pre-revolutionary tradition," Kozlov contends, "the literary realm remained the principal setting in which alternative ideas emerged, dissent was voiced, and opinions were formulated and exchanged."[11] Journalists, too, however, felt empowered by the sense that the government was seeking in to "reinvent" itself. Like prosecutors with their renewed powers of oversight (*nadzor*), they sprang to point out abuses of power, expose dangerous situations, and reveal moral misdeeds.[12] As a longtime fiction writer, experienced journalist, and former military prosecutor, Dudintsev was perfectly positioned to make the leap from individual cases of injustice to larger themes of good and evil.

The Author and His Story

In his first major work, Vladimir Dudintsev took his inspiration from the travails of real frustrated inventors he met through his work for the youth paper *Komsomol'skaia pravda*. Although employed as a journalist and trained as a lawyer, Dudintsev had long harbored literary dreams. As a youngster he had been encouraged by his stepfather to write poems and stories. He had published some works in the children's newspaper *Pionerskaia pravda*, and even found a mentor in the renowned short story writer Isaac Babel.[13] As a high school student, Dudintsev successfully entered some writing competitions, but an interest in moral philosophy drew him to study law.

Dudintsev spent the purge years training to be a prosecutor. In later interviews and in a post-perestroika memoir, Dudintsev would skirt the subject of what it meant to be studying law at a time when the principles of fair trials were being undermined. He preferred to recount how he had been appalled when a girlfriend asked whom he loved more—her or Stalin. He recalled responding indignantly, "Why how can you even compare two such incomparable things! You are one thing and Stalin is something quite different. Both one and the other will find a place in [my] heart."[14] This anecdote conjures up the image of a clever, if blinkered, youth. Given the fact that Dudintsev's father—a White army soldier—was shot by the Bolsheviks during the civil war while his pregnant mother barely escaped execution, one might have expected a more sanguine political outlook. In his memoir, however, Dudintsev dispassionately recounted that he invoked his family history to dodge invitations to join the Communist Party, but confirmed that he considered himself loyal to Soviet power.[15]

Upon graduation from law school in 1940, Dudintsev went straight into officer's training classes and in the early months of World War II found himself commanding an infantry company. Severely wounded in December 1941, Dudintsev finished up his army service as a military prosecutor. On the eve of his discharge in 1945, he won a short story contest sponsored by the national youth league's newspaper *Komsomol'skaia pravda*. He then became a correspondent for the same paper, where his work included investigating readers' letters of complaint.[16]

Fig. 10-01 Vladimir Dudinstev with his son Vanya in 1963. Courtesy Russian State Film and Photo Archive.

Although Soviet citizens often began by taking their grievances to party or state officials, writing to the media was another tried-and-true avenue for individuals to pursue justice. Journalists had insufficient resources to follow up on the majority of appeals, but they had the authority to investigate and the potential to shame officials into helping petitioners.[17] Dudintsev understood the occasional powers of a word in the right ear. In 1950 the writer and his wife were sharing a single room of less than nine square meters with her mother and their two small children. In the evenings, as his wife, Natal'ia, recalled, the three adults sat at one small table, the two women, both schoolteachers, correcting student notebooks and making lesson plans, and Dudintsev hunched over his typewriter. With the birth of a third child imminent, the grown members of the family "sent a multitude of letters to a multitude of 'high-up' addresses. Letter-prayers! The last one was to [presidium member Georgy] Malenkov." Fortunately one of their appeals was answered with two rooms in a communal apartment; hence, Dudintsev gained the physical and mental space to start his novel.[18]

Given his legal background, Dudintsev was drawn to cases of inventors who complained to *Komsomol'skaia pravda* that their ideas had been stolen. He befriended some of them, published the occasional article on their plight, and helped them with their petitions and court cases. The materials from this work—designs, letters of complaint, and correspondence with ministries—formed the documentary base for *Not by Bread Alone*. In writing the novel, Dudintsev literally pieced together his subjects' stories. He collected his notes, sorted them by theme, copied them out on different-colored pieces of paper, and pasted them up on a big sheet made of pieces of heavy paper glued together. The resultant "wall newspaper" or "patchwork quilt" had a square covered with scraps of paper for each chapter.[19]

Based on the theme, readers might have expected from Dudintsev a formulaic novel of socialist realism. Dudintsev knew full well what editors expected. In the 1990s he described how he worked before his success with *Not by Bread Alone:* "The editor who invited me in (let's say of a youth newspaper or magazine), says, 'Dudintsev! Soon it will be the New Year. How about if in a week you bring us some New Year's story—one that can go straight into the next edition? Insofar as ours is a youth organ, that means, there should be young people in the story—Komsomol. Also there should be some industry, preferably metallurgy, but machine building would do. There should be socialist competition. And certainly love, so that the story is interesting. . . .' and so forth down to the obligatory happy ending."[20] Having received a concrete request, Dudintsev would lock himself in his room, smoke himself into a state, and write flat out until he had crafted a story that met all the requirements. He later conceptualized the process as that of filling an order for a product deemed to be necessary by management. In composing *Not by Bread Alone*, however, as Dudintsev later formulated it, he had responded to an unvoiced demand from society at large (*sotsialnyi zakaz*).[21]

Dudintsev began writing the inventor's tale with no immediate prospect of publication. Indeed, aware that he was violating some taboos, he did not even discuss his project with friends or colleagues. Moreover, he took the real travails of his inventor friends not just as a starting point but as the source for a plot with many ups and downs and only rare successes. Perhaps because he drew directly from the lives of inventors who had become genuine family friends, Dudintsev did not compose a tidy story line with an overwhelmingly happy ending.

Not by Bread Alone opens in 1947 in a typical Soviet industrial town, where the central avenue is named after Stalin and the boss of the main factory holds sway over the whole community. The novel revolves around the epic struggles of a physics teacher, Dmitrii Lopatkin, to realize his idea for improving the manufacturing of metal pipes. On a class trip to the local factory, Lopatkin had watched with chagrin as workers poured metal by hand into earthen forms. Although not an engineer, Lopatkin devises a machine that uses centrifugal force to cast pipes rapidly and seamlessly. His invention promises to rationalize labor in the making of a humble but ubiquitous product, but Lopatkin is blocked at all turns by a closed scientific community, which jealously guards its privileged status as gatekeeper for new ideas, and by bureaucrats who are unwilling to invest in a project that might fail.

Lopatkin's first disappointment comes when the head of the town's factory drops his patronage of the invention. Like Dunskii and Frid's "Commissar of the Mines," Dudintsev's Leonid Drozdov has tremendous powers and discretion. He can decide in an instant whether to extend favors ranging from the provision of drawing paper to the construction of a prototype. The novel opens with Lopatkin inquiring about the status of his design, which the factory has submitted to the relevant ministry. Drozdov has learned that a team headed by an acknowledged authority (likely with access to Lopatkin's drawings) has come up with a similar contrivance. Seeing no gain in helping the physics teacher, who has neither credentials nor important connections, Drozdov informs Lopatkin that his project has no future. Moreover, he explains to the inventor that he has made a fundamental error by being "an individual on his own." Drozdov pontificates: "The lone wolf is out of date. Our new machines are the fruit of collective thought. You [alone] will scarcely succeed in anything; no one will want to work with or for you." As Drozdov later elaborates to his wife, accepting the existence of some "superior beings" capable of acts of individual genius would mean relegating all the rest of society to the "common herd," something no good socialist should endorse.[22]

Drozdov's wife, the young schoolteacher Nadia, becomes the surrogate for the reader as she gradually discovers the hidden natures of both her husband and the inventor. Nadia, whose full name means "hope," starts out admiring Drozdov for his forceful ways and the long hours he puts in at the plant. She excuses his rough manners, forgives his crude interpretations of Marxism, and accepts the luxuries that come from his position. In an evocative scene, the reader first encounters a pregnant Nadia, just returned from Moscow, enfolded in a new fur coat, being fed orange segments by her doting husband as they walk through the town's snowy streets. The local children, ignorant of oranges, scramble to pick up the scraps of peel that Drozdov tosses onto the ground. Nadia, reveling in the beauty of the sunny day and wrapped up in her domestic pleasures, is strangely indifferent to the spectacle created by her privilege. Almost immediately, however, Nadia finds herself drawn into a conflict with her husband over his treatment of her former coworker Lopatkin.

Visiting the household of one of her pupils, Nadia finds that the father, an elderly worker, has taken in Lopatkin as a boarder. Lopatkin has given up teaching to pursue the dream of getting his idea approved for testing and now shares his hosts' poverty. Over a starkly simple meal of baked potatoes with salt, Nadia learns of her husband's role in Lopatkin's lack of success. She also sees how the workingman believes in Lopatkin's genius and respects his willingness to sacrifice in pursuit of an invention that will benefit the construction industry and hence all those waiting for decent housing. From this point on, Drozdov's values start to grate on her conscience. In an illuminating episode, Nadia is rushed to the hospital in danger of suffering a miscarriage, and the nurses scramble to clear other patients from the ward meant to be reserved for the elite. When Nadia realizes that their beds have been moved to the corridor to give her the proper level of privilege, she demands they be shifted back. Her husband ridicules her "uprising" and justifies the allotment of special treatment to those who have worked especially well (meaning himself, of course).[23]

For several hundred pages, *Not by Bread Alone* chronicles Lopatkin's long struggle with Drozdov and other gatekeepers in science, industry, and the government. The novel's essence can best be grasped not by tracing the convoluted and somewhat repetitive plotline but by scrutinizing Lopatkin's friends and foes. At Lopatkin's lowest moments he is saved by hidden or previously unknown allies, honest and true individuals who form a small spontaneous collective of sorts outside the bounds of formal institutions.[24]

Lopatkin's foremost ally is Nadia. Inspired and infatuated by the selfless inventor, Nadia betrays her husband by stealing away from their fine apartment in Moscow—where Drozdov has gone to serve in the central bureaucracy—to visit Lopatkin, who has come to the capital to try to get the ministry's attention. She secretly sells her fur coat to fund his research and types his petitions and complaints. In *Not by Bread Alone* the real marriage is hollow; the liaison with the inventor is pure but unconsummated except for a single night. Romance, as in traditional socialist realist novels, takes a backseat. On the last page of *Not by Bread Alone*, Nadia is recognized as Lopatkin's natural companion, his muse, but at the cost of her personhood: "Nadia said nothing. She only moved closer and disappeared; she was not there at all; there was only a clear little stream from which he might drink and refresh himself on his hard road."[25]

Lopatkin's second ally is an elderly professor who has had many disappointments of his own as an inventor. They meet in a newspaper office where Lopatkin has gone to try to interest some journalists in writing about his mistreatment at the hands of the scientific establishment. Professor Bus'ko recognizes a fellow sufferer and saves Lopatkin from having to leave Moscow with his dream unrealized. He shares his humble room, even giving Lopatkin half of his drawing board on which to work. The goodhearted but eccentric Bus'ko, however, represents a sad vision as he lives on crumbs and has all but given up on realizing his inventions despite their tremendous economic potential.

Ultimately, two allies from within the system allow Lopatkin to build his machine. The first is the young scientist Galitskii, who has become disgusted by the monopolistic behavior of those experts who disparage any invention that originated outside their own laboratories. By abandoning the Moscow elite to take up a job as a factory boss in the Urals, he reverses Drozdov's trajectory so as to take advantage of a manager's power and independence to create a haven for honest people and a site for innovation. The second insider ally is Major Badyin, who serves on a military court that sentences Lopatkin to eight years in prison. Unjust imprisonment is Lopatkin's final ordeal. Having won the support of the military for his work, Lopatkin had begun drafting an even more sophisticated version of his machine. Nadia's research in foreign periodicals had given Lopatkin a key insight, but his jealous rivals denounce him for permitting an "irrelevant person" access to classified designs. The chief judge is loath to dig into the messy details that emerge at the trial, but Badyin oversees a reinvestigation that frees Lopatkin after only eighteen months.

Lopatkin's enemies, with the exception of Drozdov, are only sketchily portrayed. They are senior scientists and naive, toadying junior designers who have had their heads turned by greed and ambition. Having reached the pinnacle of success in the Soviet system—ranks of doctor or academician—and having been appointed to head up research institutes, the experts block the door to anyone who will not assume a subservient position. These leaders must receive a share of the credit for any good work done by their underlings, and they destroy anyone whom they cannot co-opt. Lopatkin's complaints to the ministry and the press fail because the officials and journalists turn to the selfsame clique of experts for advice as to the merits of his claims against them. When by chance Lopatkin gets the minister's ear and an opportunity to pursue his invention with the assistance of expert designers, his rivals cook up the charge that sends him to prison.

The other obstacle to Lopatkin's success is the careerism rampant among the Soviet elite. Here, Drozdov stands out. A far more complex character than the selfish scientists, Drozdov is a skilled and ambitious manager who artfully works the system to ensure his personal fortunes rise. For instance, when he understands that the experts' alternative machine has led to great wastage of metals, Drozdov immediately forms a commission to investigate—not to learn what went wrong, but to put himself in a position to assign the blame to others. Drozdov is not an ideological enemy of Soviet power; however, he is selfish while alleging to be selfless. Nadia becomes "irritated by Drozdov's philosophical discourses; he knew so well when to insert glibly catchwords such as 'basis,' 'state duty,' 'collective,' and so on, using them to hide his own personal interests or weaknesses." She notes, "Drozdov, when he began to talk in these phrases, somehow, in an odd way, disarmed her, depriving her, as it were, of the power of speech."[26] Drozdov has learned to "speak Bolshevik," to use historian Stephen Kotkin's phrase, with such mastery that he cannot be reproached.[27] He supports the socialist system, but readers come to see how his aggrandizement undercuts its ends and its ideals.

Not by Bread Alone has two denouements. The first comes when Lopatkin returns from imprisonment to find that his friends have saved the plans for his invention and brought them to fruition under Galitskii's wing. The second takes place at a banquet honoring the elderly academician who heads the research institute where Lopatkin had met such resistance. Lopatkin sees that even though he has succeeded in promoting his machine over the inferior one, his opponents are not defeated in the least. He has won in the one instance, but they remind him that only by joining them will he be able to guarantee a permanent place at the trough. One of his rivals condescendingly suggests that they make peace and Lopatkin can treat himself to a car or dacha. But Lopatkin harshly counters: "Man lives not by bread alone, if he is honest." The ministry may not have held his foes to account, but he suggests his opponents read "Field Regulations, Infantry" because: "I used to be described there by the words 'single combatant.' But now we are 'a section in action.'"[28] With this analogy, Lopatkin brandishes his own collective, a small group of dreamers united by their principles.

The novel's ending violates the socialist realist model. First, the final celebration does not honor the noble inventor whose machine will save the state considerable resources. Instead it celebrates the physical longevity of one of the vain obstructionist academics. Second, the chief villain, Drozdov, having turned on those who planned to cover up the waste resulting from the alternate machine, has finagled a promotion. By contrast, Lopatkin's patron Galitskii has refused a state decoration, writing: "I did what any decent person would have done and still more, any Communist."[29] Lopatkin's machine has been saved by a party member, but not by attention from the party per se. Last, Lopatkin does not follow in the tradition of the socialist realist hero and think of "regeneration and of the glorious time that awaits future generations."[30] Instead he contemplates a road that has no end. He has not changed the system to make things easier for other inventors; he has won through perseverance and luck.

Allies and Opponents

Good fortune also played a role in the publication of *Not by Bread Alone*. Dudintsev recounts that he only dared to submit his novel for consideration after the editor of *Novyi mir,* Konstantin Simonov, asked him if he had anything a bit sharp when they chanced to meet in the spring of 1956. Inspired by the Twentieth Party Congress and Simonov's query, Dudintsev risked submitting the nearly finished novel to several editors. Simonov alone, however, embraced the book and shepherded it quickly through reviewers and censors.[31]

Simonov had good reason to want *Not by Bread Alone* for his journal. *Novyi mir* had a reputation for publishing high quality prose and poetry with a critical edge. Within the boundaries of supporting Marxism-Leninism and recognizing its embodiment in the Soviet establishment, writers of fiction, essayists, and even literary critics were allowed to tackle social problems. Even before Stalin's death, for instance, *Novyi mir* had published stories and sketches highlighting inefficiencies in the party's administration of agriculture, a topic of perennial concern for policy makers. According to the unwritten norms of "permitted dissent"—a term coined by political scientist Dina Spechler to describe precisely the kind of material published by *Novyi mir*—problems raised publically had to be resolvable within the framework of socialism. Social pragmatic criticism, to use Spechler's distinction, was even welcome insofar as it provided constructive suggestions. Criticism of the norms of socialism, however, risked being interpreted as anti-Soviet.[32] Writers, hence, had to balance many demands—to be relevant yet artistic, critical but not pessimistic, grounded in daily life and compelling.

Editors, too, walked a tightrope in choosing how many and which daring works to promote. After Stalin's demise, then editor in chief of *Novyi mir* Aleksandr Tvardovskii led the way in challenging the strictures imposed on Soviet literature. In the 1946 Central Committee decree, which singled out and condemned satirist Mikhail Zoshchenko and poet Anna Akhmatova for their lack of partymindedness and in the case of Akhmatova overly introspective works, political authorities had made clear their vision of a literature that served the goals of the regime. In his poem "Distance beyond Distance" published in June 1953, however, Tvardovskii extolled his ideal—honest, aesthetically pleasing poetry that neither lectured nor condescended to readers. In December 1953 Tvardovskii published an even more provocative piece—Vladimir Pomerantsev's essay "On Sincerity in Literature." Coinciding with the publication of *The Thaw,* which portrayed the steep price paid by an artist who chose to paint to order, Pomerantsev's paean to sincerity unsettled ideologists and some literary bigwigs.

Cultural authorities had promulgated their own critiques of socialist realism over the years, most notably decrying excessive embellishing of Soviet reality to the point that authors lost all credibility and absence of dramatic conflict stemming from fear of attributing negative elements to Soviet characters.[33] The early thaw critics, however, went much further by depicting the dark side of the need to curry favor. They showed successful Soviet intellectuals as dishonest and grasping at worst and timid and insincere at best. For such affronts, Tvardovskii became the target of verbal attacks from conservatives and in the summer of 1954, with the support of Central Committee, the heads of the Writers' Union forced his resignation in favor of Simonov.[34]

A respected poet, playwright, and war correspondent, Simonov initially reined in the cultural liberalism cultivated by Tvardovskii. Yet he, too, understood the stifling nature of the 1946 Central Committee decree on Soviet literature and wanted to publish works that would earn *Novyi mir* respect from the progressive intelligentsia. Moreover, he heard the rumblings within the Writers' Union in the wake of the Twentieth Party Congress about the need to explore the causes and consequences of the cult of personality.[35] In this moment of soul-searching and uncertainty about the extent to which Stalinist practices were to be renounced, Dudintsev's novel presented a tantalizing combination of the pragmatic criticism common in the past and the raw, sincere outcry against the stifling of individual creativity that had surfaced since Stalin's death. *Not by Bread Alone* had the added appeal of raising economic issues that fit with Khrushchev's agenda.

The post-Stalin leadership knew full well that the planned economy faced problems with managers who responded to quotas by avoiding risk and who—like their political masters—often used their positions of power to discourage critical feedback. In his opening speech to the Twentieth Party Congress, Khrushchev had raised this issue, describing such a manager as one who "sits and thinks, 'why should I get involved in this? There's a lot of fuss and what's the good, you can get a lot of unpleasantness . . . Let them do the thinking at the top, let the bosses do it. If there is a directive about it, then we'll see.'" *Not by Bread Alone* could easily be viewed rebuking cowardly managers.[36]

Moreover, *Not by Bread Alone* tackled the Soviet Union's need to promote innovation. In the 1950s the USSR was attempting to move from extensive economic growth typical of early stages of industrialization to intensive growth, which meant increasing efficiency rather than just allocating additional resources. To compete with the West in military and consumer goods, the planned economy had to produce increasingly complex machines. Planners could incentivize workers and factories to raise output; it was harder to mandate innovation. Dudintsev's novel could be of use here because, as Spechler notes, "by illustrating those problems and the need for change in a dramatic, interesting form," pragmatic prose "made it easier for the Soviet leaders to arouse public interest and in and support for reforms that they themselves realized were necessary."[37] The leadership wanted to inspire inventors—as evident by the convening of the first ever "All-Union Congress of Rationalizers, Inventors, and Innovators of Production" in the summer of 1956—and Dudintsev made the inventor a popular hero.

Yet an internal Central Committee report from late September had already listed *Not by Bread Alone* first among recent problematic pieces in *Novyi mir*. While the staffers who prepared the report did not dissect Dudintsev's novel, its political shortcomings were clear. As a retired teacher wrote in care of *Novyi mir*, "Respected author, show us where in your novel there is at least one good, normal Soviet person?" The disgruntled reader protested that he was not opposed to criticism of bureaucracy, but where were the "decent" people, and why was the hero saved only by "blind fortune"?[38] Detractors bemoaned the high proportion of negative characters and the unheroic ending, yet it was the preponderance of passionate praise that would become a liability for the novel.

The Spin

In the same month that *Novyi mir* published the final installment of *Not by Bread Alone*, a discussion of the novel organized by the Moscow branch of the Writers' Union attracted so many people that mounted police had to be deployed to control the crowd. Later called on the carpet for letting such a wild scrum develop, the writer in charge of sending out invitations, poet Evgenii Dolmatovskii, recalled that he tried to explain to Khrushchev that they always printed two thousand tickets even though the hall at the Central House of Writers (TsDL) held only five hundred. A popular topic usually attracted at best two hundred attendees.[39] The huge turnout for the discussion of *Not by Bread Alone* took everyone, including the author, by surprise. After all, as of that moment not a single review of the novel had appeared in the central press—in part because the editorial staff at the leading cultural daily were divided in their opinions of the book.[40]

As Dudintsev and his wife made their way to the TsDL building on the evening of October 22, they felt a flush of excitement followed by dismay when they realized that the doors had been shut against the throng. To get them inside Simonov had to enlist the help of the staff of the club's adjoining restaurant. Once in the hall, Dudintsev could see nothing but humanity. As he recounted later, every inch of the hall was occupied and faces could be seen peering through each open window. "This, you know, took some talent," the novelist noted, "to somehow climb up to the second floor by the drainpipes and to occupy all the windows."[41]

Fans of the novel flocked to cheer the author and to defend him for the rumor mill had warned that ideologists were not pleased with *Not by Bread Alone*. With Central Committee staffers in attendance and a rowdy crowd, Simonov sternly called for a serious discussion and emphasized that the critical novel had been written "by a man who passionately loves Soviet power and who is ready to fight on its behalf." None of the novel's opponents took the stage that day and numerous members of the Writers' Union framed the novel as a source of pragmatic criticism in line with the Twentieth Party Congress. Nonetheless, the evening would show that it also inspired commentary that breached the bounds of the permissible.[42]

The first speakers at the event strove to set a positive tone by emphasizing the socialist virtues of *Not by Bread Alone*. Vsevolod Ivanov stressed that the novel's hero was a little man who won sympathy for his stubbornness in the face of adversity—just like Charlie Chaplin. Nikolai Atarov downplayed the novelty of the book, naming Lopatkin as one in a line of honest heroes in Soviet prose. He also credited the novel's popularity to the political moment: "The Party and its collective leadership are leading the people now to wonderful changes in life," he averred, "and there is nothing surprising then that our literature and our art are striking a chord." Indeed, the fact that the book had aroused a passionate response could be seen as a good sign of the population's engagement in current affairs. In this regard, playwright Lev Slavin linked Dudintsev's novel with reportage in *Pravda* from the Congress of Inventors that cited huge numbers of unimplemented suggestions to improve efficiency in Soviet industry. "And here Dudintsev's novel tells how [such things happen] and doesn't hide some bitter truths. He doesn't say that it always happens this way. He says that sometimes it happens like this, but that it should never be so." In other words, the novel fit the model of helpful advice regarding shortcomings already being addressed.[43]

The novel's negative personages posed more of a challenge for its circumspect supporters. Letters to *Novyi mir* show that Dudintsev's villains, especially Drozdov the factory boss turned central bureaucrat, rang truest to readers. Historian Denis Kozlov argues that many readers were so outraged by Drozdov's wily ways that they readily used Stalinist language about enemies and wreckers against him. Intellectuals wishing to promote reform did not want to endorse crude scapegoating, especially of government ministers, or to justify new purges. Their strategy was to temper the image of Drozdov by suggesting he was a relic of the now defunct cult of personality or an anomaly. Hence, Atarov insisted: "Drozdov does not have the right to say—'the State, that is I.'"[44]

Yet Dudintsev's supporters had difficulty in glossing over the unequal nature of the balance of forces in the novel, a balance that was quite apparent to readers. Having finished only the first two installments of the novel, M. Chetyrkina, an elderly woman from Slaviansk in Ukraine, for instance, already wrote to *Novyi mir* on October 1, 1956, to complain about its negative tone. She declared, "It's like some wretched Dostoevsky imitation [*Priamo Dostoevshchina kakaia-to*]!" In Stalinist style, she questioned the motives of *Novyi mir*'s editors. She asked accusingly, "Where is the Communist Party [*Kompartia*] in Dudintsev? Has it been disbanded in Moscow?"[45] Simonov, well aware of such critiques, introduced Dudintsev as a patriot at the event's start and other participants in the discussion hastened to cite his wartime service and to ascribe to him positive motives. Moreover, several writers justified his grim portrayal of ranks of obstructionist, self-serving officials as necessary to arouse the people's anger against careerists.[46] "Having unmasked these people," Sergei Mikhalkov asserted, "the author with his work says:

'I believe in the Party, I believe in the people, I believe that truth will triumph!'"[47]

By casting Dudintsev as aspiring to aid the party on its path of reform, his friendly peers were dodging the question raised by the near absence of party figures among the novel's heroes. Dudintsev was not the first to try to dodge the formula of having a party official arrive in the concluding moments to fix everything. But *Not by Bread Alone* further broke with this socialist realist model by leaving his hero still on the battlefield, so to speak, with only a small group of allies around him. The near absence of positive party members and the less than triumphal ending could create the impression that good men were outnumbered in Soviet institutions. This politically fraught interpretation became the bitterest point of conflict that evening.

Just as the young students in the audience were growing impatient with the circumspect praise of the novel, Konstantin Paustovskii, fresh from his European cruise, offered a shockingly harsh and candid tirade against what he saw as a real danger—a whole stratum of privileged, crude, arrogant and ignorant "Drozdovs." The senior writer began his speech by announcing that he did not wish to discuss the literary merits of *Not by Bread Alone*, but rather its social significance as "the opening skirmish with 'Drozdovs' against whom our literature should unleash all the force of its wrath until they vanish from our society."[48]

Hailing *Not by Bread Alone* as the "merciless and life affirming truth, that truth which is genuinely needed by the people on their difficult road to the construction of a new society, a new socialist order," Paustovskii rejected previous speakers' claims that selfish bureaucrats were few and confined to the past, Paustovskii posited that there were thousands of them. Emphasizing the seriousness of the phenomenon, he argued: "The problem lies in the fact that in our country there exists and even flourishes a new social stratum, a caste of middlebrow philistines. This tribe of predators and property owners has nothing in common with the revolution, or with our regime, or with socialism."[49] Paustovskii reinforced Dudintsev's portrait of narrow-minded elites with anecdotes about the "so-called *nomenklatura* workers" whom he had met on the *Pobeda* the previous month. He heaped scorn on the political appointees who traveled in first class and who made openly anti-Semitic statements, displayed sickly suspicion, and criticized everything foreign.

Paustovskii took his analysis of the ruling Soviet elite even further by posing—and answering—the most difficult question: "Where did they come from, these 'Drozdovs'?" He postulated that top bureaucrats had thrived on the purges. Conjuring up ranks of Stalin clones, Paustovskii railed: "Their weapons are betrayal, defamation, moral assassination, and just plain assassination." He accused them of destroying others for the sake of their own welfare. "If these 'Drozdovs' had not existed, we would still have living and working among us such talented men of the arts as [director Vsevolod] Meierhold, [writers Isaac] Babel, [and] Artem Veselyi, and many others."[50] In other words, a group of people inside the Stalinist system had benefited and continued to benefit from the purges (a topic Dudintsev had skirted). Paustovskii went on to cite the reckless despoliation of the environment as evidence that Soviet officials rather than epitomizing concern for the masses, disdained them. Unlike writers who served as the nation's conscience, bureaucrats concentrated on their own interests.

The audience hung on Paustovskii's every word, straining to hear his quiet, nasal voice. One student recalled, "A storm of applause greeted every paragraph of this independent and freewheeling speech. When Paustovskii finished, a genuine ovation lasting at least two minutes burst out."[51] The author and his editor were not so thrilled. In retrospect, Dudintsev would note that Paustovskii was not entirely at fault in the novel's fall from grace; ideological watchdogs were already uneasy. To wit, in her speech later that evening, writer Vera Ketlinskaia described frenzied reactions behind the scenes in publishing houses and in the offices of the Writers' Union, where she had heard conformists complaining that the situation described in the novel was "'not typical,' a 'distortion of reality,' [and] 'this is not a hero for our time,' 'such things don't happen.'" But gazing at the representatives of the Central Committee apparat who were sitting in the front row silently taking notes during Paustovskii's radical speech, Simonov muttered: "It's all over [*Vse propalo*]."[52]

On October 22, however, no one stepped forward to attack the novel; rather its fans clashed over how best to laud it. Valentin Ovechkin, himself a critic of administrative misdeeds, praised the book, but slammed Paustovskii for "putting weapons in the hands of Dudintsev's enemies" by exaggerating the negative tones of novel. Attempting to restore moderation to the evening, Ovechkin rejected Paustovskii's generalizations. Dudintsev, he contended, never meant to tar the whole leadership. Moreover, he asked why readers used crude arithmetic to try to tote up the predominance of good or bad characters when a spirit of patriotism and support for socialism infused the whole novel. Finally, he caustically expressed surprise at Paustovskii's bold speech given his record of tame writings.[53]

Insulted and perhaps concerned that he had hurt the novel's cause, Paustovskii took the floor again to accuse Ovechkin of misconstruing his words. He had never said that Drozdov signified the country's leaders (*vyshe rukovodstvo*). On the contrary, he noted, at the Twentieth Party Congress, the leadership had empowered the people to tackle the "Drozdovs" of the world. Furthermore, Paustovskii expressed dismay at Ovechkin's disrespectful interpretation of his speech: "Obviously—I completely forgot about this—one is obliged to start every conversation with the basics; it's mandatory to declare one's Soviet convictions, as if everything that a writer has done over the course of his life counts for naught." Last, Paustovskii addressed the conundrum that faced all who had succeeded under Stalin. "Ovechkin asks why I did not touch on these issues in my books—for the very same reason that Ovechkin himself and all other writers did not raise these issues with such openness as at present." He admitted he had tried to avoid writing about the person at the center of the cult and claimed he had concentrated instead on inspiring people to embrace values such as honesty and humanity that stood counter to the cult's essence. Each member of the audience, he implied, would have to decide if avoidance equaled cowardice or even collaboration.[54]

In their closing speeches, both Dudintsev and Simonov strove to leave the audience with a reassuring message. *Not by Bread Alone* was part of a tradition of critical literature written in a spirit of *partiinost'*. Deploying a metaphor that conjured up his wartime service record, Dudintsev rejected his colleagues' characterization of him as a path breaker: "I went, as they say, behind the tanks that went in front and laid heavily into the foe. Then they parted and gave me room. I stepped out and spent my ammunition and afterwards . . . I am sure that the same tanks now will move forward and say even sharper words in literature."[55] Simonov, meanwhile, disparaged Paustovskii's initiation of comparisons of who said Stalin's name how many times. After all, one could hardly write honestly about Soviet history without mentioning the leader. Attributing Paustovskii's confusion to the difficulty of absorbing new revelations, he urged writers to speak with care. It was a mistake for Paustovskii to paint all those in first class with one brush and equally misguided to not look for "Drozdovs" and "Galitskiis" among all classes, including among the ranks of writers. Solemnly reminding writers of their particular responsibility in rooting out consequences of past mistakes, Simonov expressed confidence that Dudintsev's novel would help secure a good future.[56]

At the end of the discussion, the chair read a note from the floor signed by a group of students from the Literary Institute: "Look around the hall: dozens of people are madly taking notes on the orators' speeches. An honest, truly party-minded conversation is taking place! The conversation will not end tomorrow or the day after. But for the sake of the matter it is vital that the essence of today's discussion reaches the broad mass of readers without distortion." The students wanted *Literaturnia gazeta* to publish a transcript of the event, and the audience voted overwhelmingly in favor. A week later, however, the newspaper published a much-abbreviated account with heavy editorializing. It charged Paustovskii with "drawing a series of untrue conclusions and generalizations [including] considering 'Drozdovs' a mass phenomenon." This dry judgment, however, by no means settled the matter. Instead, a bootleg transcript of Paustovskii's speech circulated among emboldened intellectuals and curious youth. Physics students at MGU even reprinted it in their wall newspaper.[57]

Into the Line of Fire

In the short run, Dudintsev and Simonov celebrated the event's upbeat ending with dinner and drinks in the adjoining House of Writers restaurant. If success were measured by popularity, Dudintsev had surely succeeded. And yet, while writers often cited reader response as a positive indicator of their work being in tune with Soviet ideals, the reviews that counted most would come from the top. The absence of a definitive signal from above would last one more month. In the meantime, the leaders of the prose section of the Moscow Writers' Union calmly discussed the organizational lessons from the event at their meeting the next week and Dudintsev prepared for speaking engagements at MGU and LGU.[58]

In November, however, young people would redirect the discussion of *Not by Bread Alone* away from literary themes and into the realm of activism. To stormy applause from an overflowing auditorium at LGU, Revol't Pimenov, for instance, would use the novel as a jumping off point for deep criticism that included the post-Stalin Soviet system, declaring: "It's not just in the sphere of inventions that we have such a state of affairs that arises when secret networks of people [form] using nearly boundless power and declaring a monopoly on the truth. Such a situation exists in history, literature, art, philosophy, biology, physics, linguistics and politics. For these monopolists of the truth, the most horrifying things, to use the words of the novel, are "openness [*glasnost'*], debate, comparison."[59]

In describing the fate of thwarted inventors as they struggled against indifference and egotism, Dudintsev had ended up illuminating ways in which the system of centralized planning and one-party rule malfunctioned. The Secret Speech endorsed criticism as a principle and hence some readers of the novel felt empowered to stray from rubric of cult of personality to tackle wider economic and management issues. Questions in the wake of the Twentieth Party Congress had included concerns about wage levels and inequity in housing and access to education. Now, according to literary specialist Raisa Orlova, ordinary readers recognized the "Drozdovs" in their own workplaces and the personification of a smooth-talking and hypocritical bigwig made it easier for them to broach the desire for more just economic relations.[60]

Dudintsev's reminder that among those who thrived under socialism were callous, calculating operators had also sparked a debate about whether opportunists were rare or the norm. Sergei Dmitriev noted in his diary that the hero and his small band of eleven allies—"were too few for the 39th year of socialist revolution, which had supposedly created an unprecedented moral-political unity of Soviet society." Dmitriev concluded, "Judging by the novel, such unity really has been created, it exists. Only it's a moral-political unity of a society of careerists, bureaucrats, graspers, louts, traitors, and conmen." Yugoslav Milovan Djilas's heretical theory of a "new class" of opportunists within the Communist Party had not penetrated the USSR in 1956, but Paustovskii, Dmitriev, and others had been struck by a similar disturbing notion.[61]

In discussions of *Not by Bread Alone,* it would become clear that the very naming of such a group of insulated, privileged public "servants" legitimized reform in some eyes, but constituted slander of the party in others. Already in October an astute reader, who liked the first two parts of the novel but not the ending, had prophetically warned that Lopatkin's salvation by only a few honest people and happy coincidence "discredits us in the eyes of our friends and enemies." "Every honest Polish, German, English, Chinese worker or intellectual who reads your novel," he predicted, "will see the terrible force of the Stalinist bureaucratic, anti-popular system, but will not see the means for its real . . . overcoming."[62] The novel, in other words, had crossed over into unconstructive criticism.

November would reveal an unfortunate coincidence—the timing of the novel's enthusiastic embrace overlapped with political turmoil in the socialist bloc. The participation of Hungarian students and intellectuals in an armed insurrection seemed to fulfill party pessimists' fears about the consequences of weakening control over culture and politics. Consequently, Dudintsev, his novel, and his most vocal fans would all feel the party's wrath.

11 | NOVEMBER

WINDS FROM THE EAST

In the last days of October 1956, Revol't Pimenov signed his full name under a frank letter protesting Soviet military "interference in the internal affairs of Hungary." He then mailed copies to some twenty deputies of the Soviet legislature whose addresses he had managed to search out. Rather than write to Communist Party First Secretary Khrushchev, the head of genuinely most powerful Soviet institution, Pimenov chose to act as if he were in the democracy the USSR purported to be. Therefore, he called on his elected representatives to assert control over the dispatch of troops outside of the country's borders. Not surprisingly, several deputies forwarded his impudent missive straight to the KGB. However, Pimenov really attracted the attention of the authorities—and of his peers—when he spoke out at the discussion of *Not by Bread Alone* at Leningrad State University on November 10. There he not only denounced monopolists and bureaucrats in all spheres of Soviet life but also battled complacency by criticizing otherwise intelligent people who justified patently unfair practices such as anti-Semitic quotas in higher education.[1]

Pimenov would later admit that he had only skimmed Dudintsev's long novel before the event with the author. He had been too busy that fall tracking diverse political developments in the socialist bloc. Information about discord in Eastern Europe and the description of an insular bureaucracy in *Not by Bread Alone*, however, both fed his determination to push for more change at home. Pimenov believed that the Secret Speech's commitment to ending repression and accepting more criticism had opened up the possibility for more responsive politics. In November 1956 he sought to stir up the bold discourse that he imagined could begin to shape public opinion, which in turn might influence policy makers. The organized discussion of *Not by Bread Alone* served as a platform for him to raise the consciousness of a larger audience to what he saw as the flaws of the Soviet system and the consequences of passivity. His confrontational tactics, commitment to sweeping democratization, and overweening self-confidence put Pimenov in a distinct minority. However, the cheers he received from Leningrad students reflected a broader craving among Soviet youth for more freedom to debate politics and art.

In the fall of 1956, Soviet dormitories resounded with heated arguments as students analyzed *Not by Bread Alone,* discussed Soviet rapprochement with Yugoslavia and antagonism with Poland, and puzzled over news from Hungary. November and December also saw young people in Moscow and Leningrad flocking to the Pushkin State Fine Arts Museum and the State Hermitage to enter into lively disputes over whether Picasso was a genius or a charlatan. Sensations on the cultural scene as well as fast paced changes in foreign affairs prompted Soviet citizens—with students in the forefront—to form their own judgments on art, on the role of the USSR in the international socialist movement, and invariably on the nature of the ideal post-Stalinist state. Students from different institutions began to voice identical demands to be allowed to test new ideas, to have open disagreements be tolerated, and to have authorities persuade rather than dictate. I argue that in late 1956 raw emotions and a whirlwind of controversies drew once reticent or formerly complacent students into genuinely political debates and that desire for free speech only grew when confronted by resistance from the establishment.

Polemical articles in wall newspapers, unauthorized leaflets, diaries, private letters, unsanctioned meetings, and even casual speech show that in the autumn of 1956 many Soviet young people were avidly following cultural and political controversies in what were then called the "fraternal people's democracies." Looking west to Eastern Europe and even beyond, and displaying a certain confidence that the rules for speaking out had changed. The preoccupations of politicized youth in Moscow and Leningrad—admittedly a subset of young people—expose the scope of questions that arose among attentive citizens as more information flowed in from abroad and as other socialist states grappled with de-Stalinization. Ironically, young people would demand that the authorities trust them to think for themselves just as the Hungarian events shook Soviet party leaders' confidence in the strength of socialism. The subsequent crackdown on exuberant freethinkers (*vol'nodumtsy*) would produce a new generation of political prisoners, Pimenov among them.[2] November 1956 saw the limits of tolerance being reset, while December would show the coercive power of a disoriented, fractured, but entrenched Communist Party.

Pimenov's writings in 1956 as preserved in his KGB file as well as his memoirs and those of several others in his circle provide a rich base for examining the politicization of one small group of Soviet youth. Pimenov's escalating activism and growing circle of allies demonstrate how fast-paced developments that autumn stimulated freethinkers.[3] However, Pimenov and his "co-conspirators" were not alone in their incautious, sometimes deliberately provocative political speech in late 1956; I examine here several cases from Moscow and Leningrad of conflict between students and authorities regarding—in roughly chronological order—rapprochement with Yugoslavia, publication of *Not by Bread Alone,* unrest in Poland, the Hungarian uprising, and the Picasso exhibit. The minority who publicly tested the limits on free speech around these issues generally found support among their peers who avidly read incendiary student writings, clapped for bold speeches, and sometimes even protested the punishment of freethinkers in their institutes and universities. Hence, the persecution and sometimes prosecution of freethinkers sheds light on their contemporaries' attitudes, including toward the renewal of harsh punishments for "anti-Soviet agitation and propaganda."[4]

Looking to the "Near Abroad"

Back in May 1956, the twenty-five year-old Pimenov and his friend Ernst Orlovskii had written a letter to the Soviet newspaper *Literatur-*

naia gazeta praising the appearance of two Yugoslav periodicals—*Borba* (Struggle) and *Politika* (Politics)—among other socialist bloc publications for sale, yet complaining that they were available only in limited numbers at a single newsstand in Leningrad. Noting that *Pravda* had recently reported that Yugoslavs could now subscribe to Soviet newspapers, Pimenov and Orlovskii complained about Soviet citizens' inability to do the same for Yugoslav periodicals. They couched their request in politically correct language, noting: "Over the course of a long time, we have been following the successes of the construction of socialism abroad, the achievements in economics, science, culture, and sport" and adding that access to the Yugoslav press would greatly help them "to understand the diverse forms of socialism."[5] In fact, Pimenov anticipated correctly that the Yugoslav media would continue to outstrip its Soviet counterpart in reporting on political developments. *Borba* had already provided more details about the Secret Speech than any Soviet editions. At MGU students had sought it out in late March as they waited impatiently to hear Khrushchev's report.[6]

Moreover, like many in the Soviet Union, Pimenov and Orlovskii were curious about Josip Broz Tito, the Yugoslav partisan and communist leader who had fallen sharply out of favor with Stalin. In the eyes of liberal youth, Stalin's hatred for Tito now only redounded in the Yugoslav's favor. Aleksandr Gidoni, another Leningrader later caught up in the crackdown on freethinkers, frankly idolized Tito, even proclaiming him the "Lenin of his time" at a meeting of students that December. The twenty-year-old Gidoni admired Tito for his popularity with the peoples of Yugoslavia, his wartime record, and for coming up with a national path to socialism—the very qualities that had sparked Stalin's jealousy.[7] Stalin meant for the USSR to be the unquestioned center of the new postwar socialist "camp," and he had sensed in Tito a strong rival. In his typical Manichean fashion, Stalin had dubbed the Yugoslavs "traitors" and "enemies," forced the other Soviet satellite states to join a trade blockade against them, and encouraged the naming of Yugoslavs as villains in East European show trials. Khrushchev's steps toward reconciliation with Tito, therefore, seemed a potent symbol of change.

In the summer of 1956, Tito spent nearly three weeks touring the USSR and engaging in high-level talks. This visit built on a warming promoted by Khrushchev's own trip to Belgrade in 1955 during which he had conceded that the Soviets carried the lion's share of the blame for the Soviet-Yugoslav rift.[8] Though wary of being roped again into an unequal alliance, the Yugoslav leaders wanted to end their isolation from Moscow and its European allies. Moreover, though not aspiring to membership in the Warsaw Pact, Yugoslav leaders had looked favorably on its formation the previous year as evidence that the post-Stalin USSR might be ready to begin to base its relations with allies on formal, mutually binding rules rather than imperial dictates. Finally, since they saw themselves as victims of Stalin, the Yugoslavs welcomed Khrushchev's report on the cult of personality.[9]

During Tito's extended sojourn in the USSR in June 1956, the Soviet press trumpeted newly amicable relations with Yugoslavia as Khrushchev played the genial host. Perhaps drawing on his experience in Britain that spring, Khrushchev set out to show Tito a warm popular welcome and hence paraded him in front of excited crowds. In Leningrad an atmosphere of celebration prevailed as hundreds of thousands lined the streets to catch a glimpse of the mysterious Yugoslav leader once reviled by Stalin. Indeed, Gidoni ran all around the city until he finally caught a glimpse of his hero. In Stalingrad so many people turned out for Khrushchev and Tito's visit to the famous battlefield at Mamaev Kurgan that they overwhelmed security.[10]

Those who could not see Tito in person got to know him through three weeks of front-page coverage starting off with *Pravda*'s publication of his biography and formal portrait on the eve of his visit. The leading Soviet newspaper then reported daily on Tito's stops in the USSR from his arrival at the Ukrainian border until his departure. Coverage included his speeches and photos, including one showing Khrushchev and Tito surrounded by Muscovites on Pushkin square. Informality and a lack of barriers marked a sharp contrast from Stalin's aloofness and demonstrated Khrushchev's confidence in Russians' reception of him and his guest. Moreover, though Khrushchev and other members of the presidium were not entirely comfortable with Tito's persistent advancement of his own agenda, they treated him with outward respect and ultimately signed a joint declaration committing Moscow to cooperation "based on complete voluntarism, equal rights, friendly criticism, and a comradely character to the exchange of opinions on contested issues."[11]

Fig. 11-01 Josip Broz Tito speaking to a rally at the Dynamo Stadium in Moscow, June 1956.
Courtesy Russian State Film and Photo Archive.

The Yugoslavs also pushed to get their message to the Soviet public that rapprochement was based on the Soviet side's realization of the positive aspects of diversity within the cause of socialism. As reported verbatim in *Pravda*, Tito lectured a large Soviet audience at Moscow's Dynamo stadium: "In the reports of your Party's XXth Congress, you read that there exist different paths to socialism; you read that each country has its own specific qualities which give birth to its own path to one and the same goal, to socialism. So our path differs a little [*neskol'ko*] from the path along which you are going, but we have the same goal and differences in paths shouldn't hinder the very closest cooperation between countries that are building socialism."[12] Such a concession to pluralism seemed to reinforce Khrushchev's promises of a break not only with Stalin, but also with his practices of classifying as enemies all those who strayed from his party line. It also legitimized curiosity as to the nature of the Yugoslav model.

Although Soviet readers found few concrete details about the Yugoslav national path in their media, the decision to start selling Yugoslav periodicals (albeit in small quantities) in the USSR offered a real channel of contact with Eastern Europe. Aleksandr Gidoni, like Pimenov, became an avid consumer of the Yugoslav press in the spring 1956. Moreover, as a graduate student—he had recently finished an undergraduate degree in history in just two years—Gidoni had easy access to other young people and he shared his fascination with anyone who would listen. He would later boast that he was considered quite the specialist in the endless discussions of "fashionable Titoism" that took place in his dormitory at Leningrad State University. In retrospect, Gidoni admitted, "Of course, the degree of my 'Yugoslav specialization' was very relative. For instance, I had only the vaguest notion about the affair of [Milovan] Djilas and [Vladimir] Dedijer, about the Italian-Yugoslav conflict over Trieste, about the genuine problems in Yugoslavia itself even as regards nationalities."[13] Yet the Yugoslav press provided a different, if also limited, view of the ideal socialist state and economy, as well of developments elsewhere in the bloc. Pimenov's friend Ernst Orlovskii, for instance, would rely on *Borba* to create a timeline of the Hungarian uprising.[14]

For those interested in alternatives to Soviet-style socialism, the importance of access to foreign socialist newspapers increased in the summer and fall of 1956 as Poland became the site of increasing cultural and political unrest. Pimenov himself later confessed that, busy with a mathematical paper in the summer of 1956, he had not initially taken note of the June events in Poznan, which featured only on the back page of Soviet newspapers. When his mathematics students asked him in October what he thought of the "revolution" in Poland, Pimenov's first reaction was to retort: "Don't utter such stupidities. Solve your problems." However, intrigued by his students' jumbled accounts—which likely drew on foreign radio broadcasts—Pimenov went home and started reading. "By the next day," he reminisced, "not even smoke remained from mathematics. For the next four months, I lived exclusively for politics."[15]

Pimenov tuned in to Polish affairs at a moment of great change. On October 19, the divided leaders of the Polish communist party had convened a three-day plenum to address prevalent unrest among workers and intellectuals. Without consulting their Soviet allies, they selected as their new first secretary Władisław Gomułka, a veteran communist who had been jailed as a result of political purges between 1951 and 1954 and only restored to the party in August 1956. "From prison—to first secretary!" Pimenov would exult in a letter to his father later that month.[16] The readmission of a rehabilitated person to the highest circles of power seemed another sign that Poland had raced ahead of the Soviet Union in acknowledging and grappling with the negative aspects of Stalinism. Polish intellectuals already had taken the lead in questioning the strictures of socialist realism, as Pimenov and other liberals knew from an April article by Jan Kott from *Przegląd Kulturalny* that circulated widely among students in an informal translation.[17]

Khrushchev and other Soviet leaders, however, were alarmed by the disarray within the Polish party that had led to such a choice for first secretary. They knew their Polish counterparts had been struggling to maintain order after using force in Poznan to disperse crowds led by factory workers angry about changes in the work quota system and price rises. In the June incident, thousands of protesters had marched on the center of Poznan and at one point even attacked government buildings and police stations and seized weapons. Polish armored and infantry divisions quelled the disturbance at the cost of approximately sixty civilians killed and more than six hundred wounded. The blatant and unrepentant deployment of violence against workers, however, sparked various smaller protests throughout Poland that summer and fall. Heading into October, the Polish party was facing ever more frequent and open calls for de-Stalinization of the political system and a reduction of Soviet influence across the board.[18]

As a stalwart communist who had shed the Stalinist taint by dint of his own suffering, Gomułka had the potential to mend some of the divisions in the party and society. However, his initial selection led to more contention. Stunned not to have been asked about this major personnel change and alarmed by reports of increasingly common anti-Soviet rhetoric in the public sphere, Khrushchev took several presidium members and flew uninvited to Warsaw. He also activated Soviet military units near the city. Clearly not having internalized the idea that the satellite states were to be treated equals, he greeted the Polish leaders with an intemperate tirade. Only after protestations that Khrushchev's crude threats contradicted the norms of socialist solidarity and fervent reassurances from Gomułka that the Poles valued Soviet friendship did Khrushchev calm down and call off troop movements toward Warsaw. Tense negotiations left Gomułka in charge and affirmed the Polish-Soviet alliance. Gomułka's leadership skills and sway over the public stood him in good stead in getting the Soviets to deescalate. Khrushchev would later claim a long-standing good opinion of Gomułka, but evidently he worried that Stalin's tacit approval for his imprisonment might have turned him against the Soviet Union.[19]

Readers of the Soviet press, however, knew very little about the wave of anti-Soviet outbursts and pro-reform demands that had unsettled the Polish leadership. The Soviet media had reported only tersely on events in Poznan and consistently attributed them to outside intervention. *Pravda,* for instance, titled its first reportage on June 30 "Enemy Provocation by Imperialist Agents in Poznan" and cited an initial Polish explanation that "disorder" had stemmed from carefully planned provocations by a "reactionary underground" and foreign agents.[20] In mid-July *Pravda* allowed that there were some economic reasons why Polish workers were inveigled into joining the demonstration but focused on preaching vigilance against radical opinions. It quoted Polish first secretary Ochab's assertion that the press could not be allowed to distort facts or socialist theories, denigrate the people's achievements, defame the Soviet-Polish relationship, or provide a platform for bourgeois propaganda.[21]

In actuality the Polish communist leadership had been permitting critical voices in the press and in the public sphere for quite some time. Since Stalin's death the Polish media had been publishing relatively frank articles about the extremely poor state of the domestic economy. Moreover, the Polish literary press in 1954–1955 repeatedly reported criticism of socialist realism for stifling individuality. Journalists also joined in with, as one analyst noted, "numerous reports covering sore spots in socialist society . . . agricultural conditions, public morality, juvenile delinquency, alcoholism, prostitution, administrative excesses and the like." The youth weekly *Po Prostu* had even critiqued state and party institutions. When Khrushchev and his entourage arrived uninvited in Warsaw on October 19, they brought a sheaf of offensive articles with them. Moreover, they issued a warning of sorts by commissioning an attack on the Polish press that appeared in *Pravda* the next day.[22]

Pravda's sudden scathing denunciation of several Polish authors prompted Pimenov to pen a new letter. Unlike his moderately worded appeal for the opportunity to subscribe to Yugoslav journals, this epistle minced no words. In a turnabout to "Anti-Soviet Statements in the Pages of the Polish Press," Pimenov titled his response "Anti-Democratic State-ments in the Pages of the Soviet Press" and touted the virtues of discus-sion with citations to Lenin, Tito, and Indonesian president Sukarno, who also had also visited Moscow that summer. He concurred with *Pravda* that, "Yes, recently a lot of sharp and new statements have ap-peared in the Polish press." Judging some of them to be "untrue and hasty," Pimenov argued nevertheless, "Some of them are doubtlessly true, others ought to be debated." Moreover, he defended such "slanderers" as the lit-erary figures Jan Kott, Julian Przyboś, and Antoni Słonimski, calling them "searchers" and claiming that the Polish writers were "agonizingly striv[ing] to erase from memory the shameful years of fearing their own shadows; they want socialism to become a heavenly kingdom of freedom and creativity. They are seeking such a path . . . So sometimes they err." Here Pimenov admitted his own shortcomings—he did not comprehend cubist paintings. "But," he chided the editors of *Pravda*, "I don't label the cubists 'anti-socialists.'" By contrast, he concluded: "*Pravda*'s 'own' corre-spondent is not a seeker . . . He is a sentry."[23]

Unlike the majority of its readers, Pimenov—thanks to his perusal of the Polish press—had a good idea about why *Pravda* had savagely at-tacked Polish intellectuals. He, however, found plenty of ammunition in the *Pravda* piece to defend his point of view without letting on that he was familiar with outside sources. For instance, in defending Jerzy Putrament, who had allegedly maligned the state of the Polish economy, Pimenov made no specific claims about conditions in Poland but cited a comment by Khrushchev that earlier agricultural policies in the USSR had led to a dead end. Therefore, Pimenov proposed that perhaps *Pravda* would like to publish a piece entitled "Anti-Socialist statements by Comrade Khrushchev." Pimenov further goaded the establishment by suggesting that Putrament might be arguing that since the Soviet model had failed, it was time to try the Yugoslav one. The stance of "our own correspondent" in Poland that presented the Soviets as the utmost arbiter of what was socialist seemed to be a throwback to the era of the cult of personality.

In pursuit of his own free speech agenda, Pimenov compared the *Pravda* journalist to a policeman who wanted "put a muzzle" on anyone with dissident views. Speaking for the younger generation, he contended that *Pravda*'s tactic of labeling those Polish authors with whom it took issue as "slanderers" solved no problems because it did not persuade. Instead, it harkened back to the purges. In conclusion Pimenov challenged the editors of *Pravda* to show their commitment to pluralism by publishing his letter: "The government in the country of socialism is designed to realize the will of the people. And the will and opinion of the people is not just the will and opinion of the 'mister our own correspondent'; my opinion is also part of the opinion of the people. To withhold this from the people means to misinform public opinion."[24] Pimenov did not really believe in the representative nature of the existing Soviet state, but he wanted to leverage the regime's avowal of a democratic legitimacy to increase its accountability. Hence when news came of Soviet intervention in Hungary a week later, Pimenov sent his protest directly to deputies of the Supreme Soviet, despite its rubber stamp nature.

In the fall of 1956, Pimenov calculated that "legal means" of opposition—namely, expressing opinions at meetings or in signed letters to official institutions—provided the best hope for change. To that end he began to try to mobilize allies. He and his friends looked to controversial cultural events to identify and connect with other curious young people. Throughout November and December an exuberant Pimenov would engage new acquaintances, including much younger students from the Leningrad Library Institute. They in turn would press him to adopt more radical forms of organization and propaganda especially in light of events in Hungary and the role of student activism there.

Revolution or Counterrevolution?

Hard on the heels of the tussle with the Polish leadership, Khrushchev had to turn his attention to Hungary, where the local communist party also faced internal rifts exacerbated by the Secret Speech and social pressure for reform. Unlike Poland, where the Stalinist first secretary

Bolesław Bierut had conveniently died of natural causes on the heels of the Twentieth Party Congress, Stalin's Hungarian favorite Mátyás Rákosi remained at the helm of his party. However, his authority eroded under calls from within the party elite to investigate and prosecute Stalin era crimes and to promote reformers, most notably Imre Nagy. Dissatisfaction arose outside the party, as well. In March 1956 young people had organized a discussion forum—the Petőfi Circle—that in July drew some six thousand to a discussion about free press. Shortly thereafter, Anastas Mikoyan arrived from Moscow to help steer Rákosi out of his post while engineering a more moderate replacement in the person of Ernő Gerő. The new leader, however, proved incapable of calming tensions as was evident when tens of thousands gathered on October 6 to witness the reburial of Lazlo Rajk, the former interior minister who had become the victim of a show trial in 1949.

Simmering discontent exploded in Budapest on October 23. A demonstration by students in sympathy with their Polish peers who were trying to organize an independent youth league turned into a massive march joined by workers and military cadets and ending with chants of "Russians go home" and a rally of hundreds of thousands in front of the Hungarian parliament. In one eventful night, which cannot be covered in full here, a massive statue of Stalin in Budapest was toppled, and the reformer Imre Nagy reemerged. Martial law could not quell the disorder and on the night of October 24, Soviet troops entered Budapest. Urban warfare in the capital, as well as strikes and violence in provincial cities followed. Soviet troops temporarily withdrew at Nagy's request on October 29 to be replaced by Hungarian armed forces in an effort to calm the situation. However, unhappy with reports of continued unrest, violent attacks on communists, especially members of the Hungarian secret police, and a fiercely anti-Soviet atmosphere, Khrushchev reconsidered. On November 4, after consultations with Tito and other socialist leaders and following much vacillation, Khrushchev dispatched more tanks and troops to quell the Hungarian uprising.

Not surprisingly, the seemingly sudden crisis in Hungary (which coincided with conflict between Egypt, Britain, and France over the Suez Canal) drew the attention of the Soviet public to the international sphere. On November 3 historian Sergei Dmitriev noted in his diary that "the main topic of all conversations is events in Hungary." It seemed clear to him that "open military intervention of the USSR against Hungary" was imminent, and indeed the next day he expressed his shame at that turn of events, adding, "Even though the Hungarians are being suppressed not by the Russian people but by the communist power of the USSR, the Russian people are silent, behaving themselves like a nation of slaves."[25] And yet, as he himself had noted the previous day, they were not entirely silent. Private conversations, however, were not the same as public expressions. Yet the passion of both those Russians appalled by the Hungarian "counterrevolution" and those dismayed by "Soviet imperialism" was so strong that incautious words bubbled up most noticeably among young people.

Discussions of Hungary were everywhere in student circles that November. At the All-Union State Institute of Cinematography (VGIK), students debated in the dorms at night past lights-out, swapped news in the corridors, and asked difficult questions in the classrooms. There an older student, a party member, would trigger the arrest of two classmates when he wrote a denunciation to the KGB about a fellow student's interpretation of the Hungarian events as a revolution rather than a counterrevolution. The young man in question had argued that American propaganda alone could hardly account for the uprising given the huge number of Hungarians who had turned out against the system. He also alleged that those being lynched in Hungary were most likely Stalinists whom the people rightfully blamed for copying the good and bad from the USSR.[26]

At MGU, too, party members expressed concern about the vociferous and unguided discussions taking place in dormitories. At a party meeting in the School of History, one participant reported that he had heard young people were debating whether Yugoslavia was indeed an example of socialism and whether one could speak of a cult of Tito.[27] Most student conversations, however, went unrecorded and unpunished. What remain from the moment for historians—and what attracted the full scrutiny of the Soviet secret police—are writings, especially leaflets manufactured on a small scale and pasted on walls or scattered on public transport. While not providing a full view of student views on Hungary, these documents cast light on how some young people connected Soviet intervention with Stalinist practices.

Two philology students at Moscow University wrote, "Friends! On the bayonets of your countrymen thousands of patriots in Poland and Hungary are being destroyed, hundreds of thousands of honest people are arrested, tortured, and killed in the other nations of the so-called 'people's democracies' and here in the USSR." They fretted, "Our government, covering itself with high-sounding phrases, is pushing the peoples of the whole world toward a new war with its aggressive behavior." They added, "It relies on your support, on your silence. Aren't you ashamed friends?" In their long leaflet, Andrei Terekhin and Vladimir Kuznetsov poured out their fury in prose and verse.[28]

Poetry had brought the two classmates together. Both Terekhin and Kuznetsov admired "decadent" verse excluded from the socialist realist canon. Through his father, a distinguished professor of linguistics at MGU, Kuznetsov had access to prerevolutionary and rare editions, which he shared with a small, close-knit group of poetry-loving classmates. Kuznetsov also participated in "tourist" hikes and both young men were involved with student publications, but they considered themselves to be free spirits. Terekhin especially was not a disciplined student. He frequently skipped class and had a reputation for indulging in drink and telling tactless jokes. But the Soviet invasion was no laughing matter to them.[29]

Kuznetsov would recall that his excited interest in the first reports of student demonstrations in Hungary gave way to bitterness when he learned of intervention by Soviet military units. He and his friends could not believe that the Soviet government was using force in a friendly state at the very moment it was criticizing British and French "imperialism" in Egypt. Over the November holiday marking the thirty-ninth anniversary of the Bolshevik Revolution, Terekhin and Kuznetsov borrowed a married friend's empty dorm room and his typewriter. In a single burst of energy they wrote and typed a dozen copies of their proclamation. Once they had pasted one up near the elevators in the dorm at MGU, they scattered the others on buses and trams. Kuznetsov said they felt an emotional relief afterward, though they entertained no expectations that their gesture would change anything.[30]

Boris Pustyntsev, one of a group of Leningrad students sentenced in 1957 for producing anti-Soviet leaflets and discussing ideas for an alternative political party, also admitted that he and his friends wrote and distributed a tract in November 1956 without realistic a hope of change. He described it as more of a feeling of "necessity" to protest what they saw as agonizingly wrong policies toward Hungary. He and his loose circle of friends—they did not call themselves "freethinkers," but recognized one another as individualists and outsiders—disagreed on many issues of the day, with some favoring Yugoslav-style socialism, others calling themselves Leninists, and still others being apolitical, but they all condemned intervention in Hungary.[31]

As Pustyntsev later explained, he and his friend Aleksandr Golikov sat down together in a mood of outrage to pen their leaflet. Their text began: "Citizen Students! Cracks have appeared in the communist citadel. The proof lies in events in Hungary and Poland where popular freedom was crushed under the treads of Soviet tanks." They took their typescript to their circle of friends, but not all of them agreed with this exposition. A second draft opened: "Students! Stalinism continues to exist. The banner of Leninism has been trampled. This is evident in the increased despotism in our country. This is evident in the events in Poland and Hungary where freedom was trampled under the treads of Soviet tanks." The first text asked students if they knew about the calls for freedom being raised by their peers; the second inquired whether it was time for Soviets to rise up and ended: "Down with despotism, the domination of a narrow clique, down with bureaucracy from top to bottom!" Hence, while Hungary was the catalyst for action, these young people ended up focusing on what they knew better—the situation at home. Moreover, for them the government's perceived misdeeds abroad reflected the legacies of Stalinism and the scourge of bureaucracy inside the USSR.

While student accounts of November 1956 are replete with mentions of genuine questions about what was going on in Hungary and real arguments with some defending Soviet actions, the texts composed by politically engaged young people in the immediate wake of the Soviet intervention in Hungary are characterized by agitation, bitterness, and a rejection of euphemisms. For instance, when Pimenov organized his views into twenty "Theses on the Hungarian Revolution," he deliberately used the word *revolution* to challenge official rhetoric about a "coup" or "counterrevolution." Similarly, he eschewed the labels "fascists" or "bourgeois elements" to describe participants in the unrest but spoke rather of "the masses."[32]

In his theses, Pimenov combined erudite reasoning and inflammatory bombast. He argued, for instance, that the Hungarian events could not be a putsch because those dissolve quickly in the case of failure, whereas fighting continued broadly across Hungary even after Soviet intervention. Yet he also referred to Khrushchev and the other presidium members as "the true comrades in arms and students of Joseph the Bloody" and accused them of having "thrown off their masks of liberalism." Graduate student Viktor Sheinis, a new acquaintance of Pimenov's that fall, criticized Pimenov's theses for a lack of Marxist rigor. Yet when Sheinis wrote his own "scientific" analysis of the roots of the Hungarian uprising, he also acted out of strong emotion. Fifty years later he summed up the essence of his article more in terms of a cri de coeur: "The main idea was as follows: Lenin would not have acted like this. This was Stalinism; this was a violation of Leninist principles."[33] Pimenov, who had soured on socialism, and Sheinis, who wanted to purify it, joined in condemning the Soviet use of force against the people of Hungary.

In the spirit of moral renaissance in the wake of having been beguiled by the Stalin cult, student writings combined specific demands to withdraw from Hungary with exhortations to try to realize the promise of civic input. Kuznetsov and Terekhin reminded readers that the regime relied on their acquiescence. Pustyntsev and friends lamented, "The political initiative of the people has disappeared and in its place have come silence and whispers" and similarly asked readers: "Aren't you tired of keeping silent?" Pimenov offered a more abstract notion of opposition: "The force of the state must be countered with force—foremost the force of public opinion." In concrete terms he urged people to seek out alternate news sources—whether the BBC or the Yugoslav press—to form their own opinions, and to voice them in party or youth league meetings or by writing appeals to the Soviet press and to the government. Soviet students should follow the lead of their central European counterparts in initiating discussions about political reform and then—if enough momentum built—the Soviet government might have to reckon with public opinion, "and then one can hope that a repetition of the Hungarian tragedy will become impossible."[34]

Pimenov followed his own advice. He wrote to members of the Supreme Soviet and the press and spoke out at the discussion at LGU. Garnering snippets of information from foreign media sources and from friends, he and his girlfriend Irena Verblovskaia began to compile and share a bulletin about events not covered in the Soviet media.[35]

Pimenov also actively sought to broaden his connections with like-minded people each of whom might reach out to his or her own friends. His fiery speech at the Dudintsev event attracted the interest of other politicized youth, including Boris Gal'pernin, who was seated nearby. Gal'pernin exchanged phone numbers with Pimenov afterward and introduced him to a circle of other young university graduates including his wife—journalist Irma Kudrova—her childhood friend Viktor Sheinis and his wife, Alla Nazimova, who taught Marxism-Leninism at a Leningrad institute. Deeply interested in politics (though from a Marxist perspective), Sheinis and his crowd met repeatedly with Pimenov and Verblovskaia and their friends to discuss current events as well as Pimenov's unpublished articles on the history of non-Bolshevik revolutionaries in Russia.[36]

Pimenov also collected younger acquaintances in late 1956. Most notably he sought out the first-year Library Institute student Boris Vail' after reading a vituperative article in a local paper in which Vail' and several classmates were ridiculed and derided for their pessimistic and allegedly fatuous writings. The Library Institute students, like many others that fall, had created an informal outlet for expression, in this case a handwritten journal entitled "Heresy" (*Eres'*) with poetry and prose composed by sometimes pseudonymous student authors. Pimenov's friend Orlovskii had met Vail' through a new club in Leningrad dedicated to Esperanto and so with some confidence that he would be open-minded and sympathetic to democratic ideas Pimenov sought him out in his dormitory.[37]

Vail' recalled later that he felt an immediate kinship with this "snub-nosed blond fellow in glasses." He had imagined that somewhere in the city there must exist opposition organizations and he immediately took Pimenov for "a man from the Center" who could answer his questions about politics and let him in on secret doings. Unlike the older Marxists who loved to debate theory but recoiled from any talk of actions or organizations, Vail' and the half-dozen classmates he would recruit to meet Pimenov were attracted precisely by the idea of conspiracy and risky deeds. They wanted to figure out how to print proper leaflets and demanded a program. In late November and early December, however, Pimenov advocated only what he dubbed legal forms of opposition, which meant advocating for wider circulation of critical works including *Not by Bread Alone*, insisting on pluralism of opinions in Komsomol or

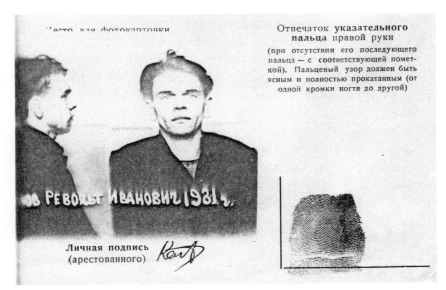

Fig. 11-02 Revol't Pimenov's mug shot from his March 1957 arrest. Courtesy Research and Information Center Memorial, St. Petersburg.

other meetings and in the media, and collecting and disseminating information omitted from the press.[38]

All of the young people around Pimenov keenly felt the "information blockade" as Sheinis labeled it and tried to surmount it in various ways. Graduate students like Sheinis and Orlovskii had access to a special restricted reading room at Leningrad's Public Library, where some Western papers were available. A student of foreign languages, Pustyntsev sometimes caught English-language BBC broadcasts. Russian-language broadcasts were heavily jammed in Moscow and Leningrad, but Vail' got information from Voice of America via a friend back in Kursk. Western sources, however, were perceived—at least by Sheinis and Pimenov—as tendentious and hence requiring care in interpreting.[39] East European media, which had become available that spring, was also ideological but had the advantage of being legal. Verblovskaia, had begun to study Polish as a student some years earlier when she chose to research the workers' movement in Poland for her history thesis. In the summer and autumn of 1956 she followed literary events in Poland and at Pimenov's request began to translate political materials from the Polish press for their group of friends. Orlovskii found Serbo-Croatian easier to puzzle through and concentrated on what he saw as more interesting Yugoslav journals.[40]

In some institutes, exchange students from Eastern Europe also provided a channel for dissemination of information, as they received newspapers and journals from their embassies and sometimes owned shortwave radio receivers. Moreover, when it came to developments in their home countries that fall, a few Poles and Hungarians took it upon themselves to explain alternate perspectives to their Soviet peers in the dormitories. For instance, a Polish student in MGU's mathematics department, Wladyslaw Turski, the son of the rector of Warsaw University, arranged special readings from the Polish press and shared information gleaned from the BBC and VOA, as well as offering his own interpretations of events. After being called on the carpet by the secretary of the party bureau of the department and the deputy dean, Turski gave further cause for reproach as he informed his classmates that "your *partburo* forbids me from talking with you." Meanwhile at LGU, Gidoni observed: "[Hungarian students], as well as the Poles who were seized by the news about changes in Warsaw, began to gather [*mitingovat'*], unintentionally attracting our students as well."[41]

In theory students could take political questions to their teachers of Marxism-Leninism, but these teachers tended to be strict ideologues who rebuffed "provocative" questions. They could turn to the party or Komsomol, but these organizations shied away from debates, which were perceived as risky. At MGU certainly, the Komsomol in many departments preferred to encourage amateur arts, lectures relating to subject matter for courses, and social work.[42] In practice, therefore, political speech emerged among unsupervised youth in marginal spaces. Pustyntsev's circle met at in a room in a communal apartment where a friend lived without parents; Pimenov lived with Verblovskaia, who had her own apartment owing to her mother's death. At LGU Gidoni, an orphan, treated his dorm's foyer—the *prokhodnaia komnata* (literally the room through which one must walk)—as a salon of sorts. There he discussed current events and wrote in his journal, on one occasion penning a maudlin ode to the dead in Poznan.[43]

In November and December a new forum emerged for unguarded speech—the halls of the Picasso exhibit. Confusion about modern art would prompt students to come together inside and then outside of the museums to pool their knowledge on a seemingly permitted and non-political topic. In the wake of Hungarian events, however, the union of students from different institutes not only alarmed university and party authorities but prompted a crackdown. For Pimenov, the repression of an open-air discussion of the exhibit marked a turning point in his thinking; it made him doubt the efficacy of legal methods of criticism.

Under the Sway of Picasso

Five days after he analyzed *Not by Bread Alone* in his diary, Sergei Dmitriev visited an unprecedented exhibit of Pablo Picasso's works at Moscow's Pushkin State Museum of Fine Arts. The historian noted: "His works leave no one indifferent—they wound, excite, upset, intrigue, disappoint, attract, and repulse." Returning for a second visit on November 3, Dmitriev found the two rooms housing Picasso's paintings and drawings uncomfortably noisy because of the intense discussions among patrons. Escaping to a visiting show of nineteenth- and twentieth-century Belgian art, he encountered more diversity and concluded: "Each artist has his own personality, paints his own pictures, and decides artistic problems in his own way." On his way out, Dmitriev marveled at the long lines of people waiting in the cold for admission. He also related rumors that police had been summoned to the museum to break up a fight between fans and critics of Picasso.[44]

The Picasso exhibit did stir lively, sometimes heated, discussions. The young writer Daniil Granin, recently returned from his European cruise, described the ruckus he encountered when the exhibit moved to the Hermitage in December: a varied public—ranging from students to military officers—were debating whether Picasso was a "genius" or a "psycho." Among viewers' comments at the exit, he read remarks, including, "I feel like I'm on a ship, it's rocking and there's nowhere to run" to which another person scribbled the suggestion that he make haste to an exhibit by Aleksandr Gerasimov, the dean of socialist realism and a vocal opponent of "formalism."[45]

Writing for a wall newspaper at MGU, philology student Aleksandr Chudakov observed that in the Pushkin Museum supporters of Picasso were few compared with opponents. Many visitors were perplexed and even angered by the wild diversity of his often abstract works. Historian Eleonory Gilburd contends that some exhibition goers who were used to "socialist aesthetics in which the ordinary viewer was the supreme judge" interpreted Picasso's very inaccessibility as an affront and perhaps a deception. However, others blamed their own inadequacy as cultural consumers due to their isolation from world art.[46]

For young people especially, the exhibit opened their eyes to possibilities in art far beyond socialist realism. Perhaps more importantly, the startlingly modern and diverse nature of the works on display prompted museumgoers to both seek out and offer opinions. Chudakov marveled at the contrast between the Picasso exhibit—where strangers struck up conversations and gathered round groups of debaters—and typical exhibitions by Soviet artists, where "in half-empty halls calm and silence prevail [and] visitors move from room to room without pausing." In recalling the event later, poet Anatolii Naiman, then a student at the Leningrad Institute of Technology, observed: "The artwork itself took second place for those who filled the halls. First in importance was air—the ozone of freedom that blew into the museum straight from the Left Bank and the Right Bank of the Seine." Here was a vicarious taste of Paris that created a strange moment in which "total strangers found themselves bound together by an unexpected closeness, a feeling, a romantic adventure—and the reverse: pointless ties were broken, former friends fell away, arguments erupted."[47] Picasso's freewheeling creativity became a stimulus that empowered (or forced) people to make their own judgments of taste and principle.

Though Picasso's early works might have been familiar to older Russian intellectuals, by 1956 his name was best known among the public in regard to his dove emblem for the Soviet-supported international peace movement. Moscow's Museum of Modern Western Art had been shuttered in 1948, and impressionist and modernist works had been relegated to storerooms in other Soviet museums. A "tentative rehabilitation of impressionism" had begun in 1954, but exposure to Western artists remained limited and contentious in 1956.[48] Indeed, only Picasso's status as a communist and partisan of peace made it possible for Ilya Eherenburg to bypass the Soviet arts bureaucracy and to arrange the exhibit honoring the artist's seventy-fifth birthday. The show was an-

Fig. 11-03 Visitors to the Picasso exhibit at the Pushkin Museum of Fine Arts, Moscow 1956.
Photograph by David Douglas Duncan. Courtesy Harry C. Ransom Center.

nounced by the Soviet-French friendship society in mid-September and opened in the last days October—giving its institutional hosts no time to train guides or prepare explanatory material.[49]

The lack of official direction to aid viewers in interpreting Picasso's works empowered amateurs to opine enthusiastically if not knowledgeably. In Leningrad, Vail' reported, students from the Academy of Arts stepped in as unofficial guides offering some information as to Picasso's place in the art world. But student viewers wanted even more. In Moscow, undergraduates at the State Pedagogical Institute invited their peers from other colleges to gather for a discussion of the Picasso exhibit only to find themselves in trouble with their deans and subjected to an investigation by the Komsomol. In Leningrad students similarly sought premises for a discussion. When arrangements at the city's stately Public Library fell through at the last moment, those who had gathered decided to recruit more people and to meet in the open air. They chose a date one week away, December 21, and a symbolic place, Arts Square, and tasked one another with spreading the plan by word of mouth. Vail' notes that at his small institute, people learned of the proposed "discussion" or "demonstration" from different sources, evidence of the effectiveness of informal links. The news, however, also reached the city party committee where the overlap of the date with Stalin's official birthday added to mounting concern about "unhealthy" political moods among youth.[50]

On the cold, dark evening of December 21, several hundred young people converged on Arts Square from different directions. Vail' stood alone—he had been turned down by one classmate who said she did not want to get arrested and stood up by a second—and tried to estimate how many had come for the discussion. His task was complicated because the square was occupied first by soldiers drilling and then by a fleet of street-cleaning machines. Moreover, nearby benches were occupied by plainclothes KGB and uniformed policemen were stopping passersby and asking for their identification. Several hundred young people, therefore, were crowded into spaces and intersections along the periphery of the square, while many no doubt turned back upon catching sight of the strange activities. Unsure what to do, Vail' was excited to hear young people muttering: "Hertzen [Street] 34" as they passed among the clumps of bystanders. Soon a large group had made its way to the building of the Leningrad branch of the Soviet Artists' Union, where a discussion of a recent exhibition was underway. When the time came for audience participation, they hijacked the program.[51]

The highlight of the evening was a passionate speech by Conservatory student Iuliia Krasovskaia. The fair-haired young woman began deprecatingly: "As regards the Picasso exhibit, I am not an apologist for Picasso as many of those making noise right now obviously think." She assured the alarmed hosts, "I am not planning to interpret his works and to evaluate them. Maybe I am not grown up enough, maybe it isn't real art." Like Naiman, however, she had taken pleasure in the "atmosphere of lively arguments" in the Hermitage's usually quiet halls. While Pimenov missed the discussion because he had to teach that evening, Krasovskaia echoed his sentiments on the virtues of hearing competing viewpoints. She rejected the notion that "the party ought to fight against any tendencies other than socialist realism." Instead, speaking for her generation, she proclaimed, "This is ridiculous. Let socialist realism win in a battle with all the other trends, let it affirm itself in this battle, and then we will believe in it."[52]

Krasovskaia also spoke out about how insulted she had felt when the police had chivvied the students along, warning them not to disturb the peace when they only wanted to discuss art. To applause from her peers, she compared the repressive actions that evening to the infamous "Arakcheev regime" from the time of Alexander I. Two days later she would really feel the police's power when they detained her on suspicion of anti-Soviet agitation and propaganda. Though Krasovskaia was released after several weeks without being formally charged, official tolerance for noisy freethinkers had reached its limit. Gidoni, too, would be arrested the day after the failed Picasso discussion. Police had confiscated the library card he had shown for identification on Arts Square but had not detained him on the spot, giving him time to destroy an incriminating leaflet he had been writing about Hungary. Nevertheless, his political statements over the course of 1956 became grounds for a two-year sentence. Meanwhile surveillance of Pimenov intensified. In March 1957 Vail', Pimenov, two of their friends, and soon thereafter Pimenov's father and girlfriend, as well, would be arrested and ultimately all sentenced for anti-Soviet agitation and propaganda on the basis of their writings and actions in late 1956.[53]

A Perfect Storm

Controversies over international and domestic developments swept relentlessly through intellectual circles and university campuses in the fall of 1956. Political talk took its place alongside discussions of music, love, and careers and intertwined with debates about art and literature. It was not the first or the last time Soviet students tested the bounds of permissible dissent, but conversations and activism mushroomed in the context of a perceived new atmosphere of candor at home and of a fresh opening to the outside world. As Gidoni would later proclaim, "We [young people] literally broke through the darkness created by feeble information about all that was occurring in the world of politics, science and art."[54] Some youth in the 1950s—the so-called style-apers (*stilyagi*)—obsessively sought out Western pop culture. Gidoni stood in a very long line for tickets to an American performance of *Porgy and Bess* and sought out works by existential philosophers such as Sartre and Camus and literature by Faulkner and Hemingway. However, although he found Western culture interesting, Gidoni's real passion was politics, and Tito was his idol.

For many freethinkers in 1956 the "nearby" West of Poland, Hungary, and Yugoslavia was at least, if not more, fascinating than the distant West represented by France, England, or the United States. Neither the students nor the Soviet leadership, however, knew quite what to make of the Yugoslav model or the rapid erosion of political unity in Warsaw and Budapest. As Gidoni would recall in his memoirs, when he challenged his interrogator after his arrest in December 1956 to characterize him, the man responded: "First of all, you are a Titoist; second, you are a revisionist; third, you are a Horthyite [follower of the fascist wartime Hungarian leader]; fourth, you're a Trotskyite; fifth, you're a Right Socialist; and all in all you're a petty-bourgeois democrat."[55] Of course, no one person could hold all these views simultaneously, but the list reflects the colorful, inchoate sweep of ideological diversity that blossomed that year under the influence of developments elsewhere in the socialist bloc. It also references the jumble of sometimes contradictory official explanations of sources of unrest.

While few students engaged in deliberate acts of political opposition—one classmate reacted to news about Kuznetsov's and Terekhin's arrests by describing writing leaflets as "suicidal"[56]—many seem to have sympathized with their political curiosity. Judging by the responses to arrests that took place in dormitories—the VGIK students and Gidoni in December 1956 and Vail' in March 1957—their peers reacted with shock and profound sympathy. At VGIK students spontaneously gathered in one of the auditoriums of the institute the next morning and demanded to know the basis of the arrests. Gidoni's roommates, too, talked back, invoking the criminal procedural code, the constitution, and the Twentieth Party Congress to deter the KGB from searching the belongings of the other students in the room. One philology student even told the judge at the trial in early 1957 that if Gidoni were convicted of "slandering Soviet reality," then "you need to arrest half the university, since thousands of students think the same as Gidoni."[57]

Soviet students had been raised to believe that an interest in current affairs was normal even obligatory for educated Soviet people. November 1956, however, found students caught between their desire for free speech and their fear of repercussions. At MGU's *filfak*, Geta Krainova, a good student, a fan of classical music, and the daughter of a party official, wished for a moderate path. Writing to her high school–aged sister about the "ferment" in the university and the closing of a student club in late November 1956, she criticized radicals and conservatives: "The authorities are afraid to set up any debates because any debate is transformed into a political meeting. Nice? The authorities are behaving very basely: they are expelling for the most innocent statements—in the [wall] newspaper or at a meeting, they're expelling even for citing those whom one is not supposed to cite." She predicted caution would hold people back, but a few weeks later she wrote that they had managed to hold a critical but not rowdy Komsomol conference at which students had raised their own interests as well as broader problems of economic inequality and press freedom. "Our souls simply rested for those two days, we were sunning ourselves with such sudden optimism," she reported to her sister. Moreover, she concluded that "they" would have to listen because "this is [happening] not just here, but in many institutes, among students as a whole and I think not just among students, though students are always the first to begin."[58]

The authorities were indeed listening but drawing a different conclusion—that students were in the vanguard of something dangerous and should not be trusted. The thaw had to end, at least for the time being.

12 DECEMBER

THE BIG CHILL

The year that started with a Secret Speech ended with a secret letter. On December 19, 1956, the Central Committee of the CPSU in effect replied to Pimenov and other proponents of open debate with a classified missive to be read out at party meetings. The letter demanded increased vigilance against the "unhealthy moods" and verbal attacks on the Soviet system spawned by the "worsening of the international situation." Just two days later, Leningrad authorities heeded the new line when they mobilized soldiers, police, and plainclothes KGB to block the unauthorized gathering of "Picassoites." Khrushchev, too, changed his tune. At the Kremlin's festivities to usher in 1957, he would rail against "those who divide Soviet leaders into Stalinists and anti-Stalinists, hoping in this way to cause a split in the Soviet and other Communist parties." According to the Yugoslav ambassador, the hall full of party elite spontaneously applauded when Khrushchev proclaimed that they all shared Stalin's dedication to fighting for the working class and for communism.[1]

December bore witness to a rhetorical retreat from criticism of Stalin and an offensive against reform-minded scholars, critical writers, and "freethinkers." Whereas Tito's visit and Polish liberalization had inspired student radicals, the violent disintegration of communist rule in

Hungary energized people who feared for the Soviet system's stability. Even as December saw an upsurge in conservative pronouncements, however, those who defended old orthodoxies and advocated for greater party control over literature and academe did not operate at will. Party leaders—Khrushchev included—were irresolute over what lessons to extract from the Hungarian crisis. The uprising in Budapest could be interpreted as proof that the Secret Speech had undermined the authority of socialism and therefore needed to be walked back. Yet pent-up anger over show trials and persistent traces of Stalinism played a role in igniting conflict in Poland and Hungary and hence implied a need for more de-Stalinization. While Khrushchev hemmed and hawed about the causes of unrest in central Europe, his colleagues' patience with his brash "diplomacy" and garrulous grandstanding was wearing thin.

The mood of uncertainty at the top was felt beyond the Kremlin walls. As Sergei Dmitriev noted in his diary on December 12: "Some await the 'tightening of the screws,' a broader application of Article 58 [of the criminal code against anti-Soviet propaganda and agitation], a reinforced clamping shut of mouths under the virtuous pretext of protecting the purity of Marxism-Leninism. Others suggest that the era of liberalism and playing at democracy is not yet obsolete . . . but even those are convinced that liberalism and democracy will exist only within limits."[2] But what might these limits be? The Central Committee's call for vigilance might represent a reversal of the promise of more discussion or a corrective to the burgeoning free speech movement. Khrushchev, after all, had not retracted his condemnation of the cult of personality.

December would bare the party's commitment to controlling the public sphere but show that it was operating in a new context of its own creation. The Secret Speech had disrupted the Soviet narrative of constant progress. Details of unjust arrests and executions could not be forgotten; nor could the soul-searching that followed be undone. Those who had been adults in the 1930s might not have wanted to reexamine their own behavior, but the very term *cult* suggested that they ought to at least reconsider their susceptibility to propaganda. Meanwhile many young people were relishing the novelty of cultural openness and political flux. I argue that in December the unsteady and partial nature of the thaw would both embolden conservatives and radicalize freethinkers—hence widening the gap between them. The Central Committee's letter would stall, but not reverse, the post-Stalin liberalization that had accelerated with the Secret Speech. In fact, the experience of being silenced would force moderate reformers as well as radical students to consider the merits of more drastic political change.

Blowing Hot and Cold

The classified December letter "On Intensifying Party Organizations' Work among the Masses and the Thwarting of Anti-Soviet Attacks and Hostile Elements" began with a recitation of the Soviet Union's accomplishments since World War II. Its successes, in fact, were credited for having so enraged the imperialists that they had increased their efforts to undermine socialism as evident in Hungary. Fortunately, with the help of the USSR, the "attempt by means of counterrevolution to destroy the dictatorship of the proletariat in Hungary, to overthrow the people's government, to destroy the socialist system, to restore the reign of landowners and capitalists, to impose a fascist regime in Hungary, and to create a new hotbed of war" had been averted.[3] However, the conflict had highlighted the persistence of external threats and internal weaknesses; hence the need for renewed vigilance.

While citing the party's intentions to continue strengthening "socialist legality" and promoting "Soviet democracy," the Central Committee painted an alarming picture of the potential harm that loomed if party members neglected ideological threats. In language both emotional and formulaic, the letter warned that "under the influence of international reaction, the pathetic remnants of anti-Soviet elements in our country" were "trying to exploit all of the difficulties that we face and all of our shortcomings for their vile ends." These hostile persons were slandering the party and state, spreading rumors, and belittling the socialist alliance. Moreover, the letter invoked Lenin to remind communists that they had a duty to act when "chaos" flourished in the arts under the guise of "spontaneity."[4] Ideological control needed to be bolstered, not diminished as some intellectuals had been suggesting.

Among those called out for malicious or careless behavior since the Twentieth Party Congress were Konstantin Paustovskii for his speech at the discussion of *Not by Bread Alone* and Anna Pankratova's journal *Voprosy istorii* for publishing allegedly one-sided and incorrect articles on party history. Several instances of demagogic speeches in institutions of higher education were cited as evidence of widespread "unhealthy moods" among the young. Meanwhile former prisoners were mentioned as a hazard. Although most of those released were deemed to have been integrated into productive work and social-political life, the directive concluded that "there are people among the returnees who are malevolently inclined against Soviet power, especially from among former Trotskyites, right opportunists and bourgeois nationalists."[5]

Having identified the threats facing the socialist system, the Central Committee instructed party members on the need to improve political education and to react assertively to any signs of opposition. Indeed, law enforcement received its own specific advice: "Communists working in the procuracy, courts, and state security organs should vigilantly stand guard over the interests of our socialist state, attentively seek out enemy elements, and, in accordance with the laws of Soviet power, should cut short their criminal activities in a timely fashion." Rather than behaving tentatively in light of the gross abuses of the Stalin era, police, prosecutors, and judges were to react decisively toward anti-Soviet persons. Dmitriev's friends who predicted that Article 58 of the criminal code would come back into fashion were correct.[6]

Behind the decision to circulate such a letter lay two months of shattered nerves among the Soviet leadership over disarray in Poland, near "capitulation" in Hungary, and subsequent diplomatic fallout from Soviet intervention. The depth of anti-Russian sentiment and the fragility of social control in Poland and Hungary forced the presidium members to confront not only their allies' resentment toward Soviet domination but also socialism's seemingly shallow roots in central Europe. Khrushchev knew many presidium members blamed his report on the cult of personality for awakening antisocialist or antiregime forces in Poland and Hungary. However, he castigated local party leaders and intellectuals there for failing to control the message of the Twentieth Party. Why hadn't they been able to convert the break with Stalin into a strengthening of support for socialism? Why hadn't they held their people's confidence as he had done—or should he be worried, too?

In making the Secret Speech, Khrushchev had recognized from the start that in the short run the party's enemies would try to leverage the admission of errors against the USSR. But he acted with the conviction of one who having suffered and profited from Stalin's whims never blamed the system for having empowered Stalin in the first place. Marxism-Leninism had thrived before the cult of personality and could do so without it, he believed. By owning up to mistakes of the past, Khrushchev predicted that the party would demonstrate its confidence. Therefore, he had pushed for the report and pressed for its broad dissemination. By keeping the report an official secret, Khrushchev ducked questions about accountability; however, he also deprived reform of a solid foundation. The Secret Speech became a resource that the first secretary could wield when he wished to justify changes, but it did not bind him (or anyone else) to anything. Without a text in the public sphere, Khrushchev retained the right to hedge and to harangue, to act the radical but not the repentant.

Before Polish October and the Hungarian uprising, Khrushchev's speeches and actions had reflected his satisfaction at his own maneuvering. Elbowing Bulganin aside, he had acquitted himself well in Britain in April. Over objections from Molotov, he had demonstratively mended the breach with Tito in June. And by July it was evident that his gamble on the Virgin Lands had paid off with a massive harvest. The Central Committee's December letter with its call for renewed vigilance, therefore, reflected a dramatic tumble in Khrushchev's spirits and a shift in the balance within the new collective leadership. Khrushchev's sour mood at the end of 1956 can best be appreciated in contrast to his upbeat sentiments just a few months earlier.

On August 6, 1956, Khrushchev made an unscripted speech to a meeting of his own workplace party cell—a group composed of employees of the Central Committee. Using a word that evoked the liberation of the serfs, he had expounded his belief that the Secret Speech had been necessary to "emancipate" (*raskrepostit'*) people to work well and think creatively. He had credited his Secret Speech with progress even in agriculture. "How can this be?" Khrushchev asked his audience. He explained, "Comrades, I really do link the rise in milk yields with the liquidation of the cult of personality. It's well known that the 'mood' of the cows is created by their feed, and the feed is created by people, the *kolkhozniki* [state farm peasants]." In a quasi-Lysenkoist vision, the spirit of emancipation had been passed from the first secretary to the farmers to the fodder and thence to the animals. The optimism generated by the break with the past was generating popular enthusiasm that would be harnessed toward economic development, thereby boosting satisfaction with socialism.[7]

In August, moreover, the first secretary was prepared to be magnanimous toward those whose moods did not match his own. He recognized that many intellectuals were dazed by the sudden change of policy toward Stalin. He counseled his fellow apparatchiks: "We need now to help writers, we don't need to be strict toward them, and I would even say we don't need to show harshness as some would like . . . we need to explain patiently to them all that has taken place."[8] As for himself, Khrushchev boasted that he did not waste time going back to count up how many times he had praised Stalin in his speeches. Having changed his own fate, Khrushchev felt empowered to focus on the future. Soul-searching seemed like an occupational hazard for the intelligentsia, not a task for public servants. Khrushchev was too busy congratulating himself and making plans for the economy to look over his shoulder.

Yet even before the debacle in Hungary, not everyone in Khrushchev's audience agreed with the wisdom of the attack on Stalin. Many shared Voroshilov's fear that "the baby would be thrown out with the bathwater." Both the April 5 editorial in *Pravda* against anti-Soviet outbursts and the June 30 decree "On the Cult of Personality" represented efforts to spin the Secret Speech in a conservative direction by declaring that major damage had already been repaired by the restoration of collective leadership and by warning against passivity in cases of wrongheaded interpretations of Khrushchev's report. The December letter reflected even more strongly the views of those who felt that dogma needed to be reinforced. Party history was one arena where conservatives had never let down their vigilance, and in the winter of 1956 the case to limit reforms met with real success in this realm. For Anna Pankratova, the heat of reform was about to give way to the chill of orthodoxy.

"In the Spirit of the Decisions of the Twentieth Party Congress"

Though Pankratova had felt obliged to warn the presidium of the alarming political questions she had encountered after her lectures in March, the historian had not shrunk from grappling with the legacy of the Stalin cult. With her energetic deputy Eduard Burzhdalov, Pankratova had used the editorial powers of *Voprosy istorii* to follow through on her commitment to correcting certain omissions and distortions that had sprung up under the cult of personality. Pankratova and Burzhdalov's take on how to reform Russian and Soviet history without "throwing out the baby with the bathwater" was evident in the journal's first post-Congress edition.

The lead editorial for the March 1956 issue praised Stalin's leadership in constructing communism, including in the fight against Trotskyism, but accused historians of having exaggerated his role, admittedly with Stalin's own encouragement. Following the compromise reached at the tense presidium meetings leading up to the Secret Speech, the early years of Stalin's rule remained above criticism. Megalomania and violations of the law were condemned but scant attention was paid to the identities or experiences of victims. *Voprosy istorii*, however, did not provide a definitive new line on party history. Instead, Pankratova and her editors counseled historians, ideologists, and teachers that "overcoming the cult of personality does not consist of dropping some quotations and crossing out names."[9] Stalin, in other words, could not be purged from Soviet history books but somehow had to be adroitly cut down to size within a story of progress and victories.[10]

Moreover, *Voprosy istorii* cautioned historians that the delivery of comprehensive answers via directives from on high was a thing of the past. Now scholars would be tackling problems "by means of free exchange of opinions, creative discussions, and serious scientific research."[11] Although it went without saying that Marxism-Leninism would continue to shape Soviet social sciences, Pankratova and her allies plainly endorsed radically different ground rules for their profession.

The editorial board of *Voprosy istorii* not only avowed pluralism; it also reflected it. Pankratova numbered among those who found change painful and distressing. However, her deputy Burzhdalov, like Khrushchev, focused on the sense of emancipation wrought by naming the terrible truth about the repressive policies and fearful atmosphere of the past. He told the editorial staff in March 1956: "Consciously or unconsciously we deceived and incorrectly educated our people. Each one of us should feel this sorrow. But, along with that we should experience a feeling of great upsurge, great joy that now our science is moving onto a broad path . . . and a feeling of great creative uplift and enthusiasm should seize us in light of this new and radical turn, which cannot be compared in the least to all the little turns and reorientations or more accurately zigzags that we experienced previously."[12] Burzhdalov became a vocal proponent for reform of the historical profession in the summer of 1956. His writings, sharp speeches, and frank answers to questions at readers' conferences in Leningrad and Kiev, however, angered some historians, including Central Committee staffers, who held the position of collective overseers of orthodoxy. Burzhdalov enjoyed readers' conferences, which included teachers and enthusiastic amateurs, but ideological gatekeepers disliked having sensitive issues discussed with those outside the ranks of leading party historians.[13]

In letters to Khrushchev and the Central Committee, as well as in publications in party periodicals and local newspapers, antireform historians fought back. Targeting Burzhdalov rather than the high-ranking Pankratova, they took his words out of context and sometimes resorted to crude name-calling, yet also cast light on real differences of opinion about Soviet history and about how historians should work. A senior historian from Leningrad's Institute for Party History, for instance, denounced Burzhdalov's reply to a questioner at the June readers' conference who asked whether historians could publish 100 percent truthful material given the capitalist encirclement. Burzhdalov had asserted that the threat from abroad was exaggerated—a liberal pronouncement in June, but one that looked treacherous by December. Conservatives also twisted his statement that historians and editors no longer had to wait for commands and directives to move ahead to mean that he was renouncing party supervision. Others objected to the notion that one could write in a neutral or positive way about the actions of Trotsky or Zinoviev in 1917 knowing that they had later become enemies of the party.[14]

In 1956 Pankratova agreed with Burzhdalov's insistence that the journal defend its pursuit of reform. Hence, they responded forcefully when the theoretical journal *Partiinaia zhizn'* (Party Life) published a harsh critique of their journal that summer. Historian and experienced party functionary Evgenii Bugaev, who joined the Central Committee's department of propaganda in 1956, had accused *Voprosy istorii* of its own lack of objectivity in choosing facts and Burzhdalov in particular of giving undue credit to the Mensheviks and Socialist Revolutionaries in 1917. Bugaev further claimed that the journal was indiscriminately discarding Soviet historians' works of the past two decades while excessively praising bourgeois historiography. He concluded that the journal's editors needed to work more slowly and carefully and eschew "cheap sensationalism."[15] Pankratova and Burzhdalov not only rebutted the particulars of his critique, but countered: "*Perestroika* of historians' work has only begun and is going slowly. In these conditions, warnings against 'haste' and imaginary excesses are objectively hampering the realization of the decisions of the Twentieth Party Congress in the realm of historical sciences."[16] In other words, the editors of the journal were the true loyalists.

In the light of events in central Europe and increasingly freewheeling discussions of historical issues among Soviet students, however, resistance to *Voprosy istorii*'s liberalism only increased that fall. In October the journal's foes organized critical "discussions" at which prepared speakers took turns finding fault with its recent issues. In mid-November Pankratova learned that in one such meeting at her old department of party history at MGU she and her editors had been and accused of trying to rehabilitate Trotskyites and revise Leninism. Sergei Dmitriev, who was present at one of several sessions at MGU, observed that the level of vitriol reminded him of the worst days of the anticosmopolitan campaign of 1949. "Stalinists have noticeably perked up everywhere," he wrote in his diary. He also noted that those in the academy incapable of doing proper history rightly understood reforms as endangering their positions. Not surprisingly then, dogmatists were using their considerable powers to try to silence Burzhdalov and other reformers.[17]

Pankratova herself, however, had powerful connections and plenty of experience with ideological battles. Although her complaints to her political patrons that fall had produced few results, Pankratova was shocked to find *Voprosy istorii* singled out in the December Central Committee letter, which charged: "Distortions in illuminating questions of the CPSU's history, which are carried out under the guise of correcting shortcomings and overcoming the consequences of the cult of personality in historical science, are abetting the invigoration of revisionist views and moods among unstable persons who are not free of the weight of bourgeois ideology, and are being actively used by anti-Soviet elements."[18] Pankratova reeled at the notion that her actions were duplicitous and destructive. She saw herself as "acting in the spirit of the Twentieth Party Congress" to fix mistakes identified by the party and as helping teachers and scholars navigate ideologically tricky terrain.[19]

Pankratova's remonstrations and explanations, however, did not find a warm reception among her highly placed comrades that winter. Khrushchev did not stand by her. In March 1957 he allowed the Central Committee to replace the majority of *Voprosy istorii*'s editorial board. Moreover, even though she had agreed to sacrifice Burzhdalov and other board members, Pankratova was silenced at the meeting that decided her journal's fate. She did not get to deliver her prepared remarks in which she blamed herself for not having taken "heed in proper measure of the signals from the Party press." Two months later from a hospital bed, she would sign into press the long delayed March 1957 issue. Suffering from heart trouble, Pankratova allegedly did not read the new board's opening editorial that admitted to all the charges lobbed against the journal during the previous year. Perhaps she glanced at the congratulatory notice regarding her sixtieth birthday. She died a few days later, on May 25, 1957.[20]

In the last fifteen months of her life, Pankratova had tried hard to make good on her vows to help undo the negative consequences of the Stalin cult. She had handled troublesome questions stemming from the Secret Speech and had helped gulag survivors. She had allowed her staff to debate every article considered for publication and had worked with authors to revise their submissions to meet new times. She had tried—and failed—to shift the field of history away from slanderous attacks masquerading as academic discussions. Pankratova did not outlive the age of tendentious "dressing-downs" (*prorabotki*) of those who strayed from an unstable orthodoxy. Her daughter said she felt betrayed by Khrushchev and other former allies who neither came to her aid nor defended their promise of a return to Leninist forms of discourse.[21] The first secretary himself, however, had gone from feeling buoyant to feeling besieged. He, too, found himself reluctantly toeing a more conservative party line after the bloodshed in Budapest.

Indeed, in their first issue the new editors of *Voprosy istorii* would quote at length a fresh pro-Stalin outburst from Khrushchev. His assertion that "we are all Stalinists" on New Year's Eve had not appeared in the Soviet press. However, two weeks later *Pravda* reported Khrushchev's remarks at a reception at the Chinese Embassy, where he railed against those in the West who "accused us of being Stalinists." Moreover, in a statement that appealed to the new editors of *Voprosy istorii,* he had explained: "We criticized Stalin not because he was a bad communist, but because he permitted some serious mistakes . . . The main thing for Marxist-Leninists is defending the interests of the working class, the cause of socialism, and battling the enemies of Marxism-Leninism—in this lays the main thing and, as they say, God grant every communist knew how to do battle like Stalin did."[22]

Khrushchev Cornered

Not coincidentally, both of Khrushchev's rants on the topic of Stalin were made at diplomatic soirees. Foreign policy problems lay at the root of Khrushchev's testiness in late 1956. He had to iron out relations with the Polish leadership, a process that included economic concessions, and cope with instability in Hungary. Special albums of photographs sent by the Soviet embassy in Budapest had helped persuade Khrushchev that his decision to intervene against Imre Nagy's wishes was correct. Nevertheless, the images of battered bodies of communist loyalists lying in the gutters or strung up from lampposts left lingering feelings of trauma.[23] Moreover in vacillating over policy toward Hungary, Khrushchev had been caught unsure of his instincts—perhaps sparking a recollection of Stalin's warnings that the presidium members would be "like blind kittens" without him. In late 1956 fallout from the intervention was spoiling Soviet relations with the West and ruining Khrushchev's much touted rapprochement with Yugoslavia.

Conflict with Tito spiked when the Soviets detained Imre Nagy and his aides as they left their safe haven in the Yugoslav embassy in Budapest after receiving false guarantees of safety from the new Hungarian government. Tito had lashed back at this dirty trick with a speech on November 11 in which he disputed Soviet aspersions that the Yugoslavs had played a counterrevolutionary role by supporting Nagy. Tito put the blame for unrest in Poland and Hungary squarely on Stalin and Stalinists. The Secret Speech had been a major step forward for the Soviet leaders, he allowed. However, now they needed to understand that the cult of personality was only "the product of a system." Tito suggested

Fig. 12-01 Khrushchev at a reception at the Polish Embassy, November 18, 1956. Photograph by David Douglas Duncan. Courtesy Harry C. Ransom Center.

that the roots of political weakness in Soviet-style regimes lay "in the bureaucratic apparatus, in the method of leadership and the so-called one man rule, and in the ignoring of the role and aspirations of the working masses." Furthermore, he faulted Stalinists for ongoing resistance to "democratization and the decisions of the 20th Congress."[24] In short, if Khrushchev really wanted to overcome the consequences of the Stalinist dictatorship, he had more work to do both to fix his party and to repair the CPSU's relations with the Soviet people.

Predictably, Tito's "Pula Speech" enraged Khrushchev. Not only had he staked his reputation on reconciliation with the Yugoslavs but he despised the term *Stalinist*.[25] Khrushchev saw himself as a communist, not a Stalinist. Moreover, he saw the party as encouraging and channeling participation in service of the people's own needs and therefore as genuinely democratic in its means and ends. For Khrushchev the successful recruitment of Komsomol volunteers for agricultural and industrial projects was just the latest evidence that Soviet citizens were striving to build communism not out of fear and coercion, not at the direction of domineering bureaucrats, but in a mood of solidarity with the party.

Khrushchev did admit faults in management and inadequacies in manufacturing. He did not deny that the East was behind the West in consumption, nor did he claim impeccable governance in all corners of the economy. In his memoirs, he would even admit to having seen examples of waste in his cherished Virgin Lands program.[26] But Khrushchev took pride in being aware of shortcomings as well as successes of the communist modernization project. Unlike Stalin, Molotov, and some other presidium members, Khrushchev traveled widely throughout the USSR and routinely poked his nose into coal mines, cafeterias, dairy barns, and the like. He liked to see things for himself and propose his own schemes for improvements, such as the turn to prefabricated construction that would accelerate the provision of housing for the masses.

Khrushchev saw plenty of room for improvement in the Soviet economy and willingly identified areas needing attention. However, in the winter of 1956 Khrushchev was not prepared to stomach systemic criticism from heretical Yugoslavs or impertinent ingrates at home. There would be a price for criticizing the regime, and Vladimir Dudintsev would be among the first to pay it.

Fig. 12-02 Children playing as new apartments go up in the Iugo-Zapadnyi region of Moscow, 1956. Photograph by L. Porter and S. Preobrazhenskii. Courtesy Moscow Central Archive of Audiovisual Documents.

With a Red Scarf on His Chest

Although the December Central Committee letter had singled out Paustovskii as having "besmirched Soviet practices and our cadres" with his speech about *Not by Bread Alone*, it was Dudintsev who most sharply felt a reversal of fortune in December. The author had already been buffeted by the passionate reception of his novel in November. At an event with the author hosted by the MGU *filfak*, for instance, a graduate student had called for people to exert control from below over important institutions and to wild applause had invoked Heine—"Beat the drum without fearing!" Dudintsev, by contrast, tried to temper his fans' zeal.

At LGU, for instance, in response to a note from the audience asking, "Doesn't it follow that the system must be reconstructed?" Dudintsev parried that the system should not be confused with the forces that made it up. The novelist explained that he was fighting together with positive forces and they were overcoming the negative ones.[27]

Even though he recoiled from their radical moods, Dudintsev recognized his young fans as idealists. He wrote many decades later: "All these students stamped their feet in the name of communism, for the purity of the idea." They appreciated that he "wrote the novel with the sensation of the red [pioneer's] scarf on my chest." But their passion for undefined political change frightened ideologues and Dudintsev could predict the consequences. The enforcers of orthodoxy would overreact and their disproportionate response would in fact erode young people's faith in the system.[28] Indeed, while the MGU philology students were chanting "Lenin Prize, Lenin Prize," a different response was being prepared within the Central Committee. Its staffers concluded that the novel's vivid portrayal of careerists and the hero's almost accidental victory made it fodder for "slanderous fabrications about how the socialist system allegedly does not facilitate creativity and innovation, [and] gives birth to stagnation and bureaucracy." With Paustovskii's speech about *Not by Bread Alone* circulating in typescript, they saw a need for stronger guidance.[29]

On December 2, 1956, *Izvestiia* printed an authoritative appraisal of *Not by Bread Alone*. Its reviewer denounced Dudintsev's "hero" as an "individualist" and "egotist." In a remark calculated toward young audiences, she marveled: "[The inventor Lopatkin] graduated from university, but the novel never even mentions his classmates although student years bind people for their whole lives."[30] In other words, Lopatkin was a loner and misanthrope, not a victim of exclusion. Dudintsev clearly had underestimated the strengths of Soviet collectives while overestimating the prevalence of careerists. According to the critic, having selectively taken facts out of context, *Not by Bread Alone* became a "half-truth, which is in fact a lie." Having in effect called Dudintsev a fool and a liar, the article ended on a self-congratulatory note by claiming it had helped a talented author understand his mistakes and assisted readers in finding their way amidst an "unhealthy furor" (*nezdorovyi azhiotazh*).

Perhaps not surprisingly, the day after the review appeared Revol't Pimenov fired off a letter taking *Izvestiia*'s critic to task. He accused the reviewer of wanting a trite ending, and asked: "Would it have been better to show at the end of the novel some Mr. Party Committee [*Partkom Partkomych*] who would explain to Lopatkin that it is harmful to stand outside the collective and to Drozdov that it is harmful not to promote innovation, and then all three could go off hand in hand to the successes that await them?" Pimenov insisted such a template did not deserve to be called "socialist realism," but instead ought to be labeled "anti-popular idealism" as such a rosy picture hampered the fight against real evils in Soviet society. Just as Dudintsev predicted, Pimenov considered the condescending review proof of the sway of obstructionist bureaucrats.[31]

Pimenov was not alone in bridling at the deliberately chilling message sent by the review in *Izvestiia* and a similar one in *Literaturnaia gazeta*. In letters to *Novyi mir* in December many readers complained about unfair attacks on *Not by Bread Alone*. One compared *Izvestiia*'s appraisal to a criminal indictment (*obvinitel'nyi akt*). And in a ten-page letter, Galina Zimchenko from Kiev lamented in part: "[It is] as if a little window was opened in long sealed up the room of a sick person. And in the given case, we the readers are the sick person. We are so cosseted . . . that we have gotten quite weak and already don't have the strength to think or speak. We have grown accustomed to agreeing with everything, to always nod in affirmation. And now a stream of fresh air has entered the room, the patient has inhaled a lungful and has begun to ponder. But [the critic] has taken fright and run to slam shut the window."[32] Students, too, understood that the publication of authoritative editorials signified the arrival of "Mr. Party Committee." They were once again supposed to receive wisdom from above rather than participate in a dialogue.[33]

The fears of the novel's fans that the author like his hero was suffering at the hands of the "Drozdovs" would be further confirmed in the New Year. At a Writers' Plenum in March 1957, Dudintsev repeated his faith in the artistic quality of his novel and affirmed his loyal sentiments in writing it. He even claimed that he had downplayed the poor state of technology in the USSR, citing as evidence the fate of Soviet fighter planes in the first days of the war. Moreover, Dudintsev pointed out that the imposition of curbs on constructive criticism was backfiring.

Every day, he recounted, readers sent him copies of letters they had written to the press in support of *Not by Bread Alone* because they knew he would never see them in print. Readers felt they had been muzzled. Comparing the treatment of the Soviet public to that of English children whose mothers kept them on harnesses, he observed that it did not bode well for the future of the country if people could not be trusted to express themselves.[34]

In the wake of the ideological retrenchment that winter, Dudintsev's self-defense could not save him. On the contrary, Konstantin Simonov used it to distance himself from the novelist. At the March Writers' Plenum he declared Dudintsev was just as irresponsible as Paustovskii and withdrew his journal's support for *Not by Bread Alone*. Simonov accused Dudintsev of acting like a victim when he should have understood that embrace of his novel by foreigners and enemies of the USSR meant that his position must have been wrong. He now judged Dudintsev as hopelessly embittered—why else did he recall Soviet Union's wartime losses rather than its victories? Simonov even twisted Dudintsev's metaphor about mothers using leashes on their children to mean that Dudintsev wanted to cast off party leadership and the dictatorship of the proletariat—a statement that was met with cries of "Not true!" When Dudintsev got a final chance to speak, he could only repeat that he had "died" from Simonov's words.[35]

The stubborn author did suffer a professional death of sorts. The Central Committee did not outlaw *Not by Bread Alone*—they already had a scandal brewing over Pasternak's *Doctor Zhivago*. Instead, they allowed the novel to be translated into many languages but permitted only a token edition at home with the express purpose of showing people that they had not banned it. Meanwhile, Dudintsev received no royalties for the translations of *Not by Bread Alone* and had to fight in court to keep the advances paid for broken contracts for Soviet editions. In 1957 he would struggle to feed his large family and would sell off the fancy furniture he had acquired in his brief interlude of wealth. But friends sent crates of food, helped with cash, and offered long-term loans.[36] Moreover, Dudintsev used the experience of being ostracized to help him understand the suffering of Soviet biologists who opposed Lysenko. Thirty years later, his second novel, *White Robes*, would become one of the sensations of Gorbachev's perestroika. Once again Dudintsev would win readers' attention with a portrayal of an unequal battle against an immoral elite fostered by the Soviet system.

Dudintsev's experience of being publicly condemned, though still privately embraced, in 1956–1957 reflects how far the Soviet system and its adherents had come since the height of Stalinism. Though denigrated and humiliated, Dudintsev was not arrested. His works were not confiscated, and most of his friends and admirers stood firm in their approval of his novel. Paustovskii, too, kept his membership in the Writers' Union even as he witnessed the cancellation of the liberal almanac *Literaturnaia Moskva*, which he and some colleagues had launched that spring. However, he paid, as well. In late November 1956 he joined other notable writers, liberals and conservatives, in signing a public letter rebuking French writers' criticism of the Soviet invasion of Hungary. Historian Vladislav Zubok suggests that Paustovskii, Ehrenburg, and other liberals acceded to this request because "they probably intended to save the literary 'renaissance' that, as they hoped, might still continue."[37]

With ups and downs, the thaw in the arts would persist over the course of the Khrushchev era. In the spring of 1957, however, Paustovskii's sense of being in danger would grow to the point that he actively sought to reassure the leadership of his loyalty. In an episode revealed only after the end of the Soviet Union, it emerges that Paustovskii asked to be received at the Central Committee. According to Petr Pospelov's speech at the closed June 1957 Plenum, after Khrushchev delivered a harsh tirade against at a special picnic for writers on May 13, 1957, Paustovskii sought him out and the two men later conversed for three hours in the course of which Paustovskii asked Pospelov to pass along copies of his books to the first secretary and to convey to him that he was a "Soviet writer." Moreover, when Pospelov showed the writer photocopies from the Western press praising his remarks about *Not by Bread Alone*, Paustovskii promised to find a way to "disassociate" himself from them. In citing this meeting as evidence that strongly worded reprimands worked, Pospelov casually added: "This is a man who in October [1956] made an anti-Soviet speech, and if he'd delivered another such speech he'd have needed to be arrested."[38]

Dudintsev had warned an unruly student audience in November that when driving on a road full of bumps and potholes one had to know how to step on the brakes in a timely fashion. His attempts at moderation had led students to judge him a coward, but Dudintsev ended up paying for his fans' far-reaching interpretations of his novel. The party, with Khrushchev's acquiescence, had stopped what they saw as a treacherous skid, but Dudintsev had been thrown from the vehicle. He would survive, but for the party elite his name would become synonymous with recklessness.[39]

Survivors and Victims

Battles over the arts and social sciences reflected serious differences of opinion about the limits of pluralism, but even graver splits lay in wait. Khrushchev denied the Yugoslav charge that the presidium was split into Stalinists and anti-Stalinists, but he would find out the hard way in June 1957 that many of his top colleagues were ready to discard him and abandon his new proposals for reorganizing management of the economy. Having ignored warnings from Snegov and Shatunovskaia among others that too many Stalinists remained at the top, Khrushchev discovered Molotov, Kaganovich, and Malenkov among those conspiring to oust him from the post of the first secretary. Ironically, by observing the new "softer" rules of the game and confronting Khrushchev at a meeting of the presidium rather than arresting him, they left Khrushchev room to maneuver. By shifting the discussion from the presidium, where he found himself outnumbered, to the Central Committee, Khrushchev would rally enough protégés and allies to turn the tables on what was soon dubbed the "anti-party group." Though Khrushchev would be sent into early retirement for his "hare-brained schemes" in 1964, in the summer of 1957 he used the revived commitment to inner-party rules to defeat his rivals.[40]

The extraordinarily blunt and combative discussions at the emergency Central Committee Plenum that stretched over a week in June 1957, however, reveal Khrushchev's vulnerability based not only on the fiasco in Hungary but also on his leadership style and blunt talk on many subjects, including Stalin. His colleagues would take Khrushchev to task for his impulsive statements—such as a public boast that the USSR would catch up with the United States in production of meat by 1960—and his own concentration of power. Molotov would even quote Lenin's critique of Stalin's rudeness against Khrushchev. However, Khrushchev was able to construe Molotov's behavior as "factionalism" undermining the unity of the party. Khrushchev could also point to economic growth, especially in agriculture, and Molotov's objections to the reforms that had produced it. In this and in other areas, Khrushchev cast his rivals as being stuck in old Stalin era thinking. But it was complicity in and lack of repentance for the purges that Khrushchev and his allies wielded most ferociously to discredit the members of the "anti-party group."

Khrushchev and Minister of Defense Georgii Zhukov called out Molotov, Kaganovich, and Malenkov in particular for having signed off on death sentences of thousands of innocent party comrades. Zhukov cited dates, statistics, and marginal notations to drive home the callous cruelty with which the top leaders had approved the executions of colleagues and subordinates. Close association with Stalin—and Khrushchev would argue that the key members of the anti-party group were closer to the dictator than he was—became a potent weapon in this internal party battle. None of the elite wanted to touch the issue of broad accountability, but individual sins came in handy in close combat.[41]

Having learned in detail about the horrors of the NKVD torture chambers, execution lists, and concentration camps, Khrushchev, like many communist loyalists, generally preferred to avert his gaze. As Shatunovskaia regretfully noted, he never asked for a final report from the commissions that had traveled through the gulag in 1956. He never spoke out about the terrible treatment of Soviet POWs or about victims of famine. Nor did Khrushchev authorize publicity about rehabilitations. And when at the emergency Plenum Kaganovich challenged him to account for his activities in Ukraine in the late 1930s, Khrushchev ignored him. Yet toward the Plenum's end, Khrushchev brought up an instance where he successfully deflected Stalin's paranoia about enemies in the Moscow party organization and a moment in 1947 when he tried to get Stalin interested in hunger in Ukraine. However, though he clearly had been thinking about his own role, Khrushchev excluded himself from those in the inner circle when it came to responsibility for policies of repression. Moreover, he approved Zhukov's contention that some members of the presidium had since "earned the trust of the Central Committee and of the entire Party with their honest work and directness."[42]

Khrushchev believed in redemption and, though he came out on top of the Soviet system, he identified himself as a survivor, as well. After all, one aspect of the terror was what historian Lynne Viola has labeled the "unstable nature of the 'victim.'" "In the Stalinist context," Viola observes, "the enemy was internal. He could be anyone."[43] As a party official, Khrushchev had been particularly susceptible to being caught up in one of the group cases spun by NKVD investigators in the 1930s. His later membership in Stalin's inner circle carried its own danger. Perhaps a sense of the ease with which he could have become a victim motivated Khrushchev to reconnect with his former colleagues Snegov and Shatunovskaia and to listen to some pleas from the relatives of friends executed unjustly. But I contend that Khrushchev did not credit his survival just to luck; he wanted to believe that his survival and his success stemmed from hard work and loyal service—with his willingness to tackle thankless jobs extending to taking on the task of revealing Stalin's mistakes.

Khrushchev's great-granddaughter Nina tells that in retirement he read and liked Eugenia Ginzburg's unpublished gulag memoir as well as taboo Solzhenitsyn's novel about prisoner scientists. But his wife could not finish them. A believer in the just motives of the revolution, she could not stomach reports of rampant injustices carried out in its name. Perhaps she agreed with Kaganovich, who admitted at the June Plenum that he had "loved Stalin" and felt sick at the sudden "campaign" against him. "We debunked Stalin and unwittingly in front of the whole world debunked 30 years of our work, not having wanted to do so," he had ruminated. As a result, "Now we speak about our achievements, the great battle of our Party, [and] our people with shame. We shouldn't do this."[44] Khrushchev understood that the less the public discussion of whether the party had made mistakes or carried out crimes, the easier for people not to think about such things.

But in 1956 the rough outline of the regime's abuses of power as provided in Khrushchev's report was supplemented for many people by the whispered stories of returning survivors of prisons and exile. The poet Anna Akhmatova famously opined upon learning of the Secret Speech: "Now the prisoners will return and the two Russias will look each other in the eyes; the one that imprisoned, and the one that was imprisoned."[45] Since those in power preferred to look away, more often the survivors encountered not the direct gaze of their former interrogators or bosses, but the agitated regard of those who had preferred not to know or who, aware of their own vulnerability had stood helplessly to the side. Coping with living proof of the terror turned out to be hard for everyone, even those eager to help survivors.

In March 1956 Akhmatova's friend Lidiia Chukovskaia, whose husband was executed in 1938, found herself pondering why she did not feel more joy at greeting friends who were returning from camps and exile. She decided that the reason was not "shame for silence, one's own and our general one" because "after all, to speak up then meant to dig your own grave and lie in it. Alive. And to place your loved ones there by your side as well." Akhmatova suggested that the problem was that while Chukovskaia wanted to link up the day of separation with the day of reunion, all that had come in between could not be erased. Survivors struggled with the same dilemma of how much to tell, how much to try to forget. Shalamov, for example, could not pretend as his wife wished that he had been away on a business trip. Nor could he put aside his unpublishable Kolyma tales. As painful as it was for Chukovskaia and Akhmatova to hear of their friends' suffering, the two women also would not look away from those in need, from their own damaged lives, and in Akhmatova's case from a son who survived.[46]

For those willing to see, the returned were everywhere in the summer of 1956. Even as she prepared for her European cruise, Elena Katerli housed a newly freed friend at her dacha. Pankratova found ways to employ colleagues who had returned, and Dunskii and Frid reconnected with their film school classmates. Although out of the spotlight, the "problematic people," as Barkova described herself, flooded the reception rooms of the procuracy, lined up in housing offices, and timidly looked for work. The fortunate had families or friends to help them, but the wounds inflicted by unwarranted and brutal imprisonment were hard to heal in a society that expected survivors to gratefully and gracefully pick up where their lives had been interrupted. While the bureaucracy slowly and warily grappled with rehabilitation paperwork, issues of justice remained taboo.[47] There were no apologies—public or private—from the state, only certificates that pithily declared convictions reversed or vacated. Moreover, Barkova's prediction that people could still be punished for incorrect thinking came true in her case.[48]

Having finally been rehabilitated for her first two cases, Barkova would be arrested in November 1957 based on denunciations by suspicious neighbors. Barkova and her housemate Valentina Sanagina would be accused of listening to foreign radio stations and naming their cat after "a leader of the Party and government." An investigation would bring to light Barkova's sardonic and apocalyptic writings. Yet at her trial a year later, she pled not guilty to anti-Soviet propaganda and agitation. She refused to accept that her drafts should be treated as proper works. Moreover, she boldly stated: "I consider that the leader of the government is carrying out a duplicitous policy: first he curses the previous leadership, then he starts to defend it. I know that in three-four years it is hard to change a previous policy, and even now we are afraid to speak the whole truth—[that] as before people are put on trial for anything." As for her manuscripts, she had been published once and Barkova still imagined a day when new ideological shifts might mean she could rework her stories for publication. In 1957, however, her lack of repentance combined with "expert" opinions that her works slandered Soviet institutions, however, got her another ten-year sentence.[49]

In a labor camp outside Kemerovo in the summer of 1958, Barkova would meet another woman who felt she had been unjustly convicted. Just as Barkova had wondered following her first arrest back in 1934, Irena Verblovskaia asked herself why a powerful state seemed to need to make an "enemy" out of an ordinary and powerless individual. Swept up in the case against her common-law husband, Revol't Pimenov, Verblovskaia shared many of his liberal views, especially regarding free speech. She had translated articles from the Polish press for him and helped collect bits of unpublished news for his bulletin "Informatsiia," but she did not consider herself a criminal or a conspirator. As she put it later, "I was a humble young teacher who never allowed herself to make any anti-Soviet statements—not because I was cautious but because I never even thought about doing so."[50]

Pimenov had been more deliberate in his political activities in 1956 and hence was more accepting of the price. For him the courtroom became another platform. As Verblovskaia later saw it, Pimenov had made the strategic choice: "As if before him stood an interested public, he seemingly was addressing the future generation." Using the knowledge gained by reading about the trial of Lopatkin in *Not by Bread Alone* to address the court properly, Pimenov tried to get the judge to understand his theory of legal opposition and to accept his distinction between antigovernment and anti-Soviet views. The prosecutor, by contrast, compared the young people's conspiratorial aims to the actions of Hungarian counterrevolutionaries. Yet, perhaps swayed by the parade of sympathetic young witnesses who denied that the accused held extreme views, the judge initially condemned Pimenov to six years, Vail' to three, and Verblovskaia to two. On appeal, however, the prosecutors got the sentences increased to ten, six, and five years, respectively.[51]

Despite the long sentence he received, Pimenov was heartened by the behavior of the witnesses at his group's trial in September 1957. Many of them denied that the views expressed by Pimenov and Vail' were "anti-Soviet," and some bravely repudiated the formulas that investigators had inserted in the records of their interrogations. Moreover, on the last day, one friend held aloft the book version of *Not by Bread Alone* that had come out while Pimenov was in prison, while another waved the newly reissued *Ten Days That Shook the World*, an American's account of the 1917 revolution that featured Bolsheviks who had later been demonized in show trials. Pimenov later wrote that he understood their actions: "As if to say look, what you were fighting for is being realized."[52] The free speech movement had not been extinguished.

The difficulty in definitively silencing freethinkers can be seen in the subsequent political "careers" of both Pimenov and Vail'. The two young men clung to their commitment to free speech and freedom of information, principles central to the dissident movement of the 1970s–1980s in which both participated. Pimenov and Vail would be arrested and convicted again in 1970 for circulating self-published texts (*samizdat*). Physicist Yuri Orlov who was fired for his untimely speech on democratization in March 1956 also became a stalwart of the human rights community in the 1970s. Like Pimenov and Vail', he kept searching for ways to influence the system. But the regime countered with its own innovations: Vail' would be permitted to emigrate to the West in 1977, while Orlov—a founder of the Moscow Helsinki Watch Group—would be expelled from the USSR in 1986. Pimenov, however, stayed on in semiexile in Komi after his second prison term. When competitive elections became possible in 1990, he won a seat in the Russian Supreme Soviet, where he served on the Constitutional Committee.

Yet in 1956 the loss of liberty stung. Vail', who had hung on Pimenov's every word and recruited his classmates to join in what he hoped would be an opposition circle, realized that he had sacrificed a lot. Awaiting trial, he composed a poem full of longing for his student days:

> If you've got money in your pocket
> You should hurry to the café
> There in the café it's warm and cozy
> There [Yves] Montand sings from the radio.

Vail reminisced about "jazz sweeter than chocolate" and lamented, "Everything has disappeared: night, exams, silence."[53] The price for playing at politics was high, and the rewards for conformity many. While some lucky young Russians would mingle with foreigners at the 1957 International Youth Festival in Moscow, he would be in prison.

For the majority of liberal minded students in 1956, the lesson of December was that they had misjudged the degree of emancipation granted by the Twentieth Party Congress. In rallying behind the anti-bureaucratic message of *Not by Bread Alone* and in arguing about Picasso in the halls of the Hermitage, they had felt a new liberty. As one former MGU philology student wrote later of the gleeful commotion at the meeting with Dudintsev: "In the hall there reigned an unbelievable excitement. [Students] spoke not so much about the novel as about life in the Stalin era. It was all like in a dream. It seemed (and we believed) that great and irreversible changes were in the air."[54] They had felt free, but freedom was contingent. In December they got a sharp reminder that what the party had given, it could take away. What was allowed to Khrushchev was not allowed to everyone.[55]

A New Normal?

The Central Committee Letter of December 1956 reminded people that although they remained in force the decisions of the Twentieth Party Congress were subject to interpretation from above—and not necessarily from below. There was to be no Russian equivalent of the Petofi Circle and certainly no unauthorized gatherings. The Soviet media worked relentlessly in December to show that calm prevailed throughout the bloc, especially in Hungary. *Ogonek,* for instance, featured images of mundane activities in Budapest with reassuring captions: "In the city the metro is working," "Newspapers are being sold," and "Trade in vegetables [is taking place]." The traces of the uprising were portrayed as superficial and easily fixed. Khrushchev, too, attempted to cast reform in the Soviet Union as unaffected by events in central Europe. On November 4, 1956, in a meeting of Central Committee members and party activists, he ruminated: "We need to look at everything anew, to clean all the gears and cogs, and to remove the rust where it has built up so that our relations are built on correct Bolshevik, Marxist-Leninist principles. We need to correct comrades who just pay lip service to the decisions of the Twentieth Congress, but interpret them in their own way and persist in working according to old methods."[56] Cleaning the Soviet machine, however, was not the same thing as considering it critically.

Aleksandr Iakovlev, later dubbed the "architect of perestroika," observed in 2001 that the next logical step after the Secret Speech should have been to look at what it meant that Stalin was "great follower and continuer of Lenin's cause."[57] But such an intellectual leap was impossible not just for Khrushchev but for many others who believed in the goals of the revolution and who had pursued them for better and for worse through the Stalin years and beyond. Khrushchev, like Pankratova, defined himself as both a servant of the party and as an activist within it. In times of difficulty, he fell back on the tried-and-true metaphor of battle and the traditional tactic of mobilizing enthusiasts. For party loyalists the correct reply to the question where is Soviet power was always wherever we are. The appropriate remedy for anti-Soviet outbursts and unhealthy moods was for right thinking communists to educate and proselytize their countrymen into a spirit of confidence in and gratitude for the party's wisdom.

Khrushchev's report on the Stalin cult, however, had plunged many Party members into a state of anxious uncertainty even as it liberated them to criticize the old regime. 1956 became a year of questions and questioning, but also a year of silences, some strategic, some self-imposed, and others ordained from above. Khrushchev—as he would remind an audience of restive writers in May 1957—went much further than Dudintsev or anyone else in 1956 in exposing the regime's weaknesses. But, as he would lecture the intelligentsia, "I criticize for the purpose of correcting these shortcomings." Dudintsev, by contrast, according to Khrushchev "relished" exposing the USSR's failings. In fact, I contend that Dudintsev straddled the line between pragmatic dissent and systemic criticism. Had the antibureaucratic aspects of the novel not received so much fervid attention from readers, he might have been hailed for promoting the efforts of inventors to rationalize production.[58] But the line between the permissible and the forbidden was not only set from above, but sometimes applied ex post facto.

Reform from above did not fail per se in 1956, but it bumped up against its inherent limits. The leadership remained unaccountable and inconsistent. The collective security pact within the presidium held to the extent that Khrushchev's rivals did not arrest him when they lost patience with him in the summer of 1957. But it proved lacking in terms of defining politics; hence Kaganovich's failed attempt to defend himself by arguing, "The Presidium has the right to its opinion and the members of the Presidium have the right to express their point of view."[59] At the same time, awareness that they could not carry on as before meant that the party elite were seeking new ways of building popularity, making peace, and legitimizing the communist project. With the myth of party infallibility shattered, a cycle of the political elite seeking (and often later rejecting) new solutions had been launched.

However, the Secret Speech not only shook up the party; it also affected Soviet society, particularly the intelligentsia and educated youth. Khrushchev's report—despite its secrecy, omissions, and euphemisms—opened the way for pent-up questions about policies on many fronts. The crackdown in late 1956 showed that the regime could still frighten critics into recanting or falling silent and would still punish perceived "anti-Soviet" speech. However, the experience of discussion and debate and the pleasurable process of finding like-minded people had already transformed a generation.

Although December 1956 reminded young people of the danger of engaging in politics, for some at least the shame of having propagated the cult of Stalin, having believed press reports about "enemies of the people," or having swallowed Lysenko's unscientific conclusions would motivate them to stick by their convictions. They did not change their opinions of *Not by Bread Alone* or go back to praising Stalin. Indeed, for many freethinkers, the regime's retrenchment in December only proved that reform needed to be deeper. They would continue to seek opportunities to promote debate and cultural experimentation.

The crackdown on critical speech in December 1956 reflected the perils of reform from above for the ruling party. But it also showed the power of words and ideas in forming public opinion. There was no going back in terms of restoring a cult of the leader or a complete monopoly on speech. Ahead would lie decades of renegotiation of the boundaries of criticism. Moscow's silenced spring of 1956 was the beginning of the end of Soviet rule, but only the beginning.

EPILOGUE

In February 1956 Nikita Khrushchev dared to open a Pandora's box from which spilled scraps of terrible information about the abuses wrought by the ruling Communist Party on its own people. Revelations about the purges and Stalin's monopolization of power in turn sparked uncomfortable questions about who was to blame and what needed to be done to make amends. In the Greek myth, Pandora closes the lid just in time to keep hope from escaping. Khrushchev, by contrast, acted with hope by his side. The first secretary was motivated not by curiosity but by conviction. He believed that by airing some of the regime's dark secrets in a controlled and limited way he and other party loyalists could liberate themselves from guilt over the past and reinvigorate the party. He reckoned that freed from the myth of Stalin's infallibility, the party could restore "socialist legality" and open itself up to constructive criticism, both of which would lead to better governance.

From the very start, however, contradictions were evident in the notion of a monopolistic party-state declaring it could fix problems caused by its own lack of democracy and accountability. Even the most profound immediate consequence of the renunciation of Stalinist practices—the freeing of political prisoners—reflected a gap between means and ends. Living in exile in Inta in the summer of 1956, Valerii Frid heard the Supreme Soviet's traveling commissions referred to as *troikas*—the same term used for the three-person panels that had sentenced people in lieu of proper courts during the purges.[1] Once again, an institution created by the party and accountable only to it operated outside the legal system with great leeway and haste but little procedure to decide the fates of tens of thousands of vulnerable prisoners. As Ol'ga Shatunovskaia found, the composition of these commissions made a difference—those that did not include a rehabilitated party veteran sometimes approved fewer releases. Clearly, members were not all alike in their views of the purges. And yet Shatunovskaia had been told by Khrushchev that there were no plans for sweeping personnel change in the institutions of power. He expected her to believe that secret policemen, prison guards, judges, and prosecutors would all willingly adapt to the "Leninist path" prescribed from the center.

The spirit of the party dictatorship was also felt in the nature of the Secret Speech itself. As the writer Lidiia Chukovskaia noted, it was hard to fully rejoice over the fact that Stalin's reputation had finally and deservedly been blackened when it depended on a word from on high. "On command, we all glorified, and now on command we'll all curse him," she wrote in her private notebook.[2] To be told how to think presumed on the same shameful obedience of the purge years. Moreover, such abrupt commands potentially rang hollow. Unknown numbers of people in 1956 resisted the order to change their opinions of Stalin. An anonymous letter to the editor of the journal *Kommunist* from a technical specialist at the Gorky automobile plant dated November 14, 1956, for instance, reported: "The workers are saying that if Joseph Vissarionovich [Stalin] were here he wouldn't have permitted bloodshed in Hungary . . . But these leaders like Khrushchev (the "traveler" as we call him) having wined and dined the spy Tito, have lost their heads and don't know what to do with their collective leadership."[3]

It was not so easy to dislodge the very public and prolonged cult of Stalin with a Secret Speech that rested on anecdotal evidence and unpublished documents. Many listeners were offended by Khrushchev's unlikely story that Stalin had tracked the course of the war on a globe. Moreover, Khrushchev's folksy manner and open curiosity about the outside world stood in sharp contrast to Stalin's reserved demeanor and isolationist rhetoric. Not everyone welcomed the abrupt change in leadership styles. Yet to provide a more persuasive rationale for reform would have meant giving camp survivors a chance to speak, revealing more about the flaws of Stalin's rule, and exploring the causality of the purges. Given that Khrushchev and other "survivors" of Stalin's inner circle remained in power, they had little incentive to broaden the blame for the terror beyond Stalin, Beria, and a few other rogues.

As it was, the manner of sharing the Secret Speech and its reception demonstrated the inherent difficulties in balancing controlled discourse and a new policy of more openness. Marietta Chudakova, then a second-year student at MGU's *filfak*, remembers that the party functionary prefaced his reading out of the speech to her class by announcing that it "was not up for discussion" (*obsuzhdenie ne podlezhit*). This instruction was met with a loud groan from the audience. Students had learned about the essence of the report "On the Cult of Personality and Its Consequences" through the rumor mill and hence were expecting a different atmosphere. Fifty years later, Chudakova reasoned that their vocalization of disappointment showed that they already had begun to change. The collective expression of frustration was a liberty that they would not have taken a few years earlier. In the moment, however, the dominant feeling was that the party was rejecting their curiosity.[4]

Yet, as Anna Pankratova's experience showed, everyone had questions. The inquiries she received in the immediate aftermath of the Secret Speech exposed problems with the concept of "cult of personality" both as an explanatory device and as a prescription for reform. As one of Pankratova's listeners astutely pointed out, by placing all causality and culpability on Stalin alone Khrushchev had executed a sort of reverse cult—the man who had once gotten all the credit for socialism's development now got the entire fault for its flawed execution. Historians, teachers, and propagandists expected a more Marxist, or at least less individualistic, explanation for how Soviet institutions could have been subverted into instruments of terror and disinformation. Meanwhile, Revol't Pimenov was already asserting in April 1956 that the party had created a new cult of the Central Committee. What did it matter, he argued, whether it was one person or a select few at the top as long as they dictated to all the rest?

To contemplate the extirpation of the "consequences of the cult of personality" implied thinking about how to prevent a recurrence. Here

Pimenov, a genuinely anti-Soviet critic, stood ready to challenge the idea that top party leaders could earn redemption by renouncing illegal methods of investigation and freeing political prisoners. Where was the guarantee that the temptation to purge would not recur? Like the physicists at the Thermal Technical Laboratory, Pimenov was full of ideas for mechanisms to inject democratic accountability into socialism. Khrushchev's promise of a return to inner party democracy and a restoration of "Leninist" norms, by contrast lacked specifics, perhaps deliberately. Party leaders were not accustomed to being constrained by laws or their own pledges. As the conflict at the June 1957 Plenum would demonstrate, there was no consensus on what constituted fair criticism even within the presidium.

As 1956 unfolded, discussions about the Secret Speech and other political and cultural novelties expanded in a variety of spaces—in party meetings and editorial offices, but also in classrooms, dormitories, corridors, and apartments. Everywhere, the questioning of the reigning narrative of party history, of the politicization of science and the arts, and of the nature of the Soviet bureaucracy revealed a shortage of satisfactory answers. Pankratova's experience with teaching the teachers showed both a dire need for guidance and a lack of experience in independent thinking on the part of those charged with answering for the party. Not surprisingly, passivity became the bane of party watchdogs. From March through December regime, party insiders struggled to find a new mix of persuasion and intimidation that would dissipate "unhealthy moods" while forestalling the need for repressive measures.

The waxing and waning of liberalization over the course of 1956 illustrates how directives for change from above did not translate into dependable change from within. Khrushchev's report, for instance, freed Pankratova up to cast off some of the falsehoods and cautions she had adopted in writing Soviet history for Stalin. Yet it proved a weak shield when she came under fire for presenting a more complex narrative of the revolution. Ultimately, the "spirit of the Twentieth Party Congress" could not trump the tradition of *partiinost'*. If being a worthy communist meant following the leadership in all its zigzags, then perhaps Pankratova deserved her final dunning. One wonders if she remembered at the end how her audience had laughed at her in March 1956 for saying this was not the first time she had had to reform herself.

Sincerity and *partiinost'* proved hard to reconcile even in discussions about the restoration of Leninist norms.

Pankratova's subordination to party dictates for and against reform offers an important reminder that while not all members of the establishment defended the status quo, not all who backed change were heroic advocates for free speech. Reginald Zelnik concluded about Pankratova: "We should imagine her as neither devil or angel, but as someone who did some harm and also much good as she tried to steer a course through the rough seas of Soviet life."[5] Khrushchev too swung between tyrant and populist, policeman and liberator. According to his son-in-law, Khrushchev recounted more than once that he "trembled" when he had to meet newly returned camp survivors because "I knew these people would be coming into my [office] shadows of the people they had once been."[6] Yet in the winter of 1956, he ignored survivors' needs, praised Stalin, endorsed force in Hungary, and backpedaled on permitting criticism at home.

In a historiography of the "thaw," Stephen Bittner has argued pointedly that analysts should not make the thaw out to be a bipolar struggle between reformers and conservatives. I have demonstrated that many individuals at all levels did not fall neatly into such categories. Indeed, the year 1956 shows that one might have come to loathe Stalin but still not tolerate independent thought; one could hate bureaucracy, but respect the party; one could be a proud Komsomol, and disdain official judgments about "bourgeois genetics." In 1956, reactions to the new party line were raw and often inconsistent. In a context where discussion of the purges remained taboo, people had to sort out their beliefs in relative silence. Denis Kozlov refers to the thaw as a moment of "the *unmaking* of Soviet subjectivity," essentially a time in which old certainties were rejected and people were motivated "to seek new forms of self-expression and new grounds for intellectual stability rather than absorbing themselves in the old, now manifestly inadequate political language."[7] In the first year after the "Word," many were still gazing upward, expecting the state to solve problems; yet others looked to literature, to each other, and even outside the Soviet Union for models and inspiration.

Though true believers like Elena Stasova refused to entertain the question of for what had they sacrificed, other Soviet citizens succumbed to more soul-searching. Many artists and intellectuals had embraced the ideals of the revolution and attempted to mold their lives and careers to reflect the party's standards. Yet in 1956 Konstantin Paustovskii was lamenting the sacrifices he made in his writing to serve the goal of industrialization. He assured the leadership that he was a "Soviet writer," but under the influence of European culture he had lambasted the ranks of crude party apparatchiks. Meanwhile, Anatoly Gladilin, in the vanguard of the yet unnamed "Youth Prose Movement," was seeking to be a mirror, rather than an "engineer of the human soul." He by no means rejected the regime's project of building a better society, but he wanted to strip away its pompous ideological veneer.

The year 1956 revealed that despite the reality of repressions and violence, Stalin's "children" had taken to heart ideas of social justice, altruism, and honest labor. As Vladislav Zubok has concluded: "The educated cadres trained for Stalinist service turned out to be a vibrant and diverse tribe, with intellectual curiosity, artistic yearnings, and a passion for high culture. They identified not only with the Soviet collectivity, but also with humanist individualism. This was the unintended result of the Stalinist educational system, the high ideals of self-cultivation and self-improvement, and the pervasive cult of high culture that it propagated."[8] At once grateful for the generosity of a state that allowed access to higher education, that housed them and fed them, albeit modestly, the students of the 1950s expected respect in turn for their diligence and devotion. They wanted to be trusted to think for themselves and to act responsibly. They did not abandon the idea of collectivism. Instead, they sought to build their own genuine, self-constituted groups—to be individualists but not egotists—and to set their own challenges.

Without their elders' burden of accounting for their behavior in the 1930s, Soviet young people focused on the present with optimism about the potential for decentralization. Yet as they clashed with monopolists in science, uncovered corruption in cafeterias, and encountered waste and callousness on the frontiers, they could not escape thinking about the faults in the post-Stalin system—especially when their complaints were rebuffed or even punished. Young people of 1956 may have been last naive generation of Soviet idealists in part because of the sharp revanche after Hungary that saw students expelled from the universities and some young radicals put behind bars. As Boris Vail' realized in prison, there was a lot to lose in 1956. The chance to study, to explore the far reaches of the Soviet Union, to pursue one's ambitions, to catch a whiff of Parisian air in the halls of the Hermitage—all this remained for those who kept their criticism within bounds.

The incident at the Thermal Technical Laboratory and the debate about Dudintsev's novel demonstrate that Pimenov and Vail' were not alone in challenging monopolies in politics and the media. However, they were unusual among young people in their deliberate rejection of the existing system. Pimenov later reasoned that in his case mathematical training made him sensitive to flaws in the state's logic; for him a single false proposition negated the whole equation. His wife, however, had "undergone a different evolution—she had been attracted to opposition by the thaw and not the frosts."[9] Many young people, in fact, concentrated on the positive prospects of reform, especially cultural openness. They thought about how honest people might steer the party away from errors by offering critical feedback and how their generation might do things differently.

The desire for change, in other words, did not necessarily imply an antisystem bias. Historian Julianne Fürst found for the late Stalin period that "a closer examination of individual subjectivities reveals that challenging directives and norms from above does not signify automatic opposition, let alone resistance . . . Partial support was joined with resigned acceptance . . . Critical anger was often rooted in enthusiastic support."[10] In 1956 anger about the purges was combined with excitement that the party itself had initiated reform. Even Pimenov had danced for joy when he first heard of the contents of the Secret Speech. If the party made good on promises of more trust, more debate, and more self-criticism, then reform might really allow more individualism and free expression.

The year 1956 had its partial victories. Gladilin saw his frank novel about a disappointed youth published—though the material he gathered that summer about corruption and disorganization at the construction site initially proved unpalatable to editors. Students were disappointed in the attack on *Not by Bread Alone*, but they found a hero in Paustovskii. Although Lysenko had not been discredited publicly, by the end of the year his domination of biology was crumbling. That fall, classmates asked Natal'ia Liapunova what to read about "real" genetics, and Nikolai Timofeev-Resovskii lectured at LGU. Moreover, the sisters and their friends came through the ordeal of being dressed down for heretical views with their commitment to honesty and independence reinforced. It seems no accident that Elena's husband, fellow biologist Nikolai Vorontsov, was the only one of Gorbachev's ministers to reject outright the coup attempt of August 1991. Boris Yeltsin would use his scribbled transcript of the fateful cabinet of ministers meeting to prove to Gorbachev the depth of rot inside the CPSU.[11]

Khrushchev's liberalization turned out to be transformative but precarious. The essence of the thaw, then, may be its oscillation between openness and discipline. The overall unsteady nature of liberalization in the 1950s and 1960s makes it difficult to draw clear temporal bounds around the thaw. Indeed, Bittner cautions against drawing too sharp a line between Stalinism and thaw, or thaw and stagnation, arguing of the time: "It was not Stalinism, to be sure. But neither was it a 'robust spring' that produced democratization and an autonomous civil society."[12] Certainly the post-Stalin USSR witnessed neither genuine democratization nor the emergence of independent social groups. Yet I argue that Khrushchev's denunciation of Stalin, despite its problematic form, marked a threshold, drew a line that carried with it certain visceral expectations.

When Irma Kudrova, detained as a witness against Pimenov, refused to cooperate, her interrogator summoned her father, a party member and a high-ranking manager. At first he was angry at her refusal to admit her acquaintance with Pimenov against photographic evidence. But when he found out she had been detained all day without food, he wheeled on the secret policeman and spluttered, "What's this? What year is this outside? Does the Twentieth Party Congress mean nothing to you?"[13] Chastened, the investigator released Kudrova into her father's custody for the night. Similarly, Khrushchev and the other top leaders schemed and swore, but they did not resort to arrests when they fell out in the summer of 1957. The politics of the thaw may only look genuinely liberal when compared with what went before and what came after, but they clearly marked a fundamental change in thinking about what was acceptable against "internal enemies."[14]

The thaw did not end in December 1956. More testing of censorship and more tirades by Khrushchev lay ahead. However, the year 1956 is often remembered by Russians who came of age at the time as the brightest moment of hope in a decade of unstable reform. For them, the momentum of the cultural spring and the momentous break with the Stalin cult outweighed the chill that set in after events in Hungary. Both the Liapunovas who tried to escape politics and Pimenov and student radicals who embraced them had the chance to pursue and defend their passions in 1956. The young geneticists and the "freethinkers" found ways to break the silences imposed on them. The setbacks of December 1956 could not erase their words or hold them back forever.

AFTERLIVES

Balandina, Nina (1935–2014), graduated with a degree in applied mathematics from MGU. She worked as a programmer in a secret research institute and later in computer linguistics for a private firm. Her daughter is a molecular biologist.

Barkova, Anna (1901–1976), served out most of her third sentence for anti-Soviet activity in a labor camp in Mordova. Released early in 1965, with the intervention of prominent writer Konstantin Fedin, she was rehabilitated and received a room in a communal apartment in Moscow. She spent the last days of her life in a hospital, where she suffered from terrible delusions of being back in prison.

Dunskii, Iulii (1922–1982), together with Valerii Frid authored many successful screenplays, including *There Served Two Comrades* (1968) and a television serial based on Sherlock Holmes (1979). Late in life he married architect Zoya Osipova. Suffering badly from asthma, he took his own life.

Frid, Valerii (1922–1998), after Dunskii's death threw himself into teaching a new generation of filmmakers at VGIK. He also continued to write for the screen. During perestroika, he was finally able to use some of his gulag material for the screenplay *Lost in Siberia* (dir. A. Mitte, Moscow, 1991). Frid also wrote a well-received witty memoir of his time in prison and labor camps.

Gidoni, Aleksandr (1936–1989), was arrested in December 1956 and received a "light" sentence of two years, but he got a second sentence for political activities in the prison camp in Mordova. Under duress he briefly worked as an informer in the camp. Upon early release in 1960, he was not allowed to return to Leningrad. He worked as a teacher and continued his education. In 1973 his wife asked for political asylum exile while on a tourist trip in Italy. Two years later, the Soviet government allowed the rest of the family to join her. They settled in Canada, where Gidoni worked for a Russian-language newspaper.

Gladilin, Anatoly (1935–), quit the Literary Institute before graduation and briefly headed up the literary section of the youth newspaper *Komsomol'skaia pravda* before taking up writing full time. He openly defended the writers Andrei Sinyavskii and Iulii Daniel when they were tried in 1965 for publishing works abroad. Finding publication of his novels increasingly problematic, in 1976 Gladilin emigrated to the West, where he worked for Radio Liberty. Author of many novels, he currently lives outside Paris.

Granin, Daniil (1919–), an engineer by training, he served in World War II (though recently controversy has emerged over whether he was a political officer or a simple soldier as claimed in his autobiographical works). A prolific and respected author of short stories, essays, and novels including *The Bison* (based on the life of Nikolai Timofeev-Resovskii), his recent travels included a 2014 visit to the German Bundestag, where he delivered a powerful speech on the siege of Leningrad.

Liapunova, Elena (1936–), earned a PhD in biology and specialized in zoology and cytology. She and her husband, Nikolai Vorontsov (1934–2000), worked in Novosibirsk's Akademgorodok in the 1970s. She heads a laboratory at the Kol'tsov Institute of Developmental Biology.

Liapunova, Natal'ia (1937–), earned a PhD in biology and taught for several years in the Department of Biophysics at Moscow State University. She is currently a senior researcher at the Laboratory for Cytogenetics of the Russian Academy of Medical Science's Center for Medical Genetics in Moscow.

Orlov, Yuri (1924–), worked, after being fired from the Thermal Technical Laboratory, for the Institute of Physics of the Armenian Academy of Sciences and returned to Moscow only in 1972, after which he became deeply involved in the human rights movement. In 1976 he became a founding member of Helsinki Watch Committee. He subsequently lost his job, was sentenced to five years of hard labor, and was expelled from the Academy of Sciences. Deprived of his Soviet citizenship in 1986, he emigrated to the United States and continued his work on experimental physics at Cornell University.

Paustovskii, Konstantin (1892–1968), was able in the 1960s to realize his dream of more travel through Europe, including another visit to Paris and a long stint on the island of Capri. He continued to promote liberal writers, most famously in the almanac *Pages from Tarusa*, which passed censorship at a regional publishing house only to cause a scandal in Moscow. He also spoke out for Siniavsky and Daniel. The writer also signed a collective letter against Leonid Brezhnev's perceived rehabilitation of Stalin.

Pimenov, Revol't (1931–1990), was released early from his 1957 sentence thanks to intervention on his behalf by several renowned scholars. While continuing his mathematical work, Pimenov wrote articles for *samizdat,* for which he was arrested again in 1970. Sentenced to five years of exile, he spent them in a village in the northern Komi region, after which he relocated to its capital Syktyvkar and worked in the local branch of the Academy of Sciences. In 1990 Pimenov won election to Russian Congress of People's Deputies, where he served on the constitutional committee until his death from cancer.

Shalamov, Varlam (1907–1982), published poetry collections with Soviet publishing houses in 1961, 1964, 1972, and 1977. However, his prose about the gulag—most famously, *Kolyma Tales*—appeared only in the West and without his formal permission. Shalamov divorced Ol'ga Nekliudova in 1966; he subsequently had a relationship with Irina Sirotinskaia, who would play an important role in preserving his literary heritage. A longtime sufferer of Meniere's disease, the solitary writer was placed in a nursing home after his health deteriorated sharply in 1978.

Shatunovskaia, Ol'ga (1901–1990), retired from party work in 1962. During perestroika she gave several interviews on the fate of the commission on which she had served that investigated the show trials and the Kirov murder and whose materials were never published.

Snegov, Aleksei (born Iosif Falikzon, 1898–1989), left the Ministry of Internal Affairs in 1960 and retired from party work in 1964. He continued to take a strong interest in the history of the party and Stalin in particular. In 1967 he was briefly expelled from the party for continuing to speak out among historians about Stalin's crimes.

Stasova, Elena (1873–1966), was a delegate to the Twenty-Second Party Congress in 1961. She remained an active behind-the-scenes advocate for prisoners until the end of her life. Already a decorated revolutionary, she received numerous additional state awards—including her third and fourth Orders of Lenin—in the 1960s. Her ashes are buried in the Kremlin walls.

Timofeev-Resovskii, Nikolai (1900–1981), and his wife resettled in 1964 in the town of Obninsk, near Moscow, where he headed the department of radiobiology and genetics at the Institute of Medical Radiology of the USSR Academy of Medical Sciences until 1969. After retirement, he continued to work as a consultant. He received many international honors. He was rehabilitated posthumously only in 1992.

Vail', Boris (1939–2010), received an additional two-year term for participating in an underground organization in the prison camp where he was serving his sentence for involvement in "anti-Soviet activity" with Pimenov. Released in 1965, he returned to Kursk, where he married, worked in the local puppet theater, and studied part time to be a teacher. In 1970 he was sentenced to five years in exile for distributing *samizdat*. He emigrated to the West in 1977. After settling in Denmark, he worked in the Royal Danish Library.

Verblovskaia, Irena (1932–), was able, not long after her release from a labor camp in 1962, to return to St. Petersburg, where she became a professional tour guide specializing in the literary history of the city.

Verblovskaia is the author of a book on Anna Akhmatova and also a memoir. She was officially rehabilitated in 1991.

Vidali, Vittorio (aka Comrade Carlos, 1900–1983), went on to be elected to the Italian parliament after the dispute over Trieste was decided in favor of Italy. He remained hostile to Tito, and some viewed the publication of his diary of the Twentieth Congress in 1974 as a pretext for criticizing Yugoslavia. He is now best known for his romantic relationship with the photographer Tina Modotti.

NOTES

Abbreviations

ARAN   Arkhiv Rossiiskoi Akademii Nauk (Archive of the Russian Academy of Sciences)

GARF   Gosudarstvennyi Arkhiv Rossiiskoi Federatsii (State Archive of the Russian Federation)

NITs Memorial   Nauchno-Informatsionnyi Tsentr Memorial Sankt Peterburg (Scientific-Informational Center of the St. Petersburg Memorial Society)

RGALI   Rossiiskii Gosudarstvennyi Arkhiv Literatury i Iskusstva (Russian State Archive for Literature and Art)

RGANI   Rossiiskii Gosudarstvennyi Arkhiv Noveishei Istorii (Russian State Archive of Contemporary History)

RGASPI   Rossiiskii Gosudarstvennyi Arkhiv Sotsial'no-politicheskoi Istorii (Russian State Archive of Social and Political History); RGASPI-M refers to the former Komsomol archive (Tsentr khraneniia dokumentov molodezhnykh organizatsii), which was merged with RGASPI in 1999

RGAKFD   Rossiiskii Gosudarstvennyi Arkhiv Kinofotodoku-mentov (Russian State Archive of Film)

TsAOPIM Tsentral'nyi Arkhiv Obshchestvenno-Politicheskoi istorii Moskvy (Central State Archive of Social and Political History of Moscow) now merged into the Central State Archive (TsGA) of Moscow

Prologue

1. Lidiia Chukovskaia, *Zapiski ob Anne Akhmatovoi (1952–1962)* (Paris: YMCA-Press, 1980), 2:133.

2. "Khrushchev's Secret Speech," included in Strobe Talbott, trans. and ed., *Khrushchev Remembers* (New York: Bantam Books, 1971), 677.

3. Quotations from speeches by Ludmilla Alexeyeva and Igor' Vinogradov, respectively, at the seminar "Shestidesiatniki-I" held by the Liberal Mission Foundation on May 21, 2006 (see http://www.liberal.ru/articles/1258).

4. My thinking on decision making by reformers and hardliners has been shaped by Adam Przeworski's *Democracy and the Market: Economic and Political Reforms in Eastern Europe and Latin America* (Cambridge: Cambridge University Press, 1991).

5. Dina Spechler coined the term *permitted dissent* to describe criticism tolerated by and even sometimes solicited by the regime. Dina R. Spechler, *Permitted Dissent in the USSR: Novy mir and the Soviet Regime* (New York: Praeger, 1982).

6. Alexeyeva in "Shestidesiatniki-I."

7. On the split between private tastes and publically performed rhetoric, see Alexei Yurchak, *Everything Was Forever, until It Was No More: The Last Soviet Generation* (Princeton, NJ: Princeton University Press, 2005).

8. I consciously speak of Russians and Russia in this book since my research focuses on what was then the Russian Republic and is now the Russian Federation. The focus on Russia means that short shrift is given to some important aspects of 1956: notably, pro-Stalin demonstrations in Georgia in March, the return of deported nations to the Caucuses, and tension in eastern Soviet borderlands caused by rehabilitation of nationalists and intervention in Hungary. These topics have been covered in Timothy K. Blauvelt and Jeremy Smith, eds., *Georgia after Stalin: Nationalism and Soviet Power* (Abingdon: Routledge, 2016); Nicolas Werth, "The 'Chechen Problem': Handling an Awkward Legacy, 1918–1958," *Contemporary European History* 15, no. 3 (2006): 347–356; Amir Weiner, "The Empires Pay a Visit: Gulag Returnees, East European Rebellions, and Soviet Frontier Politics," *Journal of Modern History* 78, no. 2 (2006): 333–376; Amir Weiner, "Déjà Vu All Over Again: Prague Spring, Romanian Summer, and Soviet Autumn on Russia's Western Frontier," *Contemporary European History* 15, no. 2 (2006): 159–194.

9. Historians who have explored the thaw from diverse angles include Alan Barenberg, Stephen Bittner, Miriam Dobson, Deborah Field, Ol'ga Gerasimova, Slava Gerovich, Eleonory Gilburd, Polly Jones, Denis Kozlov, Karl Loewenstein, Benjamin Tromly, Gleb Tsipursky, Elena Zubkova, and Vladislav Zubok. William C. Taubman has written a multifaceted and balanced biography of Khrushchev. Khrushchev's memoirs are available in three newly edited and translated volumes; his son Sergei N. Khrushchev has written several books of memoir and analysis and his great-granddaughter Nina Khrushcheva recently published a reflection on family history.

1. January

1. On 1953 as a year of social as well as political turbulence, see Miriam Dobson, *Khrushchev's Cold Summer: Gulag Returnees, Crime, and the Fate of Reform after Stalin* (Ithaca, NY: Cornell University Press, 2009), 21–49.

2. On the reopening of Kremlin, see William C. Taubman, *Khrushchev: The Man and His Era* (New York: W. W. Norton, 2003), 263. In the first twelve months that the Kremlin was opened, some five million visitors toured its grounds. See "5 millionov ekskursantov v Moskovskom Kremle," *Trud*, July 20, 1956, p. 1.

3. N. F. Kargina, "1955. Nachalo," in *Vremia, ostavsheesia s nami: filologicheskii fakul'tet v 1955–1960 gg.: vospominaniia vypusnikov* (Moscow: MAKS Press, 2006), 3:250–252; Chermen B. Borukaev, *Drobinki* (Novosibirsk: Izd. SO RAN, NITs OIGGM, 2000), 121–122.

4. Susan Reid observes that such "petit-bourgeois" domestic fashions were to be considered bad taste just a few years later. In the Stalin era, however, solid furniture and cozy textiles were signs of solidity and status. See Susan Reid, "Cold War in the Kitchen: Gender and the De-Stalinization of Consumer Taste in the Soviet Union under Khrushchev," *Slavic Review* 61, no. 2 (Summer 2002): 247–249.

5. A. Barto, "Novaia Snegurochka," *Pravda*, January 1, 1956, p. 2.

6. Varlam Shalamov, *Novaia kniga: vospominaniia, zapisnye knizhki, perepiska, sledstvennye dela*, comp. I. V. Sirotinskaia (Moscow: EKSMO, 2004), 444–450.

7. Biographical details for Barkova are drawn from L. N. Taganov, *"Prosti moiu nochnuiu dushu . . ." Kniga ob Anne Barkovoi* (Ivanovo: Talka, 1993); L. N. Taganov, "Zhizn' i tvorchestvo Anny Barkovoi," in *Anna Barkova: . . . Vechno ne ta*, comp. L. N. Taganov and O. K. Pereverzev (Moscow: Fond Sergeia Dubova, 2002), 446, 509. On the gradual softening of the camp regime starting in March 1953 and continuing in the aftermath of 1954 prisoner strikes and

uprisings, see Steven A. Barnes, *Death and Redemption: The Gulag and the Shaping of Soviet Society* (Princeton, NJ: Princeton University Press, 2011), 208–210, 232–233; Alan Barenberg, *Gulag Town, Company Town: Forced Labor and Its Legacy in Vorkuta* (New Haven, CT: Yale University Press, 2014), 121–112.

8. Letter from Iulii Dunskii to Mikhail Levin, January 17, 1955 [*sic*], in *Sluzhili dva tovarishcha: Kniga o zhizni kinodramaturgov Dunskogo i Frida*, comp. Z. B. Osipova (Moscow: Zebra E, EKSMO, 2002), 248.

9. Letter from Nikolai Timofeev-Resovskii to Aleksei Liapunov, January 5, 1956, in N. V. Timofeev-Resovskii, *Istorii rasskazannye im samim, s pis'mami, fotografiiami i dokumentami* (Moscow: Soglasie, 2000), 490.

10. These interpretations of *thaw* are eloquently explained in Katerina Clark, "'Wait for Me and I Shall Return': The Early Thaw as a Reprise of Late Thirties Culture?" (paper presented at "The Thaw: Soviet Society and Culture in the 1950s and 1960s," Berkeley, CA, May 2005). Historian Stephen V. Bittner also addresses the thaw metaphor and its shortcomings over time. For him, the key elements of the metaphor are "impermanence, uncertainty, insta- bility." Stephen V. Bittner, *The Many Lives of Khrushchev's Thaw: Experience and Memory in Moscow's Arbat* (Ithaca, NY: Cornell University Press, 2008), 13. Denis Kozlov and Eleonory Gilburd emphasize the anticipatory aspect of the thaw and suggest it be construed as a "constitutive event" in "The Thaw as Event in Russian History," in *The Thaw: Soviet Society and Culture during the 1950s and 1960s*, ed. Denis Kozlov and Eleonory Gilburd (Toronto: University of Toronto Press, 2013), 31.

11. Bittner, *Many Lives*, 12.

12. Yuri Orlov, *Dangerous Thoughts: Memoirs of a Russian Life*, trans. Thomas P. Whitney (New York: William Morrow, 1991), 50–53, 63.

13. Cited in Taubman, *Khrushchev*, 21. My account of Khrushchev's life draws heavily on Taubman's biography and on Khrushchev's memoirs.

14. Sergei Khrushchev, ed., *Memoirs of Nikita Khrushchev*, vol. 1, *Commissar (1918–1945)*, trans. George Shriver (University Park: Pennsylvania State University Press, 2004), 16.

15. Ibid., 28.

16. Taubman, *Khrushchev*, 91.

17. For the latest research on the Kirov assassination and its tangled after- life, see Matthew E. Lenoe, *The Kirov Murder and Soviet History* (New Haven, CT: Yale University Press, 2010).

18. Speech of May 1937 cited in Taubman, *Khrushchev*, 99.

19. Ibid., 99–103.

20. Khrushchev, *Memoirs*, 1:121.

21. Cited in Taubman, *Khrushchev*, 122.

22. Tat'iana Rybakova, *"Schastlivaia ty, Tania!" o "Detiakh Arbata" i ne tol'ko* (Moscow: Vagrius, 2005), 41.

23. K. P. Chudinova, "Pamiati nevernuvshikhsia tovarishchei," in *Imet' silu pomnit'*, comp. L. M. Gurvich (Moscow: Moskovskii Rabochii, 1991), 9–10.

24. Orlov recounts in detail his political conversations in 1946 and the pressure to avoid NKVD informers (*Dangerous Thoughts*, 80–89). On veterans' attitudes more generally, see E. Iu. Zubkova, *Obshchestvo i reformy 1945–1964* (Moscow: AIRO, 1993), 33–44. Mark Edele offers a more sophisticated analysis of political views of veterans based on attitudes toward specific policies or alternative ideas that undermined overall regime legitimacy in "More Than Just Stalinists: The Political Sentiments of Victors 1945–1953," in *Late Stalinist Russia: Society between Reconstruction and Reinvention*, ed. Juliane Fürst (London: Routledge, 2006), 167–191.

25. "Iz dnevnikov Sergeia Sergeevicha Dmitrieva," *Otechestvennaia istoriia* 3 (1999): 144.

26. While stable compared with the late 1930s, postwar politics included a serious purge of the Leningrad party organization in 1949, the exclusion of Molotov and Mikoyan from Stalin's inner circle, and expansion of the presidium to twenty-five members in 1952. For details, see Yoram Gorlizki and Oleg Khlevniuk, *Cold Peace: Stalin and the Soviet Ruling Circle, 1945–1953* (Oxford: Oxford University Press, 2004); Sheila Fitzpatrick, *On Stalin's Team: The Years of Living Dangerously in Soviet Politics* (Princeton, NJ: Princeton University Press, 2015), 171–223.

27. Rybakova, *"Schastlivaia ty, Tania!,"* 32.

28. Sergei Khrushchev, ed., *Memoirs of Nikita Khrushchev*, vol. 2, *Reformer (1945–1964)*, trans. George Shriver (University Park: Pennsylvania State University Press, 2006), 83–84.

29. Taubman, *Khrushchev*, 240.

30. On Beria and relations more generally among Stalin's heirs from 1953 through 1955, see Fitzpatrick, *On Stalin's Team*, 224–240. For Beria as reformer, see Sergo Beria, *Beria, My Father: Inside Stalin's Kremlin*, ed. Francoise Thom, trans. Brian Pearce (London: Gerald Duckworth, 2001). Quotation from Elena Zubkova, "The Rivalry with Malenkov," in *Nikita Khrushchev*, ed.

William Taubman, Sergei Khrushchev, and Abbot Gleason (New Haven, CT: Yale University Press, 2000), 69.

31. Beria, *Beria, My Father;* Taubman, *Khrushchev,* 256.

32. For details of Khrushchev's political maneuvering, see Taubman, *Khrushchev,* 257–269.

33. Lenoe provides fascinating evidence of how Khrushchev relied in inner-party battles on his ally Ivan Serov, who replaced Beria. He also reveals fierce contention among presidium members in 1956–1957 over reevaluating the show trials of the 1930s (*Kirov Murder,* 591–600).

34. Khrushchev, *Memoirs,* 2:207.

2. February

1. For instance, foreign parties were ranked according to their political prominence in their home countries. The most highly regarded delegations would receive gifts of hunting rifles, record players, cameras, and so forth. M. Iu. Prozumenshchikov, *XX S"ezd KPSS. Preodolenie . . .* (exhibition catalog) (Moscow: Rosarkhiv, 2006), 14; for the call to convene the Congress, see "Zapiska N. S. Khrushcheva chlenam Prezidiuma o sozyve XX S"ezda KPSS," April 7, 1955, and "Vypiska iz protokola no. 115. Zasedaniia Prezidiuma TsK KPSS," April 8, 1955, in *Doklad N. S. Khrushcheva o kul'te lichnosti Stalina na XX S"ezde KPSS: Dokumenty,* comp. V. Iu Afiani and ed. K. Aimermakher (Moscow: ROSSPEN, 2002), 167–168.

2. "Protokol no. 184. Zasedanie 30 ianvaria 1956 g.," in *Prezidium TsK KPSS 1954–1964. Chernovye protokol'nye zapisi zasedanii. Stenogrammy. Postanovleniia,* ed. A. A. Fursenko (Moscow: ROSSPEN, 2003), 1:88–93. On Khrushchev's inconsistent attachment to "peaceful coexistence," see Vladislav Zubok and Constantine Pleshakov, *Inside the Kremlin's Cold War: From Stalin to Khrushchev* (Cambridge, MA: Harvard University Press, 1996), esp. 184.

3. On treatment of Stalin the press in 1953–1956, see A. V. Pyzhikov, "Problema kul'ta lichnosti v gody khrushchevskaia ottepel'," *Voprosy istorii* 4 (2003): 47–50; Jane P. Shapiro, "The Soviet Press and the Problem of Stalin," *Studies in Comparative Communism* 4, nos. 3–4 (1971): 179–209.

4. Vittorio Vidali, *Diary of the Twentieth Congress of the Communist Party of the Soviet Union,* trans. Nell Amter Cattonar and A. M. Elliot (Westport, CT: Lawrence Hills, 1984), 6.

5. S. A. Mikoyan, "Aleksei Snegov v bor'be za 'destalinizatsiiu'," *Voprosy istorii* 4 (2006): 77.

6. Cited in Roy Medvedev, *Khrushchev: A Biography* (Garden City, NY: Anchor Press, 1984), 67.

7. According to Sergo Mikoyan, Snegov credited his avoidance of immediate execution to his decision to recant his false confession at trial, a brave act given that it meant a return to prison and more torture ("Aleksei Snegov," 75).

8. Medvedev, *Khrushchev,* 66–67, 69. Matthew Lenoe, *The Kirov Murder and Soviet History* (New Haven, CT: Yale University Press, 2010), 562.

9. Mikoyan, "Aleksei Snegov," 70.

10. Ibid., 69; personal communication from Andre Broido.

11. Miriam Dobson, *Khrushchev's Cold Summer: Gulag Returnees, Crime, and the Fate of Reform after Stalin* (Ithaca, NY: Cornell University Press, 2009), 78.

12. William Taubman, *Khrushchev: The Man and His Era* (New York: W. W. Norton, 2003), 276–277.

13. Ibid., 292.

14. Ibid., 277. In his memoirs, dictated after his fall from power in 1964, Khrushchev generally takes a harsher line on Stalin, calling him a criminal who deserved to have been tried for his crimes. See Sergei Khrushchev, ed., *Memoirs of Nikita Khrushchev,* vol. 2, *Reformer (1945–1964),* trans. George Shriver (University Park: Pennsylvania State University Press, 2006), 209–210.

15. Khrushchev, *Memoirs,* 2:203–204. Khrushchev does not lay out the timeline for his decision making and in some places his recollection of the timing of events conflicts with the documentary record.

16. Ibid., 211.

17. On the use of the Leningrad Affair against Malenkov, see Taubman, *Khrushchev,* 263–265. On Khrushchev's use in 1956 of Molotov and others' records of participation in the worst of the purges, see Lenoe, *Kirov Murder,* 570, 575.

18. Anastas Mikoyan had already asked Lev Shaumian to use his position as head of the Soviet Encyclopedia project to compile data on the fates of the 1934 Congress delegates; see Mikoyan, "Aleksei Snegov," 71.

19. "Pis'mo O. G. Shatunovskoi A.I. Mikoianu o repressiiakh v 1937–1938 gg. i ubiistve S. M. Kirova," no later than December 31, 1955, and "Pis'mo A. V. Snegova N. S. Khrushchevu o vydache emu postoiannogo gostevogo bileta na XX s"ezd KPSS," January 20, 1956, in *Doklad N. S. Khrushcheva . . . dokumenty,* 170–171, 173. For a chronology of preparations for the Congress, see Iu. V. Aksiutin and A. V. Pyzhikov, "O podgotovke zakrytogo doklada N. S. Khrushcheva XX S"ezdu KPSS v svete novykh dokumentov," *Novaia i noveishaia istoriia* 2 (2002): 108–109.

20. "O kul'te lichnosti i ego posledstviiakh," February 25, 1956, in *Doklad N. S. Khrushcheva . . . dokumenty,* 3; for more on Rodos's career, see

Donald Rayfield, *Stalin and His Hangmen* (New York: Random House, 2004), 357–358. On his sentencing and execution, see "Rodos—ostrov v arkhipelage GULAG," *Novaia gazeta,* special issue *Pravda Gulaga,* September 22, 2010. Valerii Rodos, *Ia—syn palacha* (Moscow: OGI, 2008).

21. "Protokol No. 185. Zasedanie 1 fevralia 1956 g." in *Prezidium TsK KPSS, 1954–1964,* 1: 95–97.

22. Ibid.

23. Ibid.

24. "Protokol No. 187. Zasedanie 9 fevralia 1956 g." *Prezidium TsK KPSS, 1954–1964,* vol. 1, 99; "Postanovlenie Prezidiuma TsK KPSS 'Vopros Ministerstva oborony SSSR'," *Prezidium TsK KPSS, 1954–1964, Postanovleniia 1954–1958,* ed. A. A. Fursenko (Moscow: ROSSPEN, 2006), 2:197.

25. Anastas Mikoyan, *Tak bylo: Razmyshleniia o minuvshem* (Moscow: Vagrius, 1999), 591–592.

26. "Doklad Komissii TsK KPSS dlia ustanovleniia prichin massovykh repressii protiv chlenov i kandidatov v chleny TsK VKP(b), izbrannykh na XVII s"ezde partii, Prezidiumu TsK KPSS," February 9, 1956, in *Doklad N. S. Khrushcheva . . . dokumenty,* 185–230.

27. Ibid., 197.

28. "Protokol No. 187," *Prezidium TsK KPSS, 1954–1964,* 1:99–103.

29. On the role of former prisoners as truth tellers, see Khrushchev, *Memoirs,* 2:209.

30. Mikoyan credited Khrushchev with clever maneuvering to ask a broader set of party members if they wanted to hear about the cult (*Tak eto bylo,* 594). On who would give the report, see Roy Medvedev, *All Stalin's Men,* trans. Harold Shukman (Garden City, NY: Anchor Press, 1984), 84. Khrushchev may have used the prospect of Snegov speaking to scare presidium members into accepting him as a more moderate speaker. Ironically, Snegov's draft speech was not nearly as far-reaching or frank as Khrushchev's Secret Speech. Snegov's draft speech is reprinted in *Doklad N. S. Khrushcheva . . . dokumenty,* 177–185.

31. Vidali, *Diary,* 14–15. It is unclear how much revision occurred before the publication of this diary; given the level of detail about events attended, conversations held, weather, and so forth, it seems Vidali must have written a record of some sort during the Congress itself.

32. "Otchetnyi doklad Tsentral'nogo komiteta," in *XX S"ezd Kommunisticheskoi partii Sovetskogo Soiuza: Stenograficheskii otchet* (Moscow, 1956), 1:58, 79–80.

33. Aleksandr Iakovlev, *Sumerki* (Moscow: Materik, 2003), 253.

34. A few days later they responded similarly to French Communist Party leader Maurice Thorez's positive reference to Stalin; see Vidali, *Diary*, 26, 39.

35. *XX S"ezd . . . Stenograficheskii otchet*, 302.

36. Ibid., 325, 326.

37. Mikoyan, *Tak eto bylo*, 595.

38. *XX S"ezd . . . Stenograficheskii otchet*, 1:625.

39. Vidali, *Diary*, 17–18.

40. Ibid., 28–29. On enjoying the perks of being a delegate, see reminiscences of Leningrad factory worker and social activist Anna Karetnikova in Lev Lur'e and Irina Maliarova, *1956 god. Seredina veka* (St. Petersburg: Izd. Dom 'Neva', 2007), 99–100. See also interviews with Vasilii Isaev, Konstantin Galashin, and Ivan Kazanets in ibid., 101–104, 112–117.

41. Rada Adzhubei cited in Anatoly Medetsky, "A Speech to Stun Even a Daughter," *Moscow Times*, February 22, 2006, p. 1; Sergei Khrushchev cited in Vladimir Tolts's Radio Liberty series, "XX S"ezd—sorok let spustiia," part II, http//:www.svoboda.org/programs/cicles/xx/xx_02.asp.

42. Lysenko's speech is in *XX S"ezd Kommunisticheskogo partii Sovetskogo Soiuza: Stenograficheskii otchet* (Moscow, 1956), 2:348–352. Vidali remained silent not as a protest against the Congress but out of despair that, owing to the pending settlement of the territorial dispute between Italy and Yugoslavia, his party would soon cease to exist as an independent organization (*Diary*, 76, 78–79).

43. Vidali, *Diary*, 78, 75.

44. Ibid., 79.

45. Aksiutin and Pyzhikov, "O podgotovke zakrytogo doklada," 116.

46. Radio Liberty "XX S"ezd–sorok let spustia"; Dmitrii Anokhin, "Povisla tishina, i siden'ia khlopali, budto chastye vystrely," *Vecherniaia Moskva*, March 6, 2006.

47. K. P. Chudinova, "Pamiati nevernuvshikhsia tovarishchei," in *Imet' silu pomnit'*, comp. L. M. Gurvich (Moscow: Moskovskii Rabochii, 1991), 34; Aleksandr Mil'chakov, *Molodost' svetlaia i tragicheskaia* (Moscow: Moskovskii rabochii, 1988), 99.

48. Memories conflict as to whether or to what extent Khrushchev diverged from his written text. Semichastnyi insists he stuck closely to the text, while Aleksandr Iakovlev, among others, insists Khrushchev interjected in an

even harsher tone than the text. Differences exist as well regarding the length of time the reading took. Semichastnyi cited in "XX S"ezd—sorok let spustiia," part II; Aleksandr Iakovlev, *Omut pamiati* (Moscow: Vagrius, 2001), 116.

49. A complete annotated Russian text can be found in *Doklad N. S. Khrushcheva . . . dokumenty*, 51–119; Quotations here are from U.S. Department of State translation "Khrushchev's Secret Speech," included in Strobe Talbott, trans. and ed., *Khrushchev Remembers* (New York: Bantam Books, 1971), 609.

50. "Kruschchev's Secret Speech," *Khrushchev Remembers*, 614.

51. Ibid., 615.

52. Ibid., 631.

53. Future politburo member Mikhail Solomentsev, then a young delegate from Cheliabinsk, recalled, "In the midst of the session, a break was announced. During previous sessions, the delegates upon arising would immediately trade remarks and the hall of the Great Kremlin Palace would be filled with the hum of voices. Now a heavy silence hung and only the banging of seats, like occasional gunshots, broke the silence" (Anokhin, "Povisla tishina").

54. "Kruschchev's Secret Speech," *Khrushchev Remembers*, 652.

55. Ibid., 676, 677.

56. Ibid., 677. "Protokol zakrytogo utrennogo zasedaniia XX S"ezda Kommunisticheskoi partii Sovetskogo Soiuza," February 25, 1956, in *Doklad N. S. Khrushcheva . . . dokumenty*, 250–251.

57. Reminiscences of Vasilii Isaaev in Lur'e and Maliarova, *1956 god. Seredina veka*, 104.

3. March

1. Vittorio Vidali, *Diary of the Twentieth Congress of the Communist Party of the Soviet Union*, trans. Nell Amter Cattonar and A. M. Elliot (Westport, CT: Lawrence Hills, 1984), 101. Many delegates recall that they did not accept Khrushchev's claim about Stalin following the course of the war on a globe. See Vasilii Isaev and Konstantin Galanshin in Lev Lur'e and Irina Maliarova, *1956 god: Seredina veka* (St. Petersburg: Neva, 2007), 102, 112.

2. Vidali, *Diary*, 101.

3. Ibid.,102.

4. A. S. Stykalin, "XX S"ezd KPSS: Vostochnaia evropa. Razmyshleniia po itogam konferentsii," *Slavianovedenie* 1 (2008): 58–73.

5. "Postanovlenie Prezidiuma TsK KPSS 'Ob oznakomlenii s dokladom tov. Khrushcheva N. S. "O kul'te lichnosti i ego posledstviiakh" na XX s"ezde KPSS'"" in *Doklad N. S. Khrushcheva o kul'te lichnosti Stalina na XX S"ezde KPSS: Dokumenty,* comp. A. Iu. Afiani and ed. K. Aimermakher (Moscow: ROSSPEN, 2002), 253. On foreign parties, see M. Iu. Prozumenshchikov, "'Sekretnyi' doklad N. S. Khrushcheva na XX s"ezde KPSS i mezhdunarodnoe kommunisticheskoe dvizhenie" in ibid., 17–22. On the leak of the Secret Speech overseas, see Vladimir Tol'ts, "XX s"ezd—sorok let spustia," part 5, http://www.svoboda .org/programs/cicles/xx/xx_05.asp.

6. Entry for April 9, 1956, "Iz dnevnikov Sergeia Sergeevicha Dmitrieva," *Otechestvennaia istoriia* 1 (2000): 170.

7. Along with variations in when the report was heard, the atmosphere at the meetings invariably differed. Journalist Fedor Burlatsky recalled later that at the editorial offices of the journal *Kommunist:* "Three people took turns to read it out and each put something of his own emotions into the words he uttered. A young editor . . . even seemed cheerful . . . One of the older men . . . kept stumbling over every phrase, testing it for size as if weighing up the accuracy of the information and shaking his head, showing in every gesture his distrust and disapproval of what was happening"; see Fedor Burlatsky, *Khrushchev and the First Russian Spring,* trans. Daphne Skillen (New York: Charles Scribner's Sons, 1988), 64.

8. Quotation from Mikhail Gorbachev in *XX s"ezd: Materialy konferentsii k 40-letiiu XX s"ezda KPSS. Gorbachev Fond 22 fevralia 1996 goda* (Moscow: Aprel'-85, 1996), 4; on his experience in 1956, see also Mikhail Gorbachev, *On My Country and the World,* trans. George Shriver (New York: Columbia, 2000), 32; Ekaterina Dobrynina, "Dvadtsatyi s"ezd—dvadtsatyi sud," *Rossiiskaia Gazeta,* February 14, 2006.

9. N. S. Zlobin in *XX s"ezd: Materialy konferentsii,* 99.

10. Over the course of 1956, regional first secretaries submitted accounts to the Central Committee Department for Party Organs for the Russian Federation of party meetings held under their jurisdiction, including those devoted to the process of reading aloud Khrushchev's report in late March to early April. I also examined similar reports received by the Department for Union Republics. These reports vary in length and detail. Many report writers in March–April 1956 included partial or complete listings of questions posed by those in attendance. Polly Jones makes excellent use of a multitude of these reports in her analysis of responses to the Secret Speech, *Myth, Memory, Trauma: Rethinking the Stalinist Past in the Soviet Union, 1953–1970* (New Haven, CT: Yale University Press, 2013), 28–49.

11. The final version of Pankratova's report to the Central Committee has been published along with the list of questions by A. V. Novikov as "Pervaia reaktsiia na kritiku 'kul'ta lichnosti' I. V. Stalina. Po itogam vystuplenii A. M. Pankratovoi v Leningrade v marte 1956 goda," *Voprosy istorii* 8–10 (August–October 2006): 3-21, 3-22, 3-24. I also use an earlier draft of her report from documents donated by her daughter to the International Memorial Society (Moscow) and available in its archive (f. 32, op. 2, d. 4). For the readers' convenience, I cite the *Voprosy istorii* text whenever possible. Quotation here is from the final version; in the draft, she cited "great mental confusion and extreme emotional agitation."

12. Pankratova evidently gave a similar lecture on her return to Moscow. She saved the notes from audiences on March 27 and April 3, but she did not include them in her report. The Memorial Society archives preserve 130 Moscow notes. A sampling can be found in Boris Belenkin, "'V chem polozhitel'noe znachenie I. V. Stalina?': Voprosy uchitelei istorii posle XX s"ezda," *30 Oktiabria* 61 (2006) at http://urokiistorii.ru/history/soc/1367.

13. Pankratova's biography is drawn from L. V. Badia, "Etapy tvorcheskogo puti," in *Istorik i vremia. 20–50-kh godov XX veka. A. M. Pankratova* (Moscow: Izd. RUDN and Mosgorarkhiv, 2000), 10–20; and Reginald E. Zelnik, *Perils of Pankratova: Some Stories from the Annals of Soviet Historiography* (Seattle: University of Washington Press, 2005).

14. Pankratova's account cited by Badia, "Etapy," 13. Regarding Pankratova's husband, Grigorii Iakovin, and their marriage, see Boris Belenkin, "'Tan'ka! Tanechka! Tania! . . .' Zametki na poliakh poemy Nauma Korzhavina i biografii Anny Mikhailovny Pankratovoi," in *Pravo na imia: Biografika 20 veka* (St. Petersburg: NITs Memoriala, 2010), 14–22.

15. Badia, "Etapy," 15, 16; L. V. Maksakova, "Uchitel' i chelovek," in *Istorik i vremia*, 159–160; G. D. Burdei, "A. M. Pankratova–Professor Saratovskogo Universiteta v 1937–1940 gg.," in ibid., 74–76.

16. Badia, "Etapy," 16–17; Zelnik, *Perils*, 37–48, 75–76. On the Kazakh history textbook, see also David Brandenburger, *National Bolshevism: Stalinist Mass Culture and the Formation of Modern Russian National Identity, 1931–1956* (Cambridge, MA: Harvard University Press, 2002), 123–131.

17. Zelnik, *Perils*, 48.

18. Aleksandr Nekrich remembered her as sympathetic to his struggles to avoid anti-Semitic persecution in the Institute of History. He described her as "a kindly conscientious person and extremely decent by nature." See Aleksandr Nekrich, *Forsake Fear: Memoirs of a Historian*, trans. Donald Lineburgh (Boston: Unwin Hyman, 1991), 66. See also A. B. Zaks, *Eta dolgaia, dolgaia, dolgaia zhizn'* (Moscow: Gosudarstvennyi istoricheskii muzei, 2000), 124.

19. For a history of *Voprosy istorii* during the thaw, see E. N. Gorodetskii, "Zhurnal 'Voprosy istorii' v seredine 50-kh godov," *Voprosy istorii* 9 (September 1989): 69–79.

20. Valentin Beilinson recounted how Pankratova helped him in August 1953 to start the long process of petitioning for the posthumous rehabilitation of his grandfather Aleksandr Aluf, who had been one of Pankratova's teachers. Pankratova met with Beilinson to strategize about whom to ask for letters of support and even phoned party leader Otto Kuusinen to ask for his assistance; see Valentin Beilinson, *Sovetskoe vremia v liudiakh* (Moscow: Novyi khronograf, 2009), 17, 452–453. The wife of Ermukhan Bekmakhanov, one of Pankratova's Kazakh protégés, said that the historian gave him money to buy a fashionable overcoat to replace his padded labor camp jacket—Pankratova allegedly told him: "So that your rivals [*nedrugi*] don't think that your spirits have fallen, you should show up in Alma-Ata dressed like a dandy" (Merei Sugirbaeva, "'Ia poznala velikoe chuvstvo—liubov'," *Karavan,* March 4, 2011, http://www.caravan.kz/gazeta/ya-poznala-velikoe-chuvstvo-lyubov-56455/).

21. "Pis'mo A. M. Pankratovoi P. N. Pospelovu, A. M. Rumiantsevu, M. A. Suslovu i N. S. Khrushchevu, May 17, 1955," *Otechestvennye arkhivy* 5 (1992): 36.

22. "Zhaloba v TsK KPSS na rabotnikov Otdela nauki v sviazi s izucheniem raboty zhurnala 'Voprosy istorii', June 17, 1955," in ibid., 47–51.

23. Stenographers' transcripts of Pankratova's speech of March 20, 1956, at the Central Lecture Hall for the Znanie society and of her appearance at a seminar for pedagogues and curriculum specialists on March 29 and April 3 are in ARAN, f. 697, op. 1, d. 180a and 182. A version of a speech to a gathering of teachers (sometime between June and November 1956) was also published as a booklet: A. M. Pankratova and L. P. Bushchik, *Voprosy Prepodavaniia istorii SSSR v svete reshenii XX S"ezda KPSS* (Alma-Ata: Ministerstvo Prosveshcheniia Kazakhskoi SSR, 1956).

24. Pankatova admits as much in her early draft, but redacts this commentary from the final version. "Dokladnaia zapiska"—Memorial variant—l. 2. One audience member notes critically that in Khrushchev's report everything was presented "significantly more sharply." Another dares to chide her for referring to Stalin as "comrade." "Pervaia reaktsiia," *Voprosy istorii* 9 (September 2006): 4, 6.

25. Pankratova, "Vazhneishie problemy sovetskoi istoricheskoi nauki" (lecture at the Central Lecture Hall of the Leningrad branch of the All-Union Society for the Spread of Political and Scientific Knowledge 'Znanie', March 20, 1956, ARAN, f. 697, op. 1, d. 180a, ll. 2–39).

26. Ibid., l. 40.

27. Ibid., l. 46, 48.

28. Ibid., l. 50.

29. Ibid., l. 52. A listener later told Pankratova that the audience laughed because "your words 'many restructurings' struck all of us who have also had to restructure ourselves many times" (ARAN, f. 697, op. 1, d. 181, l. 217).

30. Sergei Dmitriev was already fretting about these issues after Mikoyan's criticisms of the profession at the Twentieth Party Congress. In his diary on February 16, 1956, Dmitriev compared the Soviet social sciences to a "corpse" and wryly observed that it could not be brought back to life by dint of shouting at it. He wondered whether Mikoyan's words were just for consumption by the press. See Sergei Dmitriev, "Iz dnevnikov," *Otechestvennaia istoriia* 1 (2000): 165.

31. "Pervaia reaktsiia," *Voprosy istorii* 9 (September 2006): 8–10.

32. E. Iu. Zubkova, *Obshchestvo i reformy, 1945–1964* (Moscow: AIRO, 1993), 135.

33. "Pervaia reaktsiia," *Voprosy istorii* 10 (October 2006): 6.

34. "Pervaia reaktsiia," *Voprosy istorii* 8 (August 2006): 7, 15.

35. "Pervaia reaktsiia," *Voprosy istorii* 10 (October 2006): 20; *Voprosy istorii* 9 (September 2006): 14, 16.

36. "Pervaia reaktsiia," *Voprosy istorii* 9 (September 2006): 15, 12.

37. Ibid., 13.

38. Ibid.

39. Daniil Granin, *Prichudy moei pamiati* (Moscow: Tsentrpoligraf MiM-Del'ta, 2010), 221; "Pervaia reaktsiia," *Voprosy istorii* 9 (September 2006): 13, 16.

40. "Pervaia reaktsiia," *Voprosy istorii* 9 (September 2006): 12.

41. "Pervaia reaktsiia," *Voprosy istorii* 8 (August 2006): 16, 17, 19.

42. All questions in this paragraph were reproduced in the body of Pankratova's report; see "Pervaia reaktsiia," *Voprosy istorii* 8 (August 2006): 8.

43. "Dokladnaia zapiska"—Memorial variant—l. 3.

44. Granin noted Stalin's picture had been taken down in the post office. News was spreading of spontaneous calls for Stalin's body to be thrown out of the mausoleum. He, too, heard the apocryphal anecdote about Khrushchev asking who had written the note asking why the presidium members had been silent (*Prichudy*, 222–223). The note asking whether Pankratova still loved Stalin is not included in the list submitted to the Central Committee.

Perhaps it defied classification. It can be found in ARAN, f. 697, op. 1, d. 181, l. 112.

45. K. L. Seleznev, "Stratsnyi borets za liniiu partii," in *Zhenshchiny-revoliutsionery i uchenye* (Moscow: Nauka, 1982), 42.

46. First quotation is from "Dokladnaia zapiska"—Memorial variant—l. 5; second is from Granin, *Prichudy,* 221.

47. Entry for April 3, 1956, "Iz dnevnikov," 168.

48. Igor' Kon, *80 let odinochestva* (Moscow: Vremia, 2008), 55.

49. In her draft, Pankratova labels some of the questions as "bordering on anti-party attacks"; in the final version she lets the questions speak for themselves ("Dokladnaia zapiska"—Memorial variant—l. 7).

50. "Pervaia reaktsiia," *Voprosy istorii* 8 (August 2006): 13. In the draft, Pankratova speaks more generally of "unhealthy and even anti-party moods," but offers more specific and more urgently voiced suggestions for improvements in ideological work ("Dokladnaia zapiska"—Memorial variant—l. 20).

51. "Pervaia reaktsiia," *Voprosy istorii* 8 (August 2006): 6.

52. Seleznev, "Strastnyi borets," 43.

53. Badia, "Etapy," 8.

54. Many reports from provincial secretaries to the Central Committee in mid-March include lists of questions posed at meetings dedicated to reading out the Secret Speech. These can be found in RGASPI, f. 556, op. 14, d. 43; see especially reports from Vladimir, Kalinin, Novgorod, Kabardino, Orlovsk, and Murmansk, ll. 22, 43–44, 60–64, 82–83, 93–95, 99–102. For an analysis of pro- and anti-Stalin responses, see Polly Jones, "From the Secret Speech to the Burial of Stalin: Real and Ideal Responses to De-Stalinization," in *The Dilemmas of De-Stalinization: Negotiating Cultural and Social Change in the Khrushchev Era,* ed. Polly Jones (New York: Routledge, 2006), 41–63.

55. Quotations from RGASPI, fond 556, op. 14, d. 43, ll. 93,100, 9; and "Informatsiia TsK KP Ukrainy" (April 20, 1956), in *Doklad N. S. Khrushcheva . . . Dokumenty,* 475.

56. Cited in "Spravka Ministerstva oborony SSSR 'O reagirovanii voennoslu-zhashchikh i sluzhashikh Sovetskoi Armii v chastiakh Moskovskogo voennogo okruga na doklad tov. Khrushcheva 'O kul'te lichnosti i ego posledstviiakh'," not later than June 6, 1956, in *Doklad N. S. Khrushcheva . . . Dokumenty,* 544.

57. Vladimir Kozlov, *Massovye besporiadki v SSSR pri Khrushcheve i Brezhneve, 1953-nachalo 1980-kh gg* (Moscow: ROSSPEN, 2010), 234–258;

Timothy K. Blauvelt and Jeremy Smith, eds., *Georgia after Stalin: Nationalism and Soviet Power* (London: Routledge, 2016), esp. chap. 3.

58. Cases against writers of anonymous letters can be found in *58¹⁰ nadzornye proizvodsta prokuratury SSSR po delam ob antisovetskoi agitatsii i propagande, mart 1953–1991,* comp. O. V. Edel'man (Moscow: Mezhdunarodnyi fond "Demokratiia," 1999). For an example of vandalism by students, see A. M. Vershik, "Takaia vot istoriia. Piat'desiat let nazad v marte," *Zvezda* 3 (2006): 173–186.

59. Apparently, the speech was not read out to them as a collective; instead it was kept in the political department's office and individual party members were allowed to go and read it there.

60. My account of this meeting is reconstructed from Orlov's memoirs and a report to the Central Committee of the CPSU that drew on a stenographic report of the meeting. See "Iz informatsii Politotdela Teplotekhnicheskoi laboratorii AN SSSR o zakrytom partiinom sobranii partorganizatsii po itogam raboty XX s"ezda 23, 26 marta 1956," in *Doklad N. S. Khrushcheva . . . Dokumenty,* 448–462. The transcript of the meeting must be treated cautiously as Orlov states that he learned from the institute secretary that Mezentsev altered it to make the rebels look worse. Yuri Orlov, *Dangerous Thoughts: Memoirs of a Russian Life,* trans. Thomas P. Whitney (New York: William Morrow, 1991), 118–121. Recent interviews with Vadim Nesterov and witness Boris Ioffe confirm Orlov's account and the involvement of the Central Committee in setting punishments (Lur'e and Maliarova, *1956 god,* 184–196).

61. Speeches by Avalov and Orlov in "Iz informatsii Politotdela," 449–451.

62. Orlov, *Dangerous Thoughts,* 84.

63. Speeches by G. I. Schedrin, G. M. Kukavadze, and M. E. Vishnevskii in "Iz informatsii Politotdela," 454–456. A debate on "sincerity" had been launched by Vladimir Pomerantsev's "Ob iskrennosti v literature," *Novyi mir* 12 (1953): 218–245.

64. Schedrin in "Iz informatsii Politotdela," 454.

65. Orlov, *Dangerous Thoughts,* 121; Boris Gordon, "Miatezhnyi atom," *Ogonek* 7 (2006): 29.

66. Orlov, *Dangerous Thoughts,* 130.

67. "Kommunisticheskaia partiia pobezhdala i pobezhdaet vernost'iu Leninizmu," *Pravda,* April 5, 1956, p. 2. For an insightful examination of the April editorial and other official responses over the course of 1956, see Jones, *Myth, Memory, Trauma,* 50–55.

68. Pimenov, though he did not tell the others at the time, managed to get a look at one of the printed copies of the speech; see Revol't Pimenov, *Vospominaniia* (Moscow: Panorama, 1996), 1:23–25.

69. Ernst Orlovskii, "Moi put' v dissidenty," *Neva* 6 (2006): 181.

70. Citations from Pimenov's essay have been taken from prosecutor's documents in the subsequent case against him for anti-Soviet propaganda and agitation. GARF, f. 8131, d. 43956, ll. 27–28 and d. 43957, l. 43. On his mood in April 1956, see Pimenov, *Vospominaniia*, 1:25–26.

71. Mikhail German, *Slozhnoe proshedshee* (St. Petersburg: Iskusstvo-SPB, 2000), 260.

4. April

1. Chudinova's biography is drawn from her memoirs: K. P. Chudinova, "Pamiati nevernuvshikhsia tovarishchei," in *Imet' silu pomnit'*, comp. L. M. Gurvich (Moscow: Moskovskii rabochii, 1991), 5–39; K. P. Chudinova, "V te trudnye gody . . . ," *Voprosy istorii KPSS* 12 (1989): 116–124; K. P. Chudinova, *Voprosy istorii KPSS* 1 (1990): 131–142; G. A. Kramor, "Zvezda komissara Ksenii Chudinova," *Korkina Sloboda: kraevedcheskii al'manakh* 9 (2007): 85–108.

2. Chudinova's first husband died before 1917; her second and third husbands perished in the purges. Her youngest son, Lev, would die in a children's home at the start of World War II. Her next oldest son, Kim, did escape the orphanage to live with his sister Natal'ia but died at the front. Her oldest son, Konstantin, served a prison sentence. Her three daughters survived unscathed (Kramor, "Zvezda komissara," 105–106).

3. As one exile in Krasnoiarsk wrote to her husband, a prisoner in Karaganda, "Terrible rumors about Stalin's crimes are circulating through all of Siberia. Now people are even saying that those sentenced by special commissions will be allowed to go home." Ironically, he learned of the contents of the Secret Speech sooner than she did. Letter from A. Chumakova to A. I. Boiarchikov, April 3, 1956, and from Boiarchikov to Chumakova, March 24, 1956, respectively, in A. I. Boiarchikov, *Vospominaniia* (Moscow: AST, 2003), 309–311. Exiles Valerii Frid and Iulii Dunskii heard a reading of the speech only thanks to a party member friend who escorted them in at the last minute; see V. S. Frid, *58 1/2: Zapiski lagernogo pridurka* (Moscow: Izd. Dom Rusanova, 1996), 422.

4. The public was sensitive to the issue of mass releases after the March 1953 amnesty led to a crime wave. See Miriam Dobson, *Khrushchev's Cold Summer: Gulag Returnees, Crime, and the Fate of Reform after Stalin* (Ithaca, NY: Cornell University Press, 2009), 37–43.

5. Chudinova, "Pamiati," 35–37. In justifying her fall from favor, Molotov allowed that his wife might have been too trusting in her choice of acquaintances. Albert Reiss, ed. and trans., *Molotov Remembers: Inside Kremlin Politics* (Chicago: Ivan R. Dee, 1993), 23–324. Sheila Fitzpatrick cites evidence that Zhemchuzhina and at least one other Jewish wife of a top leader responded enthusiastically to the creation of the state of Israel in *On Stalin's Team: The Years of Living Dangerously in Soviet Politics* (Princeton, NJ: Princeton University Press, 2015), 201–204.

6. Chudinova, "Pamiati," 36–37.

7. Roy Medvedev, *All Stalin's Men*, trans. Harold Shukman (Garden City, NY: Anchor Press, 1984), 102; "Postanovlenie prezidiuma TsK KPSS o vosstanovlenii v partii P. S. Zhemchuzhinoi," March 21, 1953, in *Reabilitatsiia: kak eto bylo*, comp. A. Artizov, Iu. Sigachev, I. Shevchuk, V. Khlopov (Moscow: Mezhdunarodnyi fond "Demokratiia," 2000), 1:15; Reiss, *Molotov Remembers*, 324. On the phenomenon of purge victims' loyalty to the party, see Nanci Adler, *Keeping Faith with the Party: Communist Believers Return from the Gulag* (Bloomington: Indiana University Press, 2012).

8. Kim's parents wanted to name him Reksem from RKSM (Russian Communist Union of Youth), but his grandmother filled in the birth certificate with a "human name": Aleksei. Kim was a compromise. Kramor, "Zvezda komissara," 102–104.

9. Eugenia Ginzburg, *Within the Whirlwind*, trans. Ian Boland (New York: Harcourt Brace Jovanovich, 1982), 65; A. L. Litvin comp., *Dva sledstvennykh dela Evgenii Ginzburg* (Kazan: Knizhnyi dom, 1994), 87–91.

10. Cited in El'mar Guseinov, "Ne razu ne usomnivshiisia," *Ekspress*, July 5, 1990.

11. Jana Kutin, Andre Broido, and Anton Kutin, eds., *Ob ushedshem veke rasskazyvaet Ol'ga Shatunovskaia* (La Jolla, CA: DAA Books, 2001), 284. This volume consists of Shatunovskaia's oral recollections, family reminiscences, and some documents and correspondence as collected by her daughter and grandsons. Up until 1939 at least, Shatunovskaia had written appeals and initially had attempted to rebut the accusations against her point by point. See her letter to Mikoyan of June 23, 1939, in ibid., 150–153.

12. Only these commissions could authorize rehabilitation for persons sentenced by a special commission (*troika*) or by military courts or condemned to eternal exile. "Postanovlenie prezidiuma TsK KPSS o sozdanii tsentral'noi komissii i mestnykh komissii po peresmotru del osuzhdennykh za 'kontrrevoliutsionnye prestupleniia,' soderzhashchikhsia v lageriakh, koloniiakh, tiur'makh i nakhodiashchikhsia v ssylke na poselenii," May 4, 1954, in *Reabilitatsiia: kak*

eto bylo, 1:116–117. On proposals from within the Procuracy and Ministry of Internal Affairs to create new procedures for rehabilitation dating back to December 1953, see Galina M. Ivanova, "XX s"ezd KPSS i likvidatsiia GULAGa," in *XX s"ezd KPSS v kontekste rossiiskoi istorii,* ed. A. S. Seniavskii (Moscow: Ros. Akad. Nauk, In-t Ros. istorii, 2012), 72–73.

13. Litvin, *Dva sledstvennykh dela,* 98–130.

14. O. V. Lavinskaia, "Protsess peresmotra del politicheskikh zakliuchennykh v 1954–1956 gg. i popytki nakazaniia rabotnikov gosbezopasnosti za fal'sifikatskiiu del," in *Istoricheskie Chteniia na Lubianke, 1997–2007* (Moscow: Kuchkovo pole, 2008), 307–308.

15. "Zapiska D. E. Salina v TsK KPSS o rabote otdela po spetsdelam prokuratury SSSR po reabilitatsii grazhdan vo vtoroi polovine 1954-nachale 1955 g.," March 14, 1955, in *Reabilitatsiia: kak eto bylo,* 1:196, 203.

16. On the marginalization of old Bolsheviks, see Roy Medvedev, *Let History Judge,* trans. George Shriver, rev. and exp. ed. (New York: Columbia University Press, 1989), 406–410.

17. Biographical details for Stasova are drawn from Barbara Evans Clements, *Bolshevik Women* (Cambridge: Cambridge University Press, 1997); E. D. Stasova, *Stranitsy zhizhni i borby* (Moscow: Gospolizdat, 1960); and R. I. Pikovskaia, "'Esli by eto kasalos' bytovogo razlozheniia . . .' iz vospominanii E. D. Stasovoi," in *Golosa istorii: muzeinye materialy kak istochnik poznaniia proshlogo* (Moscow: Tsentral'nyi muzei revoliutsii SSSR, 1990), 1:184–193.

18. Vittorio Vidali, *Diary of the Twentieth Congress of the Communist Party of the Soviet Union,* trans. Nell Amter Cattonar and A. M. Elliot (Westport, CT: Lawrence Hill, 1984), 17; Gennadii Zhavoronkov, "O. A. Piatnitskii," in *Vozvrashchennye imena* (Moscow: Novosti, 1989), 2:65.

19. Pikovskaia, "'Esli by'," 185, 188–189.

20. Ibid., 190–192.

21. Some of Stasova's correspondents had written to her from camp or exile before March 1953, but she seems not to have encouraged such correspondences until after Stalin's death. Letter from Stasova to Lavarishek, April 12, 1955, RGASPI, f. 356, op. 2, d. 6, l. 213.

22. Letter from Lavarishek to Stasova, April 25, 1955, and from Stasova to Lavarishek, May 15, 1955 (ibid., ll. 215, 216). Despite Stasova's efforts, Lavarishek was reinstated in the CPSU only in February 1956 (letter from Lavarishek to Stasova, February 29, 1956, ibid., l. 222).

23. Ibid., ll. 106–156.

24. Stasova helped Galina Voronskaia in rehabilitating her parents despite the fact that her father was known to have sympathized with Trotsky. Moreover, when Voronskaia phoned Stasova while on her first trip back to Moscow in 1957, Stasova immediately inquired as to whether she needed a place to stay. See G. A. Voronskaia, *V strane vospominanii* (Moscow: RuPab+, 2007), 90–93. Generosity coexisted with strict ideas about duty—including answering every letter (ibid., 94–95).

25. Contrast her correspondence with Berta Albert-Ploshanskaia and Viktoriia Shtempel (RGASPI, f. 356, op. 2, d. 4 and 18, respectively).

26. Ibid., d. 2, ll. 7–35.

27. On *tverdost'*, see Clements, *Bolshevik Women*, 60.

28. Vidali, *Diary*, 17. Stasova had written to Vidali in English in 1950, that "[I] came to the conclusion that I think too much about myself, that it is not allowed to [*sic*] be a party member." She banished her bad thoughts by focusing on Soviet achievements in economics and foreign policy (letters from Stasova to Vidali from July 23, September 24, and December 22, 1950, RGASPI, f. 356, op. 1, d. 112, l. 9ob, 12 ob, 13).

29. Letter from Stasova to Lavarishek, March 19, 1956 (ibid., op. 2, d. 6, l. 221).

30. Vidali, *Diary*, 93.

31. Ibid., 93–94. In a letter to Stasova after the Twentieth Party Congress, the son of Osip Piatnitskii wrote, "You drove me away [*prognali menia*] when I told you that there still were not such guarantees [that Leninist norms would be observed]. Now there are! And this pleases me beyond words. From all my heart I congratulate you that you and I have lived to this day" (letter from Igor' Piatnitskii to Stasova, March 14, 1956, RGASPI, f. 356 op. 1, d. 8, ll. 11, 11ob, 12, 12ob).

32. Clements, *Bolshevik Women*, 72, 141.

33. Letter from Stasova to Vidali, April 8, 1956, RGASPI, f. 356, op. 1, d. 112, ll. 63, 63ob.

34. For Grigorii Petrovskii's letters on behalf of victims and their relatives, see V. A. Bessonova, "'Medlenno idet likvidatsiia Stalinshchiny . . .' Iz perepiski G. I. Petrovskogo," in *Golosa istorii*, 1:214–233. Chudinova also helped; see Chudinova, "Pamiati," 10, 37–38.

35. Ginzburg, *Within the Whirlwind*, 390.

36. Ibid., 391–392.

37. Aleksandr Mil'chakov, *Molodost' svetlaia i tragicheskaia* (Moscow: Moskovskii rabochii, 1988), 93. Fadeev committed suicide in May 1956. He left a note expressing his anger at party mismanagement of literature.

38. Ibid., 92–93.

39. Ibid., 99.

40. Sergo Mikoyan, "Aleksei Snegov v bor'be za 'destalinizatsiiu'," *Voprosy istorii* 4 (2004): 74.

41. Unpublished interview with Roy Medvedev conducted by Leonid G. Novak (January 2004) author's archive; and Guseinov, "Ne razu." On broader reforms in the gulag, see Jeffrey S. Hardy, "Khrushchev's Gulag: The Evolution of Punishment in the Post-Stalin Soviet Union, 1953–1964" (Ph.D. diss., Princeton University, 2011).

42. Kutin, Broido, and Kutin, *Ob ushedshem,* 285–286.

43. Biographical data on Shatunovskaia drawn from ibid.

44. Ibid., 285.

45. Ibid., 282.

46. Ibid., 282–285, 326.

47. Chudinova, "Pamiati," 35.

48. For the first official mention of traveling commissions, see "Postanovlenie prezidiuma TsK KPSS o sozdanii partiinykh komissii po peresmotru del osuzhdennykh otbyvaiushchikh nakazanie v lageriakh," January 30, 1956, in *Reabilitatsiia: kak eto bylo,* 1:308.

49. Kutin, Broido, and Kutin, *Ob ushedshem,* 286.

50. Ibid., 287. Shatunovskaia seems to be referring to a February 9 resolution by the presidium, which was followed up by a ukase only on March 10, 1956. See "Zapiska komissii TsK KPSS v TsK KPSS ob otmene ukaza prezidiuma verkhovnogo soveta SSSR ot 21 fevralia 1948 g. 'O napravlenii osobo opasnykh gosudarstvennykh prestupnikov po otbytii imi sroka nakazaniia v ssylku na poselenie v otdalennye mestnosti SSSR'," *Reabilitatsiia: kak eto bylo,* 1:313, 411n17.

51. Kutin, Broido, and Kutin, *Ob ushedshem,* 287–289.

52. Ibid., 291; Mikoyan, "Aleksei Snegov," 76.

53. Kutin, Broido, and Kutin, *Ob ushedshem,* 286–287. Ivanova claims only eighteen rehabilitated persons served, but I have not been able to confirm that number ("XX s"ezd i likvidatsiia GULAGa," 84).

54. Marc Elie, "Khrushchev's Gulag: The Soviet Penitentiary System after Stalin's Death, 1953–1964," in *The Thaw: Soviet Society and Culture during the 1950s and 1960s*, ed. Denis Kozlov and Eleonory Gilburd (Toronto: University of Toronto Press, 2013), 115.

55. "Postanovlenie prezidiuma TsK KPSS 'o rassmotrenii del na lits, otbyvaiushchikh nakazanie za politicheskie, dolzhnostnye i khoziaistvennye prestupleniia'," in *Reabilitatsiia kak eto bylo,* comp. A. Artizov, Iu. Sigachev, I. Shevchuk, V. Klopov (Moscow: Mezhdunarodnyi fond "Demokratiia" and Izd. Materik, 2003), 2:32.

56. Chudinova, "Pamiati," 38.

57. Ibid., 39. Aristov's report to the Central Committee in May paid special attention to juveniles. See "Zapiska A. B. Aristova v TsK KPSS o rabote komissii prezidiuma verkhovnogo soveta SSSR po rassmotreniiu del na lits, otbyvaiushchikh nakazanie za politicheskie, dolzhnostnye i khoziaistvennye prestupleniia," May 16, 1956, in *Reabilitatsiia: kak eto bylo,* 2:96–101. On the percentage of "politicals," see Elie, "Khrushchev's Gulag," 117.

58. Shelest claims his commission interviewed 150,000 inmates and ultimately freed 8,500. However, the final total reported for all ninety-seven commissions was only 176,000. If his team reviewed thirty cases a day for six months, his total seems to be off by a factor of ten. See Petr Shelest, *Da ne sudimy budete: Dnevnikovye zapisi, vospominaniia chlena Politburo TsK KPSS* (Moscow: Edition q, 1995), 114–115. Thanks to Marc Elie for the reference.

59. Letter from Petrosian to Shatunovskaia, May 12, 1956, in Kutin, Broido, and Kutin, *Ob ushedshem,* 275–276.

60. Ibid.

61. Letters from Aleksakhin, June 3 and August 13, 1956 (ibid., 276–277). He claimed his commission rehabilitated twice as many as the others (ibid., 344).

62. Aleksandr Boiarchikov letter to his wife, Aleksandra Chumakova, June 19, 1956, in Boiarchikov, *Vospominaniia,* 315; on the tasks of camp officials, see Steven A. Barnes, *Death and Redemption: The Gulag and the Shaping of Soviet Society* (Princeton, NJ: Princeton University Press, 2011), 235.

63. "Zapiska A. B. Aristova v TsK KPSS o rabote komissii prezidiuma verkhovnogo soveta SSSR po rassmotreniiu del na lits, otbyvaiushchikh nakazanie za politicheskie, dolzhnostnye i khoziaistvennye prestupleniia," June 5, 1956, in *Reabilitatsiia: kak eto bylo,* 2:120.

64. These were the words of party veteran and camp survivor Valentina Pikina, who worked at the KPK with Shatunovskaia. Pikina was a devoted

communist who spent her time in exile rereading Lenin's works in the local library to keep her spirits up. See Dolores Poliakova and Viktor Khorunzhii, "Valentina Pikina: Tragediia vzleta," *Sobesednik* 34 (August 1988): 12–13.

65. Letters from Petrosian to Shatunovskaia May 12 and June 29, 1956, in *Ob ushedeshem*, 275–277.

66. Elie suggests that personal contact may have created support for prison reform among those officials who served on the commissions. See Shelest, *Da ne sudimy*, 114–115; Elie, "Khrushchev's Gulag," 12–13.

67. Pikina and Snegov were in the rare position of having testified in court against their former oppressors. Pikina testified in the March 1955 trial of Lev Shvartsman, who admitted to having used illegal methods of torture. See Anatolii Golovkov, "Ne otrekaias' ot sebia," *Ogonek* 7 (1988): 29. On how Shvartsman became one of the few NKVD interrogators tried in the 1950s, see "Sledovatel'—kostolom: exportnyi variant," *Pravda GULAGa* (a special edition of *Novaia gazeta*), November 8, 2010.

68. Letter from Aleksakhin, June 3, 1956, in Kutin, Broido, and Kutin, *Ob ushedshem*, 276.

69. On the Molotov commission and Shatunovskaia's role, see Matthew E. Lenoe, *The Kirov Murder and Soviet History* (New Haven, CT: Yale University Press, 2010), 563, 575–576, 592–595. Shatunovskaia would later head her own commission into the Kirov affair in 1960–1961. On Zhemchuzhina's request, see Kutin, Broido, and Kutin, *Ob ushedshem*, 290.

70. Mil'chakov, *Molodost'*, 7; Kutin, Broido, and Kutin, *Ob ushedshem*, 302.

71. "Dokladnaia zapiska A. B. Aristova v TsK KPSS ob itogakh raboty komissii prezidiuma verkhovnogo soveta SSSR po rassmotreniiu del na lits, osuzhdennykh za politicheskie, dolzhnostnye i khoziaistvennye prestuple-niia," October 17, 1956, in *Reabilitatsiia: kak eto bylo*, 2:193.

72. Shatunovskaia felt opposition right up to the time of her retirement in 1962. One of Khrushchev's aides admitted that he tried to keep her from reaching the first secretary because she had "a very bad influence on him." In urgent matters, Shatunovskaia phoned Khrushchev's wife at home and asked her to relay messages, but Shatunovskaia looked back on her use of this tactic with disgust—"How often can one phone like that?" (Kutin, Broido, and Kutin, *Ob ushedshem*, 289, 291).

73. Mil'chakov, *Molodost'*, 159–160.

74. Letter from P. S. Giul' to Stasova, March 10, 1954, RGASPI, f. 356, op. 2, d. 6, l. 1.

75. When an interviewer in 1988 asked Shatunovskaia why she hadn't kept copies of her reports on Kirov and so on and even tried to publish them, she was aghast. "And what right do I have? They were secret. I sent them to the Politburo members. I placed them in the archive. How could I publish them?" (Kutin, Broido, and Kutin, *Ob ushedshem*, 301).

76. Ibid., 289.

5. May

1. Valerii S. Frid, *58 1/2: Zapiski lagernogo pridurka* (Moscow: Iz. Dom Rusanova, 1996), 433–434.

2. Undated letter from Aleksandra Kartsivadze to Shatunovskaia, written after January 1957, in Jana Kutin, Andrei Broido, and Anton Kutin, eds., *Ob ushedshem veke rasskazyvaet Ol'ga Shatunovskaia* (La Jolla, CA: DAA Books, 2001), 364. Kartsivadze and her husband, the former secretary of the Georgian Writers' Union, were arrested in 1940. He was executed; she was later in exile in Eniseisk with Shatunovskaia.

3. M. G. Roshal', "Gori, gori, moia zvezda," in *Sluzhili dva tovarishcha: Kniga o zhizni kinodramaturgov Dunskogo i Frida*, comp. Z. B. Osipova (Moscow: Zebra E, EKSMO, 2002), 340–341.

4. Ol'ga Adamova-Sliozberg, *Put'* (Moscow: Vozvrashchenie, 2002), 7–8.

5. Nanci Adler provides the fullest analysis of experiences of returnees including emotional problems of camp survivors in *The Gulag Survivor: Beyond the Soviet System* (New Brunswick, NJ: Transaction, 2002). Her more recent work expands the investigation of survivors' psychologies. See Nanci Adler, *Keeping Faith with the Party: Communist Believers Return from the Gulag* (Bloomington: Indiana University Press, 2012). See also Orlando Figes, *The Whisperers: Private Life in Stalin's Russia* (New York: Metropolitan Books / Henry Holt, 2007); Stephen F. Cohen, *The Victims Return: Survivors of the Gulag after Stalin* (Exeter, NH: PublishingWorks, 2010).

6. Anna Barkova, "Mimo . . . mimo . . . ," in *Anna Barkova . . . Vechno ne ta*, comp. L. N. Taganov and O. K. Pereverzev (Moscow: Fond Sergeia Dubova, 2002), 168.

7. Letter from Anna Barkova to M. N. Kuz'ko, March 30, 1940, in ibid., 406–407; general biographical information from Leonid Taganov, *"Prosti moiu nochnuiu dushu . . ."* (Ivanovo: Talka, 1993); Leonid Taganov, "Zhizn' i tvorchestvo Anny Barkovoi," in *Vechno ne ta*, 446–509.

8. Taganov, *Prosti*, 24–25, 34–35. On Voronskii's role in Ivanovo, see G. A. Voronskaia, *V strane vospominanii* (Moscow: RuPab+, 2007), 184–190.

9. Taganov, *Prosti*, 35.

10. Ibid., 44.

11. Ibid., 46.

12. Letter from Barkova to S. A. Selianin and N. S. Semenov, April 19, 1922, in *Vechno ne ta*, 384–386. See also, Taganov, *Prosti*, 52–54.

13. V. D. Panov, "Obzor arkhivnykh sledstvennykh del A. A. Barkovoi," in *Barkova A. A. Izbrannoe: Iz gulagovskogo arkhiva*, comp. L. N. Taganov and Z. Ia. Kholodovoi (Ivanovo: Ivanovo Gos. Un-t, 1992), 271, 280.

14. Barkova, "Kapel'ka liubvi," in *Vechno ne ta*, 169.

15. Even former prisoners could discriminate. A friend from Kolyma, an old Bolshevik who had been rehabilitated and given an obscure bureaucratic job in Moscow, told Shalamov: "You and I got freed because we weren't guilty of anything. But those who weren't freed—that means there's something on them." Shalamov disagreed. See Varlam Shalamov, *Novaia kniga: Vospominaniia, zapisnye knizhki, perepiska, sledstvennye dela*, comp. I. P. Sirotinskaia (Moscow: Eksmo, 2004), 241.

16. Draft appeal from Barkova to the General Procurator of the USSR, sometime in February–March 1956, in *Vechno ne ta*, 422.

17. "Iz zapisnykh knizhek 1956–1957 godov," in ibid., 368–369.

18. M. A. Utevskii, "Ob A. A. Barkovoi," *Lazur'* 1 (1989): 333.

19. Letter from Barkova to Khrushchev, summer 1956, in *Vechno ne ta*, 426.

20. Barkova, "Kak delaetsia luna," in ibid., 304–305.

21. Barkova, "Iz zapisnykh knizhek," in ibid., 368–369.

22. Zinaida Stepanishcheva, *Neokonchatel'naia pravda* (Moscow: Fond Sergeia Dubova, 2005), 214; Barkova quotation from "Iz zapisnykh knizhek," in *Vechno ne ta*, 368.

23. Barkova, "Tsementnyi istukan," in *Vechno ne ta*, 169–176.

24. Shalamov, "Vospominaniia," in *Novaia kniga*, 249–250.

25. Sirotinskaia, "Vospominanie o V. Shalamove," in Varlam Shalamov, *Neskol'ko moikh zhiznei: Proza, poeziia, esse* (Moscow: Respublika, 1996), 456. See also Shalamov, "Vospominaniia," in *Novaia kniga*, 22–27.

26. Letter from Shalamov to A. Z. Dobrovol'skii, March 12, 1955, in Shalamov, *Novaia kniga*, 487.

27. Ibid., 24; Sirotinskaia, "Vospominaniie," 457. Letter from Shalamov to Dobrovol'skii, August 13, 1954, in Shalamov, *Novaia kniga*, 481. See also Valerii Esipov, *Shalamov* (Moscow: Molodaia gvardiia, 2012), 206–207.

28. Shalamov, "Vospominaniia," in *Novaia kniga*, 152–153.

29. On his wife's failings, see ibid., 255; on his daughter, see his letter to Dobrovol'skii of August 13, 1954, in ibid., 481 and to her of April 10–13, 1954, 458–460. A new biography of Shalamov cites a relative of Gudz' noting Elena was raised to believe that people were not jailed "for nothing" (Esipov, *Shalamov*, 218).

30. Shalamov, "Vospominaniia," in *Novaia kniga*, 247.

31. Letter to Dobrovol'skii of August 13, 1954, in ibid., 481.

32. Their correspondence is reprinted in ibid., 393–454. On the first meeting with Pasternak, see Shalamov, *Vospominanie*, 320–328.

33. Letter to Dobrovol'skii, March 26 1956, in Shalamov, *Novaia kniga*, 508–511.

34. Informer "I" report of June 19, 1956. Sirotinskaia has obtained eight such reports by a single informer covering a period from April 1956 through June 1959. She notes that Shalamov was aware of at least one, different, informer; see "Sledsvennye dela" in *Novaia kniga*, 1044.

35. Letter from Shalamov to Ivinskaia, March 20, 1956, in Irina Emel'ianova, *Legendy Potapovskogo pereulka: B. Pasternak, A. Efron, V. Shalamov: Vospominaniia i pis'ma* (Moscow: Ellis Lak, 1997), 311–312.

36. Letters from Shalamov to Ivinskaia, March 30 and 31, 1956, in ibid., 312–314.

37. Ol'ga Ivinskaia did not fear contacts with former prisoners; on the contrary, her daughter recalled their Moscow apartment serving as a sort of "transit point" for camp returnees (ibid., 57–59).

38. Ibid., 315–316.

39. Ibid., 56–57. Christopher Barnes, *Boris Pasternak: A Literary Biography*, vol. 2, *1928–1960* (Cambridge: Cambridge University Press, 1998), 286–287, 296–297. Ivinskaia's significance to Pasternak and her role in handling the scandal around the novel's publication in the West are hotly contested. For a recent interpretation, see Irina Emel'ianova, *Pasternak i Ivinskaia* (Moscow: Vagrius, 2006), esp. 96–97, 153.

40. *Doctor Zhivago* had been submitted to the "thick" literary journals *Znamia* and *Novyi mir*, as well as to the publishing house Goslitizdat, but none

had responded. Pasternak believed their silence spoke for itself (Barnes, *Boris Pasternak*, 299, 311–312). Sergio D'Angelo, the Italian radio journalist who brought the novel to Feltrinelli, recalls the idea of offering it to the Italian communist publisher was his in *Delo Pasternaka: Vospominaniia ochevidtsa* (Moscow: Novoe Literaturnoe Obozrenie, 2007), 12–13.

41. Emel'ianova, *Legendy*, 332–333.

42. Letter from Shalamov to Ivinskaia, May 24, 1956, in *Novaia Kniga*, 587–589.

43. Barnes, *Boris Pasternak*, 274.

44. Letter from Shalamov to Pasternak, July 12, 1956, in *Novaia Kniga*, 450–453.

45. Shalamov, *Vospominanie*, 342

46. Ibid., 343.

47. Emel'ianova describes Shalamov and Ivinskaia's relations as "a brief, true spring romance," as "pure and radiant" (*Legendy*, 336). Shalamov wrote to Dobrovol'skii on July 7, 1956, to say: "My personal affairs are all a mess and I don't know myself what tomorrow will bring" (*Novaia Kniga*, 517). For a secondhand account of Ivinskaia's recollection of the break, see B. M. Mansurov, *Lara moego romana: Boris Pasternak i Ol'ga Ivinskaia* (Moscow: Infomedia Pablisherz, 2009), 103–106.

48. Regarding his sudden transfer of affections, perhaps the clue lies in his earlier judgment, recorded in his notebook for 1954–1955: "The percent of familial happiness is higher in so-called calculated marriages than in marriages for love," Shalamov, "Zapisnye knizhki," in Shalamov, *Novaia kniga*, 273. See also letter from O. Nekliudova to Shalamov, July 24, 1956, in ibid., 602–603.

49. Letter from Shalamov to Pasternak, August 12, 1956, in ibid., 453–454.

50. Letter from Shalamov to Gudz', August 28, 1956, in ibid., 470–471.

51. Letter from Shalamova-Ianushevskaia to Shalamov, August 1956, in ibid., 471–474.

52. Letter from A. Z. Dobrovol'skii to Shalamov, December 15–20, 1956, in ibid., 524.

53. Sirotinskaia, "Vospominanie," 457.

54. Nekliudova's son has attributed the rapid onset of troubles in the marriage to his mother and Shalamov both having literary aspirations and difficult characters. He notes also that Shalamov had a deep solitary streak (speech by Sergei Nekliudov, June 16, 2011, http://www.shalamov.ru/video/20.html).

55. Letter from Iu. Dunskii to M. Levin, October 4, 1954, in *Sluzhili*, 207.

56. Frid, *58 1/2*, 269–270.

57. Kapler started his career as an actor, but he gained fame for his scenarios for the films *Lenin in October* (1937) and *Lenin in 1918* (1939). Released in 1948 after five years in Vorkuta, Kapler dared to visit Moscow illegally and had been sentenced to another five-year term, which he served in Inta (Dunskii and Frid, "Amarkord-88," in *Sluzhili*, 585). On his romance with Allilueva, see Varvara Samsonova, *Allilueva i Kapler* (Moscow: Vagrius, 2006). On the mixing of former prisoners and civilians in northern camp towns, see Alan Barenberg, *Gulag Town, Company Town: Forced Labor and Its Legacy in Vorkuta* (New Haven, CT: Yale University Press, 2014).

58. On Levin's career and political activities, see N. Leontovich and M. A. Miller, comp., *Mikhail L'vovich Levin. Zhizn', vospominaniia, tvorchestvo* (Nizhnyi Novgorod: Institute prikladnoi fiziki RAN, 1995).

59. Letters from Kapler to Dunskii and Frid, June 8, 1955, and undated in *Sluzhili*, 232–233, 239–240; quotation is from Dunskii and Frid, "Amarkord-88," in ibid., 588.

60. Dunskii and Frid received tremendous support from their family members during their imprisonment and exile, with the exception of Iulii's older brother, Viktor, a loyal communist and war veteran, who believed until after the Twentieth Party Congress that they must be guilty (Frid, *58 1/2*, 274).

61. Ibid., 423–424.

62. Letter from V. Frid to M. Levin, 20 November 1955 and letter from Iu. Dunskii to M. Levin, undated, in *Sluzhili*, 243–245.

63. V. Frid, "Posle skazki," in *Kinematograf ottepeli*, ed. V. Troianovskii (Moscow: Materik, 2002), 2:303.

64. Frid, *58 1/2*, 434–435; R. N. Iurenev, "Ochkariki," in *Sluzhili*, 93.

65. B. B. Bynina, "My ne davali kliatvy v vernosti . . . ," in *Sluzhili*, 52–53; I. A. Sergievskaia, "Valerii i Iulii," in ibid., 347–348.

66. Sergievskaia, "Valerii i Iulii," in ibid., 347–348; Z. B. Osipova, "My zhili schastlivo," in ibid., 617–633.

67. Frid, "Posle skazki," 309. E. N. Mit'ko, "Moi druz'ia-sosedi," in *Sluzhili*, 79–380.

68. Letter from Kapler to Dunskii and Frid, May 28, 1954, in *Sluzhili*, 90.

69. Frid, "Posle skazki," 303.

70. Frid would take advantage of perestroika to write a script about the gulag, *Lost in Siberia* (dir. A. Mitta, 1991), and later a memoir.

71. Sirotinskaia, "Vospominanie," 450. Shalamov preferred to write his stories in a single sitting, at a moment of high emotion. He considered the first draft to be the most honest. See Mikhail Mikheev, "O 'novoi' proze Varlama Shalamova," *Voprosy literatury* 4 (2011): 183–214.

72. Shalamov, "Vospominaniia," in *Novaia kniga*, 13.

73. Ibid., 149.

74. Shalamov, "Poezd," in *Neskol'ko moei zhizni*, 187.

75. All three stories are included in *Vechno ne ta*.

76. Cited in Panov, "Obzor arkhivnykh sledstvennykh del," 277.

6. June

1. Anatoly Gladilin, *The Making and Unmaking of a Soviet Writer: My Story of the "Young Prose" of the Sixties and After*, trans. David Lapeza (Ann Arbor, MI: Ardis, 1979), 13.

2. Ibid., 23.

3. Deborah A. Field, "Mothers and Fathers and the Problem of Selfishness in the Khrushchev Period," in *Women in the Khrushchev Era*, ed. Melanie Ilic, Susan E. Reid and Lynne Attwood (Basingstoke: Palgrave Macmillan, 2004), 96, 97, 102. Interestingly, Field notes that fathers were meant to encourage hobbies and studies, while mothers were expected to teach manners and character.

4. Larry E. Holmes, "A Symbiosis of Errors: The Personal, Professional and Political in the Kirov Region, 1931–1941," in *Borders of Socialism: Private Spheres of Soviet Russia*, ed. Lewis H. Siegelbaum (New York: Palgrave MacMillan, 2006), 212; Reminiscences of Margarita Monakhova, in L. I. Lebedeva comp., *Mozaika sudeb: Biofakovtsev MGU 1930–1960 godov postupleniia*, vol. 2, *1951–1960-e gody* (Moscow: Tovarishchestvo nauchnykh izdanii KMK, 2007), 511.

5. On the astronomy club, see Marina Stroganova in *Mozaika sudeb*, 2:484.

6. Teachers in rural areas also helped nurture students' ambitions. For instance, one young man growing up in a remote area of the Krasnoiarsk region of Siberia was persuaded by his teacher—an exile—to apply to MGU. See Iu. A. Romanov, "Ternistyi put' filolog vybiraet . . . ," in *Vremia, ostavsheesia s nami: Filologicheskii fakul'tet v 1955–1960 gg. Vospominaniia vypusknikov* (Moscow: MAKS press, 2006), 3:201. The dispersion of educated persons through exile

created centers of excellent education in far-flung places, including Inta. See Elena Kolpikova, *My iz Gulaga* (Moscow: RIPOL klassik, 2002), 143–154.

7. See, for instance, A. P. Onuchin, "Syn strelochnika–student MGU–Professor NGU," *Vypuskniki MGU v Novosibirskom nauchnom tsentre SO RAN*, http://www.prometeus.nsc.ru/elibrary/2007mgu/179–182.ssi.

8. Boris Vail', *Osobo opasnyi* (London: Overseas Publications Interchange, 1980), 36, 51; in a lightly fictionalized memoir, Gladilin has his hero join a *kruzhok* for photography—though this was not his real hobby. See Anatoly Gladilin, *Ulitsa Generalov: Popytka memuarov* (Moscow: Vagrius, 2008), 16; author's interview with Gladilin (Paris, May 15, 2015).

9. Monakhova in *Mozaika sudeb*, 2:510.

10. Quoted in Ekaterina Drobynina, "Politika. Dvadtsatyi s"ezd—dvadtsatyi sud," *Rossiiskaia gazeta*, February 14, 2006, p. 3.

11. Vail', *Osobo opasnyi*, 21.

12. Ibid., 49–51, 83.

13. Ibid., 19, 47.

14. Gladilin, *Making and Unmaking*, 24.

15. Vail', *Osobo opasnyi*, 21, 37.

16. Reminiscences of Gennadii Simkin in *Mozaika sudeb*, 2:411.

17. Yevgeny Yevtushenko, *A Precocious Autobiography*, trans. Andrew R. McAndrew (New York: E. P. Dutton, 1963), 85–87.

18. The questioner was Czech communist Zdenek Mlynar. Quoted in Drobynina, "Politika."

19. Lidiia Kliatsko, *Dnevnik studentki zhurfaka (1953–1957)* (Moscow: RIF "ROI," 2002), 49.

20. On suspicion of Khrushchev's motives, see Chermen Borukaev, *Drobinki* (Novosibirsk: Izd. SO RAN, NITs OIGGM, 2000), 50. Quotation from, Nadezhda Paneva, "Filfak v moei sud'be," in *Vremia, ostavsheesia s nami: Vospominaniia vypusknikov filologicheskii fakul'tet v 1953–1958 gg.* (Moscow: MAKS press, 2004), 1:344.

21. Gladilin, *Ulitsa generalov*, 32–34.

22. Ibid., 16–17.

23. Ibid., 33–34.

24. Gladilin, *Making and Unmaking*, 26.

25. "Navstrechu XX s"ezdu KPSS: 1.865 tysiach studentov," *Literaturnaia gazeta*, January 14, 1956, p. 1.

26. As Vail' describes the typical budget for an out-of-town student with a two-hundred-ruble stipend and a dorm room: ten or twelve went for expenses at the dormitory, a few more to Komsomol and trade union dues. Dinner in the cafeteria cost five to six rubles—so one could in principle eat only once a day on such a stipend. One could spend 120 rubles on a coupon book for cafeteria meals; then one wouldn't be tempted to fritter away money on books, drink, or movie tickets. Vail' survived with an extra one hundred rubles a month from his parents and he estimated this was a typical "allowance" (*Osobo opasnyi*, 105–106).

27. Vail' was shocked to find that he could not even take the entrance exams at the Institute of Foreign Relations [MGIMO], which was founded in 1944 and still trains Russian diplomats (ibid., 85–87).

28. G. D. Vovchenko, ed., *Moskovskii Universitet: Kratkii ocherk fakul'tetov i spetsial'nostei (dlia postupaiushchikh v MGU)* (Moscow: Izd. Moskovskogo Universiteta, 1956), 43–46.

29. Vail', *Osobo opasnyi*. He also later wondered whether his unusual non-Slavic surname—he descended from a French soldier from the Napoleonic wars—and his father's prison record made him a logical candidate to be excluded.

30. Archie Brown, *The Gorbachev Factor* (Oxford: Oxford University Press, 1997), 28–33.

31. Ibid., 28–29.

32. Statistics on class background of students and information on admissions policies are taken from Benjamin Tromly, *Making the Soviet Intelligentsia: Universities and Intellectual Life under Stalin and Khrushchev* (Cambridge: Cambridge University Press, 2013), 173–176.

33. Vail', *Osobo opasnyi*, 12, 88. Interestingly, his father urged him to use the cover story, but Vail' at first refused to believe it would be necessary.

34. Anatoly Gladilin, "Khronika vremen Viktora Podgurskogo," in *Ottepel' 1953–1956*, ed. S. I. Chuprinin (Moscow: Moskovskii rabochii, 1989), 336; Mikhail Gorbachev, *Memoirs* (New York: Doubleday, 1996), 63.

35. Letter from Mariia Tremiuk and Raisa Vostrikova to *Iunost'*, September 25, 1956, in RGALI, f. 2924, op. 2, d. 4, l. 13.

36. Gladilin, *Ulitsa generalov*, 70.

37. Valerii Ronkin, *Na smenu dekabriam prikhodiat ianvari . . . Vospomina-niia byvshego brigadmil'tsa i podpol'shchika, a pozzhe–politzakliuchennogo i dissi-denta* (Moscow: Obshchestvo "Memorial"—Zven'ia, 2003), 64–66.

38. Gladilin, *Ulitsa generalov,* 32.

39. Gladilin, "Khronika," 330, 331.

40. Kliatsko, *Dnevnik,* 58, 68–69. Gladilin, "Khronika," 342–348, 391.

41. Gladilin, "Khronika," 364.

42. Ibid., 375–376.

43. Ibid., 392.

44. Tromly explores in greater depth the role of student collectives in academic as well as sociopolitical life of the postwar Soviet university in *Making the Soviet Intelligentsia.*

45. See photo captions and reminiscences in the series *Vremia, ostavsheesia s nami.*

46. For first-year students, a *komsorg* was generally tapped by the university administration based on past Komsomol or army service. Such service was very time consuming and not always welcome.

47. E. Zhukovskaia, A. G. Muzykantova et al., "Koe-chto o 4-i nemetskoi gruppe," in *Vremia ostavsheesia s nami,* 3:227–228. Erofeev would be expelled the next year.

48. Galina Ponomareva who graduated from the MGU *filfak* in 1958 remembers the high anxiety her "apolitical" approach to Dostoevsky's *The Demons* caused her senior thesis adviser. He tried to protect himself by announcing she had written her paper "autonomously" ("Kak ia zashchishchala diplom," in *Vremia, ostavsheesia s nami,* 1:107–109).

49. Igor' Kochetkov, "Zhizn' vzakhleb," in ibid., 276–277.

50. Ronkin, *Na smenu,* 95.

51. Ronkin did later wonder if this incident came back to haunt the student who made the sacrifice when at graduation he was assigned to a job in the provincial city of Voronezh (ibid., 95–96).

52. Gleb Tsipursky emphasizes the role of fun extracurricular activities in "Pleasure, Power and the Pursuit of Communism: State Sponsored Popular Youth Culture in the Soviet Union, 1945–1968" (Ph.D. diss., University of North Carolina, Chapel Hill, 2011), esp. chap. 4.

53. Ol'ga Gerasimova gives a detailed account of role of wall newspapers and their editorial groups in testing the bounds of permissible discourse at MGU during the thaw as a whole in *"Ottepel'"*, *"Zamorozki" i studenty Moskovskogo Universiteta* (Moscow: AIRO–XXI, 2015), 331–354.

54. Valentin Nedzvetskii, "Chto iarche pamiat'," in *Vremia ostavsheesia s nami,* 1:183; Kliatsko, *Dnevnik,* 48.

55. On Komsomol patrols and perceptions of criminality in the 1950s, see Miriam Dobson, *Khrushchev's Cold Summer: Gulag Returnees, Crime, and the Fate of Reform after Stalin* (Ithaca, NY: Cornell University Press, 2009), esp. 139–141.

56. Ronkin, *Na smenu,* 72.

57. Kochetkov, "Zhizn' vzakhleb," 271, 278; Kliatsko, *Dnevnik,* 42.

58. Ronkin, *Na smenu,* 77, 80.

59. Juliane Fürst, "Friends in Private, Friends in Public," in *Borders of Socialism,* 241.

60. Marina Remneva, "My byli romantikami i liubili chitat'," in *Vremia ostavsheesia s nami,* 1:10. Ruf' Ageeva, *Tak bylo suzhdeno (zapiski Sof'i Vasil'evny)* (Moscow: Academia, 2008), 123.

61. Viktor Bulokhov, "Chto ostavit' posle sebia?," in *Vremia ostavsheesia s nami,* 1:219. On those with special knowledge of banned or disgraced writers, see G. S. Vasil'eva, "Prizvanie," in ibid., 3:291.

62. Quotations from Nedzvetskii, "Chto iarche pamiat' sokhranila," in ibid., 1:180. See also TsAOPIM, f. 478, op. 5, d. 74, l. 49.

63. Ol'ga Gerasimova has carefully pulled together eyewitness and archival evidence on the course and conduct of the boycott. On the background of the complaints, see Gerasimova, *"Ottepel'", "Zamorozki",* 95–99.

64. Speeches by students at the June 7, 1956, meeting of the primary party organization of the Philology Department; TsAOPIM, f. 478, op. 3, d. 233, ll. 69–70.

65. Anatolii Filatov, "Byt' studentom i ostavat'sia im," in *Vremia ostavsheesia s nami,* 1:138.

66. Iraida Usok, "Stranitsy proshlogo listaia . . . ," in ibid., 51.

67. Galina Sakharova, "MGU–kak mnogo v etom slove dlia serdtsa moego slilos', kak mnogo v nem otozvalos,'" and Tat'iana Lebedeva, "Kak molody my byli . . . ," in ibid., 240–241, 252–253.

68. Cited by Evgenii Taranov, "Raskachaem Leninskie gory!" *Svobodnaia mysl'* 10 (1993): 100.

69. Speech by Liia Kovaleva at the June 7, 1956, meeting of the primary party organization of the Philology Department; TsAOPIM, f. 478, op. 3, d. 233, l. 70.

70. Gerasimova found no solid evidence as to immediate repercussions for participation in the boycott (*"Ottepel'"*, *"Zamorozki"*, 107). Nedzvetskii says that no one informed on the initiators of the strike during the subsequent investigation ("Chto iarche pamiat'," 181).

71. TsAOPIM, f. 478, op. 3, d. 233, ll. 70–72.

72. Speech by Makarov, identified as a member of the party bureau, at the May 29, 1956, meeting of the Party Bureau of the School of Biology and Soil Sciences (ibid., op. 5, d. 74, l. 50).

73. Tromly provides much evidence of the party elite's expectation that students would feel indebted and hence see themselves as servants of the people (see, for instance, *Making the Soviet Intelligentsia*, 167).

74. Ageeva, *Tak bylo suzhdeno*, 121.

75. Kliatsko, *Dnevnik*, 40–47.

76. A sampling of letters received by *Iunost'* about Gladilin's novel have been preserved. These responses seem to be aimed at the editors as well as the author himself. Gladilin recalls receiving stacks of letters directly via his institute—such correspondence may have been less formulaic; see RGALI, f. 2924, op. 2, d. 14, esp. l. 37, 43a; Gladilin, *Ulitsa generalov*, 71–72.

77. Kliatsko, *Dnevnik*. She was part of the same class as Igor' Dedkov, an activist in the MGU School of Journalism in 1956 about whom much has been written. See Elena Zubkova, *Obshchestvo i Reformy, 1945–1964* (Moscow: AIRO, 1993), 137–145; Gerasimova, *"Ottepel'"*, *"Zamorozki,"* 73–81.

78. Svetlana Angelina, "Raz-kartoshka, dva-kartoshka," in *Vremia osta-avsheesia s nami*, 1:312.

79. Ibid. Ironically, a very few of the students managed to work hard enough to earn a tiny amount of money, but since the farm had no funds the "leading workers" were offered hay, which they generously donated to the farm's pigs.

7. July

1. My account of the summer of 1956 at Miassovo draws on Nina Balandina, "Miassovo, leto 1956 g.," *Voprosy istorii estestvoznaniia i tekhniki*, 4 (2000): 89–97; Natal'ia A. Liapunova, "Miassovskie seminary N. V. Timofeeva-

Resovskogo," in *Nikolai Timofeev-Resovskii: Ocherki, vospominaniia, materialy*, ed. N. N. Vorontsov (Moscow: Nauka, 1993), 302–308; and author's interview with Natal'ia A. Liapunova (Moscow, September 25, 2015).

2. Resolution of the Komsomol meeting cited by E. Ramenskii, "L'vinaia dolia," in *Lev L'vovich Kiselev: Nauka kak istochnik zhiznennogo optimizma*, comp. L. Iu. Frolova, K. L. Kiseleva, E. S. Levina, and S. E. Tvardovskaia (Moscow: U Nikitskikh vorot, 2010), 321.

3. On Lysenko's rise, see Loren R. Graham, *Science in Russia and the Soviet Union: A Short History* (Cambridge: Cambridge University Press, 1993), esp. 123–133; David Joravsky, *The Lysenko Affair* (Cambridge, MA: Harvard University Press, 1970); and Valery Soyfer, *Vlast' i nauka: Istoriia razgroma genetiki v SSSR* (Tenafly, NJ: Ermitazh, 1989). Notable recent analyses include Nikolai Krementsov, *Stalinist Science* (Princeton, NJ: Princeton University Press, 1997); Ethan Pollock, "From *Partiinost'* to *nauchnost'* and Not Quite Back Again: Revisiting the Lessons of the Lysenko Affair," *Slavic Review* 68, no. 1 (2009): 95–115. Graham points out that while a social constructivist approach "can help us to understand why Lysenkoism lasted so long, for over 30 years, showing the manifold ways in which, politically and ideologically, Lysenkoism fitted with and derived strength from Soviet society . . . [it] is less helpful in explaining why Lysenkoism was eventually abandoned"; see Loren R. Graham, *What Have We Learned about Science and Technology from the Russian Experience* (Stanford, CA: Stanford University Press, 1998), 22.

4. Mark B. Adams has compiled a list of thirteen important occurrences affecting genetics between December 1955 and December 1958—the Liapunovs and Timofeev-Resovskii were involved in five of them. Both Adams and I rely on the Liapunova sisters as informants, and hence their accounts may be privileged in our respective works. See Mark B. Adams, "Networks in Action: The Khrushchev Era, the Cold War, and the Transformation of Soviet Science," in *Science, History and Social Activism: A Tribute to Everett Mendelsohn*, ed. Garland E. Allen and Roy M. MacLeod (Dordrecht: Kluwer Academic Publishers, 2001), 258–259. Many aspects of the periodization of Lysenko's rise and demise remain disputed; see S. V. Shalimov, *Spasenie i vozrozhdenie: istoricheskii ocherk razvitiia genetiki v novosibirskom nauchnom tsentre v gody 'ottepeli' (1957–1964)* (Novosibirsk: Izd. Dom Manuskript, 2011).

5. Political pressure inspired "underground" geneticists to refer variously to their field as "'radiation biology,' 'biophysics,' 'physico-chemical biology'." See Mark B. Adams, "Genetics and the Soviet Scientific Community, 1948–1965" (Ph.D. diss., Harvard University, 1972), 186.

6. N. V. Timofeev-Resovskii, *Istorii, rasskazannye im samim, s pis'mami, fotografiiami i dokumentami*, comp. N. Dubrovina (Moscow: Soglasie, 2000),

367, 474–478. On use of lab equipment, see V. A. Goncharov and V. V. Nekhotin, "Neizvestnoe ob izvestnom: Po materialam arkhivnogo sledstvennogo delo na N. V. Timofeev-Resovskogo," *Vestnik Rossiiskoi akademii nauk* 70, no. 3 (2000): 254.

7. Timofeev-Resovskii's life story has been the stuff of biographies and novels, most notably V. V. Babkov and E. S. Sakanian, *Nikolai Vladimirovich Timofeev-Resovskii, 1900–1981* (Moscow: Pamiatniki Istoricheskoi mysli, 2002); Daniil Granin, *The Bison: A Novel about the Scientist Who Defied Stalin,* trans. Antonina W. Bouis (New York: Doubleday, 1990).

8. Biographical details are drawn from interviews of Timofeev-Resovskii made by MGU professor Sergei Duvakin between 1974 and 1978, published in Timofeev-Resovskii, *Istorii, rasskazannye*; see also Babkov and Sakanian, *Nikolai Vladimirovich Timofeev-Resovskii, 1900–1981.*

9. On party affiliations, see Graham, *What Have We Learned,* 76–77. On funding for the Kol'tsov institute, see Mark B. Adams, "Science, Ideology, and Structure: The Kol'tsov Institute, 1900–1970," in *The Social Context of Soviet Science,* ed. Linda L. Lubrano and Susan Gross Solomon (Boulder, CO: Westview Press, 1980), 180.

10. Krementsov, *Stalinist Science,* 13.

11. Ia. G. Rokitianskii, V. A. Goncharov, V. V. Nekhotin, comp., *Rassekrechennyi zubr: Sledstvennoe delo N. V. Timofeeva-Resovskogo* (Moscow: Academia, 2003), 62–65.

12. For a reassessment of Lysenko as scientist, see Nils Roll-Hansen, *The Lysenko Effect: The Politics of Science* (Amherst, NY: Humanity Books, 2005). Regarding Lysenko's failed suggestions, see Joravsky, *Lysenko Affair.*

13. On the effort to empower peasants as scientists and Lysenko's peasant credentials, see Joravsky, *Lysenko Affair,* 54–61.

14. Cited by Graham, *Science in Russia,* 128; See also Soyfer, *Vlast' i nauka,* 121–122.

15. On name-calling and repressions among biologists, see Soyfer, *Vlast' i nauka,* chap. 7; Krementsov, *Stalinist Science,* 61–64. On the use of rhetorical devices, see Krementsov, *Stalinist Science,* 45–53.

16. Joravsky, *Lysenko Affair,* 42.

17. On the victory of chromosomal explanations, see James Schwartz, *In Pursuit of the Gene: From Darwin to DNA* (Cambridge, MA: Harvard University Press, 2008). Lysenko's views are quite clearly stated in his speeches at the 1948 VASKhNIL conference; see the translation in Conway Zirkle, *Death of a*

Science in Russia: The Fate of Genetics as Described in Pravda and Elsewhere (Philadelphia: University of Pennsylvania Press, 1949), 97–134, 249–261. They are eloquently analyzed in Adams, "Genetics," 268–271.

18. A recent study of Lysenko's rhetoric shows the deliberate framing of "Michurinist biology" as one of "two distinct irreconcilable camps"—an appealing Cold War construct. See Dmitri Stanchevici, *Stalinist Genetics: The Constitutional Rhetoric of T. D. Lysenko* (Amityville, NY: Baywood Publishers, 2012), esp. 67–71, 154–158. On battles between scientists and philosophers, see also Slava Gerovich, *From Newspeak to Cyberspeak* (Cambridge, MA: MIT Press, 2002). Historian Kirill O. Rossianov has found Stalin's editorial changes to a draft of Lysenko's VASKhNIL speech, proving the high-level attention given to the dispute over genetics; see "Stalin as Lysenko's Editor: Reshaping Political Discourse in Soviet Science," *Configurations* 1, no. 3 (1993): 439–456. "Weismannist-Morganist-Mendelist" referred to German biologist August Weismann, American geneticist Thomas Hunt Morgan, and the Austrian monk and experimentalist Gregor Mendel.

19. Zirkle, *Death of a Science*, 285–290, 294–300; Krementsov, *Stalinist Science*, 232–238; Soyfer, *Vlast' i nauka*, 415–418; Nikolai Vorontsov, *Nauka. Uchenye. Obschestvo: Izbrannye trudy*, ed. E. A. Liapunova (Moscow: Nauka, 2006), 64; and Raissa L. Berg, *Acquired Traits: Memoirs of a Geneticist from the Soviet Union*, trans. David Lowe (New York: Viking, 1988). On Zavadovskii, see M. M. Zavadovskaia-Sachenko, "Moi otets Mikhail Zavadovskii," *Voprosy istorii estestvoznaniia i tekhniki* 2 (2003): 181–193. Mark B. Adams finds an impressive continuity of research considering the travails of genetics and its practitioners; see his "Science, Ideology, and Structure," 173–204.

20. T. A. Ginetsinskaia, "Biofak Leningradskogo Universiteta posle sessii VASKhNIL," in *Repressirovannaia nauka*, ed. M. G. Iaroshevskogo (Leningrad: Nauka, 1991), 115–116; Vorontsov, *Nauka. Uchenye. Obschestvo*, 64.

21. Timofeev-Resovskii, *Istorii, rasskazannye*, 345.

22. According to Babkov and Sakanian, Nikolai's brother Viktor was in exile in 1937–1939, and his brother Dmitrii had been arrested after the Kirov murder in 1934 and sent to a labor camp. Another brother, Vladimir, would be arrested in 1938 (*Nikolai Vladimirovich Timofeev-Resovskii, 1900–1981*, 8–9).

23. Rokitianskii, Goncharov, and Nekhotin, *Rassekrechennyi zubr*, 67–71, 104–107. For the essence of the dispute over Timofeev-Resovskii's wartime work, see Raissa L. Berg, "In Defense of Timofeef-Ressovsky," *Quarterly Review of Biology* 65, no. 4 (December 1990): 457–479. The last Timofeev-Resovskii heard of Foma was a postcard from Mauthausen in 1944 acknowledging receipt of a parcel. Details of his death in May 1945 became known only after the 1987 publication of Granin's novel about Timofeev-Resovskii.

24. Goncharov and Nekhotin, "Neizvestnoe o izvestnom," 249–250.

25. Ibid., 250–256; Timofeev-Resovskii, *Istorii, rasskazannye,* 350–351.

26. Timofeev-Resovskii, *Istorii, rasskazannye,* 360–361; letter from Timofeev-Resovskiis to Reformatskiis, April 4, 1954, in ibid., 466.

27. On the composition of the workforce in Sungul', see Rokiatinskii, Goncharov, and Nekhotin, *Rassekrechennyi zubr,* 138. Letter from N. V. Timofeev-Resovskii to E. A. Timofeev-Resovskaia, June 19, 1947, in *Istorii rasskazannye,* 461–462.

28. B. M. Emel'ianov and V. S. Gavril'chenko, *Laboratoriia "B" Sungul'skii fenomen* (Snezhinsk: Izd. RFIaTs-VNIITF, 2000), 11, 56–57; Mikhail Fonotov, "Tainye liudi," *Ural'skaia nov'* 13 (2002), http://magazines.russ.ru/urnov/2002 /13/fo-pr.html.

29. Letter from E. A. Timofeev-Resovskaia to N. V. Reformatorskaia, November 24, 1954, in Timofeev-Resovskii, *Istorii, rasskazannye,* 476–477. Even free workers appreciated the concentration of resources. See N. V. Luchnik, *Vtoraia igra* (Moscow: Sputnik, 2002), 6.

30. Goncharov and Nekhotin, "Neizvestnoe ob izvestnom," 256–257. On conditions in Sungul', see Emel'ianov and Gavril'chenko, *Laboratoriia "B,"* esp. 125–126, 207, 258. Andrei Timofeev was allowed to complete his degree in physics as a correspondence student at the university in Sverdlovsk, but by necessity he had to work at the Sungul' lab.

31. Letters from E. A. Timofeev-Resovskaia to the Reformatskiis, November 24, 1954, December 29, 1954, and October 31, 1955, in Timofeev-Resovskii, *Istorii, rasskazannye,* 476–478, 486.

32. Ekaterina Pavlova, "Delo sester Liapunovykh," *Znanie—Sila* 8 (1998): 34–47.

33. The letter was initially sent in early October 1955; it then circulated in Moscow and picked up additional signatures. See I. F. Zhimulev and L. G. Dubinina, "Novoe o 'pis'me trekhsot'—massovom proteste sovetskikh uchenykh protiv lysenkovshchiny v 1955," *Vestnik VOGiS* 9, no. 1 (2005): 13–33. Also see D. V. Lebedev, "Iz vospominanii antilysenkovtsa s dovoennym stazhem," in *Repressirovannaia nauka,* 264–282.

34. On Vladimir Engel'gardt and the struggle against Lysenko more generally from 1953 to 1956, see Adams, "Genetics," 237–238.

35. Lev Kiselev, "Ia vse esche ne ocharovan naukoi . . . ," in *Lev L'vovich Kiselev,* 34–35. For a student drawn to biology by Lysenko's critiques of bourgeois genetics, see reminiscences of Nina Samoilova, in *Mozaika sudeb: Bio-*

fakovtsev MGU 1930–1960 godov postupleniia, comp. L. I. Lebedeva (Moscow: Tovarischchestvo nauchnykh izdanii KMK, 2007), 2:159.

36. Pavlova, "Delo sester," 37–39.

37. Elena Liapunova said her parents believed that Lysenko's dominance would end shortly. Lev Kiselev's parents were more concerned that he would follow the example of his famous uncle, Veniamin Kaverin, and become a writer. Author's interview with Elena Liapunova (Moscow, June 8, 2008); Kiselev, "Ia esche ne ocharovan," 31.

38. On the family history, see Pavlova, "Delo sester"; Gerovich, *From Newspeak to Cyberspeak.* Quotation from Pavlova, "Delo sester," 39.

39. The students also called on scientists in their laboratories—a small delegation even visited Lysenko, who lectured them for three hours straight. See Pavlova, "Delo sester," 42; author's interview with Natal'ia Liapunova; and Vorontsov, *Nauka. Uchenye. Obshchestvo,* 64.

40. Author's interview with Elena Liapunova; quotation from speech of classmate Valerii Luk'iankenko recollected by N. D. Gabrielian and cited by Ol'ga G. Gerasimova, "Obshchestvenno-politicheskaia zhizn' studenchestva MGU v 1950-e-1960-kh gg." (Cand. Diss., Moscow State University, 2008), 63.

41. As a senior in high school, Natal'ia had even been a member of the regional Komsomol committee (*raikom*). Pavlova, "Delo sester," 42; author's interviews with Elena and Natal'ia Liapunova.

42. Pavlova, "Delo sester," 46.

43. Natal'ia Liapunova reports her father having heard the "monkey trial" reference at the AN USSR. See also Gerasimova, "Obshchestvenno-politicheskaia zhizn'," 66.

44. Pavlova, "Delo sester," 45. The sisters' class was unusually large—some three hundred biologists and sixty soil scientists—as it included a group of veterans given special preference. One alumna noted this diversity made it an "unfriendly" class. Reminiscences of Tat'iana (Krendel'eva) Pavlova, in *Novosel'e biologov MGU na Lengorakh,* comp. L. I. Lebedeva (Moscow: Tovarishchestvo nauchnykh izdanii KMK, 2011), 168.

45. By 1956 Lysenkoists were complaining about signs of disrespect within the halls of the department. TsAOPIM, f. 478, op. 3, d. 44, l. 190.

46. Natal'ia was less confrontational than Elena. She recalled that she nearly fainted with shock the summer before when Elena and some others began to perform anti-Lysenko songs at the end of the first year students' summer practicum (Pavlova, "Delo sester," 43). Notes from the audience register

dismay at her "hypocrisy" (Natalya Lyapunova and Yurii Bogdanov family archive).

47. At least two letters circulated in the School of Biology and Soil Sciences in the winter and spring 1955–1956. The first was the "Letter of Three Hundred"; the second seems to have been a complementary initiative by graduate students asking for a course in genetics to be taught at MGU (Gerasimova, "Obshchestvenno-politicheskaia zhizn'," 67–68).

48. TsAOPIM, f. 478, op. 5, d. 74, l. 2. In defense of the *kruzhok*, the one vocal anti-Lysenko member of the School of Biology and Soil Sciences, Boris Kudriashev, would quote Khrushchev and Bulganin in support of criticism at a meeting of the MGU party bureau on February 28, 1956. TsAOPIM, f. 478, op. 3, d. 44, ll. 155–166.

49. On their punishments and Kiselev's role, see Ramenskii, "L'vinaia dolia"; M. Kritskii, "Zolotoi mal'chik," in *Lev L'vovich Kiselev*, 321, 334. Elena recalls that a list of the main *kruzhok* participants was presented to the rector I. G. Petrovskii with the suggestion that they be expelled, but he refused, noting that these were among the school's best students. Kiselev suggests that Petrovskii's ties to fellow mathematician Aleksei Liapunov also played a role. Interview with Elena Liapunova; Kiselev, "Ia vse eshe ne ocharovan," 35–36.

50. Quotation from F. N. Zouzolkov [Zazolikov], TsAOPIM, f. 478, op. 3, d. 44, l. 147; interview with Natal'ia Liapunova.

51. TsAOPIM, f. 478, op. 3, d. 74, l. 10. Formerly friendly with Natal'ia, Ianushkevich formulated the harshly worded changes against the sisters (interview with Natal'ia Liapunova).

52. G. G. Polikarpov, "Shtrikhi vospominanii o Nikolae Vladimiroviche Timofeeve-Resovskom," http://www.chem.msu.su/rus/journals/chemlife /2000/risov.html.

53. On Timofeev-Resovskii and his wife's contributions to science, see N. G. Gorbushin and V. I. Ivanov, "K istorii sovetskogo atomnogo proekta: N. V. Timofeev-Resovskii i radiobiologiia," *Voprosy istorii estestvoznaniia i tekhniki* 2 (2008): 65–77.

54. S. P. Kapitsa, "Seminar v Institute fizproblem im. P. L. Kapitsy AN SSSR," in *Nikolai Timofeev-Resovskii: Ocherki, Vospominaniia, Materialy*, 301.

55. Ibid. Another account has presidium member Mikhail Suslov as the source of objections; either way, it underlines nuclear physicists' special access to party leaders. Valery Soyfer, "Akademik i student," *Kontinent* (2002), http:// magazines.russ.ru/continent/2002/113/soi.html.

56. Kapitsa, "Seminar v Institute fizproblem," 301. According to a report from the Central Committee Department for Science and Education made on February 9, 1956, some eight hundred persons attended the lecture. See Babkov and Sakanian, *Nikolai Vladimirovich Timofeev-Resovskii, 1900–1981,* 535–536.

57. Letter from P. Kralin, member of the CPSU, to A. B. Aristov, secretary of the Central Committee of the CPSU, February 10, 1956, in Babkov and Sakanian, *Nikolai Vladimirovich Timofeev-Resovskii, 1900–1981,* 534. Information on Lysenko's anger from author's interview with Valery Soyfer (Fairfax, VA, June 19, 2012).

58. Letters from Timofeev-Resovskiis to A. Liapunov, March 13 and 16, 1956, in Timofeev-Resovskii, *Istorii, rasskazannye,* 496, 498.

59. Letters from N. V. and E. A. Timofeev-Resovskii to Aleksei Liapunov of March 12 and May 18, 1956, in ibid., 496, 501; Graham, *What Have We Learned,* 81; E. N. Sokurova, "Nikolai Vladimirovich: uchenyi i chelovek," in *Nikolai Timofeev-Resovskii: Ocherki,* 211.

60. Balandina, "Miassovo, leto 1956 g.," 89–91.

61. Aleksandr I. Solzhenitsyn, *The Gulag Archipelago, 1918–1956: An Experiment in Literary Investigation, I-II,* trans. Thomas P. Whitney (New York: Harper & Row, 1973), 598–599.

62. Raisa L. Berg, "Nikolai Vladimirovich Timofeev-Resovskii," and N. A. Liapunova, "Miassovskie seminary," in *Nikolai Timofeev-Resovskii: Ocherki,* 230, 304–307.

63. Balandina, "Miassovo, leto 1956 g.," 95.

64. On Sungul', see Emel'ianov and Gavril'chenko, *Laboratoriia "B,"* 199.

65. Iurii Novozhenov, "Moguchii dukh mysli," in *Nikolai Timofeev-Resovskii: Ocherki,* 217

66. Ibid., 220.

67. V. I. Korogodin, "Shkola N. V. Timofeeva-Resovskogo," in ibid., 254–255.

68. Sokurova, "Nikolai Vladimirovich," 210; Balandina, "Miassovo, leto 1956 g.," 93.

69. On Aleksei Liapunov's activities in 1956, see letter from Timofeev-Resvoskii to Liapunov, December 26, 1956, in Timofeev-Resovskii, *Istorii rasskazannye,* 506. On his role in cybernetics, see Gerovich, *From Newspeak to Cyberspeak,* esp. 174–193. On genetics in Novosibirsk, see Shalimov, *Spasenie i vozrozhdenie.*

70. Letter from Raisa L. Berg to Timofeev-Resovskii, November 29, 1956, in Babkov and Sakanian, *Nikolai Vladimirovich Timofeev-Resovskii, 1900–1981*, 573–574; M. V. Vol'kenshtein, "Vstrechi s Nikolaem Vladimirovichem," in *Nikolai Timofeev-Resovskii: Ocherki*, 309–315.

71. Valery Soyfer recalls that in 1958 physicist Igor Tamm financed his train fare and cost of meals for a summer in Miassovo. See Soyfer, "Akademik i Student." See also Vol'kenshtein, "Vstrechi," 310; Kogorodin, "Shkola," 253; Liapunova, "Miassovskie seminary," 308; Babkov and Sakanian, *Nikolai Vladimirovich Timofeev-Resovskii, 1900–1981*, 264, 274–276.

72. Author's interview with Natal'ia Liapunova. Letter from N. V. Timofeev-Resovskii to L. A. Zenkevich, August 31, 1956, in Timofeev-Resovskii, *Istorii, rasskazannye*, 502–503; letter from A. A. Liapunov to E. A. and N. V. Timofeev-Resovskii, January 12, 1957, in Babkov and Sakanian, *Nikolai Vladimirovich Timofeev-Resovskii, 1900–1981*, 569–570. On revisiting the case, see TsAOPIM, f. 478, op. 5, d, 74, ll. 78, 90.

73. Gerovich, *From Newspeak to Cyberspeak*, 14–21.

74. Pollock, "From *Partiinost'* to *Nauchnost',*" 110.

75. Adams, "Genetics," 305–317.

76. Ibid., 309.

77. Graham, *What Have We Learned*, 70–71. One certainly sees this in the case of Nina Balandina's father. See N. A. Balandina, "Otets vsegda zhil po sovesti i liubimomu delu otdal sebia bez ostatka," in *O vremeni, o Noril'ske, o sebe . . . : vospominaniia*, ed. G. I. Kasabova, (Moscow: PoliMEdia, 2003), 3:481–509.

78. E. S. Kaliaeva, "Slovo o uchitele," *Voprosy istorii estestvoznaniia i tekhniki* 4 (2000): 143.

79. Adams, "Networks in Action."

80. Iurii Glazkov, "My vo vlasti nauki. Chto stalo s laboratoriei Zubra," *Obshchaia gazeta*, September 21, 2000, 5.

81. Iu. A. Malozemov, "Vospominaia Nikolaia Vladimirovicha," in *N. V. Timofeev-Resovskii na Urale: Vospominaniia* (Ekaterinburg: Izd. Ekaterinburg, 1998), 93.

82. On "palomniki," see M. I. Shal'nov, "Nauchnogo shkola professor Timofeeva-Resovskogo," in Babkov and Sakanian, *Nikolai Vladimirovich Timofeev-Resovskii, 1900–1981*, 565. On "the Word," see L. A. Bliumenfeld, "Ochen' korotko o N. V. Timofeev-Resovskom," in *Nikolai Timofeev-Resovskii: Ocherki*, 332; O. N. Popova, "Otkuda est'-poshla radioekologiia nasha . . . ," *Vestnik In-*

stituta biologii Komi NTsUrO RAN (March 1999), http://ib.komisc.ru/add/old
/t/ru/ir/vt/99–17/08–17.html.

8. August

1. Anatoly Gladilin, *The Making and Unmaking of a Soviet Writer: My Story of the "Young Prose" of the Sixties and After,* trans. David Lapeza (Ann Arbor, MI: Ardis, 1979), 32; Anatoly Gladilin, *Ulitsa generalov: popytka memuarov* (Moscow: Vagrius, 2008), 120. In the author's interview with Gladilin (Paris, May 15, 2015), he explained that he could show the letter from the central youth magazine to get assistance from local authorities.

2. *Sluchai na shakhte 8* (dir.Vladimir Basov, Mosfilm, 1957).

3. Elena Shulman, *Stalinism on the Frontier of Empire: Women and State Formation in the Soviet Far East* (Cambridge: Cambridge University Press, 2008).

4. Ol'ga Edel'man, "Tselina kak al'ternativa GULAGu," *Vremia novostei,* July 19, 2007.

5. Reminiscences of Antonina Kuznetsova in Lev Lur'e and Irina Maliarova, *1956 god. Seredina veka* (St. Petersburg: Neva, 2007), 353.

6. On the merits of studying "volunteers," see Shulman, *Stalinism,* 9–12.

7. Eric Naiman, "Introduction," in *The Landscape of Stalinism: The Art and Ideology of Soviet Space,* ed. Evgeny Dobrenko and Naiman (Seattle: University of Washington Press, 2003), xiii.

8. Ibid.

9. Richard Taylor, "'But Eastward, Look, the Land Is Brighter': Toward a Topography of Utopia in the Stalinist Musical," in ibid., esp. 209–213.

10. *The Brigantine Raises Sail* was serialized in *Moskovskii komsomolets* in 1959; references here are to the 1961 book edition: Anatoly Gladilin, *Brigantina podnimaet parusa: povest': istoriia odnogo neudachnika* (Moscow: Sovetskii pisatel', 1961), 3.

11. Michaela Pohl, "The Virgin Lands between Memory and Forgetting: People and Transformation in the Soviet Union, 1954–1960" (Ph.D. diss., Indiana University, 1999), 190. On Irkutsk, see Elizaveta Patrusheva, "Irkutskaia GES i LEP-220," in *S komsomol'skoi putevkoi: dokumenty, vospominaniia, ottisk* (Irkutsk: 2008), 15–27.

12. On the use of prisoners and soldiers to build secret installations, see V. N. Kuzentsov, *Atomnyi proekt za koliuchei provolokoi* (Ekaterinburg: Poligrafist, 2004); B. Emel'ianov, comp., *Raskryvaia pervye stranitsy: k istorii goroda Snezhinska*

(Ekaterinburg: Ural'skii rabochii, 1997); also see Kate Brown, *Plutopia: Nuclear Families, Atomic Cities, and the Great Soviet and American Plutonium Disasters* (New York: Oxford University Press, 2013). For biographies of construction bosses for one closed city, see A. V. Kesarev, ed., *Na sluzhbe otechestvu: sbornik vospominanii veteranov* (Snezhinsk: Administratsiia goroda, Gorodskoi sovet veteranov voini i truda i vooruzhennykh sil, 1995), esp. 7–13, 234–236.

13. Pohl, "Virgin Lands," 149–151.

14. "Oni postavili Ameriku na mesto," *Biiskii rabochii*, December 8, 2012.

15. "Pervye pis'ma," *Iunost'* 11 (1956): 68–70.

16. Gladilin, *Brigantina*, 5.

17. Before 1955 the average living space per person in Biisk was less than three square meters. See *Biisk sotialisticheskii: iz istorii rabochego klassa Biiska* (Barnaul, 1965), 219–220.

18. Gladilin, *Brigantina*, 27–29. V. A. Kozlov, *Massovye besporiadki v SSSR pri Khrushcheve i Brezhneve (1953-nachalo 1980-kh gg.)* (Moscow: ROSSPEN; Fond Pervogo Prezidenta Rossii B. N. El'tsina, 2010), 337–346.

19. Gladilin, *Brigantina*, 12–13.

20. Ibid., 3.

21. Ibid., 40.

22. Ibid., 16. Khetagurovites, too, felt awkward when they ended up in the land of Dal'stroi, where NKVD answered for most big economic projects and available jobs included administering the forced labor system (Shulman, *Stalinism*, 43–44).

23. Kozlov, *Massovye besporiadki*, 152, 158–161.

24. Although the official Soviet era history of Biisk is silent regarding the new defense-related plants, it chronicles a sudden leap in housing construction, provision of schools at all levels, and the launching of a television studio in 1957 (*Biisk sotialisticheskii*, 214, 220–221).

25. Gladilin, *Brigantina*, 29.

26. Ibid., 20, 31.

27. Anatolii A. Kuznetsov, *Prodolzhenie legendy: zapiski molodogo cheloveka* (Moscow: Detgiz, 1958); available in English as Anatolii A. Kuznetsov, *The Journey*, trans. William E. Butler (New York: New Horizon Press, 1984).

28. Gladilin, *Ulitsa Generalov*, 120–121; quotation from Gladilin, *Making and Unmaking*, 33.

29. RGASPI-M, f. 1, op. 8, d. 742, ll. 32–34.

30. Ibid., l. 28–31.

31. Housing for new recruits was sorely lacking—at the Belogorskii mining trust there was not a single barrack or even tent for the seven hundred arrivals. Shortages of basic furniture, tools, and food troubled all of the sites visited (ibid., d. 736, ll. 128–134).

32. Versions of the screenplay are preserved in RGALI: a 1956 draft (f. 2453, op. 3, d. 1078, ll. 1–760; an approved draft dated 1957 (f. 2453, op. 3, d. 1079, ll. 1–101); the script used by the director (f. 3327, op. 1, d. 5, ll. 1–102); and a copy sent out in advance of the December 26, 1957, meeting of Mosfilm's artistic council (f. 3051, op. 2, d. 40, ll. 1–85).

33. Like Stalin, Kraev once had a lovely wife, but is now left only with a daughter in attendance.

34. V. Frid, "Posle skazki" in *Kinematograf ottepeli*, ed. V. Troianovskii (Moscow: Materik, 2002), 2:304. On the villas, see Elena Kolpikova, *My iz gulaga* (Moscow: RIPOL klassik, 2009), 134.

35. M. A. Shvarts, "N-71 i K-963," in *Sluzhili dva tovarishcha: Kniga o zhizni kinodramaturgov Dunskogo i Frida*, comp. Z. B. Osipova (Moscow: Zebra E, EKSMO, 2002), 149–151; V. S. Frid, "Iz interv'iu raznykh let," in ibid., 321–322. Alan Barenberg explores relations between prison and free labor in *Gulag Town, Company Town: Forced Labor and Its Legacy in Vorkuta* (New Haven, CT: Yale University Press, 2014).

36. RGALI, f. 2435, op. 3, d. 1080, ll. 1–73. Kalatozov quotation, l. 6; Romm quotation, ll. 9–10.

37. William C. Taubman, *Khrushchev: The Man and His Era* (New York: W. W. Norton, 2003), 262–267.

38. Martin McCauley, *Khrushchev and the Development of Soviet Agriculture: The Virgin Land Programme 1953–1964* (London: Macmillan, 1976); V. N. Tomilin, "Kampaniia po osvoeniiu tselinnykh i zalezhnyikh zemel' v 1954–1959 gg.," *Voprosy istorii* 9 (2009): 81–93.

39. On targets for land to be sown, see McCauley, *Khrushchev*, 54, 79–80. On Komsomol recruiting, see RGASPI-M, f. 1, op. 9, d. 361, ll. 1–3, 15; d. 362, ll. 13–21.

40. See, for instance, the retrospective account by chemistry student Viktor Lamm, "Zhatva 1956 goda," http://www.proza.ru/2008/06/05/461; Iu. Stetsenko, "Energomash na tseline," *Politekhnik* (January 24, 2007), http://polytechnic.kpi.kharkov.ua/print/1299/article-1299.pdf.

41. Irina Matveeva, "Vdarim filologiei po tseline!," in *Vremia, ostavsheesia s nami: vospominaniia vypusnikov filologicheskii fakul'tet v 1953–1958 gg.* (Moscow: MAKS Press, 2004), 1:314–315. On *putevki* for permanent settlement, see Pohl, "Virgin Lands," 149–151.

42. *My byli na tseline* (dir. V. Troshkin and V. Khodiakov, Moscow, 1956). Matveeva, "Vdarim," 316.

43. Lamm, "Zhatva 1956"; Matveeva, "Vdarim," 316–319, quotation, 316–317.

44. Matveeva, "Vdarim," 317. Regarding issues with transport including provision of water, see RGASPI-M, f. 1, op. 9, d. 362, l. 27.

45. Stetsenko, "Energomash na tseline."

46. Matveeva, "Vdarim," 317–319.

47. Ibid., 324; L. V. Olina cited in, "'A ia edu za tumanom . . .' Tselina glazami studentov 50-kh. Rabota viatskoi desiatiklassnitsy Natal'i Neganovoi," *Stengazeta*, November 16, 2006, http://www.stengazeta.net/article.for.printing .html?id=757; Valery N. Soyfer, *Ochen' lichnaia kniga* (Novosibirsk: Infolio, 2011), 178. Osipova's remarks are from the Komsomol Conference of the Moscow State Pedagogical Institute im. Lenina, September 30, 1956, in TsAOPIM, f. 536, op. 1, d. 2, ll. 52–53.

48. Matveeva, "Vdarim," 320, 323–324. Nina Semenova in L. I. Lebedeva, comp., *Novosel'e biologov MGU na Lengorakh* (Moscow: Tovarishchestvo nauch-nykh izdanii KMK, 2011), 246. Lamm, "Zhatva 1956"; *My byli na tseline*.

49. Matveeva, "Vdarim," 321–323; Lamm, "Zhatva 1956."

50. Matveeva, "Vdarim," 321. On a strike, see Aleksandr Genkin in Lur'e and Maliarova, *1956 god. Seredina veka*, 380–381.

51. Ol'ga Gerasimova, "Obshchestvenno-politicheskaia zhizn' studenchestva MGU v 1950-e—seredine 1960-kh gg." (Cand. diss., Moscow State University, 2008), 131–132. On speaking out about wage issues, see Iurii Aksiutin in Lur'e and Maliarova, *1956 god. Seredina veka*, 377.

52. Matveeva, "Vdarim," 323. Quotation is from Lamm, "Zhatva 1956."

53. Soyfer, *Ochen' lichnaia kniga*, 178. See also Sergei Khakaev in Lur'e and Maliarova, *1956 god. Seredina veka*, 388.

54. The students from the Mining Institute, for instance, arrived on July 16, but harvesting began only on August 10. RGASPI, f. 556, op. 15, d. 10, l. 59. *My byli na tseline*; Soyfer, *Ochen' lichnaia kniga*, 180–181.

55. On building more storage facilities after 1956, see Nikolai Karpukhin in Lur'e and Maliarova, *1956 god. Seredina veka,* 383; on fluctuating harvests, McCauley, *Khrushchev,* 91.

56. Aleksei Botov, "Ia tozhe byl na tseline," *Pinezh'e,* April 29, 2004, http://arhpress.ru/pinega/2004/4/29/11-p.shtml.

57. Matveeva, "Vdarim," 323; Tomilin, "Kampaniia," 85–86.

58. Botov, "Ia tozhe byl na tseline"; Viacheslav Kabanov, "V bol'shoi politike," *Znamia* 8 (2010): 186. Strelianyi cited in Vladimir Tolz, "Maloizvestnaia tselina: poluvekovoi iubilei" (February 29, 2004), http://www.svoboda.org/content/transcript/24204157.html.

59. Matveeva, "Vdarim," 326. Konstantin G. Levykin reports that the accident was caused by a race between the drivers of the two open trucks during which one overturned in *Moi universitet: dlia vsekh—on nash, a dlia kazhdogo—svoi* (Moscow: Izd. Slavianskoi kultury, 2006), 320–321.

60. Both Matveeva and Tat'iana Chernaia cite this instance, with Ella Vengerova as the wit. See Matveeva, "Vdarim," 322; T. K. Chernaia, "Kak vozdukh i zemlia," in *Vremia ostavsheesia s nami: Filologicheskii fakul'tet v 1955–1960 gg.: Vospominaniia vypusknikov* (Moscow: Filologicheskii Fakul'tet MGU, 2006), 3:359.

61. Transcript of conference convened by the Bureau of Propaganda and Agitation of the Central Committee of the Russian Federation in RGASPI, f. 556, op. 15, d. 10, ll. 5–7, 13, 17–18, 29, 39, 45, 56–57, 88. Frustration with the poor organization of work in the Virgin Lands inspired the student construction brigade (*stroiotriady*) movement in which students got vocational training during the academic year.

62. "Poisk nastoiashchego v zhizni," *Iunost'* 3 (1956): 79.

63. Levykin, *Moi universitet,* 375.

64. Gladilin, *Making and Unmaking,* 34. The editor in question was Aleksandr Krivitskii—for more on the "Gray Cardinal of Simonov's *Novyi mir,*" see Denis Kozlov, *The Readers of Novyi Mir: Coming to Terms with the Stalinist Past* (Cambridge, MA: Harvard University Press, 2013), 263–280.

65. Gladilin, *Brigantina,* 30.

66. Richard C. Borden, *The Art of Writing Badly: Valentin Kataeev's Mauvism and the Rebirth of Russian Modernism* (Evanston, IL: Northwestern University Press, 1999), 191.

67. Kabanov, "V bol'shoi politike," 182–183.

68. Frid, "Posle skazki," 305. One tactic was to arrange the film's debut in Inta for a flattered audience of coal miners.

69. Gladilin, *Ulitsa Generalov,* 74.

9. September

1. K. Paustovskii, "Muza dal'nikh stranstvii," *Vokrug sveta* 1 (1957): 8.

2. For Khrushchev's schedule in 1956, see Sergei Khrushchev, ed., *Memoirs of Nikita Khrushchev,* vol. 3, *Statesman (1953–1964),* trans. George Shriver (University Park: Pennsylvania State University Press, 2007), 994–1001.

3. Central Committee resolution "Ob organizatsii poezdok sovetskikh turistov za granitsu" cited in A. N. Chistikov, "'Ladno l' za morem il' khudo?': vpechatleniia sovetskiikh liudei o zagranitse v lichnykh zapisiakh i vystupleniiakh (seredina 1950-kh-seredina 1960-kh gg.)," *Noveishaia istoriia Rossii* 1 (2011): 167. Statistics about travel can be found in Igor Orlov, "The Soviet Union Outgoing Tourism in 1955–1985: Volume, Geography, Organizational Forms" (Working Paper, National Research University Higher School of Economics, 2014), 7, 10–11, 17. On Khrushchev's views, see also Anne Gorsuch, *All This Is Your World: Soviet Tourism at Home and Abroad after Stalin* (Oxford: Oxford University Press, 2011), 13–14.

4. The "price" may have varied as Iakov Basin cites two rubles thirty kopecks for a concert, whereas the later song mentions 3.80; see Iakov Basin, "'Oni mne rasskazyvaiut za Odessu! . . . ,'" January 4, 2014, ol.ua/articles/oni -mne-rasskazyvayut-za.html. For reports of foreign performances and appearances in 1956, see "Iz dnevnikov Sergeia Sergeevich Dmitrieva," *Otechestvennaia istoriia* 1 (2000): 163–164; and "Iz dnevnikov Sergeia Sergeevich Dmitrieva," *Otechestvennaia istoriia* 2 (2000): 143–144.

5. "Razvitie inostrannogo turizma v Sovetskom Soiuze," *Pravda,* July 25, 1957, p. 2.

6. Khrushchev, *Memoirs,* 3:21–22, 81.

7. Sergei N. Khrushchev, *Nikita Khrushchev and the Creation of A Superpower,* trans. Shirley Benson (University Park: Pennsylvania State University Press, 2000), 81–85. Khrushchev, *Memoirs,* 3:50.

8. "Speech by Comrade Khrushchev at the 6th PUWP CC Plenum, Warsaw," March 20, 1956, History and Public Policy Program Digital Archive, AAN (Archive of Modern Records) PZPR 2631 Materialy do stosunkow partyjnych polsko-radzieckich z lat 1956–1958, "Przemowienie tow. Chruszczowa na VI Plenum K. C.," k. 14–87. Translated from Russian and Polish by L. W. Gluchowski (http://digitalarchive.wilsoncenter.org/document/111920).

According to Khrushchev, Stalin also reproached his colleagues, "I'm going to die, and they'll wipe you out like so many partridges—the imperialist powers will. You don't know how to defend the Soviet state" (Khrushchev, *Memoirs*, 3:50).

9. On Nikita Khrushchev's concerns about travel to Britain, see Khrushchev, *Creation*, 112–133; the term *foreign marvels* is his. On Malenkov's visit, see "Mr. Malenkov by the Sea," *Times*, March 26, 1956, p. 6.

10. Khrushchev, *Creation*, 83, 114–116.

11. Ibid., 82, 119, 121.

12. Ibid., 119.

13. On the exchange with Mrs. Eden, see Khrushchev, *Memoirs*, 3:69; quotation is from *Creation*, 125. Among other things, Khrushchev happily lectured a naval audience at Greenwich as to the obsolescence of surface ships (*Memoirs*, 3:75–76).

14. "Text of Khrushchev's Speech in London," *New York Times*, April 20, 1956, p. 3. On his attitudes toward warfare in the nuclear age, see Khrushchev, *Creation*, 104, 143.

15. "Text of Khrushchev's Speech in London," p. 3.

16. Drew Middleton, "Khrushchev Says Soviet Will Make H-Bomb Missile," *New York Times*, April 24, 1956, p. 1. The Russian press toned down Khrushchev's remarks about missile technology. See "Vystuplenie N. S. Khrushcheva," *Pravda*, April 24, 1956, p. 2. Drew Middleton, "Stassen Confers with Khrushchev on Arms Dispute," *New York Times*, April 25, 1956, pp. 1, 3.

17. "Prebyvanie v Anglii N. A. Bulganina i N. S. Khrushcheva," *Ogonek* 18 (May 1, 1956): 2–5.

18. Drew Middleton, "Russian Leaders Guests of Queen," *New York Times*, April 23, 1956, p. 1.

19. Drew Middleton, "Russians Find British Are Hard People to Sell," *New York Times*, April 22, 1956, p. 1.

20. "Vystuplenie N. S. Khrushcheva," *Pravda*, April 24, 1956, p. 2. The Soviet press reinforced the idea that protesters were not real Britons but rather unhappy émigrés. D. Kraminov and V. Nekrasov, "V Anglii v eti dni," *Pravda*, April 24, 1956, p. 3. Sergei Khrushchev makes the case that his father mistook the man's raised fist salute as a sign of hostility in *Creation*, 132–133.

21. Khrushchev, *Creation*, 118.

22. Khrushchev, *Memoirs*, 3:80.

23. "Rapid Tour of London Sights," *Times*, April 19, 1956, 10; "Sailors Tour London," *Times*, April 20, 1956, p. 6. Khrushchev, *Memoirs*, 3:78; "Vystuplenie N. S. Khrushcheva," *Pravda*, April 24, 1956, p. 2. On Bulganin's 1936 trip, see "Britain's Guests: Nikolai Bulganin and Nikita Khrushchov [*sic*]: Their Lives & Work," *Soviet News Booklet* 13 (April 1956): 5–6.

24. Churchill's advice as recollected by Khrushchev, *Memoirs*, 3:82. On Downing Street and the queen, see ibid., 68, 71–72.

25. "Changes in Soviet Leaders' Programme," *Times*, April 25, 1956, p. 6.

26. For assessments of negotiations, see Middleton, "Russian Leaders Guests of Queen"; "Khrushchev Says Soviet Will Make H-Bomb Missile," *New York Times*, April 24, 1956, pp. 1, 6; and "Stassen Confers with Khrushchev."

27. "Texts of Bulganin's Statement, Russians' Interview and Sir Anthony Eden's Address," *New York Times*, April 28, 1956, p. 4. For a fresh account of Khrushchev's 1959 trip to America, see Peter Carlson, *K Blows Top* (New York: Public Affairs, 2010).

28. For reports on eight tourist trips to England between May and October 1956, see GARF, f. 9612, op. 1, d. 373. On Pankratova's trip, see "The Court Courier," *Times*, July 25, 1956, p. 12.

29. Boris Polevoi, *Za trideviat' zemel': Dnevnik puteshestviia na teplokhode "Pobeda"* (Moscow: Gos. Izd. Detskoi Literatury, 1958); Elena Katerli, *Vosem' morei i odin okean* (Leningrad: Sovetskii pisatel', 1958). Other book-length accounts include I. Osipov, *Iz putevogo bloknota turista* (Moscow: Molodaia gvardiia, 1957); Nikolai Krivenko, *Vokrug Evropy: Zametki turista* (Moscow: Gos. Izd. Politicheskoi Literatury, 1957); I. M. Sarkizov-Serazini, *Po staromu svetu* (Moscow: Gos. Izd. Geograficheskoi Literatury, 1958).

30. Konstantin Paustovskii, "Evropeiskii dnevnik," *Mir Paustovskogo* 22 (2005): 10–18; Daniil Granin first published his essay "Chuzhoi dnevnik" in the Soviet journal *Nauka i religiia* 9 (1984): 46–63; here I use the expanded post-Soviet version in Daniil Granin, *Sobranie sochinenii v vos'mi tomakh* (St. Petersburg: Vita Nova, 2009), 8:67–106; Leonid Rakhmanov, "Puteshestvie s Paustovskim," in *Vospominanie o Konstantine Paustovskom* (Moscow: Sovetskii pisatel', 1983), 304–320.

31. *Puteshestvie vokrug Evropy . . .* (dir. T. Lavrova, Moscow, 1956). An account of the second sailing stressed the geographical diversity of participants who hailed from "Moscow, Leningrad, Kiev, Minsk, Lithuania, Latvia, Estonia, Kharkov, Gorky, Dnepropetrovsk, Odessa, Murmansk, and Magadan" and mentioned the presence of "Party, government, and managerial workers"

among the passengers (P. Satiukov, "Vtoroi reis teplokhoda 'Pobeda' vokrug Evropy," *Pravda*, July 10, 1956, p. 4).

32. "Soviet Tourists in Italy," *Times*, June 13, 1956, p. 8. In the documentary film *Puteshestvie vokrug Evropy* . . . the tourists appear to generally be between thirty and sixty with a few younger persons. A few regional trade unions reported on the makeup of their groups sent on the *Pobeda*. Odessa, for instance, sent fifty-one tourists spread across three cruises—thirty-three were men and eighteen women; twenty-seven Russians, sixteen Ukrainians, seven Jews, and one "other." Two were workers, and none were peasants. Fifteen were educators; nine were scientific or cultural workers. Seven were engineers, five were managers, five were doctors, three were leaders of enterprises, one was a white-collar worker, and four were dependents (GARF, f. 9520, op. 1, d. 316, ll. 41–44).

33. Rakhmanov, "Puteshestvie s Paustovskim." Writers on the first cruise included Lev Kassil', O. Mal'tsev, Tat'iana Tess, Vasilii Zakharchenko, Boris Polevoi, and Sergei Smirnov.

34. Quotation is from Paustovskii's speech at the discussion of Vladimir Dudintsev's *Not by Bread Alone* of October 22, 1956, as reproduced in "Obsuzhdenie romana V. Dudintseva 'Ne khlebom edinym'," *Mir Paustovskogo* 23 (2005): 37.

35. A biography of Ossetian Soviet writer Revaz Asaev notes that he was chosen by the head of the Writers Union. D. Vaneeva, "70 let plodotvornogo tvorchestva," *Iuzhnaia Osetiia*, August 16, 2006, p. 4. Female activist and metro builder Tat'iana Feodorova later noted: "I landed among [*ia popala*] the multitudinous tribe of Soviet tourists"—hence eliding the process of applying. See T. V. Feodorova, *Naverkhu-Moskva*, http://www.metro.ru/library/naverhu-moskva/.

36. Paustovskii, "Evropeiskii dnevnik," 10. Granin, "Chuzhoi dnevnik," 74–75.

37. The forms can be found in GARF, f. 9612, op. 1, d. 387, ll. 37, 38, 38 ob, 39. A trip report from England in 1956 captures a case of circumvention of rules requiring positive character references; two girl students at the Stalingrad Institute of Foreign Languages allegedly had been refused references but their parents had pulled strings to get them spots (d. 373, l. 43).

38. John Gunther, who traveled on the *Pobeda* in late 1956, was quoted prices of forty-two hundred rubles for first class and three thousand rubles for second class for the twenty-six-day summer cruises to Europe. See John Gunther, *Inside Russia Today* (London: Hamish Hamilton, 1958), 65. See also "Class Divisions for Russian Tourists," *Times*, July 14, 1956, p. 6. The number of spots seems to have been set per city or region taking into account population

and urbanity; for instance, Moldova got ten spots, while Tadzhikistan and Kyrgyzstan each had fifteen, Uzbekistan and Georgia twenty, and Estonia thirty-five. The industrial center Gorky (Nizhnyi Novogorod) got forty berths, while remote cities like Arkhangel'sk got none. Leningrad sent a total of 416 persons to capitalist countries in 1956, while Moscow sent 2,231 (GARF, f. 9520, op. 1, d. 316, l. 11, 41, 84 and d. 317, l. 9, 26, 30, 77, 91, 129).

39. Gunther, *Inside Russia Today*, 465. The documentary *Puteshestvie vokrug Evropy* . . . shows a wood-paneled music room with a grand piano, a spacious library, and a dining hall with tables set with china on white tablecloths.

40. Granin, "Chuzhoi dnevnik," 75.

41. Dutch journalist Frank Westerman discovered, ironically, that bad weather and a shortage of funds meant that Paustovskii never made it all the way to Kara Bugaz; see Frank Westerman, *Engineers of the Human Soul: The Grandiose Propaganda of Stalin's Russia*, trans. Sam Garrett (London: Harvill Secker, 2010), 90. Paustovskii and his wife had also made a short trip to in January 1956 to a Czech spa.

42. Katerli, *Vosem' morei*, 56; Paustovskii, "Evropeiskii dnevnik," 14. Granin, "Chuzhoi dnevnik," 80.

43. Polevoi, *Za tridevat' zemel'*, 4. On activities by returning tourists, see GARF, f. 9520, op. 1, d. 317, l. 16–18, 66.

44. Katerli, *Vosem' morei*, 6, 12.; K. G. Paustovskii to L. N. Rakhmanov, November 26, 1956, and to T. A. Paustovskaia, September 20, 1956, in Konstantin Paustovskii, *Sobranie sochinenii* (Moscow: Khudozhestvennaia literatura, 1986), 9:323–325.

45. Chistikov, "'Ladno l' za morem'," 73–174; Krivenko, *Vokrug Evropy*, 68, 72, 73, 79.

46. Granin, "Chuzhoi dnevnik," 76, 79. Interestingly, in Katerli's published account, the woman émigré is a sad, homeless wretch (*Vosem' morei*, 43). On the collective nature of the proposed interaction of Soviet tourists with foreigners, see Tat'iana Kaptereva-Shambingao, *Dom i za granitsei* (Moscow: Novyi khronograf, 2009), 242.

47. Konstantin Paustovskii, "Raznotsvetnye goroda," *Pervoe sentiabria* 37 (1999), http://ps.1september.ru/article.php?ID=199903710; Katerli, *Vosem' morei*, 35.

48. Polevoi, *Za tridevat' zemel'*, 103. On lack of literature for travelers, see I. Osipov, "Neskol'ko zamechanii o pervom 'kruize'," *Literaturnaia gazeta*, July 10, 1956, p. 2.

49. "Obsuzhdenie romana V. Dudintseva," 37; Rakhmanov, "Putush-estvie," 319. Granin cites two young Soviet women angrily denying the joking claim of some elderly Italian men that the local lovers were the best ("Chuzhoi dnevnik," 83).

50. For a thorough and fascinating analysis of Soviet tourism in the Khrushchev era, see Gorsuch, *All This Is Your World* (on the requirement for travelers "to perform Soviet identity," see esp. 108–109). On wardrobe, see Granin, "Chuzhoi dnevnik," 103; on palanquin carriers, see V. Sokolova, "Vstrechi," *Krestianka* 9 (September 1956): 26.

51. Granin, "Chuzhoi dnevnik," 100–101; Gamzatov cited by Daniil Granin in Nizamidin Kainbekov, "Gorets s dushoi poeta," http://www.riadagestan.ru/news/culture/literaturnyy_vecher_posvyashchennyy_90_letiyu_rasula_gamzatova_proshel_v_sankt_peterburge/?print=Y.

52. Sergei Shevyrin, "'Povedenie turistov za predelami SSSR bylo skromnym. Odnako takie turisty kak . . .'," https://www.permgani.ru/publikatsii/stati/povedenie-turistov-za-predelami-sssr-bylo-skromnym-odnako-takie-turisty-kak.html. Some 1956 reports on Soviet tourist groups to England also describe "misbehavior," such as being too friendly with individual foreigners, sneaking off from the group, showing too much concern for shopping, and making inappropriate comments in public (GARF, f. R9612, op. 1, d. 373).

53. Katerli, *Vosem' morei*, 29; Granin, "Chuzhoi dnevnik," 105; *Putushestvie vokrug evropy . . .*

54. Osipov, *Iz putevogo bloknota*, 44.

55. Polevoi, *Za trideviat' zemel'*, 115.

56. Katerli, *Vosem' morei*, 40, 53, 120; Osipov, "Neskol'ko zamechanii."

57. Tat'iana Tess, "Pod nebom Italii," *Izvestiia*, June 21, 1956, p. 4; and Osipov, *Iz putevogo bloknota*, 30–31.

58. Sokolova, "Vstrechi," 27.

59. Paustovskii, "Raznosvetnye goroda" and "Evropeiskii dnevnik," 14; Katerli, *Vosem' morei*, 48, 53–55, 93–96, 99–100; Rakhmanov, "Putushestvie," 314–315. Delectorskaya would become Paustovskii's French translator and a great friend. See Galina Arbuzova, "Anri Matiss i ego model'," *Mir Paustovskogo* 22 (2005): 30–31.

60. Rakhmanov, "Putushestvie," 305; Katerli, *Vosem' morei*, 25–26.

61. Granin, "Chuzhoi dnevnik," 82.

62. Paustovskii, "Raznotsvetnye goroda."

63. Quotation from Paustovskii, "Evropeiskii dnevnik," 12. See also letter to Galina Arbuzova, September 7, 1956, in Paustovskii, *Sobranie sochinenie*, 9:322.

64. Polevoi, *Za trideviat' zemel'*, 231; see also Krivenko, *Vokrug Evropy*, 94–95.

65. Entry for November 15, 1955, in "Iz dnevnikov Sergeia Sergeevich Dmitrieva," *Otechestvennaia istoriia* 1 (2000): 161.

66. "Moscow Prepares Guidebook for the Visitors," *Times*, April 3, 1956, p. 6; "£2 a Day for Vodka, Haircuts &c.," *Times*, August 16, 1956, p. 6.

67. Gorsuch, *All This Is Your World*, 108; Paustovskii, for instance, counseled Granin on how to smooth over the incident in which he was late for boarding the ship. Reports on Soviet tourist groups to Britain are full of examples of "helpful" tourists who try to dissuade others from talking to strangers or meeting up with new acquaintances without the consent of the trip organizer (GARF, f. R9612, d. 373).

68. Nina Katerli, "Skvoz' sumrak bytiia," in *Chemu sviditel'iami my byli: Zhenskie sud'by—XX vek* (St. Petersburg: Zhurnal 'Zvezda', 2007), 529.

69. *Britain's Guests*, 3.

70. "Obsuzhdenie romana V. Dudintseva," 37.

71. Granin, "Chuzhoi dnevnik," 76.

10. October

1. A reader in Riga noted libraries there were lending one issue at a time for twenty-four hours. A Leningrader recalled visiting three libraries only to find the relevant issues stolen. Letter from B. I. Gaiduk to *Novy mir*, February 1, 1957, RGALI, f. 1702, op. 6, d. 240, l. 15; Liudmila Ieuzitov cited in Lev Lur'e and Irina Maliarova, *1956 god. Seredina veka* (St. Petersburg: Izd. Dom 'Neva,' 2007), 418. Entry for October 26, 1956, "Iz dnevnikov Sergeia Sergeevicha Dmitrieva," *Otechestvennia istoriia* 2 (2000): 147.

2. "Stenogramma obsuzhdeniia kniga V. Dudintseva—'Ne klebom edinym' (vystuplenie Paustovskogo pravlenoe)," October 22, 1956, RGALI, f. 2464, op. 1, d. 335, quotations, l. 12, l. 23.

3. Quotation is from a conspectus of the November 2, 1956, meeting with the author at MGU, where philology students spoke also of the need for democracy and for reversing people's isolation from government. Lidiia Kliatsko, *Dnevnik studentki zhurfaka* (Moscow: RIF "ROI", 2002), 66.

4. Karl E. Loewenstein, "The Thaw: Writers and the Public Sphere in the Soviet Union, 1951–1957" (Ph.D. diss., Duke University, 1999), 295.

5. On Pasternak's decision to send his work overseas and the conse-quences, see Peter Finn and Petra Couvee, *The Zhivago Affair: The Kremlin, the CIA, and the Battle over a Forbidden Book* (New York: Pantheon, 2014).

6. Vera Dunham, *In Stalin's Time: Middleclass Values in Soviet Fiction* (Cambridge: Cambridge University Press, 1976), 26. More recently, Denis Kozlov has eloquently described Russia as a "literature centered civilization" especially during the years of Soviet power in *The Readers of Novyi Mir: Coming to Terms with the Stalinist Past* (Cambridge, MA: Harvard University Press, 2013), 2.

7. Catriona Kelly, *Refining Russia: Advice Literature, Polite Culture, and Gender from Catherine to Yeltsin* (Oxford: Oxford University Press, 2001), 272–273.

8. Loewenstein expands on the idea of literary discussions as a surrogate for more direct political civic engagement in "The Thaw." Denis Kozlov offers a sophisticated overview of the position of readers and writers and teases out "the relationship between texts and readers" (*Readers*, 11).

9. "Resolution on the Journals *Zvezda* and *Leningrad*," cited in Harold Swayze, *Political Control of Literature in the USSR, 1946–1959* (Cambridge, MA: Harvard University Press, 1962), 37.

10. Kozlov found 720 letters addressing *Not by Bread Alone* in the archives of *Novyi mir*. The majority were received in 1956–1958. Regarding *One Day in the Life of Ivan Denisovich*, he found 532 letters (*Readers*, 89; on "guild" readers, see ibid., 21).

11. Ibid., 4.

12. Thomas C. Wolfe, *Governing Soviet Journalism: The Press and the So-cialist Person after Stalin* (Bloomington: Indiana University Press, 2005).

13. Regarding Babel's arrest, Dudintsev later claimed that he was shocked and disbelieving and decided that Babel must have been preyed on by bad company. Vladimir Dudintsev, *Mezhdu dvumia romanami* (St. Petersburg: Zhurnal Neva, 2000), 40–41.

14. Ibid., 34–35.

15. V. Kardin, "Batalii mirnykh let," *Znamia* 2 (2003): 159.

16. To be more precise, Dudintsev recalled that he and (ironically) Kon-stantin Paustovskii tied for second place; no first place was awarded (*Mezhdu*, 36).

17. Wolfe, *Governing Soviet Journalism*, 35. For an example of journalistic investigation in response to a reader's letter in1956, see Igor' Kobzev, "Skuchno v Kazalinske," *Ogonek* 51 (December 16, 1956): 12–13.

18. In their new apartment, the isolated room of about fourteen square meters went to Dudintsev for his study. The other five family members happily settled into the remaining twenty square meter room (Dudintsev, *Mezhdu*, 52).

19. Dudintsev's wife was later able to help date the start of work on *Not by Bread Alone* by noting that the paper "quilt" was possible only after 1950 when they moved into two rooms (ibid.).

20. Ibid., 17.

21. Dudintsev's wife notes that the author came up with the concept of a "social order" only later (ibid., 47–48). Dudintsev knew that journals of the highest rank, such as *Novyi mir*, did not routinely place orders in such a crude fashion. But they, too, responded to shifting ideological dictates.

22. Vladimir Dudintsev, *Not by Bread Alone*, trans. Edith Bone (New York: E. P. Dutton, 1957), 27, 83.

23. Ibid., 70–77.

24. Lopatkin's ally Galitskii calls him an idealist and compares his actions to having lighted a lantern that attracts helpers like moths (ibid., 445–446).

25. Ibid., 512.

26. Ibid., 235.

27. Stephen Kotkin, *Magnetic Mountain: Stalinism as Civilization* (Berkeley: University of California Press, 1995), 222. "Speaking Bolshevik" means not only speaking as the regime would wish but playing by the unwritten rules of the game.

28. Dudintsev, *Not by Bread Alone*, 509.

29. Ibid., 505.

30. On the formula for resolution of production novels, see Katerina Clark, *The Soviet Novel: History as Ritual,* 2nd ed. (Chicago: University of Chicago Press, 1985), 260.

31. When *Not by Bread Alone* came under attack in late 1956, Dudintsev and Simonov propagated the myth that Dudintsev had been inspired by the Twentieth Party Congress, although he never could have written the long, complex novel in the short period between the Congress and its publication (Dudintsev, *Mezhdu*, 54–62).

32. Dina R. Spechler, *Permitted Dissent in the USSR:* Novy mir *and the Soviet Regime* (New York: Praeger, 1982), 29. For a history of *Novyi mir* in the

1950s, see Edith Rogovin Frankel, Novyi Mir: *A Case Study in the Politics of Literature, 1952–1958* (Cambridge: Cambridge University Press, 1981).

33. On the early thaw and debates about truth, sincerity, and so forth, in literary circles, see Katerina Clark, "'Wait for Me and I Shall Return': The Early Thaw as a Reprise of Late Thirties Culture?," in *The Thaw: Soviet Society and Culture during the 1950s and 1960s*, ed. Denis Kozlov and Eleonory Gilburd (Toronto: University of Toronto Press, 2013), 85–108.

34. My discussion of early 1950s literary debates draws heavily on Marina Zezina, "Crisis in the Union of Soviet Writers in the Early 1950s," *Europe-Asia Studies* 46, no. 4 (1994): 649–661; Loewenstein, "The Thaw"; Kozlov, *Readers;* and Spechler, *Permitted Dissent*. Regarding Tvardovskii's dismissal, see Kozlov, *Readers*, 75–78.

35. Karl Loewenstein tracks a series of contentious meetings of Moscow and Leningrad writers in which the Zhdanov decrees were subtly and openly challenged in "The Thaw," 149–153, 161–163, 179–180. See also Raisa Orlova, *Memoirs*, trans. Samuel Cioran (New York: Random House, 1983), 61–65, 204, 209–213. On Simonov's grappling with Stalinism in his literary works, see Polly Jones, *Myth, Memory, Trauma: Rethinking the Stalinist Past in the Soviet Union, 1953–70* (New Haven, CT: Yale University Press, 2013), 173–211.

36. Cited in M. J. Berry, "Science, Technology and Innovation," in *Khrushchev and Khrushchevism*, ed. Martin McAuley (London: School of Slavonic and East European Studies, 1987), 74. In May 1957 Khrushchev would admit there were places in the novel where Dudintsev echoed his own words about bureaucrats. "'A Vy sidite, kak surok, i o demokratii govorite': Vystuplenie N. S. Khrushcheva na soveshanii pisatelei v TsK KPSS 13 mai 1957 g.," *Istochnik* 6 (2003): 81.

37. Spechler, *Permitted Dissent*, 29.

38. "O ser'eznykh ideologicheskikh nedostatkakh v sovremennoi sovetskoi literature," September 26, 1956, in *Kul'tura i vlast' ot Stalina do Gorbacheva: Apparat TsK KPSS i kul'tura, 1953–1957: Dokumenty*, ed. V. Iu. Afiani and comp. K. Vodop'ianova (Moscow: ROSSPEN, 2001), 537, 541. Letter from N. Sadovoi to *Novyi mir*, December 30, 1956, RGALI, f. 1702, op. 6, d. 240, ll. 1–5.

39. Evgenii Dolmatovskii, "'Ia iz-za tebia noch' ne spal . . . ,'" *Rodina* 3 (1992): 18.

40. On October 18, 1956, the editorial board of *Literaturnaia gazeta* held a contentious meeting about whether to publish a critical review of *Not by Bread Alone*. "Stenogramma zasedaniia redkollegii po obsuzhdeniiu stat'i V. P.

Dorofeeva o romane V. D. Dudinsteva 'Ne khlebom ediny,'" RGALI, f. 634, op. 4, d. 1271, ll. 2–46. See also Vladislav Zubok, *Zhivago's Children: The Last Russian Intelligentsia* (Cambridge, MA: Harvard University Press, 2009), 75.

41. Dudintsev, *Mezhdu*, 10.

42. "Stenogramma obsuzhdeniia kniga," ll. 4–5, quotation l. 5. On expectations, see Galina Kornilova, "To, o chem zabyt' nel'zia . . . ," *Mir Paustovskogo* 23 (2005): 34; Lidiia Chukovskaia cited in, "Sovremenniki govoriat . . . ," *Mir Paustovskogo* 23 (2005): 44.

43. "Stenogramma obsuzhdeniia kniga," quotations ll. 3, 12, 7.

44. Kozlov, *Readers*, 96–98, 101; "Stenogramma obsuzhdeniia kniga," l. 14.

45. Letter from M. Chetyrkina to *Novyi mir*, October 1, 1956, in RGALI, f. 1702, op. 6, d. 241, ll. 25–26, quotation l. 26.

46. "Stenogramma obsuzhdeniia kniga," ll. 5, 20, 42, 48, 53, 56. The lone positive review in the central press echoed this argument, contending that by unmasking Drozdov, *Not by Bread Alone* could be a "useful weapon" in "the battle persistently, bravely and unwaveringly conducted by the Party for the restoration of Leninist principles of democraticism [*sic*] that were won in the days of the Great October [Revolution]"; see V. Zhdanov, "Ostryi roman o sovremennosti," *Trud*, October 31, 1956, p. 3.

47. "Stenogramma obsuzhdeniia kniga," l. 22. Mikhalkov rather put words in Dudintsev's mouth, but he was not alone. A military lawyer wrote to the journal: "You don't write in your book that the goal of this battle is Communism. But all of us readers understand this" (letter from G. I. Gaiduk to *Novyi mir*, January 2, 1957, in RGALI, f. 1702, op. 6, d. 240, ll. 15–17; quotation l. 15).

48. Quotations here are from Paustovskii's own corrected version of the transcript of his speech published as "Obsuzhdenie romana V. Dudintseva 'Ne khlebom edinym': stenogramma" in *Mir Paustovskogo* 23 (2005): 37–38. Similar corrections can be found in the transcript in RGALI, "Stenogramma obsuzhdeniia kniga," ll. 23–26.

49. "Obsuzhdenie romana," 37.

50. Ibid., 38. The writers named were all arrested in 1937–1939 and subsequently executed.

51. L. Levitskii, "Golos Paustovskogo," *Voprosy literatury* 2 (2004): 300.

52. Ketlinskaia quotation from "Stenogramma obsuzhdeniia kniga," l. 45; Simonov quotation from Dudintsev, *Mezhdu*, 12–13.

53. "Stenogramma obsuzhdeniia kniga," ll. 39–42.

54. "Obsuzhdenie romana," 35. On Paustovskii's decision to ask for the floor again, see Levitskii, "Golos Paustovskogo," 301.

55. Dudintsev was hardly the first to criticize Soviet bureaucrats. Ehrenburg's *The Thaw* similarly featured a coarse factory manager whose young wife abandons him. The year 1956 also saw publication of antibureaucratic stories by Aleksandr Yashin and Daniil Granin.

56. "Stenogramma obsuzhdeniia kniga," ll. 62–68, Dudintsev quotation l. 63.

57. Ibid., l. 68; "Obsuzhdaem novye knigi," *Literaturnaia gazeta*, October 27, 1956, pp. 3, 4; on Paustovskii's speech circulating, see Vladimir Grindin and Lazar' Lazarev cited in, "Sovremenniki govoriat . . . ," *Mir Paustovskogo* 23 (2005): 43, 45.

58. "Zasedanie biuro sektsii prozy," October 29, 1956, in RGALI, f. 2464, op. 1, d. 325, ll. 46–47.

59. "Obsuzhdenie knigi V. D. Dudintseva 'Ne khlebom edinym' Zasedanie Literaturnogo khruzhka filologicheskaia fakul'teta LGU," November 10, 1956, comp. Ernest Orlovskii, in Nauchno-Informatsionnyi Tsentr (NITs) Memorial, Revol't Pimenov Archive, razdel 3, papka 3.1, no. 26.

60. For examples of economic questions, see the report from the Central Committee of the Komsomol to the Central Committee of the CPSU, March 8, 1956, RGANI, f. 5, d. 178, l. 27. Raisa Orlova and Lev Kopelev, *My zhili v Moskve, 1956–1980* (Ann Arbor, MI: Ardis, 1988), 44.

61. "Iz dnevnikov," 148; Milovan Djilas, *The New Class: An Analysis of the Communist System* (New York: Frederick A. Praeger, 1957).

62. Letter from S. Gonikman to *Novyi mir,* October 11, 1956, in RGALI, f. 1702, op. 6, d. 241, ll. 64–65.

11. November

1. Revol't I. Pimenov, "Otkrytoe pis'mo deputatu verkhovnogo soveta SSSR," October 28, 1956, included in the ten-volume case files of the Leningrad oblast' KGB: "Po obvineniu Pimenova, Revol'ta Ivanovicha i drugikh" (nachato 25 marta 1957 okoncheno 25 iuliu 1957), tom 6, l. 170. A copy of the KGB files for the Pimenov case are held by NITs Memorial in their Revol't Pimenov Archive, "Obsuzhdenie knigi V. D. Dudintseva 'Ne khlebom edinym' Zasedanie literaturnogo khruzhka filologicheskaia fakul'teta LGU," November 10, 1956, comp. Ernest Orlovskii, NITs Memorial, Revol't Pimenov Archive, razdel 3, papka 3.1, no. 26. Pimenov here gave an example without naming the person involved—but mathematician Aleksandr D. Aleksandrov,

rector of LGU, who was presiding over the dispute, openly admitted to being that person. Benjamin Tromly suggests Pimenov antagonized Aleksandrov, his former mentor, to provoke a response in "Intelligentsia Self-Fashioning in the Postwar Soviet Union: Revol't Pimenov's Political Struggle, 1949–57," *Kritika* 13, no. 1 (2012): 167.

2. See also Kathleen Smith "A New Generation of Political Prisoners: 'Anti-Soviet' Students, 1956–1957," *Soviet and Post-Soviet Review* 32, nos. 2–3 (2005): 191–208; V. A. Kozlov and S. V. Mironenko ed., *Kramola: Inakomyslie v SSSR pri Khrushcheve i Brezhneve, 1953–1982 gg.* (Moscow: Materik, 2005). Admittedly, the study of free speech as filtered through the lens of prosecutions creates a methodological conundrum. The timing of the crackdown starting in late November 1956 creates the impression of a quantitative and qualitative rise in radical speech when in fact it may be the regime that changed, not the students. This distortion can be partially addressed by assessing what those caught over Hungary were doing in earlier months. On other means of discipline, see Gennadii Kuzovkin, "Partiino-Komsomol'skie presledovaniia po politicheskim motivam v period rannei 'ottepeli,'" in *Korny travi: sbornik statei molodykh istorikov,* ed. L. S. Eremina and E. B. Zhemkova (Moscow: Zven'ia, 1996), 88–93. On political speech at MGU, see Evgenii Taranov, "Raskachaem Leninskie gori," *Svobodnaia mysl'* 10 (1993): 94–103.

3. Revol't Pimenov, *Vospominaniia* (Moscow: Panorama, 1996), vols. 1 and 2; see his codefendants' memoirs: Boris Vail', *Osobo opasnyi* (London: Overseas Publications Interchange, 1980); Irena Verblovskaia, *Moi prekrasnyi strashnyi vek* (St. Petersburg: Zhurnal zvezda, 2011). Irma Kudrova, who was interrogated but not charged, has recently given an account in *Proshchanie s morokoi* (St. Petersburg: Kriga, 2013). Some materials from their case can also be found in GARF, f. 8131, op. 31, d. 43956.

4. There were many cases of student conflict with authorities in autumn 1956; I chose to focus here on a few well-documented instances that involved the main issues of the day.

5. Letter of May 21, 1956, NITs Memorial, Revol't Pimenov Archive, razdel 3, papka 3.17. *Borba* and *Politika* became available in March 1956; the main Polish paper *Tribuna Liudu* and East German papers were apparently available already in 1954. Ernst Orlovskii, "Moi put' k dissidenty," *Neva* 6 (2002): 184. In Moscow, too, a single kiosk near MGU sold foreign papers. Purchasers included physicist Yuri Orlov, who later recalled that while he read about Poznan exclusively in the Soviet press, he learned about Hungarian events from Yugoslav newspapers. Tat'iana Kosinova, "Nashim illiuziiam prishel konets: Pol'skii oktiabr' 1956 goda," October 31, 2006, http://www.polit.ru/article/2006/10/31/pol_1956/.

6. See transcript of the party bureau meeting of the MGU School of History for April 5, 1956, in TsAOPIM, f. 478, op. 3, d. 210, l. 11; Lidiia Kliatsko, *Dnevnik studentki Zhurfaka* (Moscow: RIF "ROI", 2002), 51.

7. Aleksandr Gidoni, *Solntse idet s zapada: Kniga vospominanii* (Toronto: Izd. "Sovremmenik", 1980), 40–42, 62–65.

8. Khrushchev would later cite his embarrassment at the Yugoslavs' disdainful reception of his attributing the purges to Beria as pushing him toward making a more decisive break with Stalin. See Sergei Khrushchev, ed., *Memoirs of Nikita Khrushchev*, vol. 2, *Reformer (1945–1964)*, trans. George Shriver (University Park: Pennsylvania State University, 2006), 215–216.

9. Veljko Mićunović, *Moscow Diary*, trans. David Floyd (Garden City, NJ: Doubleday, 1980), 11–12.

10. On Volgograd and Leningrad, see ibid., 68–70. Gidoni, *Sol'ntse*, 42.

11. For the consistent front-page coverage of the visit, see *Pravda*, June 2–24, 1956; on the walkabout in Moscow, see *Pravda*, June 4, 1956, p. 2; Mićunović, *Moscow Diary*, 61. Quotation is from "Deklaratsiia ob otnosheniiakh mezhdu Soiuzom kommunistov Iugoslavii i Kommunisticheskoi partiei Sovetskogo Soiuza," *Pravda*, June 21, 1956, p. 2.

12. Mićunović, *Moscow Diary*, 73, 81–83. Tito's speech is in "Miting, posviashchennyi druzhbe mezhdu Sovetskom Soiuze i Iugoslaviei," *Pravda*, June 20, 1956, p. 3. Ironically, Khrushchev later chewed Mićunović out because the Belgrade press abridged his speech at the same event.

13. Gidoni, *Solntse idet s zapada*, 24–26, 29–38, 40, quotation 36. Djilas, once Tito's closest ally, had fallen out with the leader and been expelled from the party in 1954. In 1955 he got a suspended sentence for spreading propaganda hostile to the state. In December 1956 he would again be prosecuted for political speech. At that date he had written, but not published, *The New Class*.

14. Orlovskii testimony in "Po obvineniu Pimenova, Revol'ta Ivanovicha i drugikh," tom. 3, l. 132 ob.

15. Pimenov, *Vospominaniia*, 1:27. No good data exist for the number of listeners to "enemy voices" in the 1956.

16. Letter to Ivan Pimenov, October 28, 1956, "Po obvineniu Pimenova, Revol'ta Ivanovicha i drugikh," tom. 5 [konvert].

17. Raisa Orlova, *Memoirs*, trans. Samuel Cioran (New York: Random House, 1983), 239; see also Peter Raina, *Political Opposition in Poland 1954–1977* (London: Poets and Painters Press, 1978), 39.

18. Pawel Machcewicz catalogues a geographically widespread, sharply anti-Soviet, and politically diverse set of protest actions in Poland in fall 1956 in *Rebellious Satellite: Poland 1956,* trans. Maya Latynski (Washington, DC: Woodrow Wilson Center Press, 2009).

19. Mark Kramer explains that a decision was made to show "patience" while attempting to negotiate an outcome that kept Poland closely tied to the USSR in "The Soviet Union and the 1956 Crises in Hungary and Poland: Reassessments and New Findings," *Journal of Contemporary History* 33, no. 2 (1998): 168–174. For background on the Polish side, see Krzysztof Persak, "The Polish-Soviet Confrontation in 1956 and the Attempted Soviet Military Intervention in Poland," *Europe-Asia Studies* 58, no. 8 (December 2006): 1285–1310. For Khrushchev's retrospective account, see Sergei Khrushchev, ed., *Memoirs of Nikita Khrushchev,* vol. 3, *Statesman (1953–1964),* trans. George Shriver (University Park: Pennsylvania State University Press, 2007), 617–630.

20. "Vrazhdebnaia provokatsiia imperialisticheskoi agentury v Poznani," *Pravda,* June 30, 1956, p. 4. In its next issue, *Pravda* noted there had been disorder in the streets and attacks on several civic buildings with some fatalities. It provided no photographs or witness reports. Subsequent coverage focused on American funding for undercover activity behind the "Iron Curtain." "Pol'skii narod kleimit organizatorov provokatsii," *Pravda,* July 1, 1956, p. 6; E. Litoshko, "Temnye dela pobornikov 'kholodnoi voiny,'" *Pravda,* July 9, 1956, p. 3.

21. "O politicheskom i ekonomicheskom polozhenii i uzlovykh zadachakh Pol'skoi ob"edinennoi rabochei partii," *Pravda,* July 21, 1956, p. 4.

22. Lawrence L. Thomas, "Polish Literature and the Thaw," *American Slavic and East European Review* 18, no. 3 (October 1959): 406–407. On *Po Prostu,* see Raina, *Opposition,* 41–43. The *Pravda* article "Antisotsialisticheskie vystupleniia na stranitsakh pol'skoi pechati" appeared in the October 20, 1956, edition (p. 3) with a dateline of October 19, the very day Khrushchev descended on Warsaw.

23. Revol't Pimenov, "Antidemokraticheskie vyskazaniia na stranitsakh sovetskoi pechati" (typescript signed and dated October 27, 1956), in "Po obvineniu Pimenova, Revol'ta Ivanovicha i drugikh," tom 6, l. 161.

24. Ibid., l. 162.

25. Entries for November 3 and 4, 1956, in "Iz dnevnikov Sergeia Sergeevicha Dmitrieva," *Otechestvennaia istoriia* 2 (2000): 149.

26. Transcript of confrontation between witness G. Shpalikov and accused V. Zlotverov, March 21, 1957, GARF, f. 8131, d. 74157, ll. 30–37. The police focused on anti-Soviet statements, and hence the interrogation record should

not be taken as a complete or neutral account of student debates. For more on this case, see Smith, "A New Generation."

27. Meeting of the party bureau for the MGU School of History, October 25, 1956, in TsAOPIM, f. 478, op. 3, d. 210, l. 73. In the School of Biology and Soil Sciences, similar concerns reigned (f. 478, op. 5, d. 72, l. 91). For a different perspective—anger that Soviet soldiers were dying on behalf of ungrateful Hungarians—see Kliatsko, *Dnevnik Studentki*, 68–69.

28. Vladimir Kuznetsov, *Istoriia odnoi kompanii* (Moscow: Izdaniia avtora, 1995).

29. Their circle included Natal'ia Gorbanevskaia, who identified Terekhin as the author of the poem in the leaflet during interrogation by the KGB. She would later go on to become a well-known poet and human rights activist. V. P. Kuznetsov, "O 40-kh i 50-kh: Dom, Shkola, filfak MGU," in *Tynianovskii sbornik*, ed. M. Chudakova, E. Toddes, and Iu. Tsiv'ian (Moscow: Knizhnaia palata, 1998), 10:776, 781–782. On Terekhin's character, see Tat'iana Kostygova, "V eti strochki mozhno gliadet', kak v glaza," in *Vremia ostavsheesia s nami: Filologicheskii fakul'tet v 1953–1958: Vospominaniia vypusnikov* (Moscow: MAKS Press, 2004), 1:378–393.

30. Kuznetsov, "O 40-kh i 50-kh," 789–790.

31. Nikolai Krishchuk, "Boris Pustyntsev: 'V piatnadtsat let ia uzhe byl antikommunistom,'" *Delo* (June 27, 2005), http://www.idelo.ru/377/21.html. Pustyntsev dated his nonconformist views to an early interest in jazz broadcasts from the United States, which he could listen to in his hometown of Vladivostok, and to an acquaintance with a survivor of the gulag. In 1956 he was also reading the Polish magazine *Po prostu* thanks to a friend who had a subscription. Kosinova, "Sobytiia v Pol'she," 200–201. Materials regarding the group case that included Pustyntsev can be found in GARF, f. 8131, d. 43956.

32. "Vengerskaia Revoliutsiia tezisy," October 28, 1956, in "Po obvineniu Pimenova, Revol'ta Ivanovicha i drugikh," tom 6, ll. 83–90. In the VGIK case, one of the two students arrested had in fact argued against the other on Hungary, contending that Western imperialists were to blame. Smith, "A New Generation," 196–197.

33. Leonid Sheinis, "Vengriia. Oktiabr' 1956-go," Sovershenno Sekretno TV, January 6, 2013.

34. "Vengerskaia Revoliutsiia tezisy," quotation, l. 90.

35. Letters from Revol't Pimenov to Ivan Pimenov, October 28 and November (illeg.) 1956, in "Po obvineniu Pimenova, Revol'ta Ivanovicha i drugikh," tom 5, konvert. On "Informatsiia," see Smith, "A New Generation."

36. Kudrova, *Proshchanie*, 128–130; Verblovskaia, *Moi prekrasnyi*, 142–143; Pimenov, *Vospominaniia*, 48–49.

37. In fall 1956 a veritable battle raged in some university departments over wall newspapers and informal journals, with the deans confiscating whole issues and students and party bureaus divided over such censorship. Marietta O. Chudakova, "1956 god (k vospominaniiam V. Kuznetsova)," in *Tynianovskii sbornik*, 808–816; and Ol'ga Gerasimova, *"Ottepel'"*, *"Zamorozki" i studenty Moskovskogo Universiteta* (Moscow: AIRO-XXI, 2015), 331–347. Pimenov, *Vospominaniia*, 1:170.

38. Vail', *Osobo Opasnyi*, 139–141, 162–163.

39. Sheinis, "Vengriia. Oktiabr' 1956-go." Pustyntsev also apparently begged English-language journals off foreign sailors. He had copies of *Newsweek* and *Time* magazine at time of his arrest. GARF, f. 8131, op. 31, d. 78804, l. 34.

40. Among the items confiscated from Pimenov in March 1957 were translations from the Polish *Politika* for October 26, 1956, and lists of articles in *Tribuna Lyudu*. Sheinis (Leonid Borisov) got hold of enough materials that he could accurately describe the divisions within the Polish Workers' Party leading up to the Plenum. Leonid Borisov, "Pravda o vengrii" (February 1957), in "Po obvineniu Pimenova, Revol'ta Ivanovicha i drugikh," tom 6, l. 79. Kosinova, "'Nashi illiuziam prishel konets.'"

41. Patryk Babiracki, "Imperial Heresies: Polish Students in the Soviet Union, 1948–1957," *Ab Imperio* 4 (2007): 232. "Zapiska otdela nauki, vuzov i shkol TsK KPSS o nepravil'nom povedenii pol'skogo studenta V. S. Turskogo," January 12, 1957, in *"Vozvratit' domoi druz'iami SSSR . . ." Obuchenie inostrantsev v sovetskom soiuze 1956–1965*, comp. T. Iu. Krasovitskaia, Z. K. Vodop'ianova, and T. V. Doracheva (Moscow: Mezhdunarodnyi fond "Demokratiia," 2013), 46–47. Gidoni, *Solntse*, 47.

42. Departmental party bureaus at MGU realized they needed to do more outreach, especially to students in dormitories. See TsAOPIM, f. 478, op. 5, d. 72, l. 91 and op. 3, d. 210, l. 1.

43. Vail', *Osobo opasnyi*, 135; Gidoni, *Solntse*, 43, 47.

44. Entries for October 31 and November 3, 1956, in "Iz dnevnikov," 148.

45. Daniil Granin, *Prichudy pamiati* (Moscow: Tsentropoligraf, 2014), 48–49; see also Gidoni, *Solntse*, 66–67.

46. Chudakov cited in M. Chudakova, "1956 god," 802. Eleonory Gilburd, "Picasso in Thaw Culture," *Cahiers du Monde russe* 47, nos. 1–2 (2006): 84.

47. Chudakov cited in M. Chudakova, "1956 god," 802; Anatolii Naiman, "Picasso in Russia 2.0," trans. Mark H. Teeter, *Moscow News*, June 15, 2010.

48. The complex situation among Soviet artists and critics is adroitly explained by Susan Reid, "Toward a New (Socialist) Realism: The Re-Engagement with Western Modernism in the Khrushchev Thaw," in *Russian Art and the West*, ed. Rosalind P. Blakesley and Susan E. Reid (DeKalb: Northern Illinois University Press, 2007), 217–239, esp. 219. On young people's awareness of Picasso, see Verblovskaia, *Moi prekrasnyi*, 144–145.

49. On the history of the exhibition, see Vladimir Volovnikov, *O Neobyknovennom gode neobyknovennoi epokhi: neizvestnaia istoriia vystavki Pablo Pikasso v SSSR v 1956 g.* (Moscow: Airo-XX, 2007), esp. 33–36, 60–67.

50. Vail', *Osobo opasnyi*, 135–136. On Moscow, see Vladimir Slepian, "The Young vs. the Old," *Problems of Communism* 11, no. 3 (May–June 1962): 57; report of Minister of Education for the RSFSR to the Central Committee, November 29, 1956, RGANI, f. 5, op. 30, d. 181, l. 83.

51. Vail', *Osobo opasnyi*, 141–144; Verblovskaia, *Moi prekrasnyi*, 144–146. For an official account, see memo from secretary of the Leningrad Obkom to the Central Committee of the CPSU, December 28, 1956, RGANI, f. 5, op. 36, d. 27, l. 102–105.

52. Transcript of speech by Iuliia Krasovskaia as preserved in the files of the procuracy, GARF, f. 8131, op. 31, d. 76945, l. 2–5, quotations l. 2, l. 3–4.

53. Pimenov was mentioned by name by the head of the Leningrad KGB in a closed meeting on problems with youth convened by the city party committee on December 13, 1956; RGASPI, f. 17, op. 56, d. 1830, l. 277.

54. Gidoni, *Solntse*, 38–39.

55. Ibid., 61.

56. Valentin Nedzvetskii, "Chto iarche pamiat' sokhranila," in *Vremia ostavsheesia s nami*, 179.

57. Smith, "A New Generation"; Gidoni, *Solntse*, 135. Igor Adamatskii also recalled a feeling of moral outrage (*oshchushchenie pravednogo gneva*) among the roommates when their dorm room at the Library Institute was searched and Vail' was taken away; see "Stranitsy vospominaniei," l. 3.

58. Letters of November 20 and December 8, 1956, in Svetlana Angelina, "Dusha, otkrytaia liudiam. Pis'ma Gety Krainovoi," in *Vremia, ostavsheesiia s nami*, 400. At MGU at least, faculty were coming to the conclusion that they needed to improve teaching about democracy and current affairs; TsAOPIM, f. 478, op. 3, d. 210, l. 88; ibid. p. 5, d. 72, l. 90.

12. December

1. Leonid Sheinis overheard local party officials in Leningrad talking about "Picassoites" (*Pikassisty*); see "Po obvineniu Pimenova, Revol'ta Ivanovicha i drugikh" (nachato 25 marta 1957 okoncheno 25 iuliu 1957), tom 4, l. 261, in NITs Memorial, Pimenov Archive. Khrushchev cited by Veljko Mićunović, *Moscow Diary,* trans. David Floyd (Garden City, NY: Doubleday, 1980), 187.

2. "Iz dnevnikov Sergeia Sergeevicha Dmitrieva," *Otechestvennaia istoriia* 2 (2000): 151.

3. "Ob usilenii politicheskoi raboty partiinykh organizatsii v massakh i presechenii vylazok antisovetskikh vrazhdebnykh elementov" in A. N. Artizov, comp., *Reabilitatsiia, kak eto bylo* (Moscow: Mezhdunarodnyi fond "Demokratiia" and izd. Materik, 2003), 2:209.

4. Ibid., 209–210, 211.

5. Ibid., 213.

6. Ibid. In June 1955 Khrushchev had told the All-Union Conference of Procuracy and Investigative Workers that he understood that the secret police and internal affairs agencies had put them in a "difficult situation." His remedy for past abuses was to put a few top bosses on trial and to order that going forward laws should be strictly followed. See N. G. Tomilina, *Nikita Sergeevich Khrushchev: Dva tsveta vremeni: Dokumenty iz lichnogo fonda N. S. Khrushcheva* (Moscow: Mezhdunarodnyi fond "Demokratiia," 2009), 1:543. Anti-Soviet convictions would reach a post-Stalin high in 1957 and 1958—1,964 and 1,416 persons as compared with 384 in 1956. "O massovykh besporiadkakh s 1957 goda . . . ," *Vestnik Arkhiva Prezidenta Rossiiskoi Fedaratsii* 6 (1995): 153.

7. Khrushchev's August 6, 1956, speech in Tomilina ed., *Nikita Sergeevich Khrushchev,* 1:579. Khrushchev would restate his belief in linkages between economics and morale in an off-the-cuff speech to writers in May 1957. See "'A Vy sidite, kak surok, i o demokratii govorite': Vystuplenie N. S. Khrushcheva na soveshanii pisatelei v TsK KPSS 13 mai 1957 g.," *Istochnik* 6 (2003): 86.

8. Khrushchev inTomilina ed., *Nikita Sergeevich Khrushchev,* 1:575.

9. "XX S"ezd KPSS i zadachi issledovaniia istorii partii," *Voprosy istorii* 3 (1956): 4.

10. As Stephen Bittner writes, "The ideological core, Marxism-Leninism, was exempted from . . . reckoning, at least on the official level. Much of Soviet politics and culture after 1953 breaks down in precisely this way: how to excise from the Soviet body politic the heretical and destructive aspects of Stalinism, on the one hand, while all the time preserving what was authentically Leninist

and Soviet on the other? This was a delicate surgery, to be sure" (http://russianhistoryblog.org/2014/05/myth-memory-trauma-the-stalinist-past-and-the-post-soviet-present/).

11. "XX S"ezd KPSS i zadachi issledovaniia istorii partii," 12.

12. Burzhdalov speech at meeting of the editorial board, March 7, 1956, ARAN, f. 697, op. 2, d. 70, l. 169. On Pankratova's feelings, see the transcript of editorial board meeting of March 9, 1956, in ibid., l. 305.

13. Roger D. Marwick notes: "Under Khrushchev, as the coercive functions of the state ceded place to its hegemonic functions, the locus of power shifted from the secret police to the party-state, which became the collective *directoire* of opinion and the practices of everyday life"; see Roger D. Marwick, *Rewriting History in Soviet Russia: The Politics of Revisionist Historiography, 1956–1974* (Houndmills: Palgrave, 2001), 32. On antipathy toward *Voprosy istorii* readers' conferences, see 53.

14. On the journal's travails in 1956, see E. N. Gordetskii, "Zhurnal 'Voprosy istorii' v seredine 50-kh godov," *Voprosy istorii* 9 (1989): 69–79. Burzhdalov's own article on the Bolsheviks' tactics after the February revolution would come under fire in the summer of 1956.

15. E. Bugaev, "Kogda utrachivaetsia nauchnyi podkhod," *Partiinaia zhizn'* 14 (July 1956): 72.

16. "O stat'e tov. E. Bugaeva," *Voprosy istorii* 7 (1956): 215.

17. L. A. Sidorova, "'*Voprosy istorii*' akademika A. M. Pankratovoi," in *Istorik i vremia. 20–50-kh godov XX veka. A. M. Pankratova* (Moscow: Izd. RUDN and Mosgorarkhiv, 2000), 81–82. Entries for November 27 and October 12, 1956, in "Iz dnevnikov" 2 (2000), quotation 150. On MGU historians in late 1956 and early 1957, see Polly Jones, *Myth, Memory, Trauma: Rethinking the Stalinist Past in the Soviet Union, 1953–70* (New Haven, CT: Yale University Press, 2013), 74–81, 90–96.

18. For correspondence between Pankratova and Burzhdalov, their opponents, and the Central Committee, see RGANI, f. 5, op. 35, d. 39. On her surprise, see letter from Pankratova to Ekaterina Furtseva of February 19, 1957, ARAN, f. 697, op. 2, d. 83. On high politics around the journal that continued even after 1957, see A. V. Savel'ev, "Nomenklaturnaia bor'ba vokrug zhurnala 'Voprosy istorii' v 1954–1957 godakh," *Otechestvennaia istoriia* 5 (2003): 148–162. Quotation from "Ob usilenii politicheskoi raboty," 211.

19. Pankratova used the phrase "in the spirit of the Twentieth Party Congress" in her July 6 letter to Khrushchev (ARAN, f. 697, op. 2, d. 61, l. 16). On the three day meeting at MGU, see her letter to the history department's party

bureau (d. 81, l.1) and to Ekaterina Furtseva of February 19, 1957 (d. 83, ll. 1–5).

20. For Pankratova's undelivered remarks, see ARAN, f. 697, op. 2, d. 84, ll. 1–18. A. V. Savel'ev concludes that Pankratova was still maneuvering to try to keep the journal under her control at the March 6, 1957 meeting in "Nomenklaturnaia bor'ba vokrug zhurnala 'voprosy istorii'," 157–158. On Pankratova's daughter as saying that Khrushchev "sold out her mother," see Aleksandr Kan, "Anna Pankratova i 'Voprosy istorii.' Novatorskii i kriticheskii istoricheskii zhurnal v Sovetskom Soiuze v 1950-e gody," in *Istorik i vremia*, 99.

21. On Pankratova's support for colleagues who had survived the camps, see entry for February 21, 1957, in "Iz dnevnikov Sergeia Sergeevicha Dmitrieva," *Otechestvennaia istoriia* 3 (2000): 152. On the dismay that once again people could be worked over for alleged political errors, see letter to Furtseva of February 19, 1957, ARAN, f. 697, op. 2, d. 83.

22. "Za Leninskuiu partiinost' v istoricheskoi nauke!," *Voprosy istorii* 3 (1957): 11. "Obmen rechami na prieme v posol'stve Kitaiskoi narodnoi respubliki," *Pravda*, January 19, 1957, p. 2.

23. Sergei Khrushchev recollects three such albums. Sergei Khrushchev, *Nikita Khrushchev and the Creation of a Superpower*, trans. Shirley Benson (University Park: Pennsylvania State University Press, 2000), 194, 202, 213. Khrushchev years later said: "Budapest was like a nail being driven into my head and it gave me no rest"; see Sergei Khrushchev, ed., *Memoirs of Nikita Khrushchev*, vol. 3, *Statesman (1953–1964)*, trans. George Shriver (University Park: Pennsylvania State University Press, 2007), 650.

24. "Speech by Josip Tito at Pula, November 11, 1956," in Csaba Békés, Malcolm Byrne, and János M. Rainer, eds., *The 1956 Hungarian Revolution: A History in Documents* (Budapest: CEU Press, 2002), 419, 420.

25. On Khrushchev's hatred of the terms *Stalinism* and *de-Stalinization*, see Mićunović, *Moscow Diary*, 158.

26. Sergei Khrushchev, ed., *Memoirs of Nikita Khrushchev*, vol. 2, *Reformer (1945–1964)*, trans. George Shriver (University Park: Pennsylvania State University Press, 2006), 329–330. Sergei Khrushchev claims that his father was anxious at the start of 1957 to get to work on domestic economic issues (Khrushchev, *Creation*, 214).

27. "Ob usilenii politicheskoi raboty," 210. On MGU, see Lidiia Kliatsko, *Dnevnik studentki zhurfaka (1955–1957)* (Moscow: RIF "ROI," 2002), 66. On LGU, see "Obsuzhdenie knigi V. D. Dudintseva 'Ne khlebom edinym' Zasedanie Literaturnogo khruzhka filologicheskaia fakul'teta LGU," November 10, 1956, comp. Ernest Orlovskii in Pimenov Archive, razdel 3, papka 3.1, no. 26.

28. Vladimir Dudintsev, *Mezhdu dvumia romanami* (St. Petersburg: Zhurnal Neva, 2000), 65.

29. "Zapiska otdela kul'tury TsK KPSS 'O nekotorykh voprosakh sovremennoi literatury i o faktakh nepravil'nykh nastroenii sredi chasti pisatelei'," in *Kul'tura i vlast' ot Stalina do Gorbacheva. Dokumenty. Apparat TsK KPSS i Kul'tura. 1953–1957,* ed. K. Aimermakher (Moscow: ROSSPEN, 2001), 572.

30. N. Kriuchkova, "O romane Ne khlebom edinym," *Izvestiia,* December 2, 1956, 3. Sergei Dmitriev recorded rumors that two conservative writers had written the review under the pseudonym Kriuchkova; see entry for December 19, 1956. "Iz dnevnikov" 2 (2000): 151.

31. Letter from Revol't Pimenov, "Proch' zashchitnikov Drozdovykh!," to *Izvestiia* December 3, 1956. Pimenov Archive, razdel 3, papka 3.17, no. 33. In this case, the literature and arts editor wrote back, "Despite some virtues, Dudintsev's novel *Not by Bread Alone* is as a whole one-sided in its depiction of our reality, thereby violating the truth of life" (letter from P. Nikitin to Pimenov, January 4, 1957, in ibid.).

32. Letters to *Novyi mir* from Boris Bindas (December 10, 1956) and Galina Zimchenko (December 22, 1956), RGALI, f. 1702, op. 6, d. 244, ll. 2–4, 46–51ob, quotation l. 46. The other harsh review was B. Platonov, "Realnye geroi i literaturnye skhemy," *Literaturnaia gazeta,* November 24, 1956, pp. 2, 3.

33. On disdain for endings in which some "Partkomych" magically appeared, see also N. B. Ermolenko, "Moi studencheskie gody," in *Vremia ostavsheesia s nami: filologicheskii fakul'tet v 1955–1960 gg.: vospominaniia vypusnikov* (Moscow: MAKS Press, 2006), 3:370.

34. "Zapiska otdela nauki, shkol i kultury TsK KPSS po RSFSR o 'politicheski vrednom' vystuplenii pisatelia V. D. Dudintseva na plenume pravleniia Moskovskogo otdeleniia Soiuza pisatelei SSSR 6 marta 1957 g." (no later than March 7, 1957), in *Kul'tura i vlast',* 626–630.

35. "Zapiska otdela nauki, shkol i kultury TsK KPSS po RSFSR o vystupleniiakh na zakliuchitel'nom zasedanii plenuma pravleniia Moskovskogo otdeleniia Soiuza pisatelei SSSR" (March 9, 1957), in ibid., 631–634. Dudintsev, *Mezhdu,* 96–99.

36. Dudintsev, *Mezhdu,* 147, 151–153, 165–170. On the printing of a miniscule edition, see the note from the Central Committee Department of Culture of January 22, 1957, reprinted in *Kul'tura i vlast',* 613–614.

37. Vladislav Zubok, *Zhivago's Children: The Last Russian Intelligentsia* (Cambridge, MA: Harvard University Press, 2009), 79. The letter "Videt' vsiu pravdu" appeared in *Literaturnaia gazeta,* November 22, 1956, p. 1.

38. N. Kovaleva, comp., *Molotov, Malenkov, Kaganovich. 1957. Stenogramma iiunskogo plenuma TsK KPSS i drugie dokumenty* (Moscow: Mezhdunarodnyi fond "Demokratiia," 1998), 104. For Khrushchev's extemporaneous speech complete with belittlement of Dudintsev, see "'A Vy sidite.'"

39. For students' perceptions of Dudintsev as showing cowardice at campus forums, see Dmitrii Urnov, "Filologicheskie fragmenty," in *Vremia, ostavsheesia s nami: filologicheskii fakul'tet v 1953–1958 gg.: vospominaniia vypusnkikov* (Moscow: MAKS Press, 2004), 1:23; and Boris Ivanov and Nikolai Solokhin in Lev Lur'e and Irina Maliarova, *1956 god. Seredina veka* (St. Petersburg: Neva, 2007), 406–407, 413–414.

40. On Khrushchev's handling of his rivals, see William C. Taubman, *Khrushchev: The Man and His Era* (New York: W. W. Norton, 2003), 317–324; Mićunović, *Moscow Diary*, 266–275. For the label "anti-party group," see *Molotov, Malenkov, Kaganovich*, 66.

41. Taubman, *Khrushchev*, 321. *Molotov, Malenkov, Kaganovich*, 32–41, 67–68, 537, 542.

42. *Molotov, Malenkov, Kaganovich*, 37–41, 68, quotation 41.

43. Lynne Viola, "The Question of the Perpetrator in Soviet History," *Slavic Review* 72, no. 1 (2013): 10.

44. Nina L. Khrushcheva, *The Lost Khrushchev: A Journey into the Gulag of the Russian Mind* (Mustang, OK: Tate Publishing, 2014), 232–233; Kaganovich remarks in *Molotov, Malenkov, Kaganovich*, 70.

45. Lidiia Chukovskaia, *Zapiski ob Anne Akhmatovoi*, vol. 2, *1952–1962* (Paris: YMCA-Press, 1980), 137.

46. Ibid., 140–141.

47. The Military Collegium of Supreme Court alone would report that it had received some thirty thousand requests for review of cases in the course of 1956 with sometimes 150 persons per day visiting their reception offices. Letter from the President of the Military Collegium of the Supreme Court of the USSR, V. Borisoglebskii, March 16, 1957, in *Reabilitatsiia: Kak eto bylo*, 2:241–242.

48. Draft appeal to the General Procurator of the USSR, sometime in February–March 1956 in L. N. Taganov and O. K. Pereverzev, comp., *Anna Barkova . . . Vechno ne ta* (Moscow: Fond Sergeia Dubova, 2002), 422.

49. V. D. Panov, "Obzor arkhivnykh sledstvennykh del," in A. A. Barkova, *Izbrannoe: Iz gulagovskogo arkhiva*, comp. L. N. Taganov and Z. Ia. Kholodova (Ivanovo: Ivanovskii Gos. Universitet, 1992), 279.

50. Verblovskaia, *Moi prekrasnyi strashnyi vek* (St. Petersburg: Zhurnal Zvezda, 2011), 158. On her acquaintance with Barkova, see I. Verblovskaia, "Poet tragicheskoi sud'by," *Neva* 4 (1989): 206–207.

51. Veblovskaia, *Moi prekrasnyi*, 157. He recalled the trial as a "holiday." Revol't I. Pimenov, *Vospominaniia* (Moscow: Panorama, 1996), 1:184–188, 194, 224.

52. Pimenov, *Vospominaniia*, 1:220.

53. Igor Adamatskii, "Stranitsy vospominaniei" (typescript dated 1971), l. 4, Pimenov Archive, razdel 5.

54. E. E. Zhukovskaia, "Vspominaia Aniu Zhuravlevu," in *Pamiati Anny Ivanovy Zhuravlevoi* (Moscow: Tri Kvadrata, 2012), 38.

55. Here I paraphrase Akhmatova's remarks upon hearing about the writer Vsevolod Ivanov clashing with *Pravda* editor Pavel Satiukov over whether they were going to discuss Khrushchev's report (Chukovskaia, *Zapiski*, 148).

56. "Esli skazal 'a', to nado govorit' i 'b': Stenogramma sobraniia partiinogo aktiva 4 noiabria 1956 g.," *Istochnik* 6 (2003): 75.

57. Aleksandr Iakovlev, "Trebuetsia ne maloe vremia," *Indeks/Dos'e na Tsenzuru* 14 (2001), http://index.org.ru/journal/14/yakovlev1401.html.

58. "'A Vy sidite'," 81.

59. *Molotov, Malenkov, Kaganovich*, 65.

Epilogue

1. Valerii Frid, *58 1/2. Zapiski lagernogo pridurka* (Moscow: Izd. Dom Rusanova, 1996), 292, 302.

2. Lidiia Chukovskaia, *Zapiski ob Anne Akhmatovoi*, vol. 2, *1952–1962* (Paris: YMCA-Press, 1980), 141.

3. Unsigned letter to A. Rumiantsev, editor of *Kommunist*, RGANI, f. 5, op. 30, d. 140, l. 196–198, quotation, l. 197.

4. Marietta O. Chudakova, "1956 god (k vospominaniiam V. Kuznetsova)," in Tynianovskii sbornik, ed. M. Chudakova, E. Toddes, and Iu. Tsiv'ian (Moscow: Knizhnaia palata, 1998), 805.

5. Reginald E. Zelnik, *Perils of Pankratova: Some Stories from the Annals of Soviet Historiography* (Seattle: University of Washington Press, 2005), 66.

6. Adzhubei quote of Khrushchev in a 1990 interview. Michael Charlton, *Footsteps from the Finland Station* (New Brunswick, NJ: Transaction Publishers, 1992), 58.

7. Denis Kozlov, *The Readers of* Novyi Mir: *Coming to Terms with the Stalinist Past* (Cambridge, MA: Harvard University Press, 2013), 9.

8. Vladislav Zubok, *Zhivago's Children: The Last Russian Intelligentsia* (Cambridge, MA: Harvard University Press, 2009), 21.

9. Revol't I. Pimenov, *Vospominaniia* (Moscow: Panorama, 1996), 1:33.

10. Juliane Fürst, "Introduction—Late Stalinist Society: History, Policies and People," in *Late Stalinist Russia: Society between Reconstruction and Reinvention,* ed. Juliane Fürst (London: Routledge, 2006), 11.

11. Timothy J. Colton, *Yeltsin: A Life* (New York: Basic Books, 2008), 202.

12. Stephen V. Bittner, *The Many Lives of Khrushchev's Thaw: Experience and Memory in Moscow's Arbat* (Ithaca, NY: Cornell University Press, 2008), 12.

13. Irma Kudrova, *Proshchanie s morokoi* (St. Petersburg: Kriga, 2013), 146.

14. Bittner makes this point more eloquently in his historiography of the term *thaw* (*Many Lives of Khrushchev's Thaw,* 9).

ACKNOWLEDGMENTS

Georgetown University's Center for Russian, Eurasian, and East European Studies (CERES), its Department of Government, and Edmund A. Walsh School of Foreign Service (SFS) kept me employed and supplied with wonderful students over the long course of the research and writing of this book. CERES and SFS also provided vital funding for research trips. I am indebted and grateful in particular to Georgetown's Harley Balzer, Angela Stent, Charles King, Jennifer Long, Benjamin Loring, and Christina Watts for their support. I am also profoundly grateful to Carole Sargent, the director of the Office of Scholarly Programs at Georgetown, for her encouragement, publishing advice, and wonderful summer writing groups.

I received a crucial research grant from the National Council for Eurasian and East European Research (NCEEER), under the authority of a Title VIII grant from the U.S. Department of State. Neither NCEEER nor the U.S. government bears any responsibility for the views expressed in this book. NCEEER's former director, the late Bob Huber, understood the travails of the independent researcher, and I remain grateful for his support.

William Taubman, my first professor of Russian politics, helped plant the seeds for this book many years ago with a research seminar dedicated to Nikita Khrushchev. His subsequent biography of the irrepressible first secretary has been a tremendous resource for me in writing this history. Meanwhile, Jane Taubman indulged my interest in Soviet-era memoirs when I was a student at Amherst College and has continued to offer sincere and timely encouragement.

I am grateful for the time and patience of my interviewees—Anatoly Gladilin (Paris); Elena and Natal'ia Liapunova (Moscow); Sof'ia Mitrokhina (Moscow); and Valery Soyfer (Fairfax, Virginia). I'm also thankful for the warmth and generosity of the families of Valerii Frid and Iulii Dunskii—namely Marina Romanovskaia, Julia and Alex Wolf, and Zoya Osipova. I am especially grateful to Zoya Osipova for allowing and facilitating the reproduction of photographs from her family archive. The descendants of Ol'ga Shatunovskaia—Andre Broido and the late Jana Kutina—not only published her invaluable oral histories but discussed her life with me. I am grateful to them and to Anton Kutin for permission to use family photographs. Serguei Parkhmenko fortuitously shared his grandparents' photographs from their 1956 cruise on the *Pobeda*.

Staff at numerous Russian archives—RGANI, GARF, RGASPI, RGASPI-M, RGALI, RGAKFD, and the Moscow City Archive branches, formerly known as TsAOPIM and TsAADM—assisted me in locating documents and images from 1956. I am particularly grateful to the spectacularly efficient Elena Kolikova and Marina Chertelina at RGAKFD and Irina Tarakanova at the Archive of the Russian Academy of Sciences in Moscow. I also received valuable assistance from the State Literary Museum, the Museum of the History of Moscow State University, the K. Paustovskii Literary Museum-Center, the International Memorial Society (Moscow); the Scientific–Informational Center of Memorial Society (St. Petersburg); the Andrei Sakharov Museum; the House on the Embankment Museum; the Museum of the History of the Criminal Justice System of Kuzbass; and the website Shalamov.ru.

In the United States, the Harry Ransom Center at the University of Texas Austin allowed me access to color photographs of Moscow in 1956 from the David Duncan Douglas Collection. I also benefited from the University of Denver's phenomenal digitization of the archive of the late Ogonek photographer Semyon Fridlyand. Staff at the European

Reading Room at the Library of Congress provided help in finding resources over the course of many visits.

Among my Moscow friends, special thanks are due to Olga Kazmina, who knows how to make everything fun, and to Boris Belenkin, who sparked my interest in Anna Pankratova twenty-five years ago and who has encouraged and assisted me ever since.

My colleagues Kathryn Hendley, Margaret Paxson, Hope Harrison, Anne Gorsuch, Deborah Kaple, and Vladislav Zubok all offered encouragement during the framing and writing of the book. Stephen F. Cohen assisted me in researching the life of Aleksei Snegov and finding his portrait. Anton Vinogradov helped with research for Chapter 11 and brought his meticulous proofreading skills to the first half of the manuscript. Charles King recommended me to his wonderful mapmaker, Chris Robinson. I'm also grateful to Stephen Bittner for his helpful comments on the manuscript. All shortcomings, however, should be ascribed solely to the author.

Kathleen McDermott at Harvard University Press whisked me through the publishing process and introduced me to a great set of critics at the Fourteenth Annual Conference "Recovering Forgotten History: The Image of East Central Europe in English-Language Academic Textbooks." There, under the auspices of Professor Andrzej Kaminski and Eulalia Łazarska of the Foundation for Civic Space and Public Policy, I received very useful feedback from Professors Boris Sokolov, Patryk Pleskot, Piotr Bajda, and Dr. Juraj Marusiak.

The biggest thank-you goes to my family, including my ever-supportive parents, Michael and Eleanor Smith, and my always helpful big sister, Pamela Nakahata Smith. My supremely patient husband, William Pomeranz, has been my number one cheerleader and best sounding board. Kira Pomeranz was an infant when I hit upon the idea for this book; she now knows how to spell *Khrushchev* and so much more. She has put up with my many absences, countless hours spent in front of my own glowing screen, and endless dinner-table discussions about Russia.

INDEX